Love at Fourteen

Fuka Mizutani

2

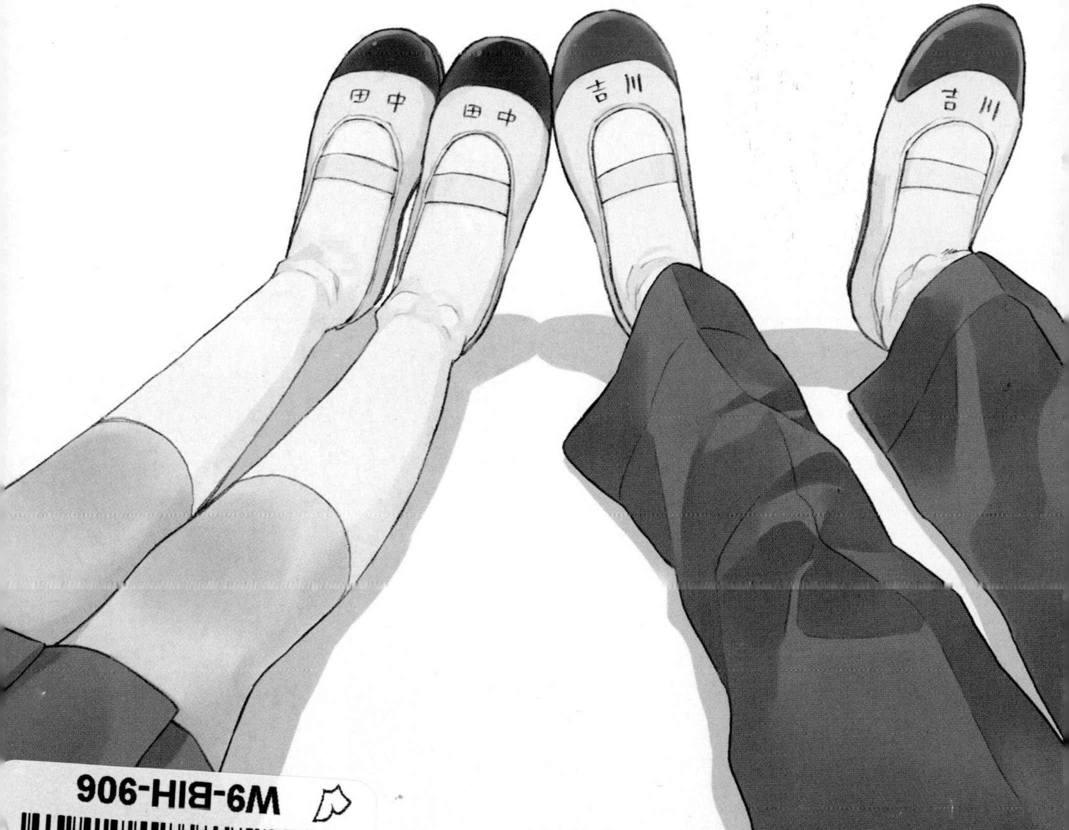
田中
田中
吉川
吉川

SHOES: TANAKA/YOSHIKAWA

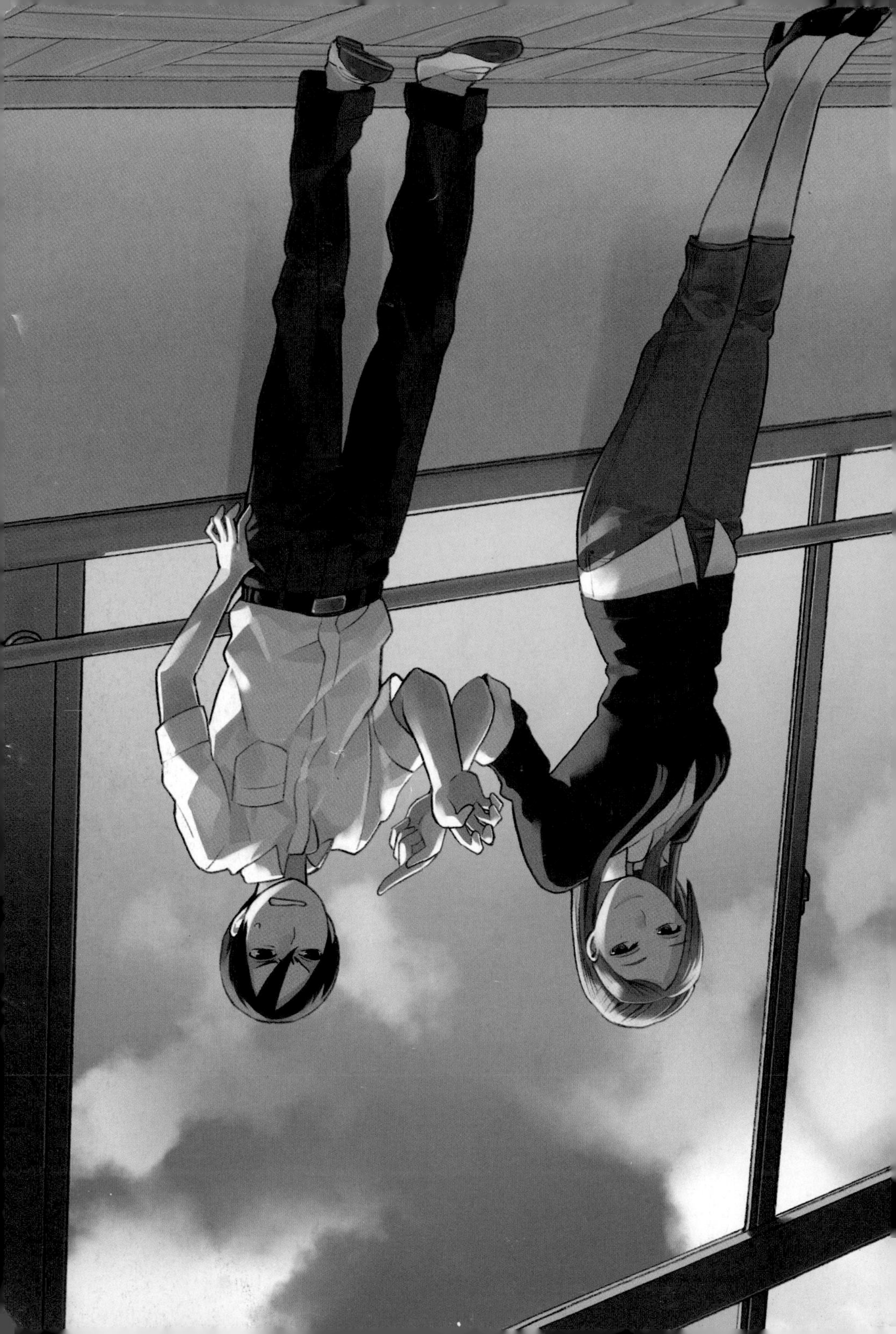

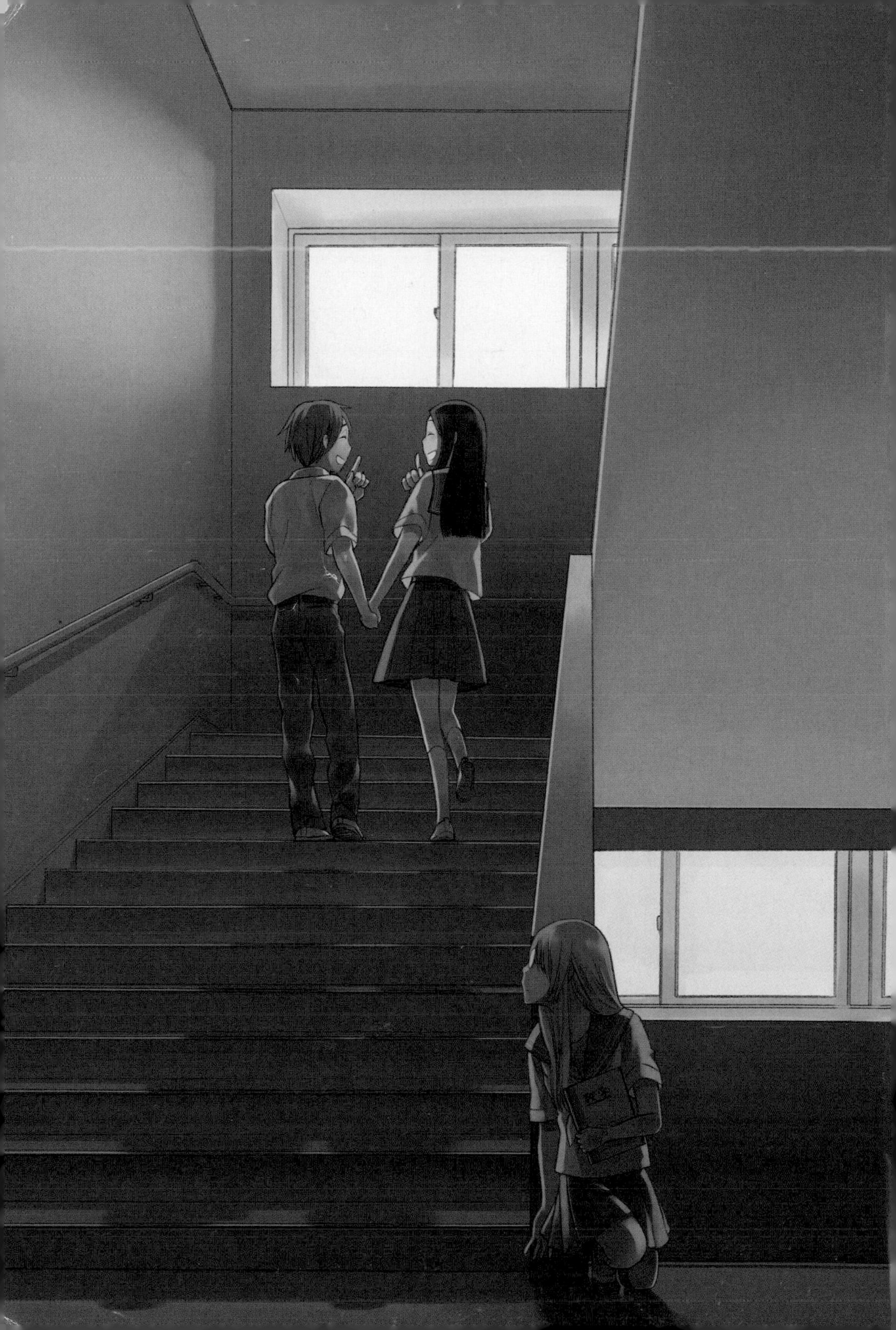

Contents

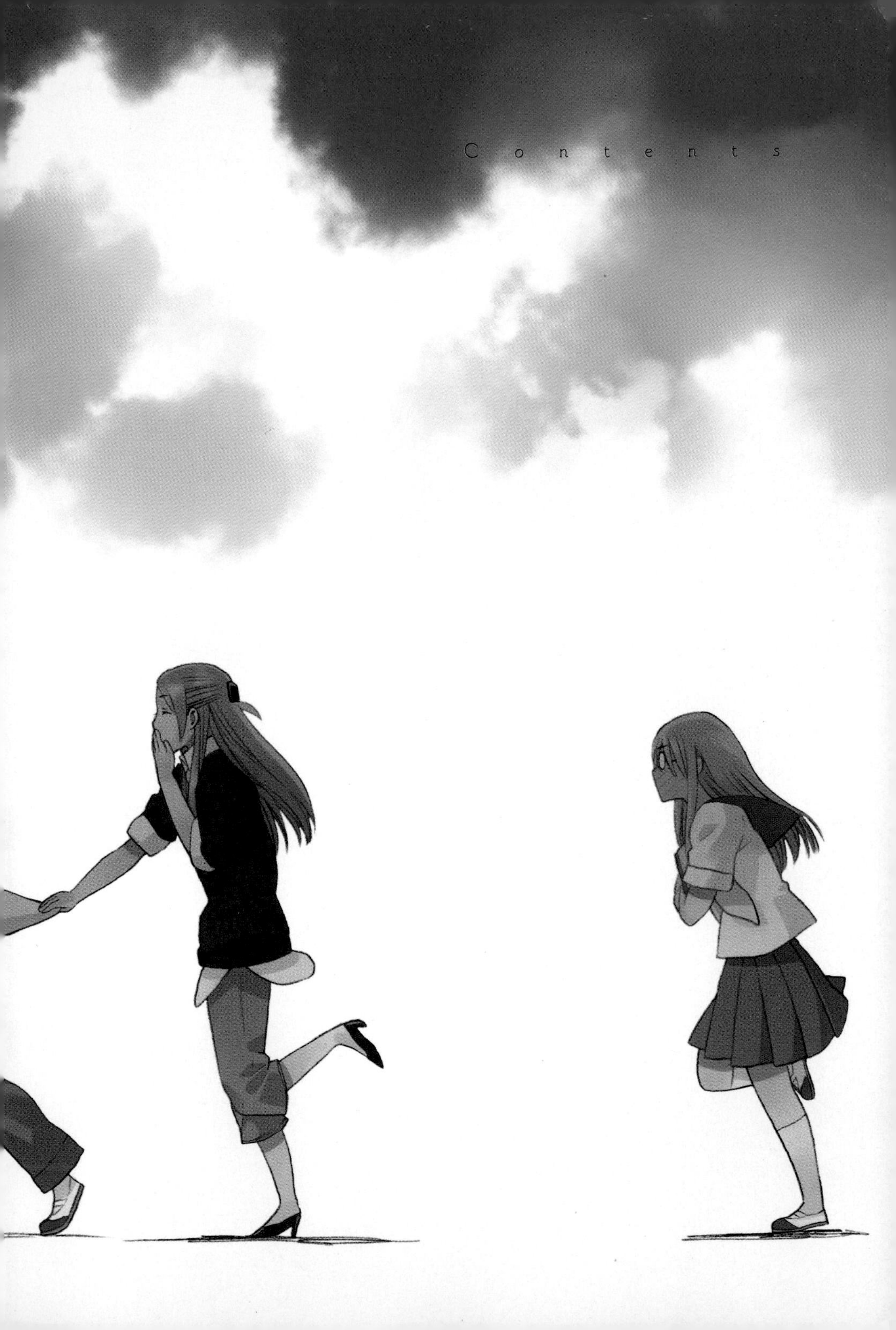

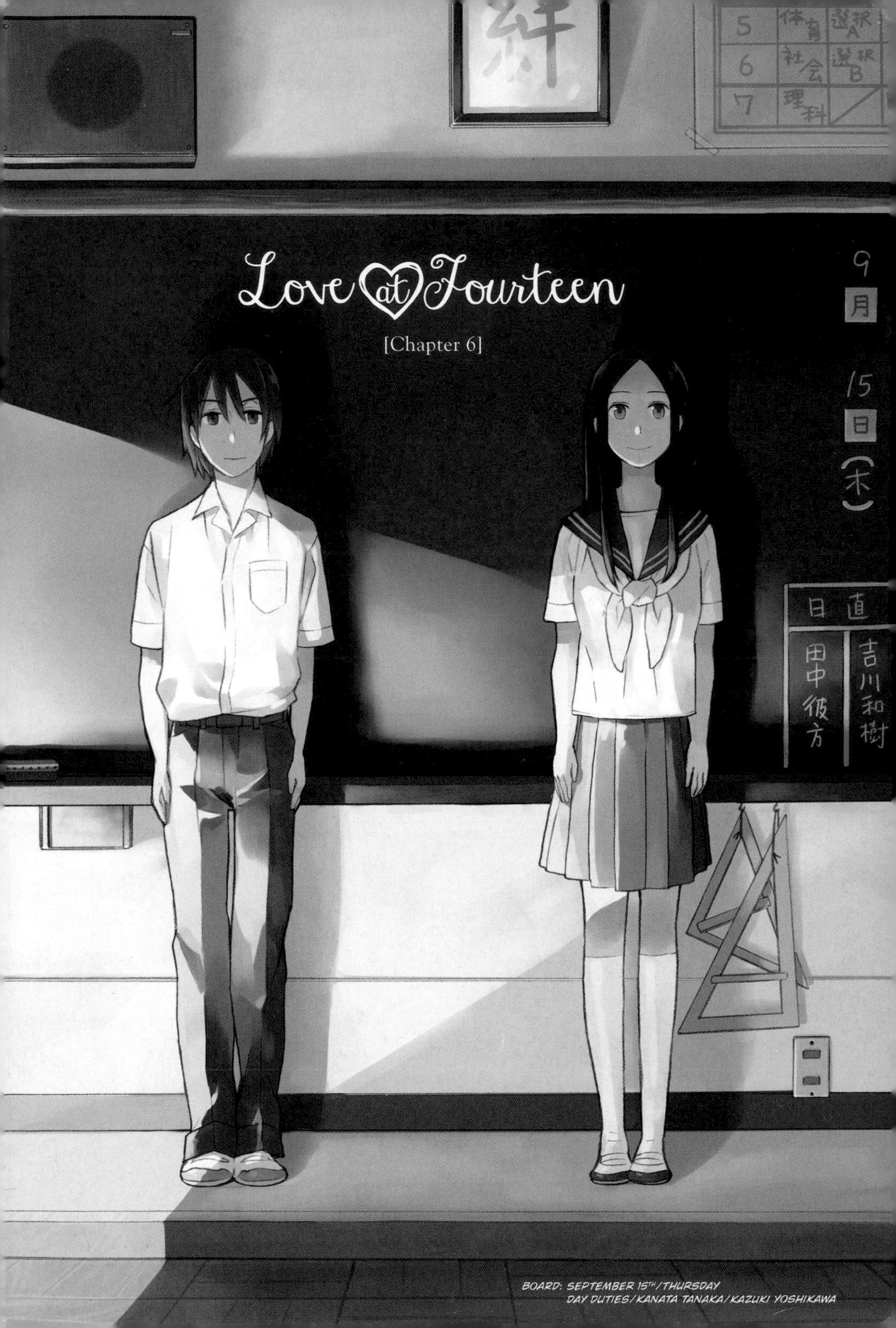
絆
5 体育 選択A
6 社会 選択B
7 理科
Love at Fourteen
[Chapter 6]
9月15日(木)
日直
吉川和樹
田中彼方
BOARD: SEPTEMBER 15TH/THURSDAY
DAY DUTIES/KANATA TANAKA/KAZUKI YOSHIKAWA

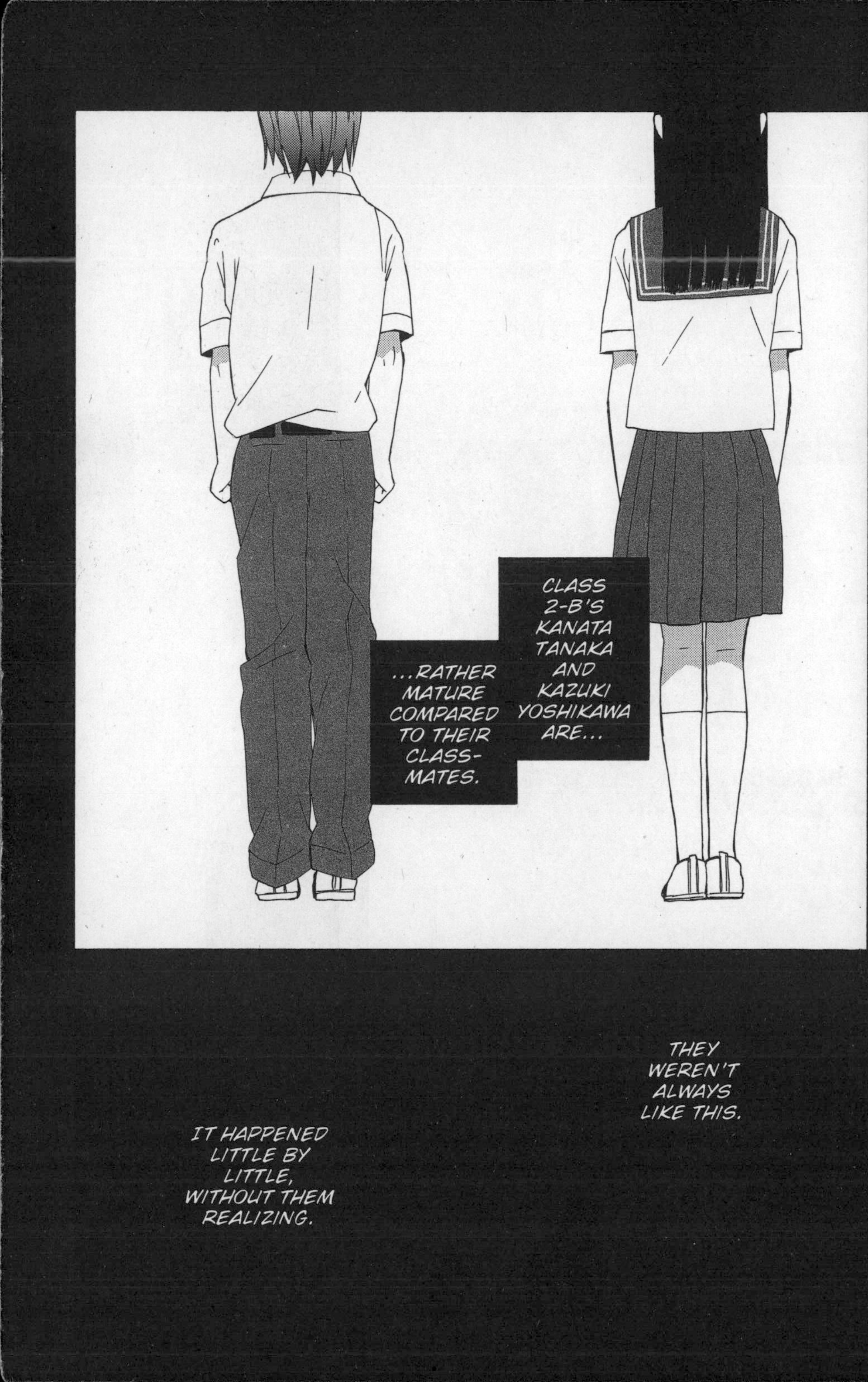
CLASS 2-B'S KANATA TANAKA AND KAZUKI YOSHIKAWA ARE...
...RATHER MATURE COMPARED TO THEIR CLASS-MATES.
THEY WEREN'T ALWAYS LIKE THIS.
IT HAPPENED LITTLE BY LITTLE, WITHOUT THEM REALIZING.

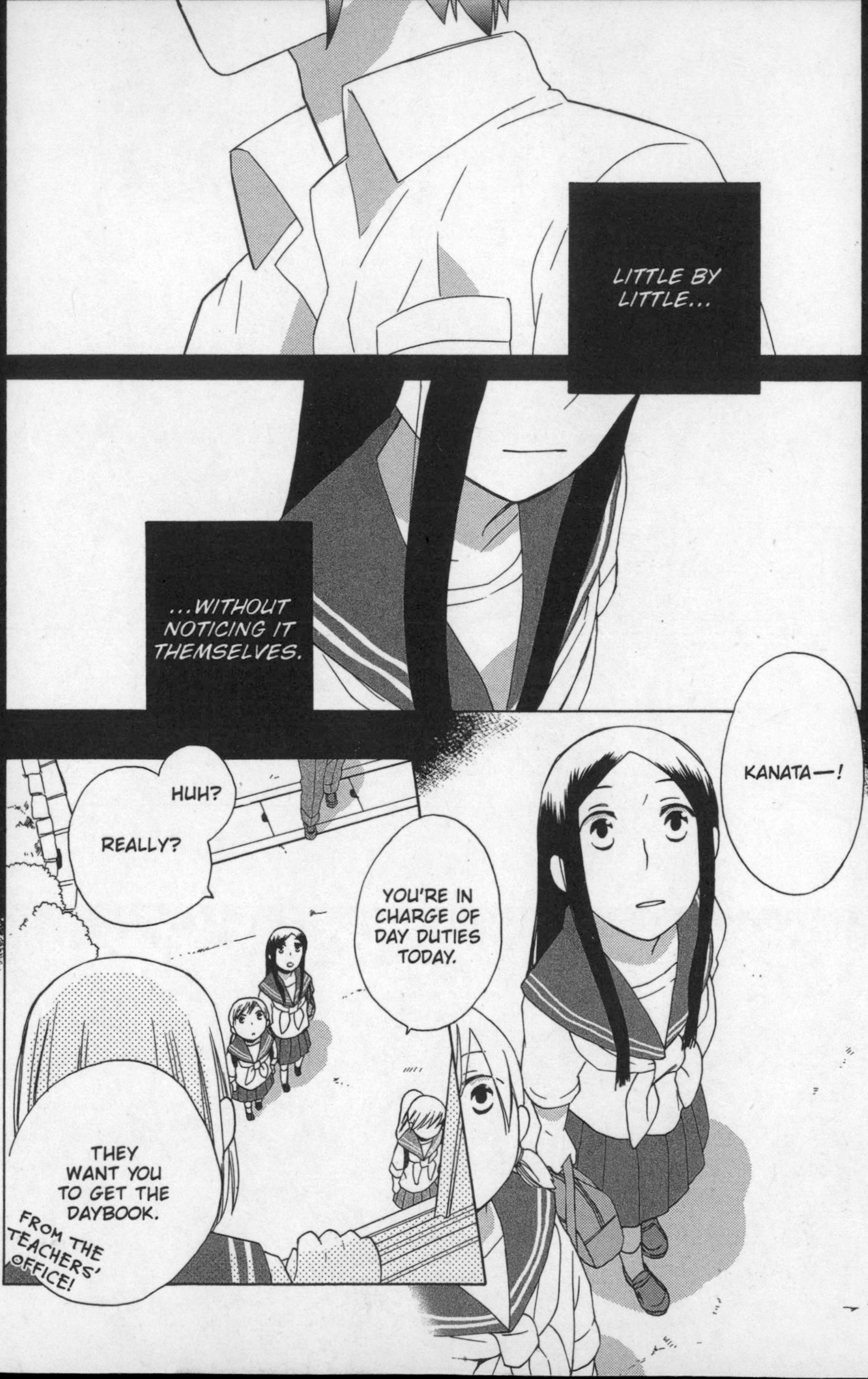
LITTLE BY LITTLE...
...WITHOUT NOTICING IT THEMSELVES.
KANATA—!
YOU'RE IN CHARGE OF DAY DUTIES TODAY.
HUH?
REALLY?
THEY WANT YOU TO GET THE DAYBOOK.
FROM THE TEACHERS' OFFICE!

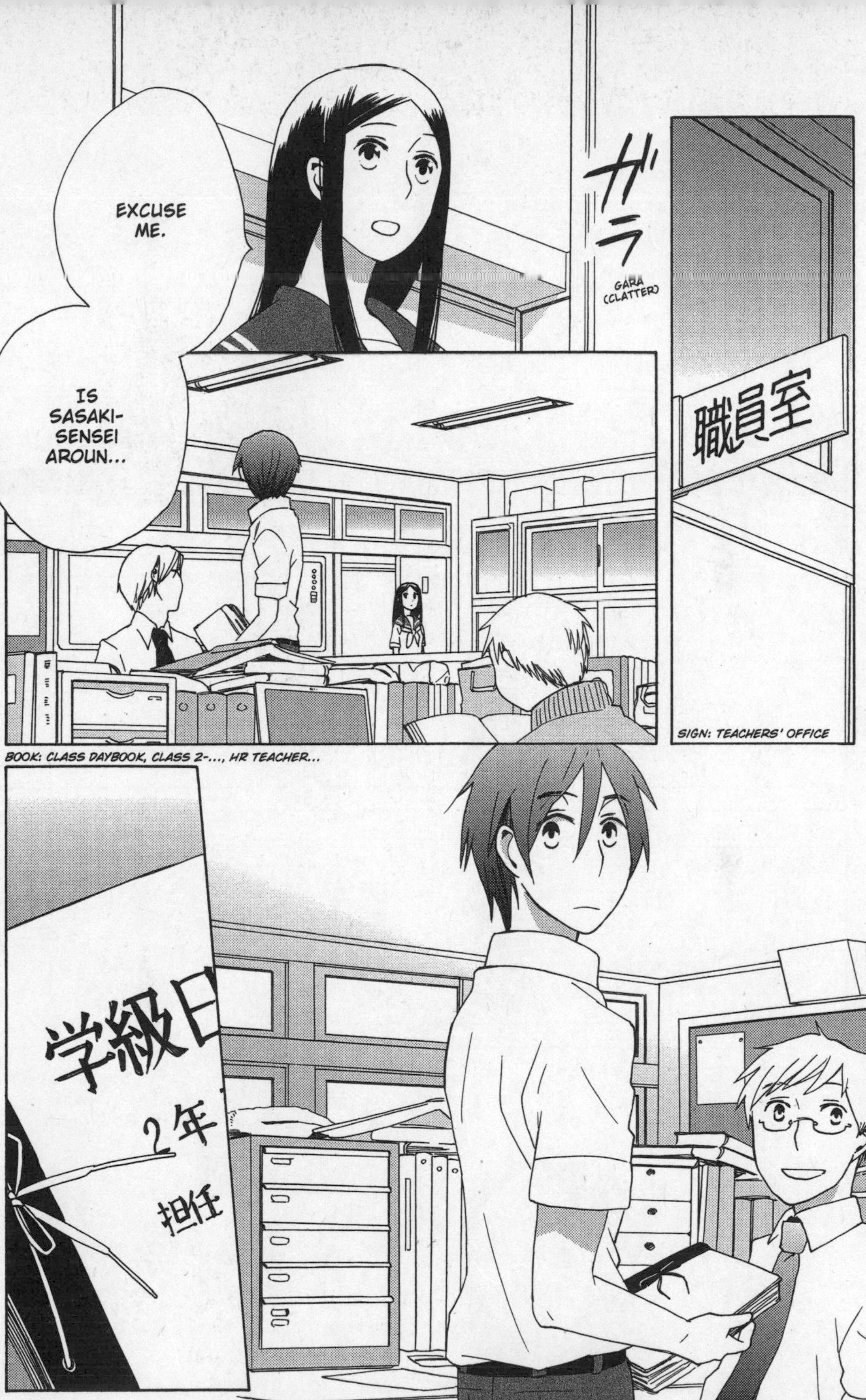
ガラ
GARA (CLATTER)
職員室
SIGN: TEACHERS' OFFICE
EXCUSE ME.
IS SASAKI-SENSEI AROUN...
BOOK: CLASS DAYBOOK, CLASS 2-..., HR TEACHER...
学級日
2年
担任

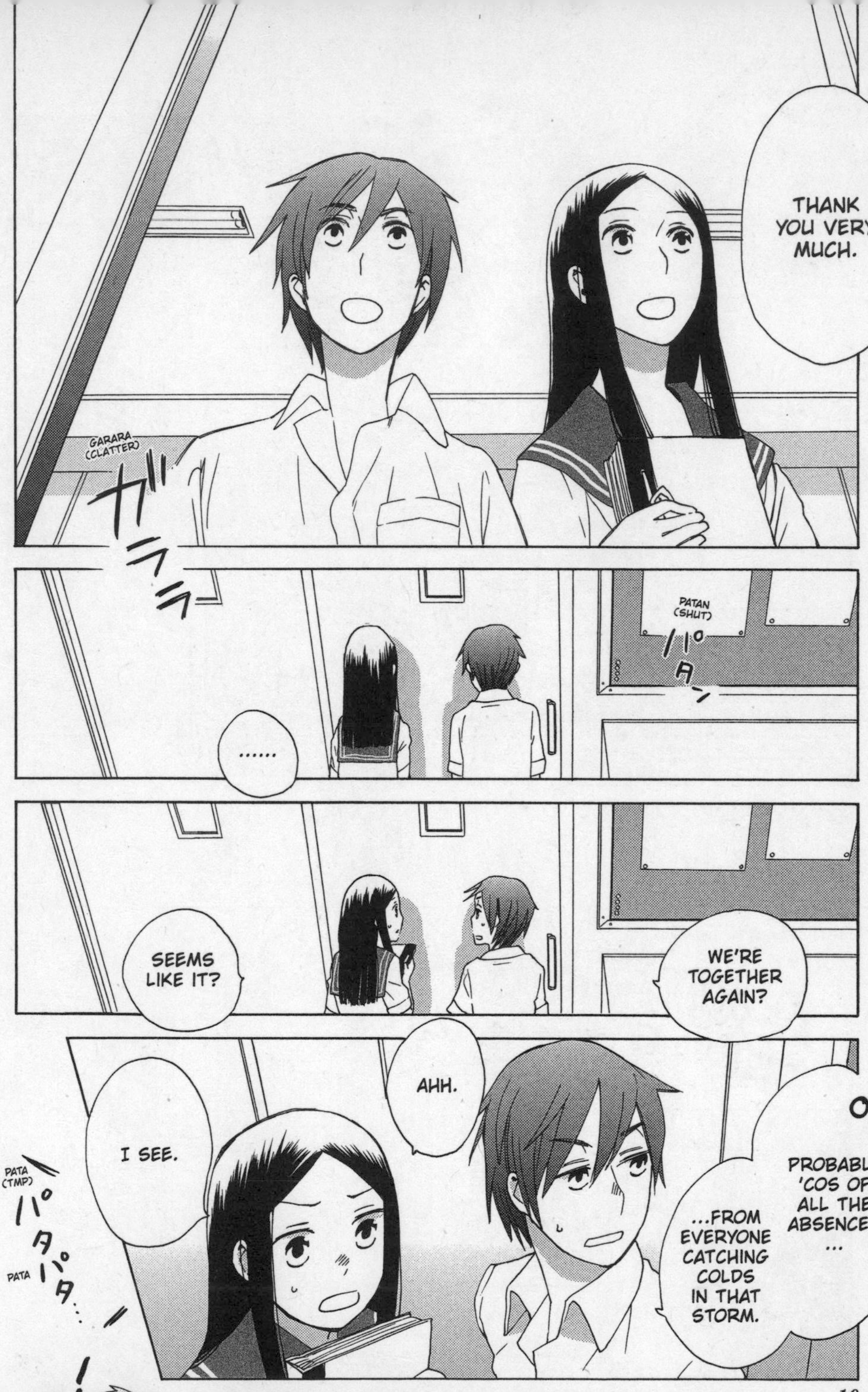
THANK YOU VERY MUCH.
GARARA (CLATTER)
PATAN (SHUT)
......
WE'RE TOGETHER AGAIN?
SEEMS LIKE IT?
OH.
PROBABLY 'COS OF ALL THE ABSENCES ...
...FROM EVERYONE CATCHING COLDS IN THAT STORM.
AHH.
I SEE.
PATA (TMP)
PATA
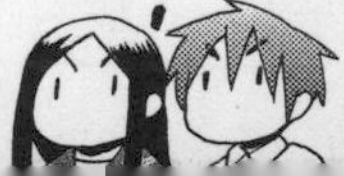

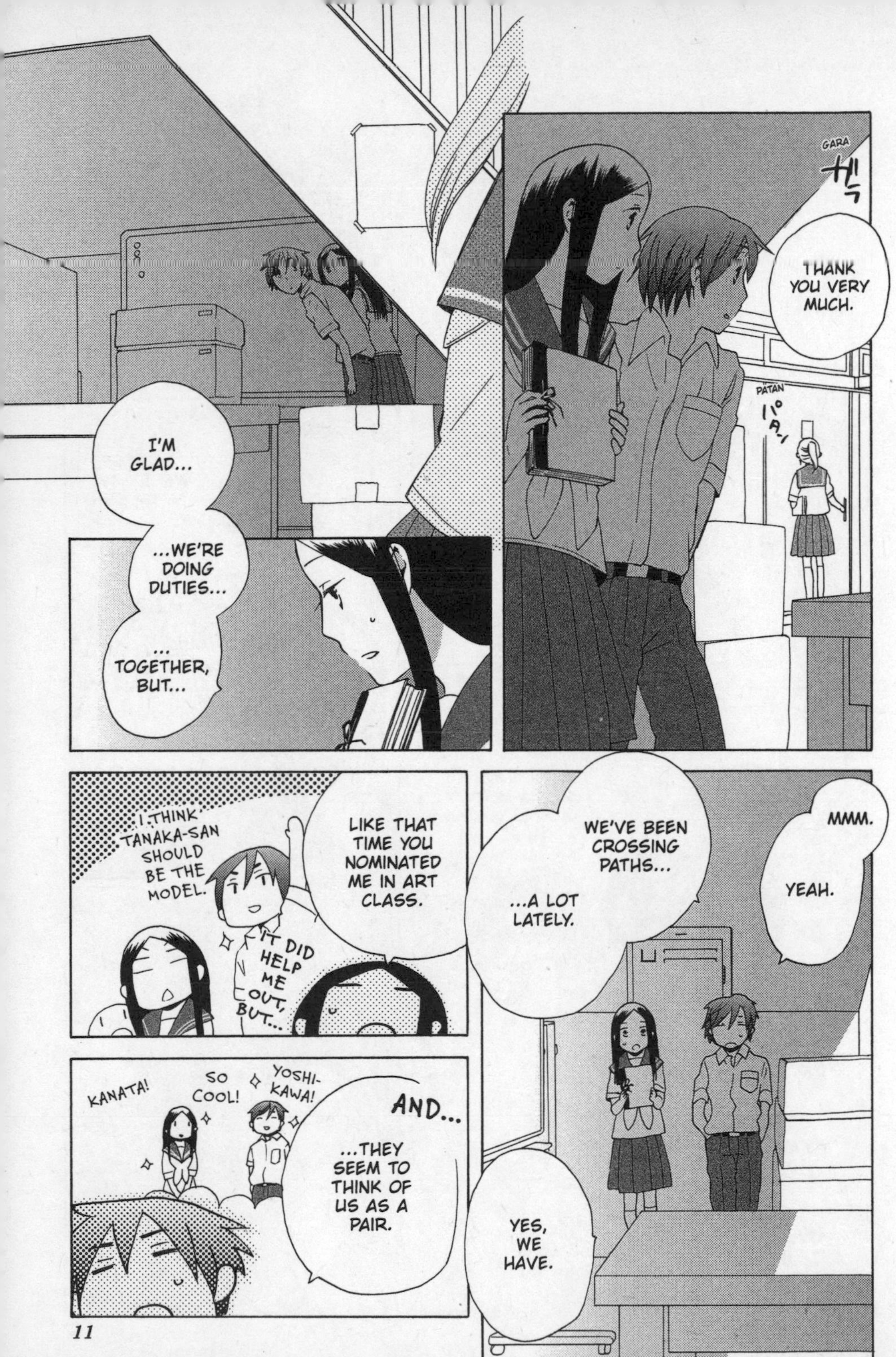
GARA
THANK YOU VERY MUCH.
PATAN
I'M GLAD...
...WE'RE DOING DUTIES...
... TOGETHER, BUT...
MMM.
YEAH.
WE'VE BEEN CROSSING PATHS...
...A LOT LATELY.
YES, WE HAVE.
LIKE THAT TIME YOU NOMINATED ME IN ART CLASS.
I THINK TANAKA-SAN SHOULD BE THE MODEL.
IT DID HELP ME OUT, BUT...
AND...
...THEY SEEM TO THINK OF US AS A PAIR.
YOSHI-KAWA!
SO COOL!
KANATA!

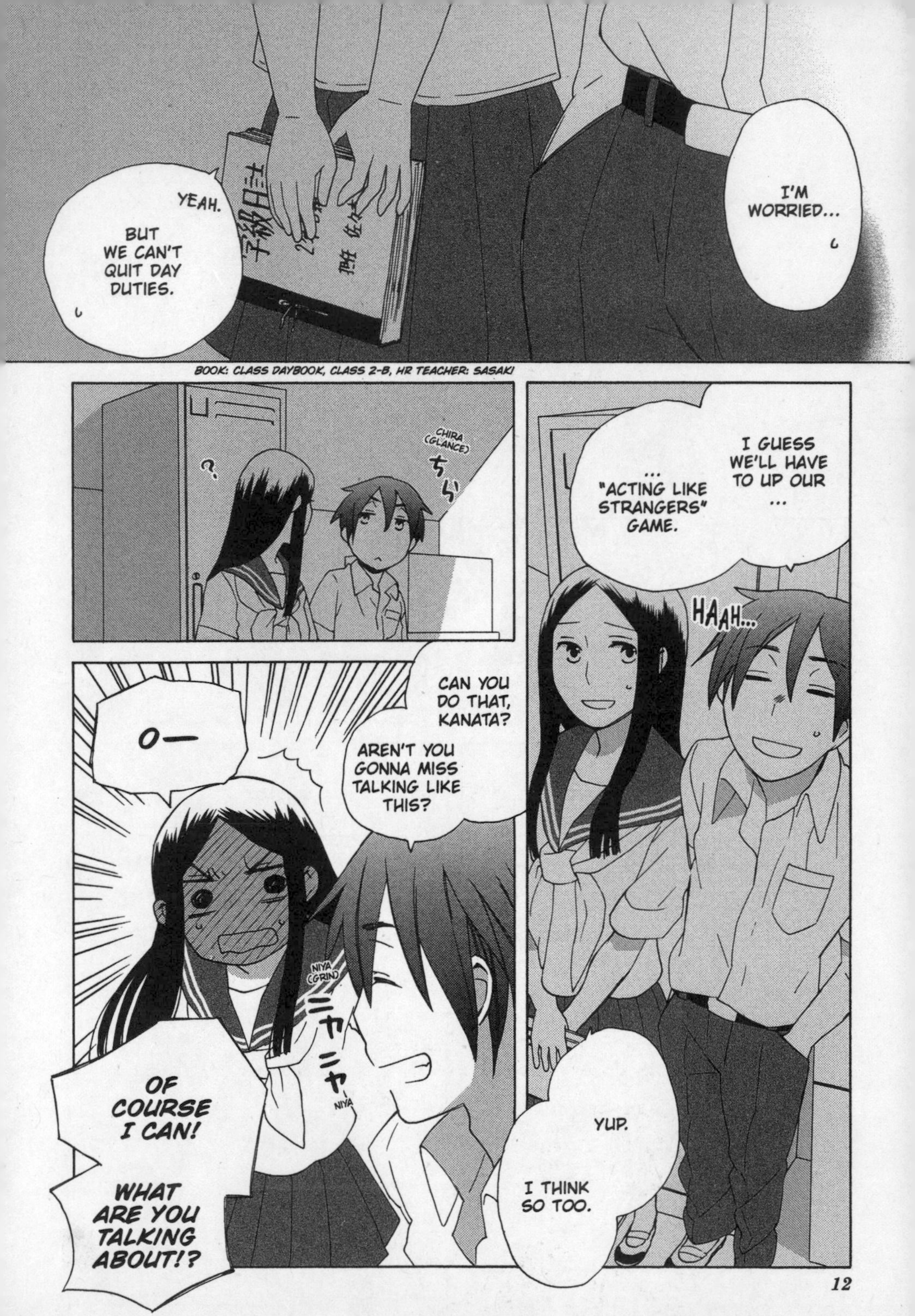
I'M WORRIED...
YEAH.
BUT WE CAN'T QUIT DAY DUTIES.
BOOK: CLASS DAYBOOK, CLASS 2-B, HR TEACHER: SASAKI
I GUESS WE'LL HAVE TO UP OUR ...
... "ACTING LIKE STRANGERS" GAME.
HAAH...
YUP.
I THINK SO TOO.
CHIRA (GLANCE)
ちら
?
CAN YOU DO THAT, KANATA?
AREN'T YOU GONNA MISS TALKING LIKE THIS?
NIYA (GRIN)
ニヤニヤ
NIYA
O—
OF COURSE I CAN!
WHAT ARE YOU TALKING ABOUT!?

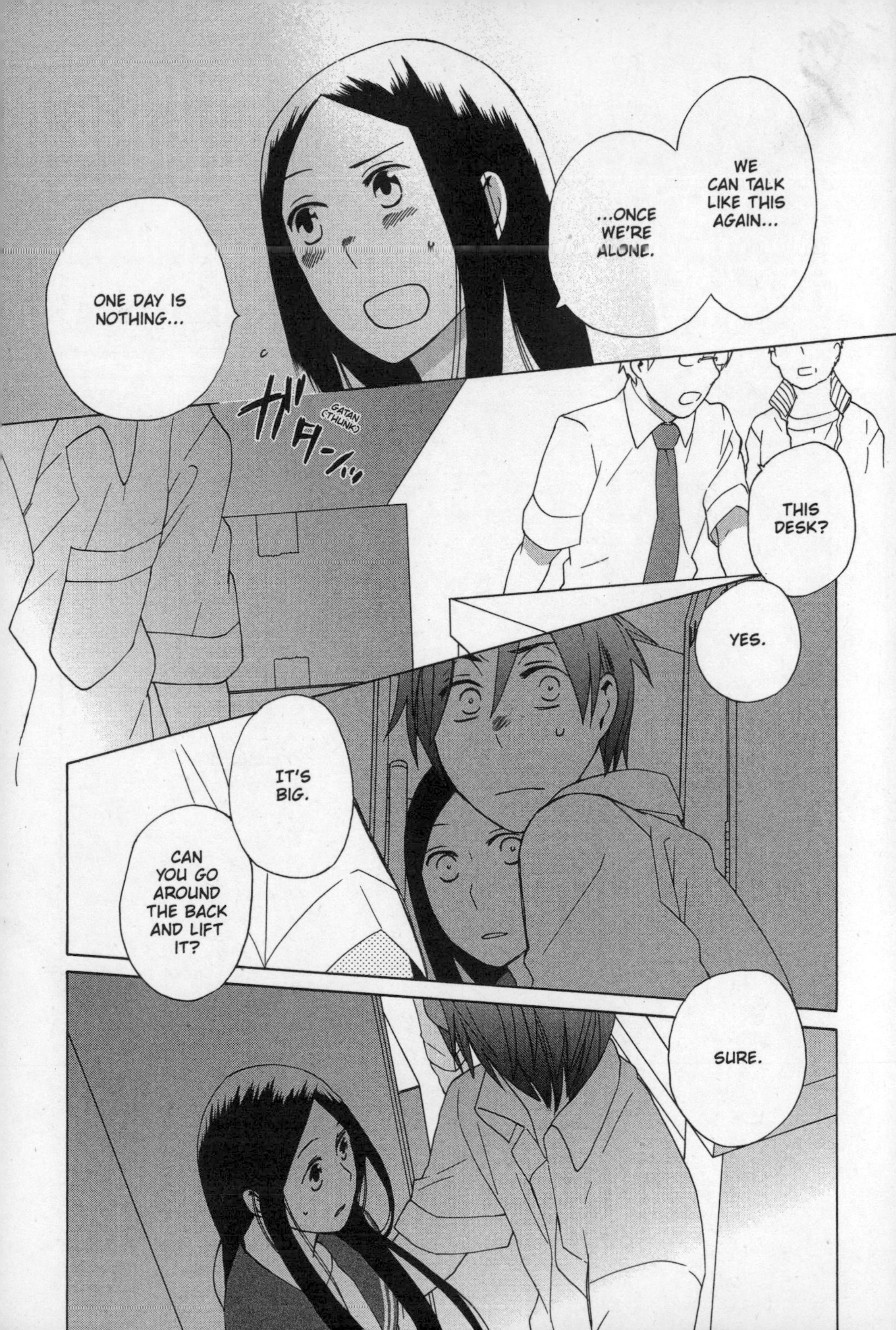
WE CAN TALK LIKE THIS AGAIN...
...ONCE WE'RE ALONE.
ONE DAY IS NOTHING...
THIS DESK?
GATAN (THUNK)
YES.
IT'S BIG.
CAN YOU GO AROUND THE BACK AND LIFT IT?
SURE.

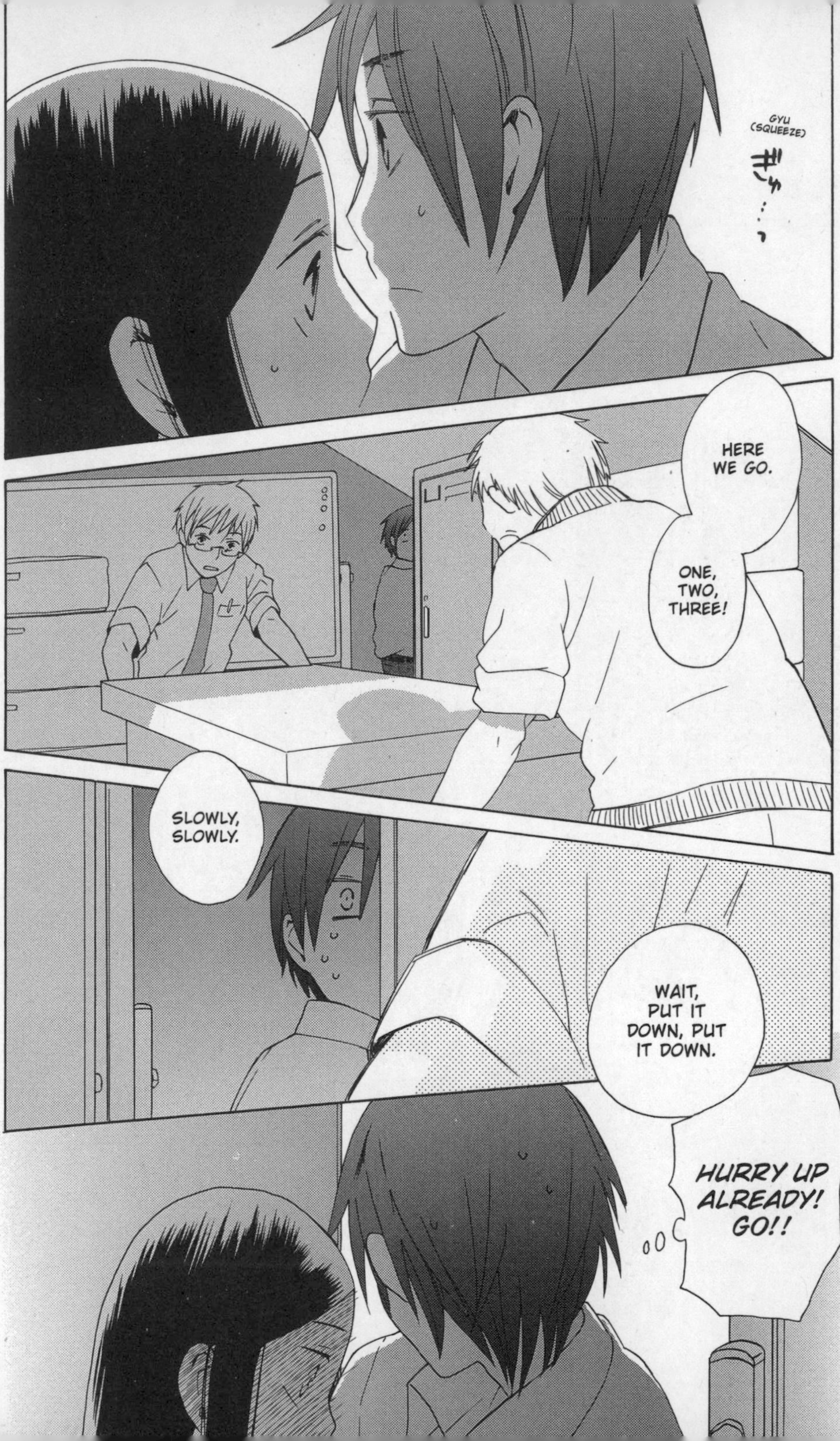
GYU (SQUEEZE)
ぎゅ…っ
HERE WE GO.
ONE, TWO, THREE!
SLOWLY, SLOWLY.
WAIT, PUT IT DOWN, PUT IT DOWN.
HURRY UP ALREADY! GO!!

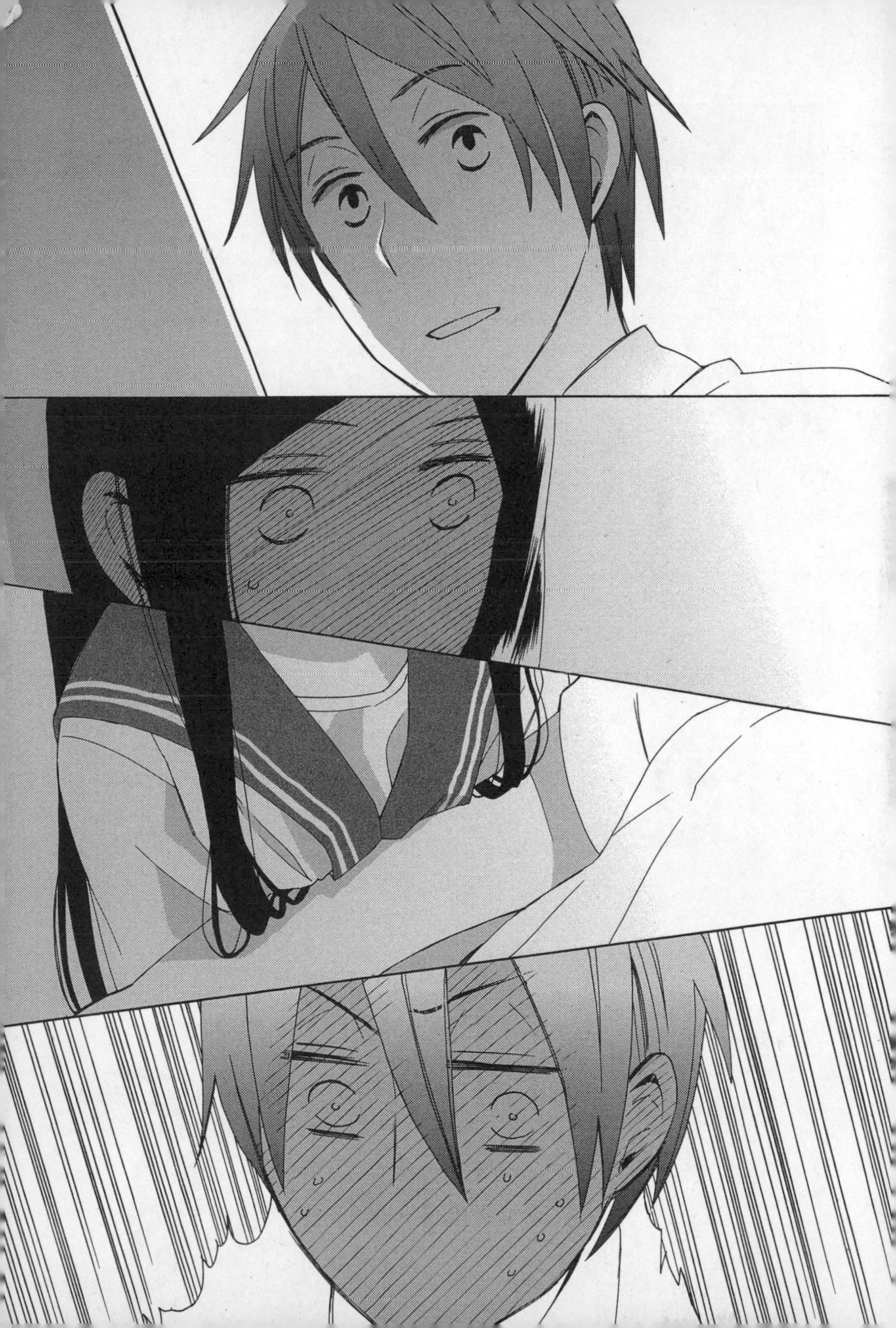

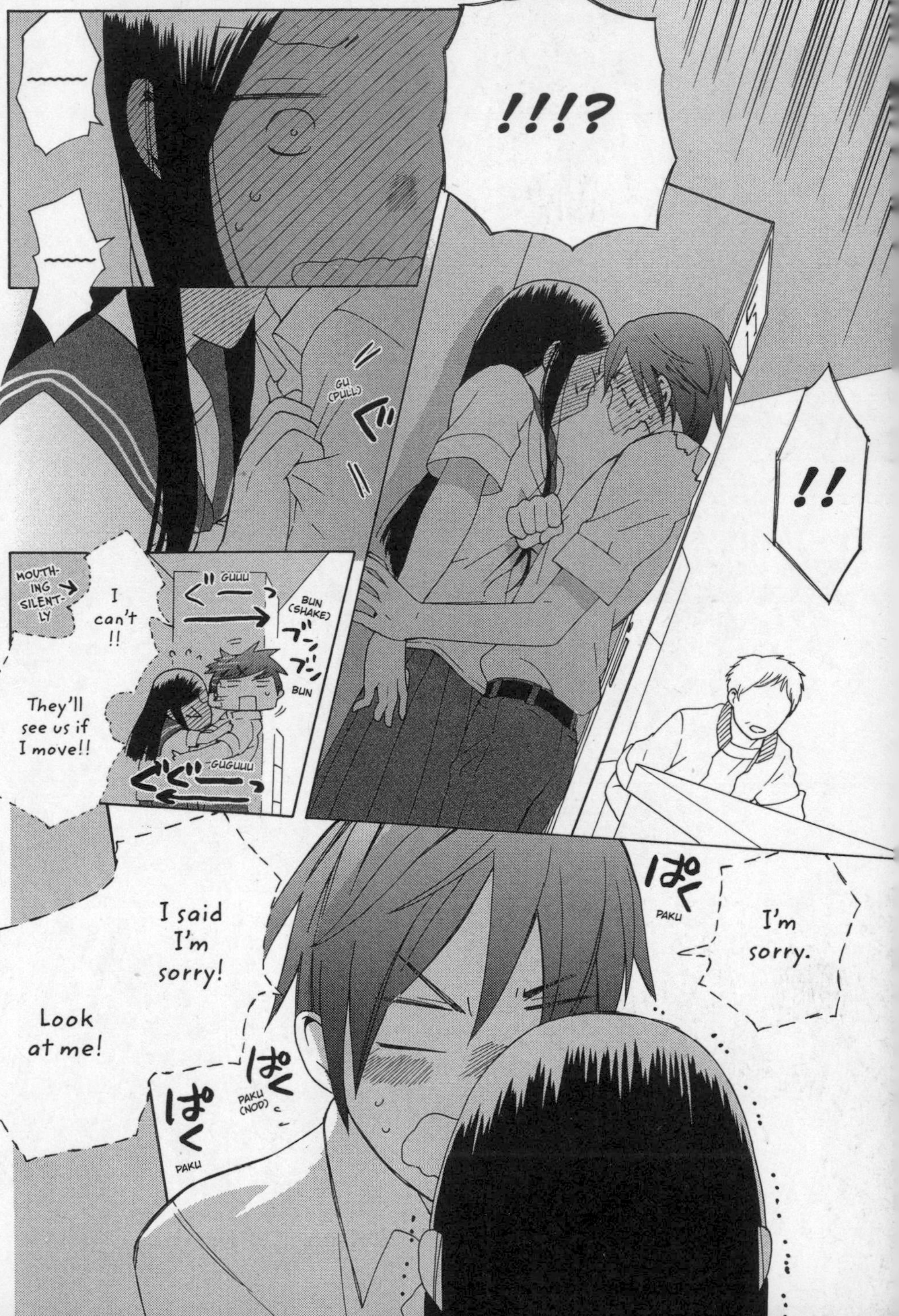
!!!?
!!
~~~~~
~~~~~
GU (PULL)
MOUTHING SILENTLY
I can't !!
They'll see us if I move!!
GUUU
BUN (SHAKE)
BUN
GUGUUU
ぱく
PAKU
I'm sorry.
I said I'm sorry!
Look at me!
ぱく
PAKU (NOD)
ぱく
PAKU

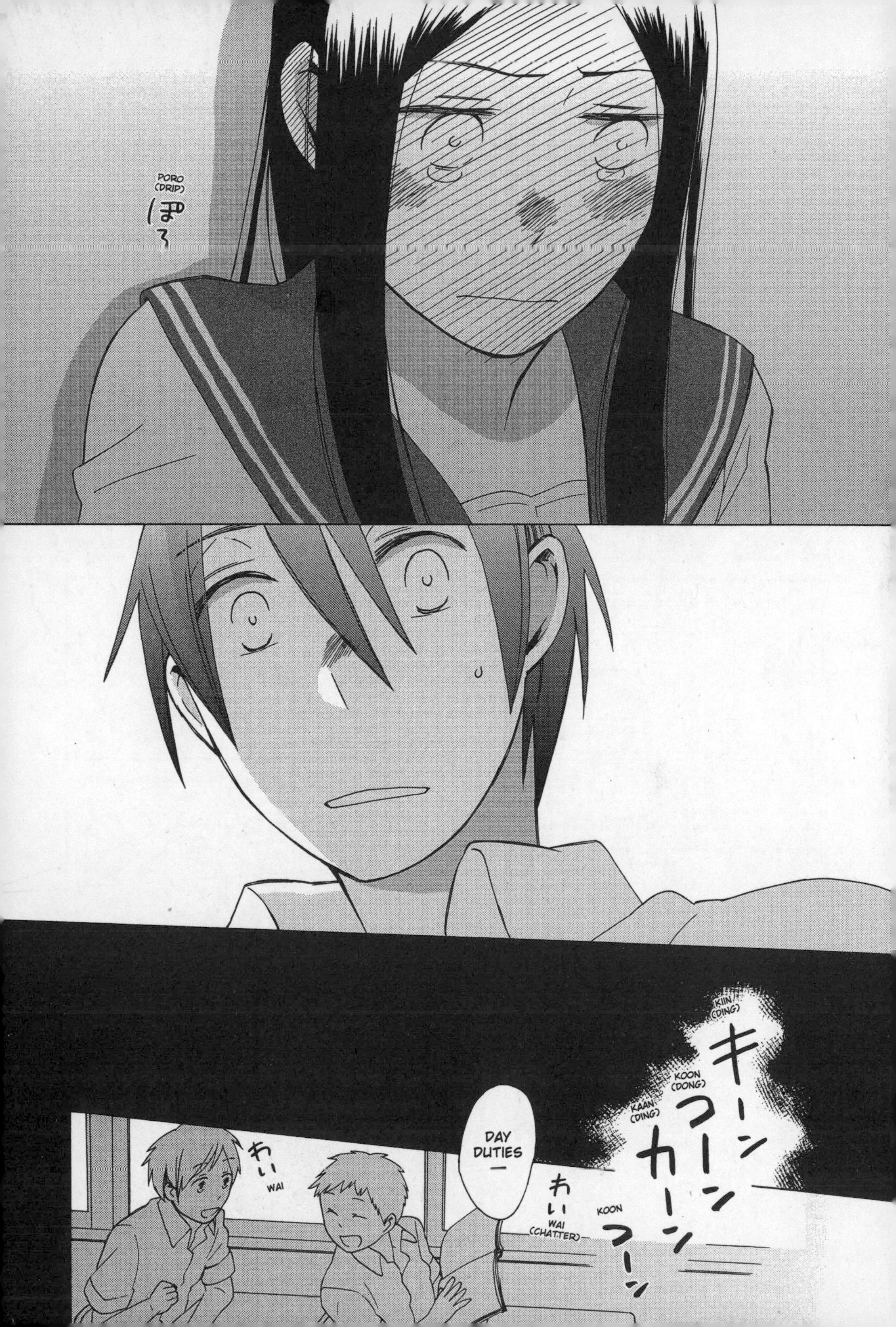
PORO (DRIP)
ぽろ
キーン
KIIN (DING)
コーン
KOON (DONG)
カーン
KAAN (DING)
コーン
KOON
DAY DUTIES—
わい
WAI (CHATTER)
わい
WAI

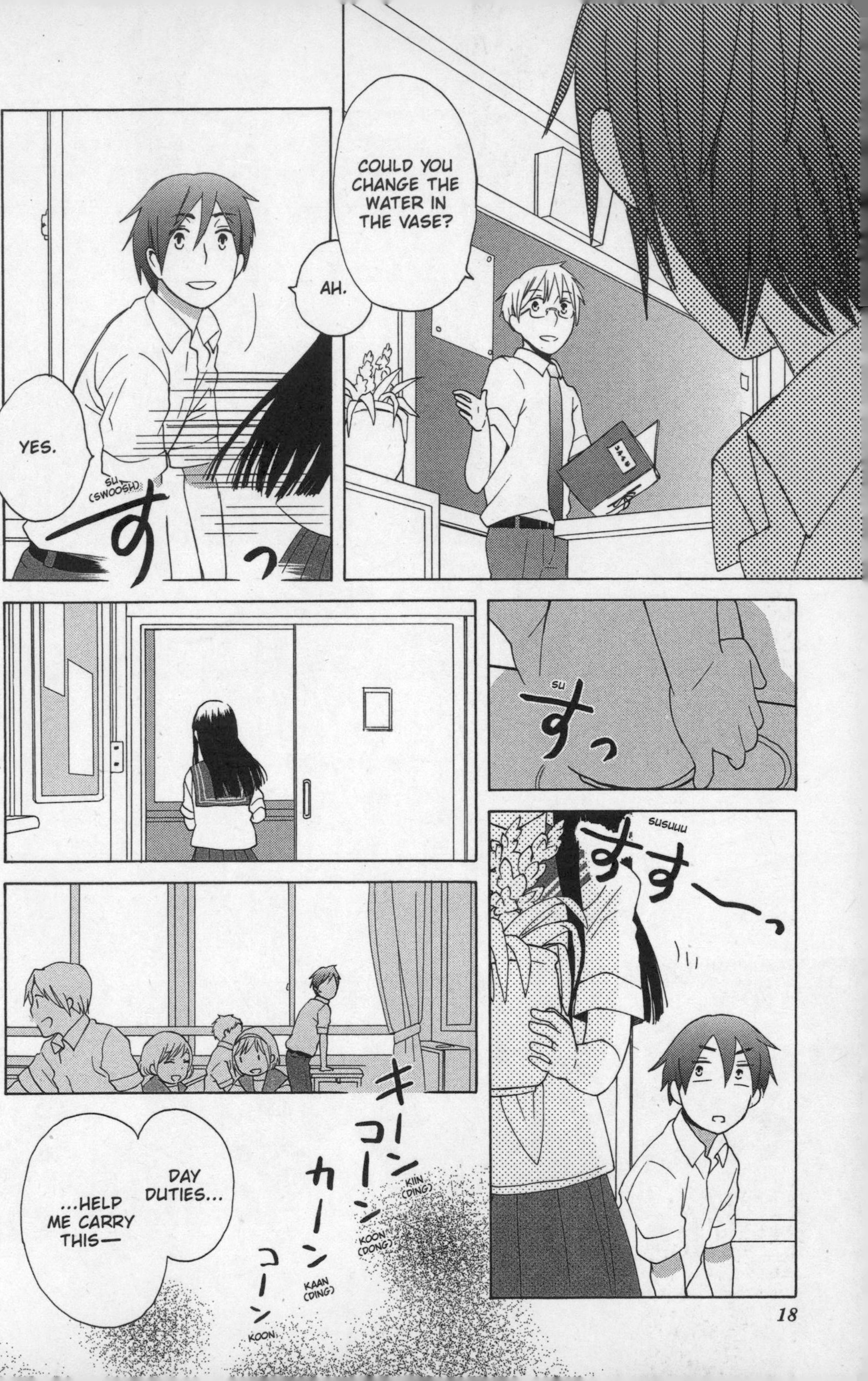

COULD YOU CHANGE THE WATER IN THE VASE?
AH.
YES.
SU (SWOOSH)
SU
SUSUUU
KIIN (DING)
KOON (DONG)
KAAN (DING)
KOON
DAY DUTIES...
...HELP ME CARRY THIS—

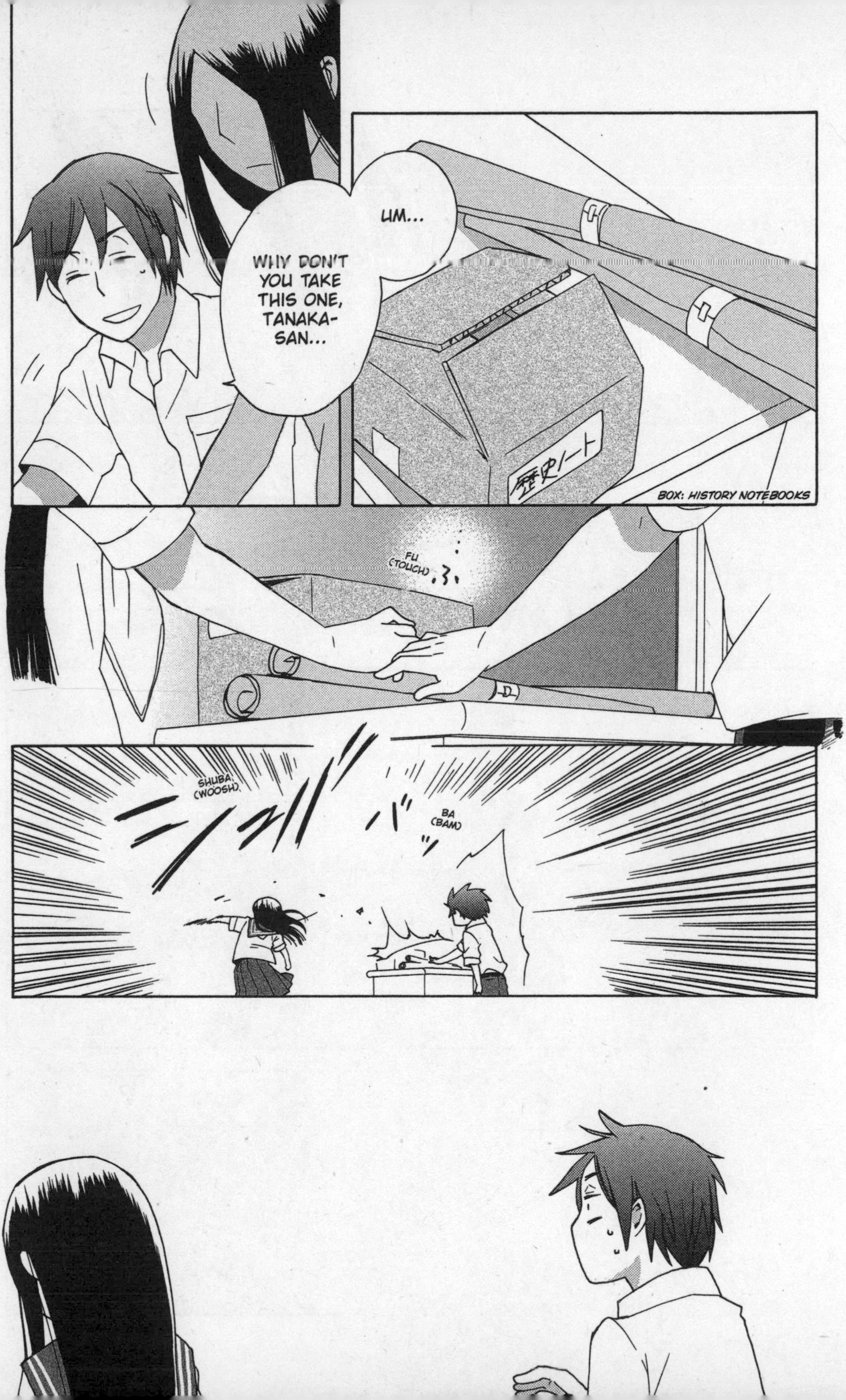
UM...
WHY DON'T YOU TAKE THIS ONE, TANAKA-SAN...
歴史ノート
BOX: HISTORY NOTEBOOKS
FU (TOUCH) ふ
BA (BAM)
SHUBA (WOOSH)

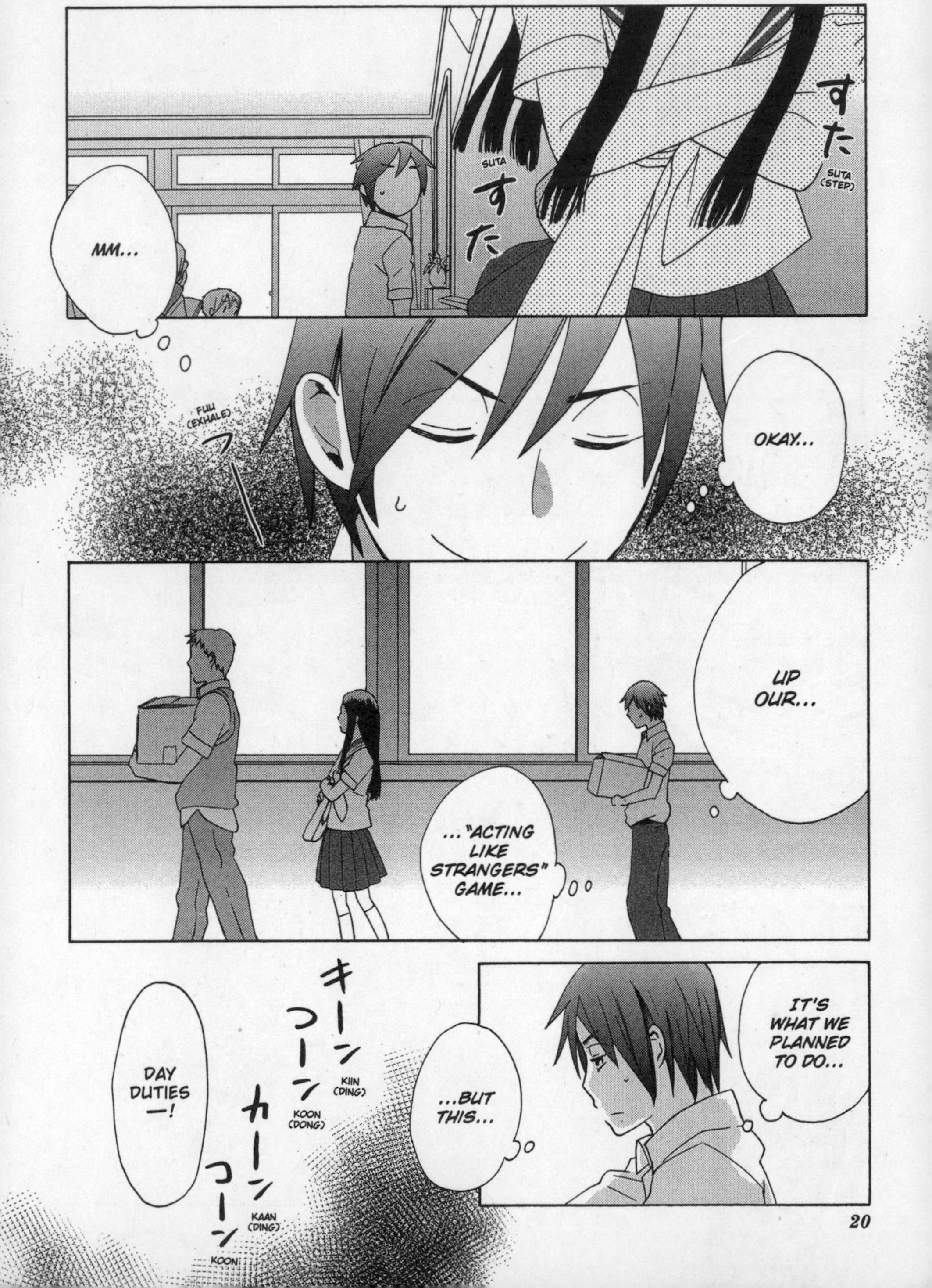
すた
SUTA (STEP)
SUTA
すた
MM...
OKAY...
FUU (EXHALE)
UP OUR...
..."ACTING LIKE STRANGERS" GAME...
IT'S WHAT WE PLANNED TO DO...
...BUT THIS...
キーン
KIIN (DING)
コーン
KOON (DONG)
カーン
KAAN (DING)
コーン
KOON
DAY DUTIES—!

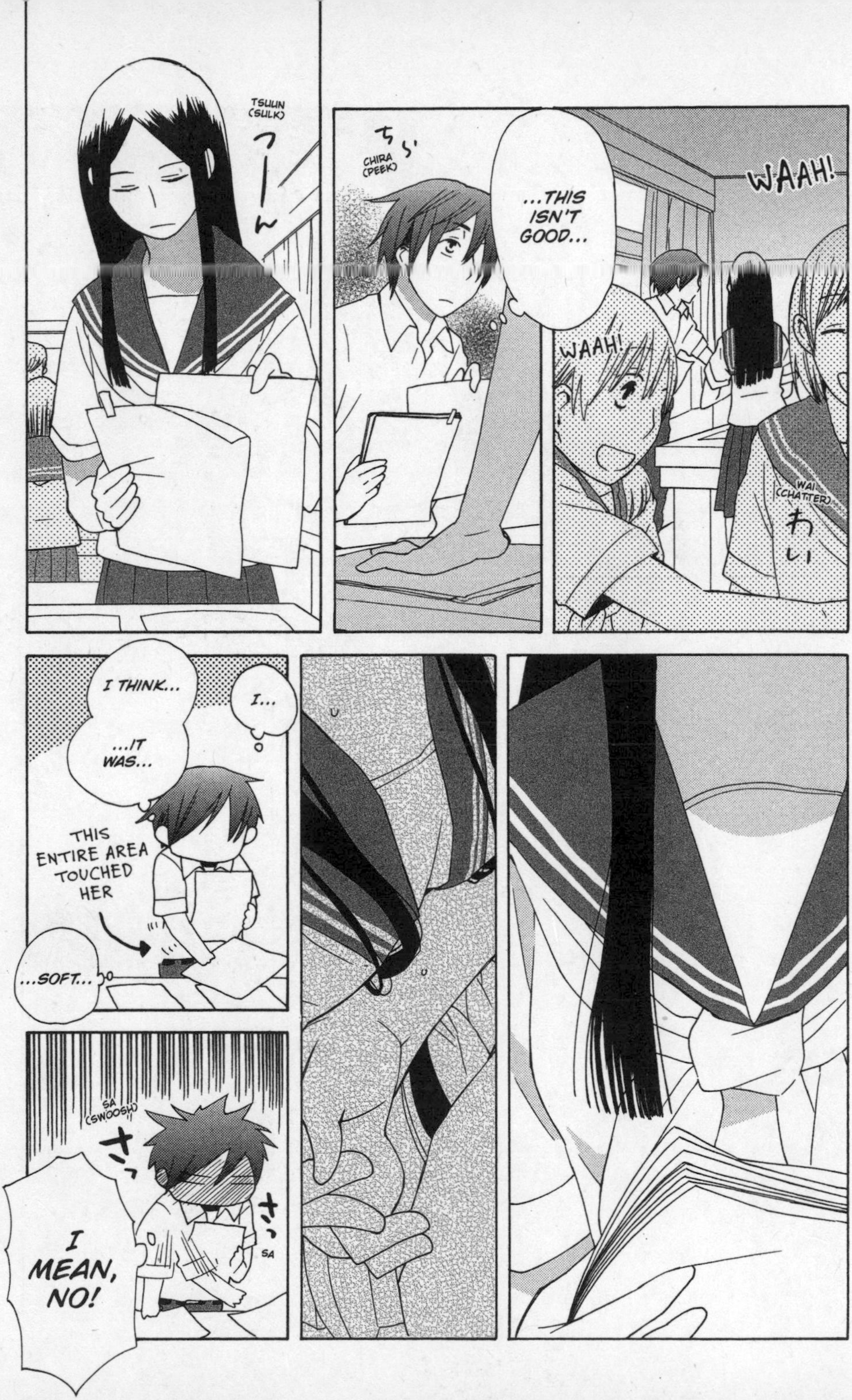
WAAH!
WAAH!
WAI (CHATTER)
わい
CHIRA (PEEK)
ちら
...THIS ISN'T GOOD...
TSUUN (SULK)
つーん
I...
I THINK...
...IT WAS...
THIS ENTIRE AREA TOUCHED HER
...SOFT...
SA (SWOOSH)
さっ
さっ
SA
I MEAN, NO!

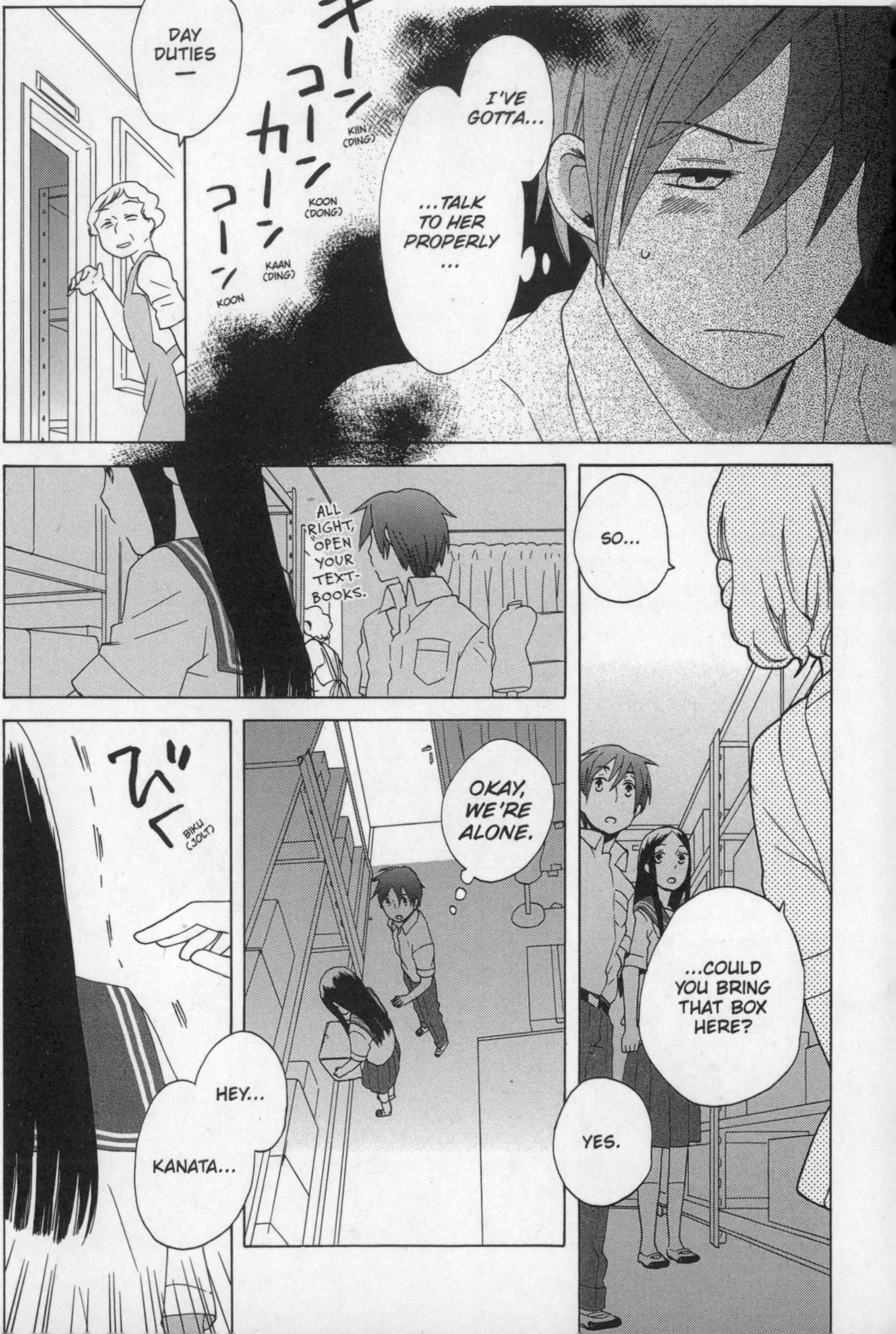
I'VE GOTTA...
...TALK TO HER PROPERLY...
キーンコーンカーンコーン
KIIN (DING)
KOON (DONG)
KAAN (DING)
KOON
DAY DUTIES —
SO...
...COULD YOU BRING THAT BOX HERE?
YES.
ALL RIGHT, OPEN YOUR TEXTBOOKS.
OKAY, WE'RE ALONE.
びく
BIKU (JOLT)
HEY...
KANATA...

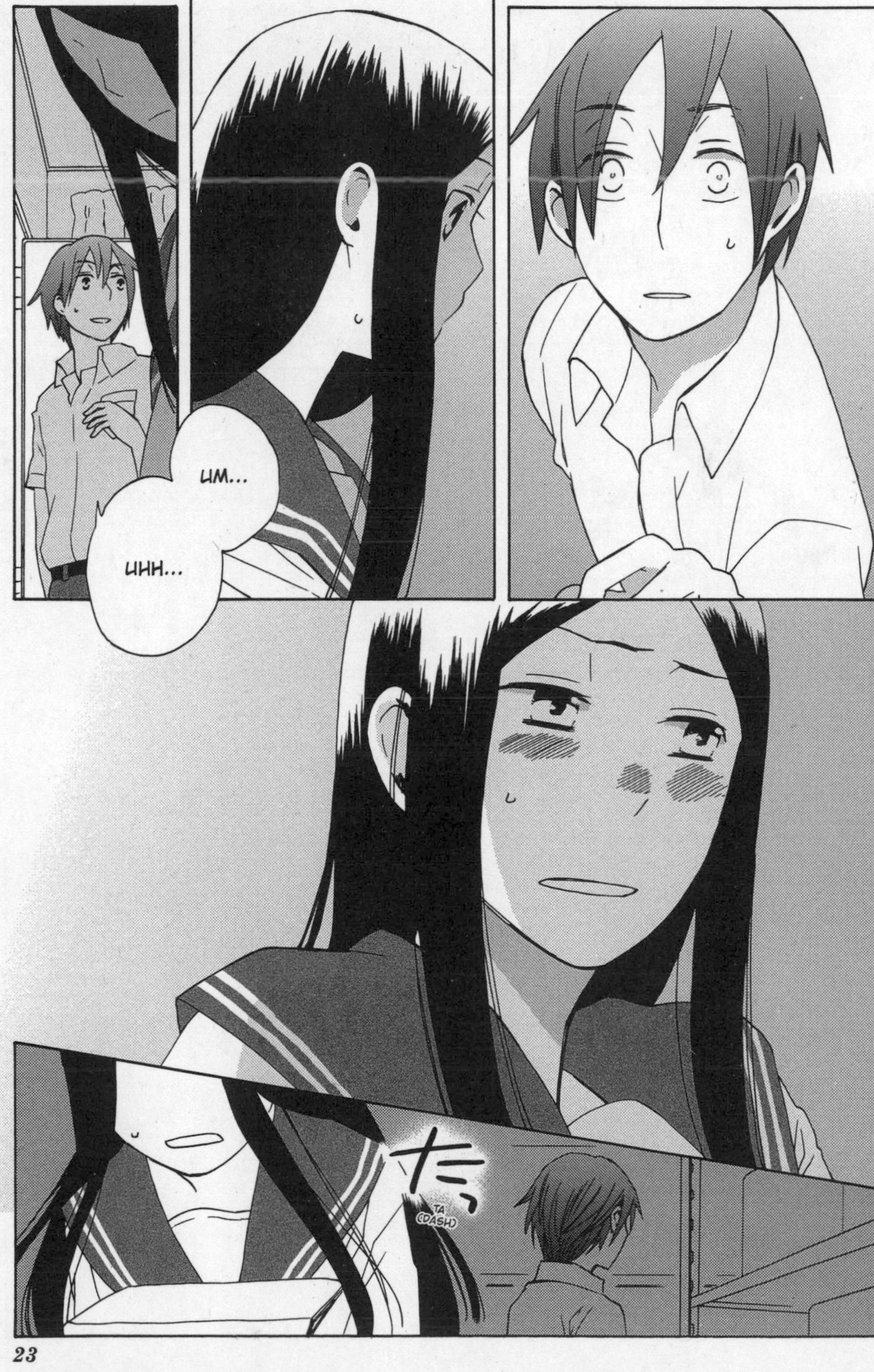
UM...
UHH...
たっ
TA (DASH)

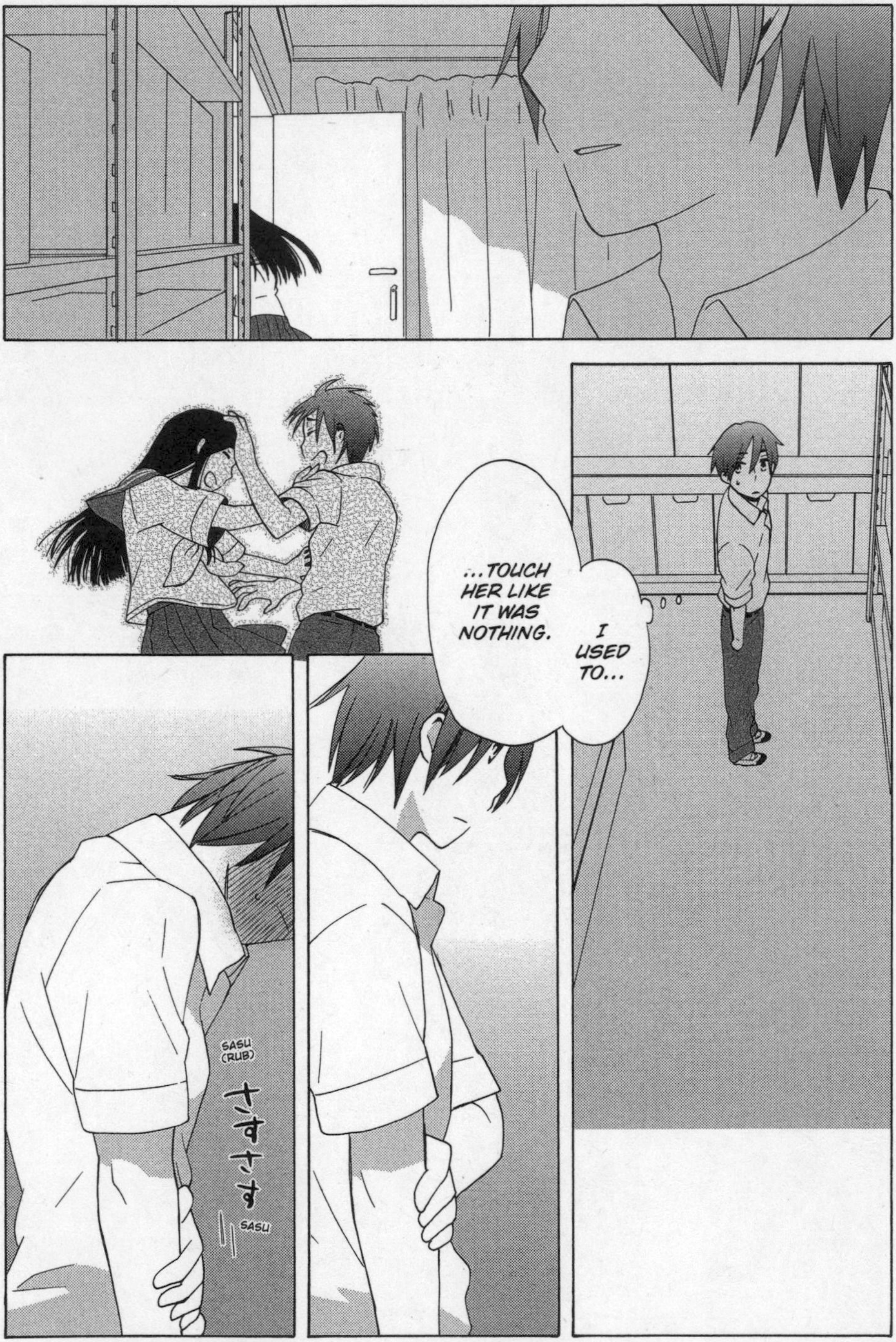
I USED TO...
...TOUCH HER LIKE IT WAS NOTHING.
SASU (RUB)
さすさす
SASU

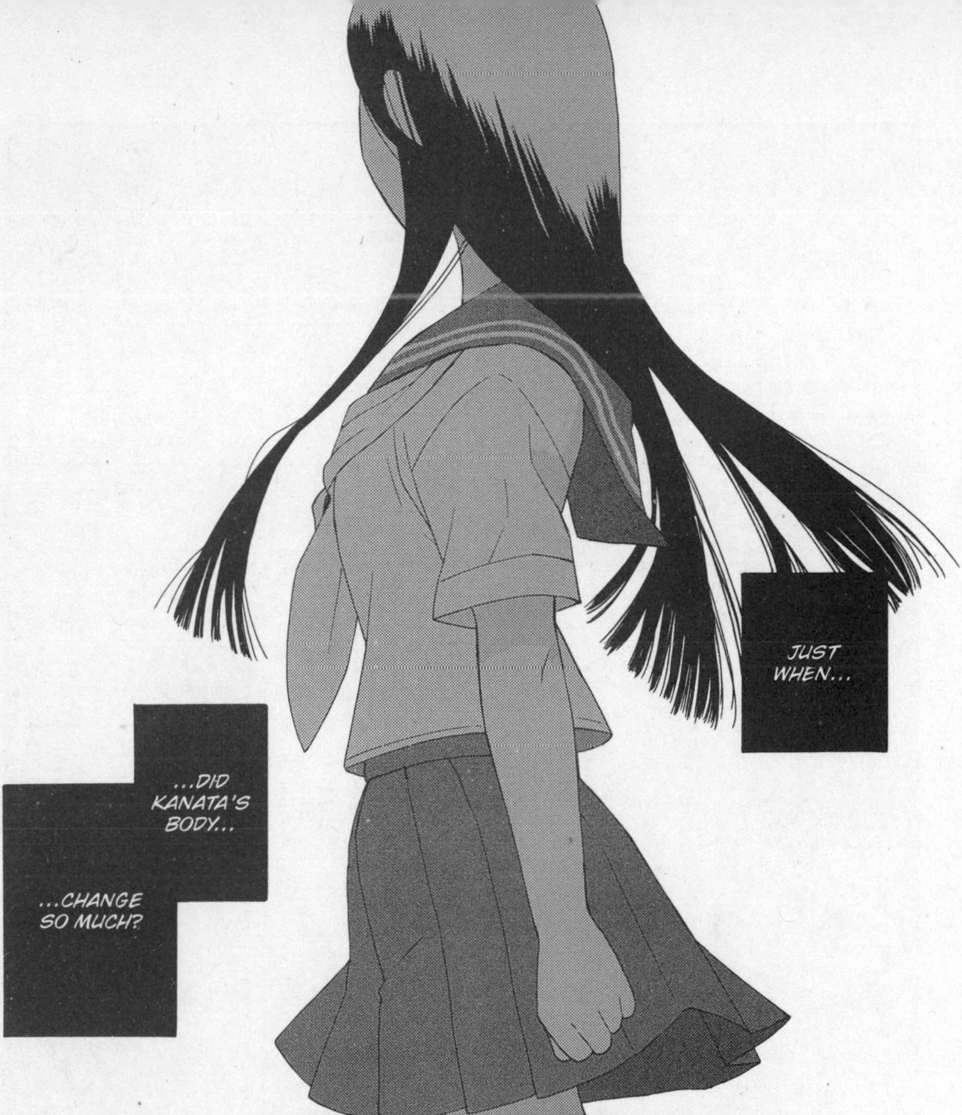
JUST WHEN...
...DID KANATA'S BODY...
...CHANGE SO MUCH?

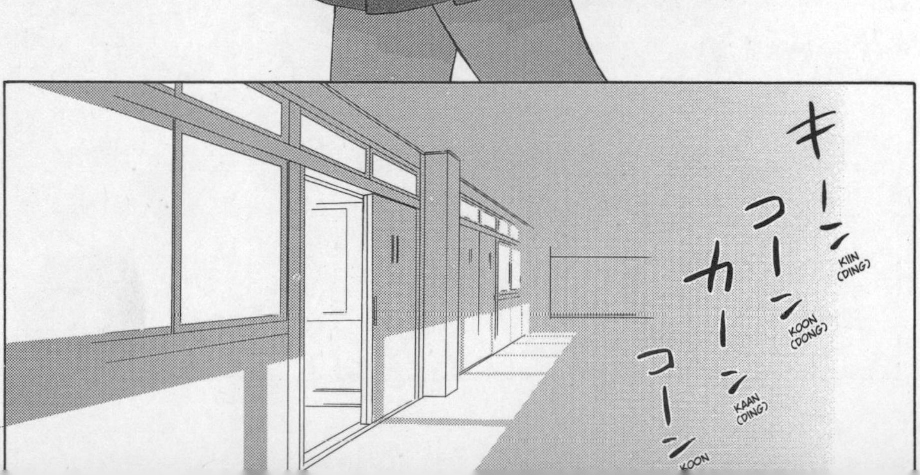
キーン
KIIN (DING)
コーン
KOON (DONG)
カーン
KAAN (DING)
コーン
KOON

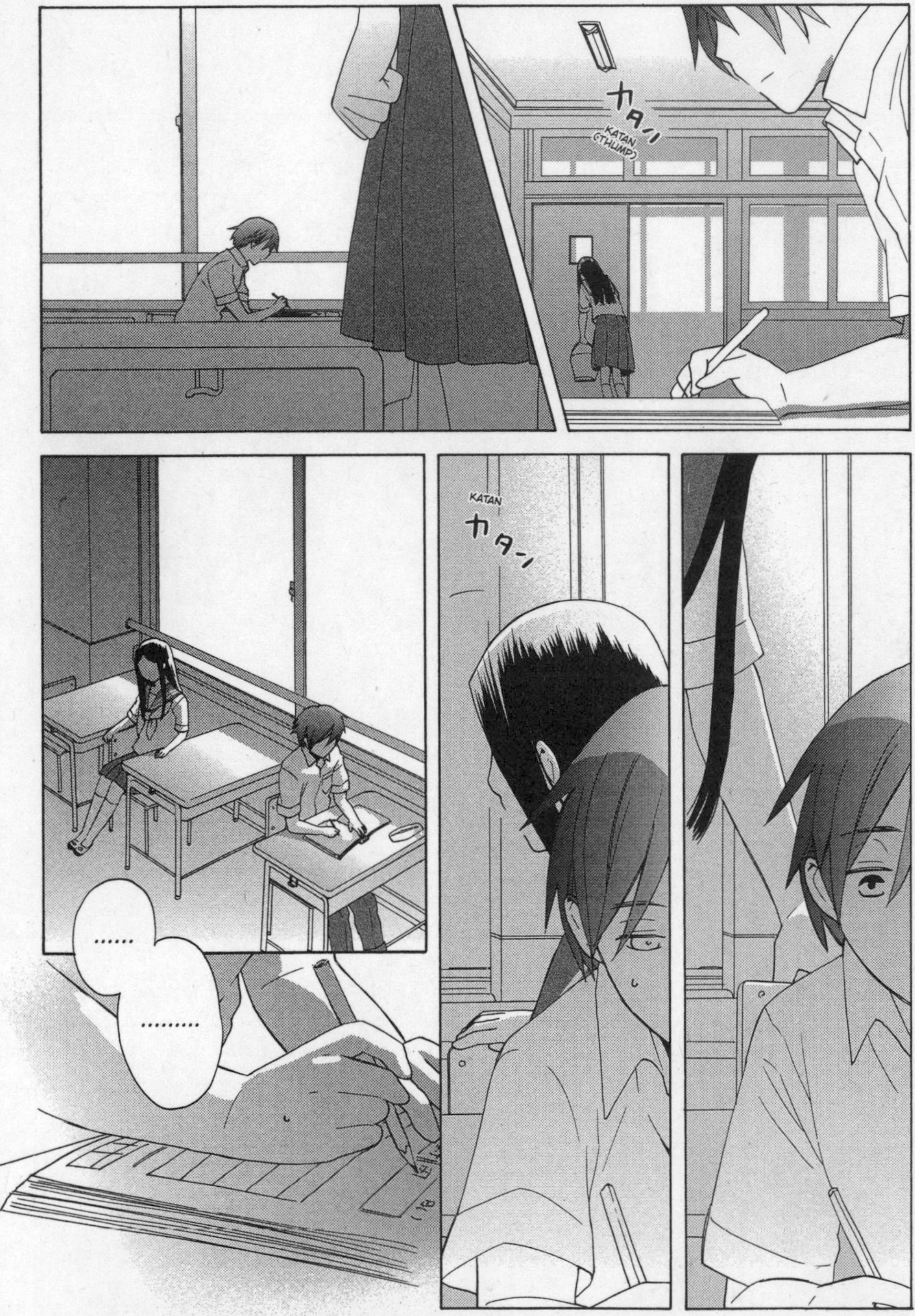
カタン
KATAN (THUMP)
KATAN
カターン
......
....

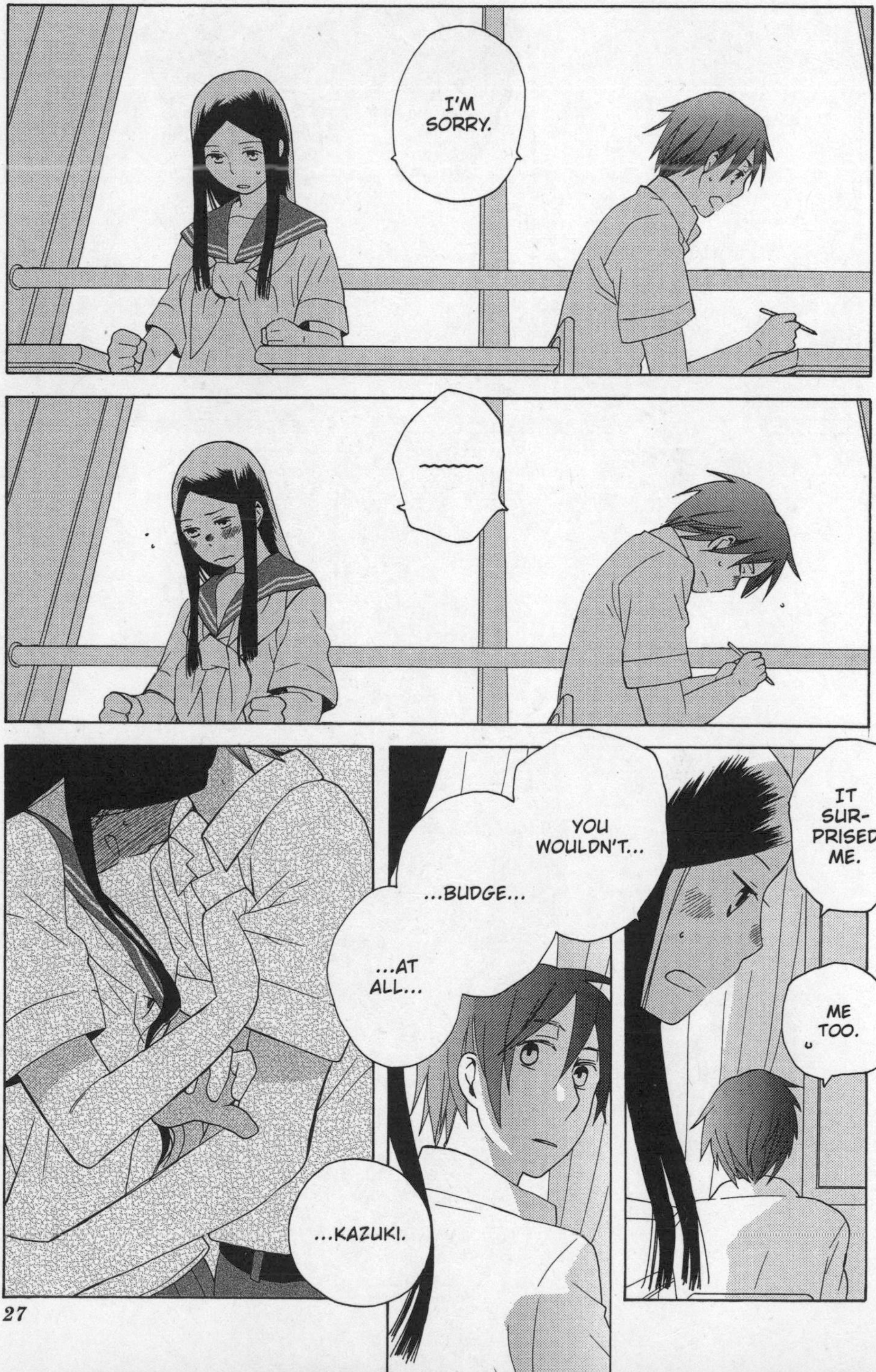
I'M SORRY.
IT...
IT SURPRISED ME.
ME TOO.
YOU WOULDN'T...
...BUDGE...
...AT ALL...
...KAZUKI.

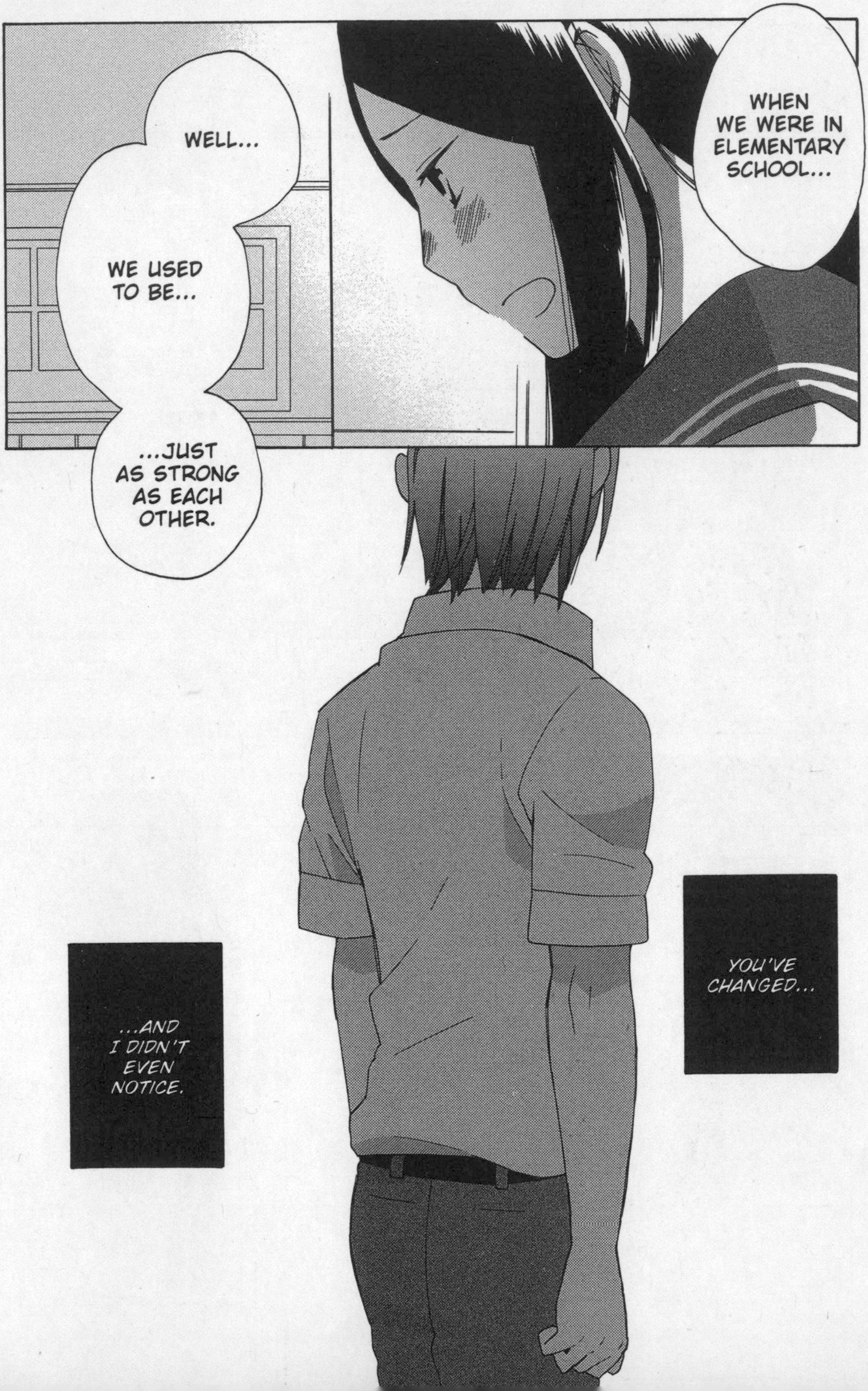
WHEN WE WERE IN ELEMENTARY SCHOOL...
WELL...
WE USED TO BE...
...JUST AS STRONG AS EACH OTHER.
YOU'VE CHANGED...
...AND I DIDN'T EVEN NOTICE.

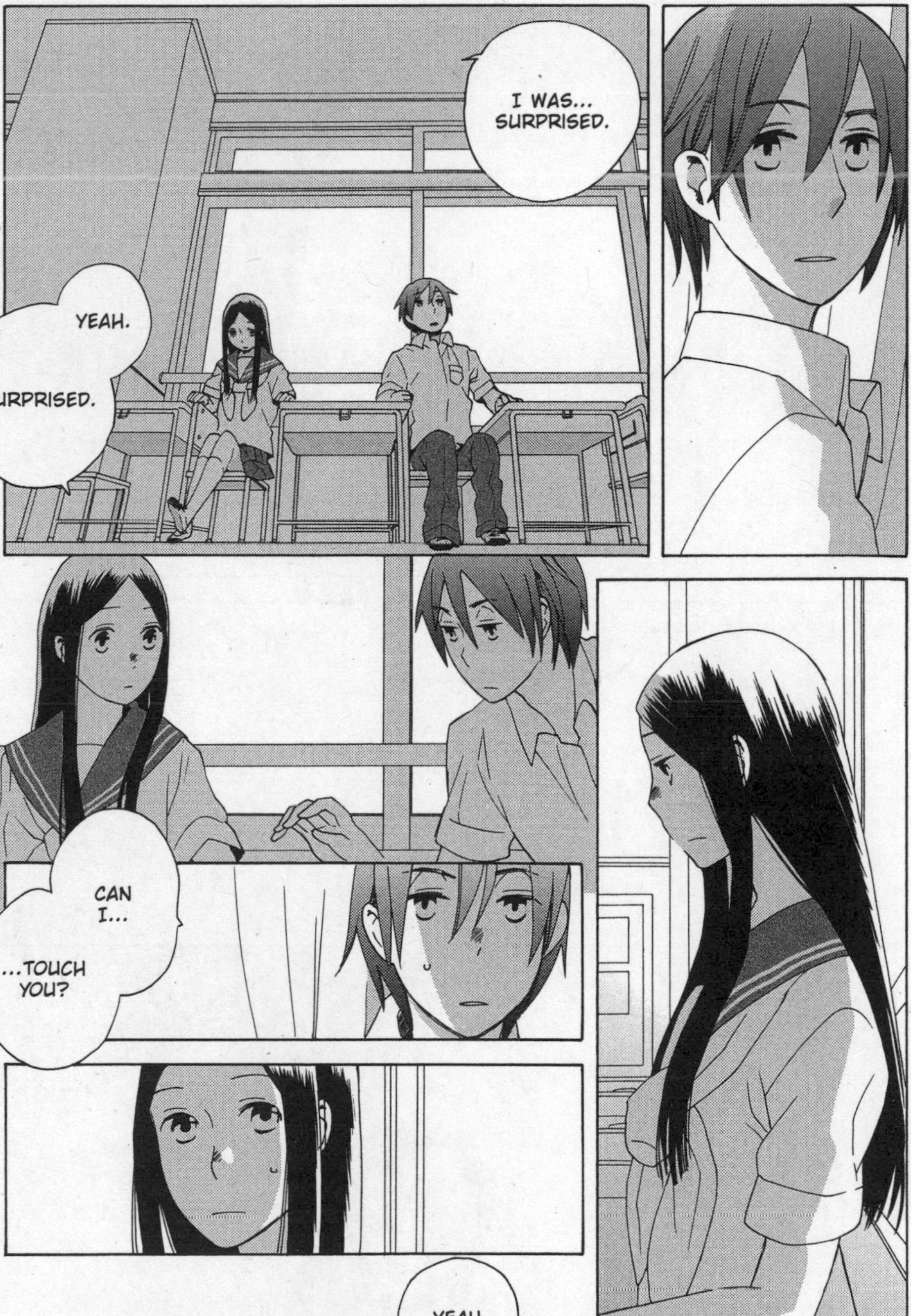
I WAS... SURPRISED.
YEAH.
SURPRISED.
CAN I...
...TOUCH YOU?
YEAH.

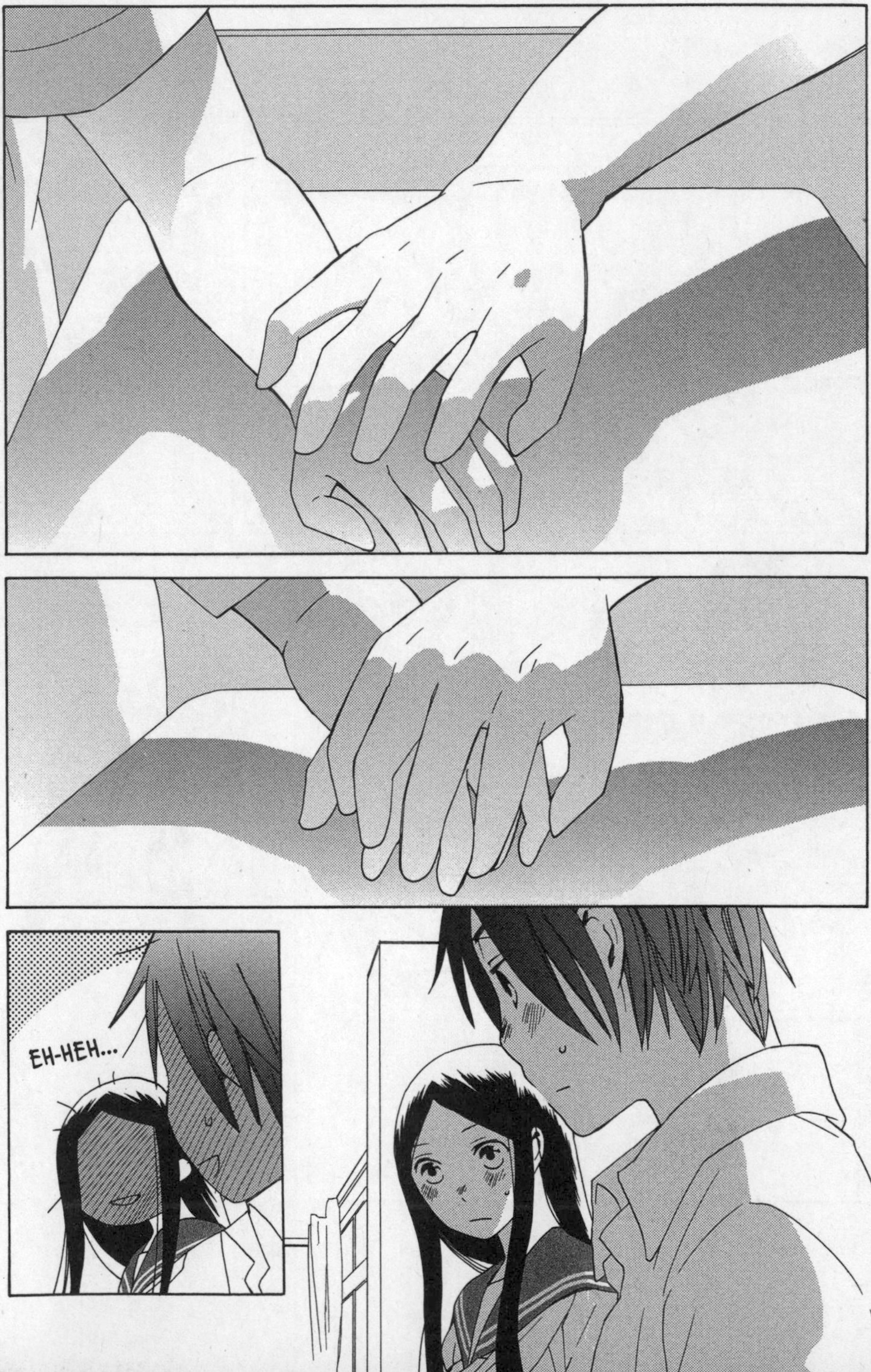
EH-HEH...

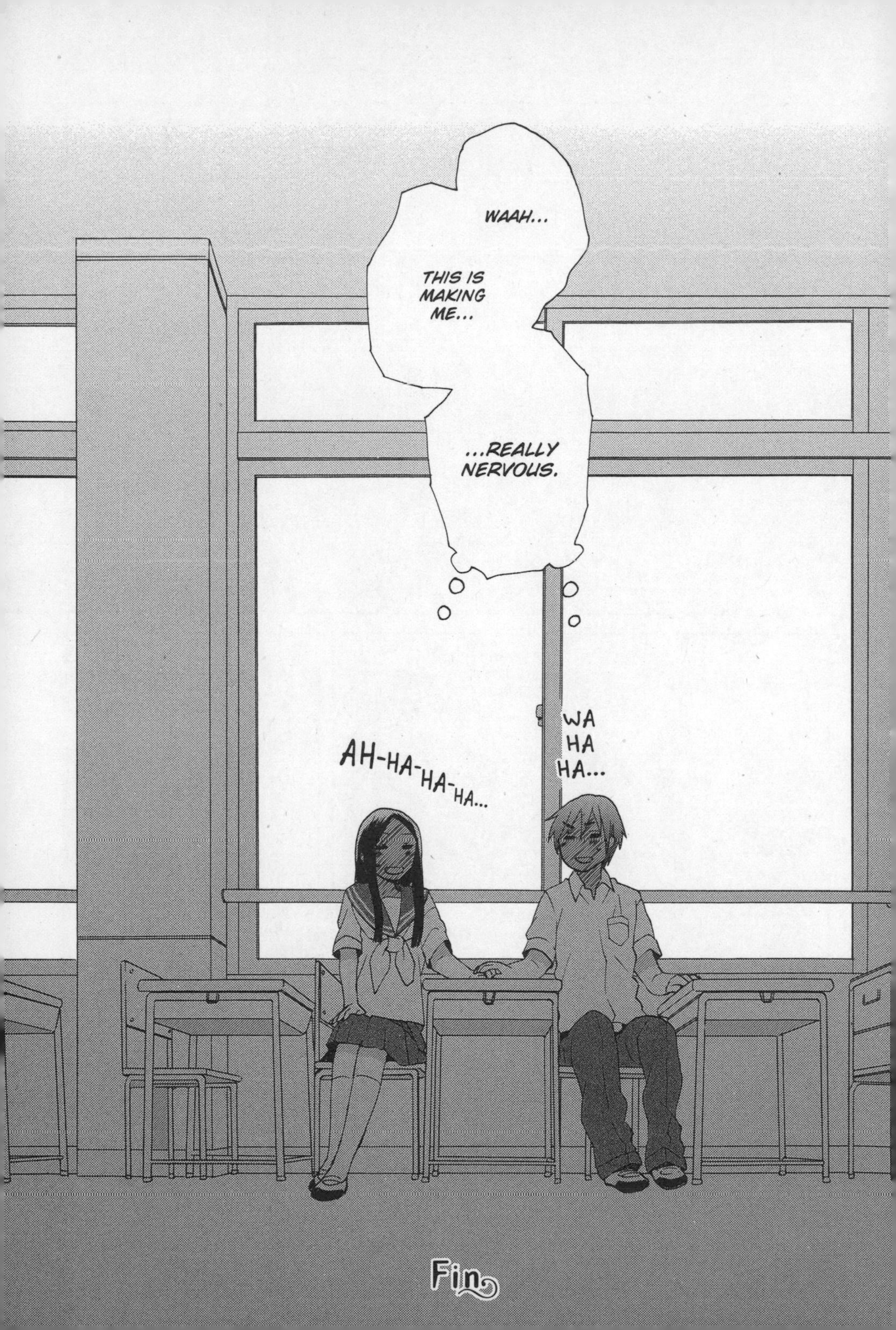
WAAH...
THIS IS MAKING ME...
...REALLY NERVOUS.
WA HA HA...
AH-HA-HA-HA...
Fin

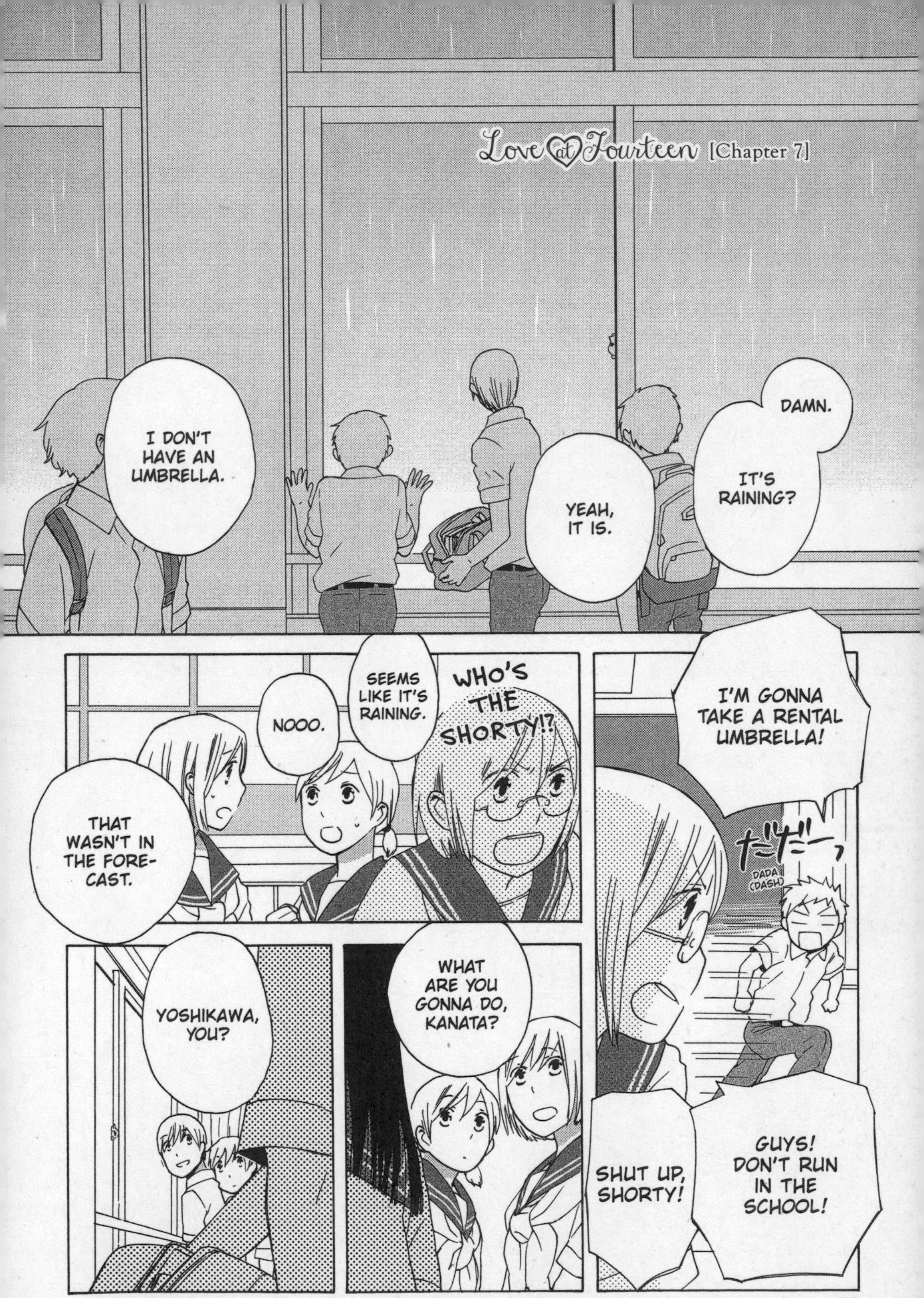
Love at Fourteen [Chapter 7]
DAMN.
IT'S RAINING?
YEAH, IT IS.
I DON'T HAVE AN UMBRELLA.
I'M GONNA TAKE A RENTAL UMBRELLA!
ダーダー
DADA (DASH)
GUYS! DON'T RUN IN THE SCHOOL!
SHUT UP, SHORTY!
WHO'S THE SHORTY!?
SEEMS LIKE IT'S RAINING.
NOOO.
THAT WASN'T IN THE FORE-CAST.
WHAT ARE YOU GONNA DO, KANATA?
YOSHIKAWA, YOU?

Love at Fourteen

[Chapter 7]

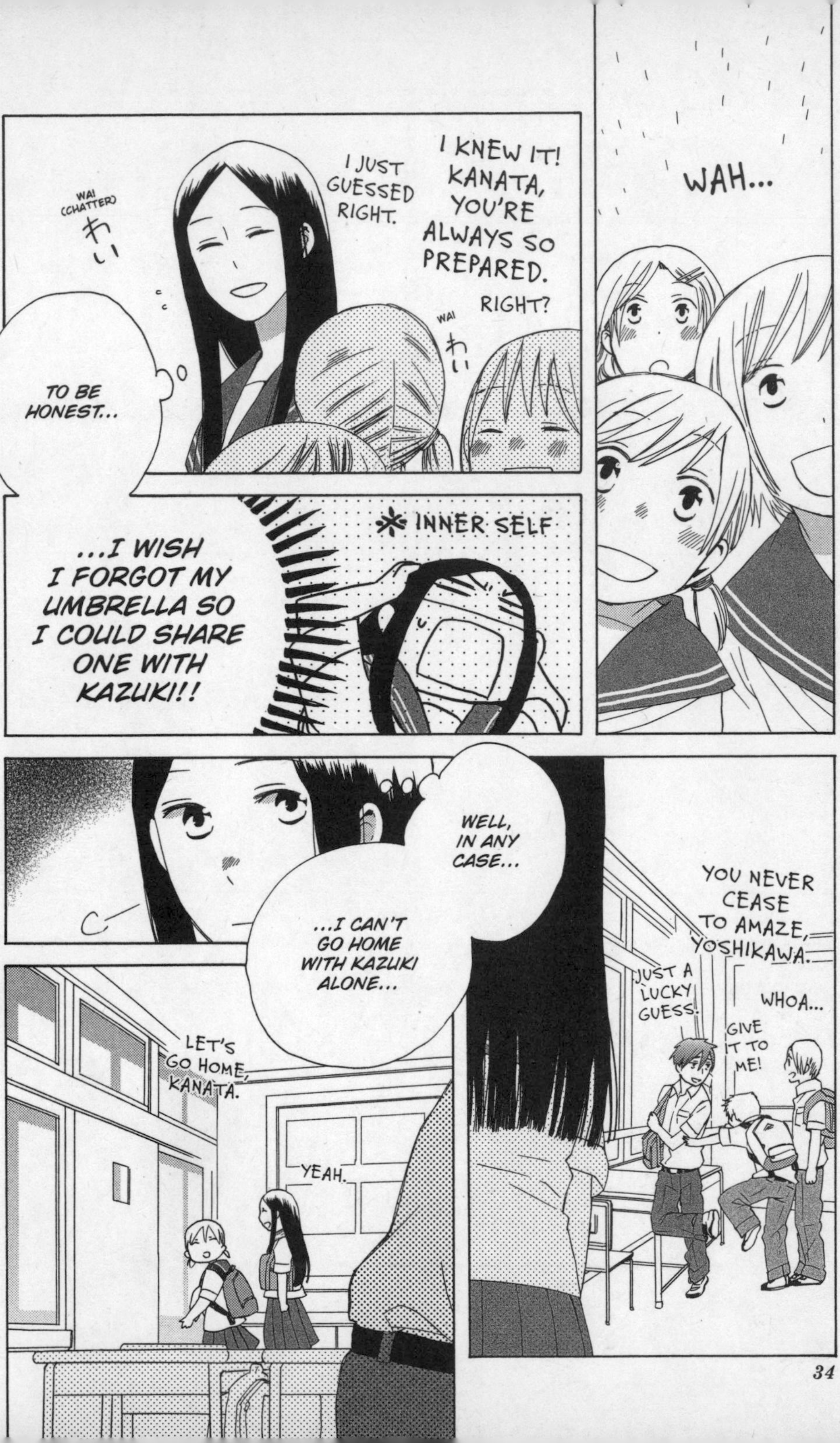
WAH...
I KNEW IT! KANATA, YOU'RE ALWAYS SO PREPARED.
I JUST GUESSED RIGHT.
WAI (CHATTER) わい
WAI わい
RIGHT?
TO BE HONEST...
※ INNER SELF
...I WISH I FORGOT MY UMBRELLA SO I COULD SHARE ONE WITH KAZUKI!!
YOU NEVER CEASE TO AMAZE, YOSHIKAWA.
JUST A LUCKY GUESS.
WHOA...
GIVE IT TO ME!
WELL, IN ANY CASE...
...I CAN'T GO HOME WITH KAZUKI ALONE...
LET'S GO HOME, KANATA.
YEAH.

SIGN: RENTAL UMBRELLA. WRITE YOUR CLASS AND NAME.
PLEASE RETURN DRY. CHECK ☑ ONCE YOU RETURN IT.

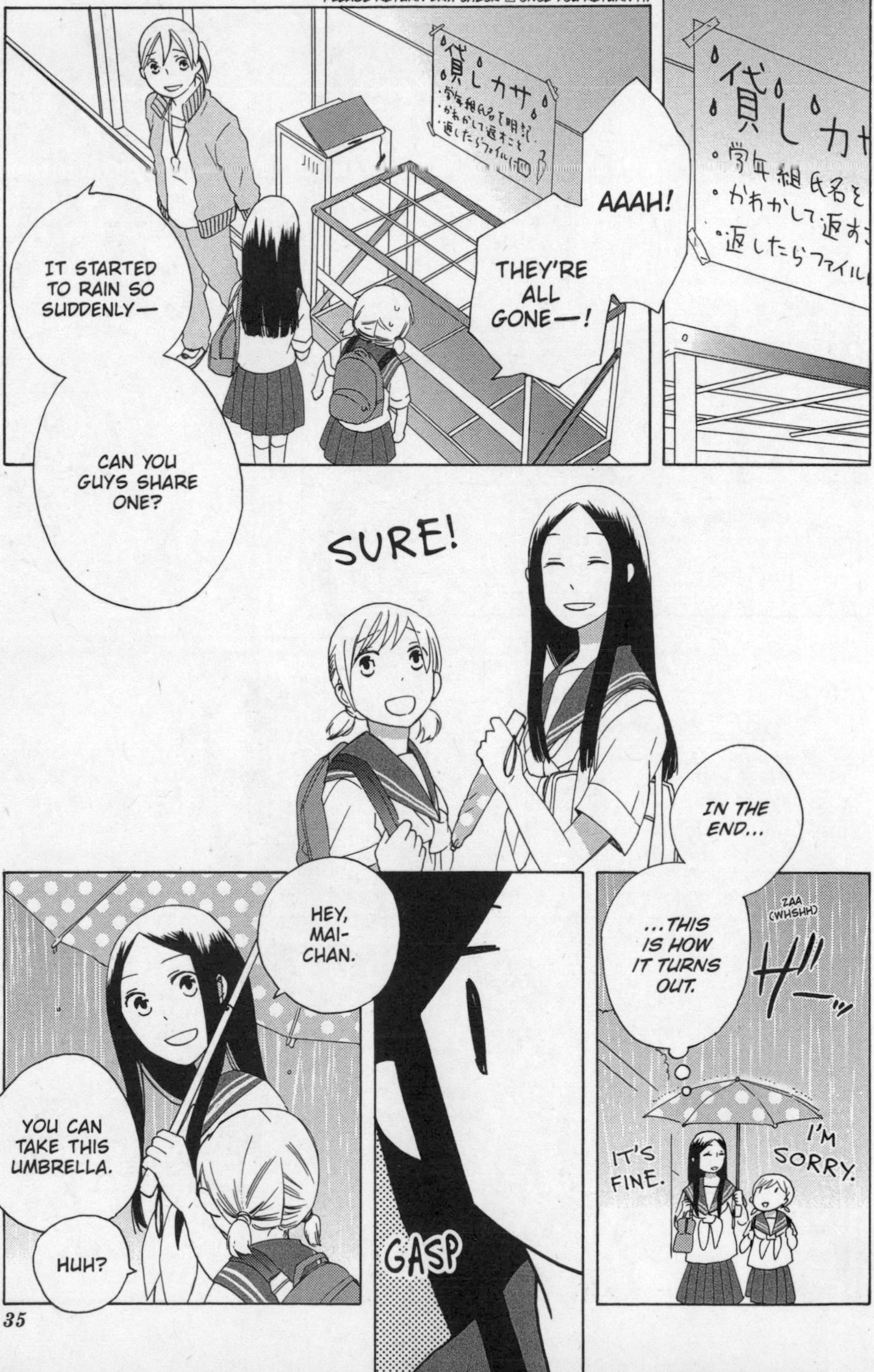

貸しカサ
AAAH!
THEY'RE ALL GONE—!
IT STARTED TO RAIN SO SUDDENLY—
CAN YOU GUYS SHARE ONE?
SURE!
IN THE END...
...THIS IS HOW IT TURNS OUT.
ZAA (WHSHH)
I'M SORRY.
IT'S FINE.
GASP
HEY, MAI-CHAN.
YOU CAN TAKE THIS UMBRELLA.
HUH?

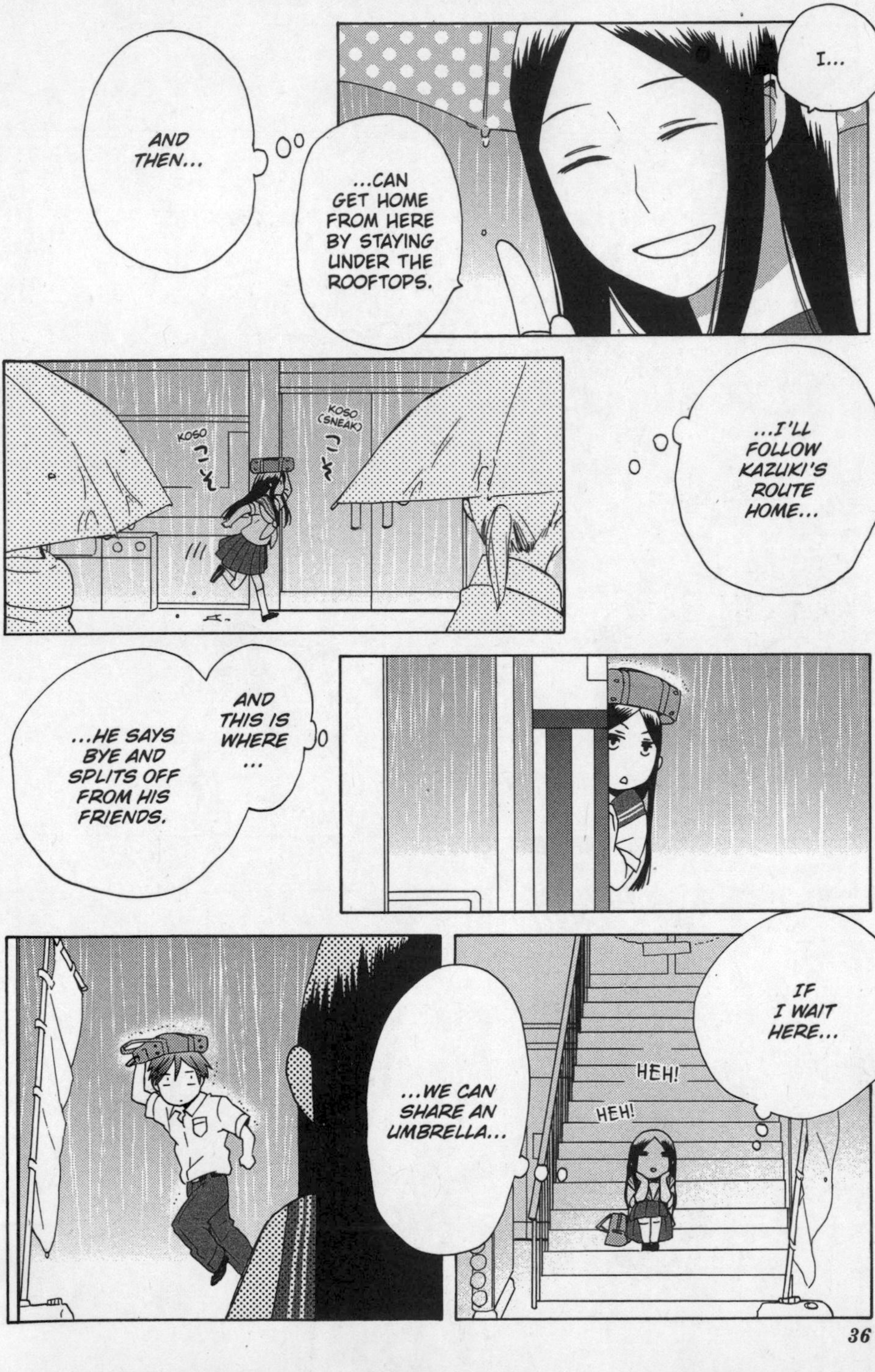
I...
...CAN GET HOME FROM HERE BY STAYING UNDER THE ROOFTOPS.
AND THEN...
...I'LL FOLLOW KAZUKI'S ROUTE HOME...
KOSO (SNEAK)
こそ
KOSO
こそ
AND THIS IS WHERE ...
...HE SAYS BYE AND SPLITS OFF FROM HIS FRIENDS.
IF I WAIT HERE...
HEH!
HEH!
...WE CAN SHARE AN UMBRELLA...

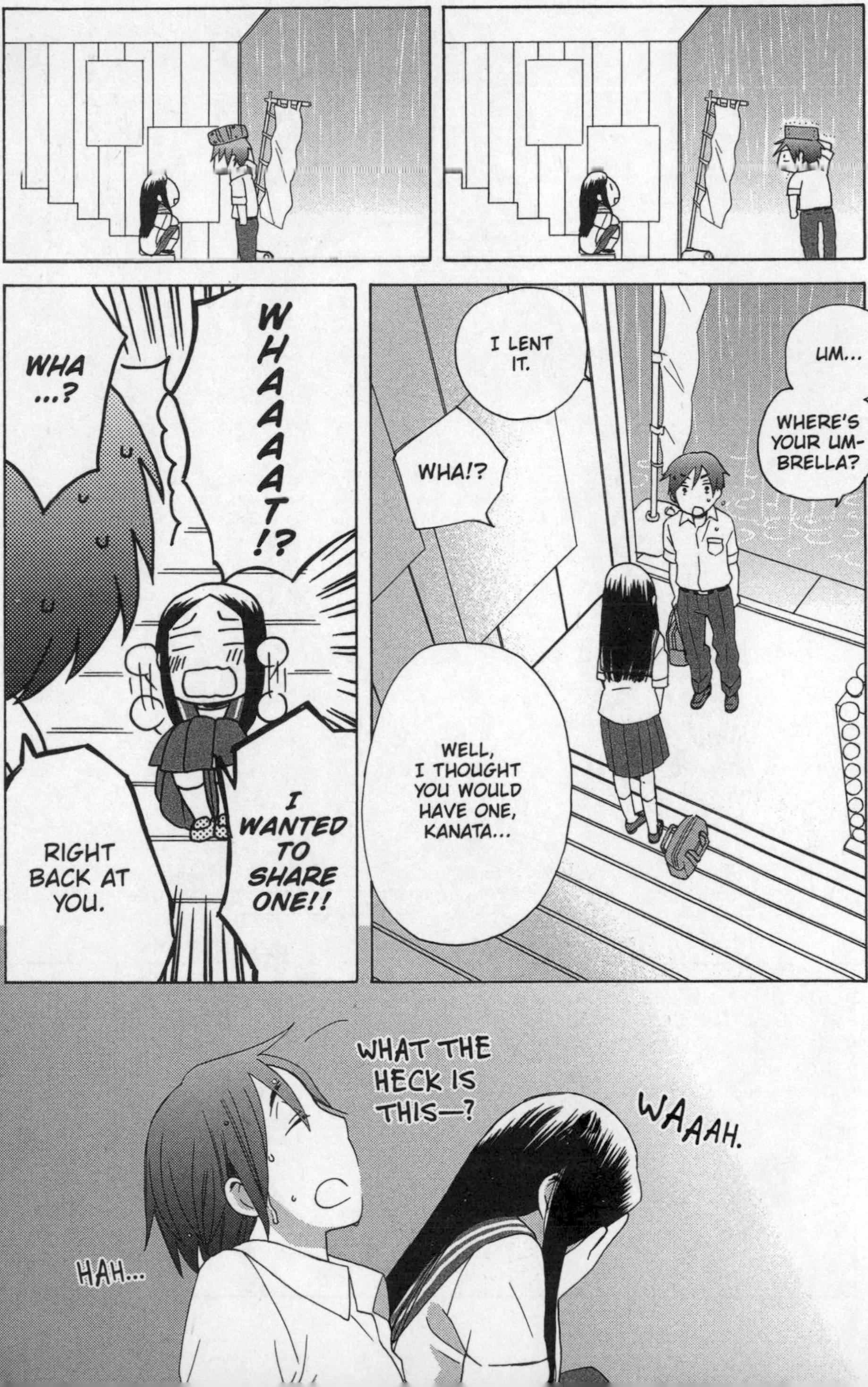
UM...
WHERE'S YOUR UM-BRELLA?
I LENT IT.
WHA!?
WELL, I THOUGHT YOU WOULD HAVE ONE, KANATA...
WHAAAAAT!?
I WANTED TO SHARE ONE!!
WHA...?
RIGHT BACK AT YOU.
WAAAH.
WHAT THE HECK IS THIS—?
HAH...

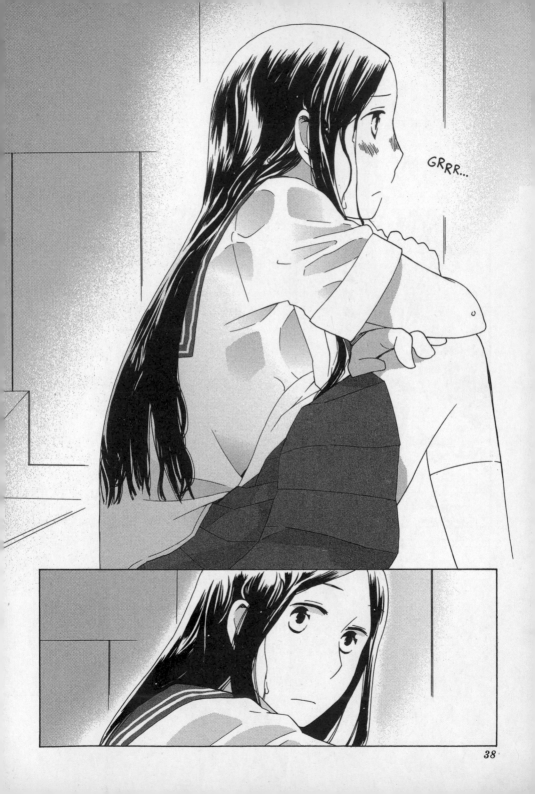

GRRR...

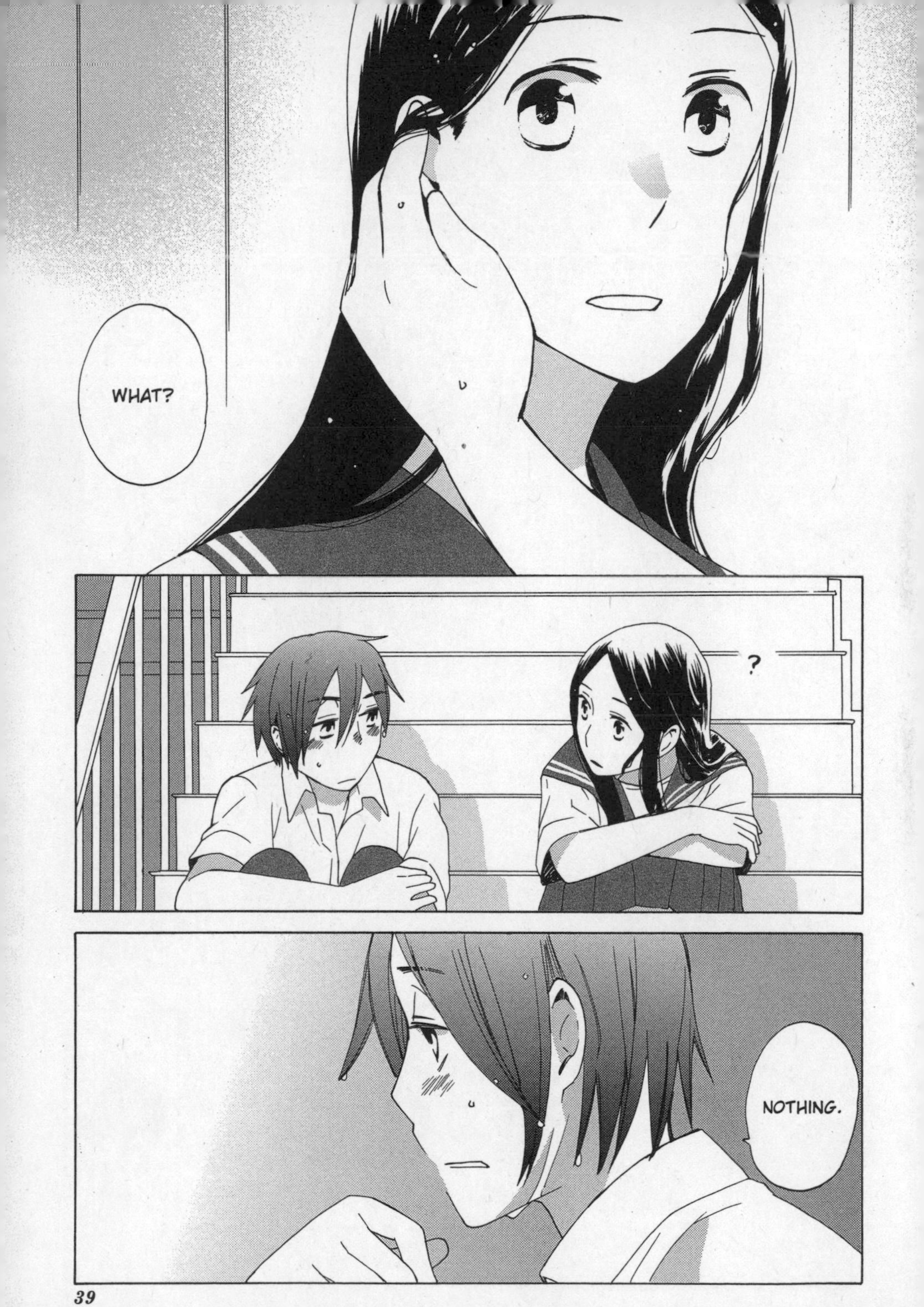
WHAT?
?
NOTHING.

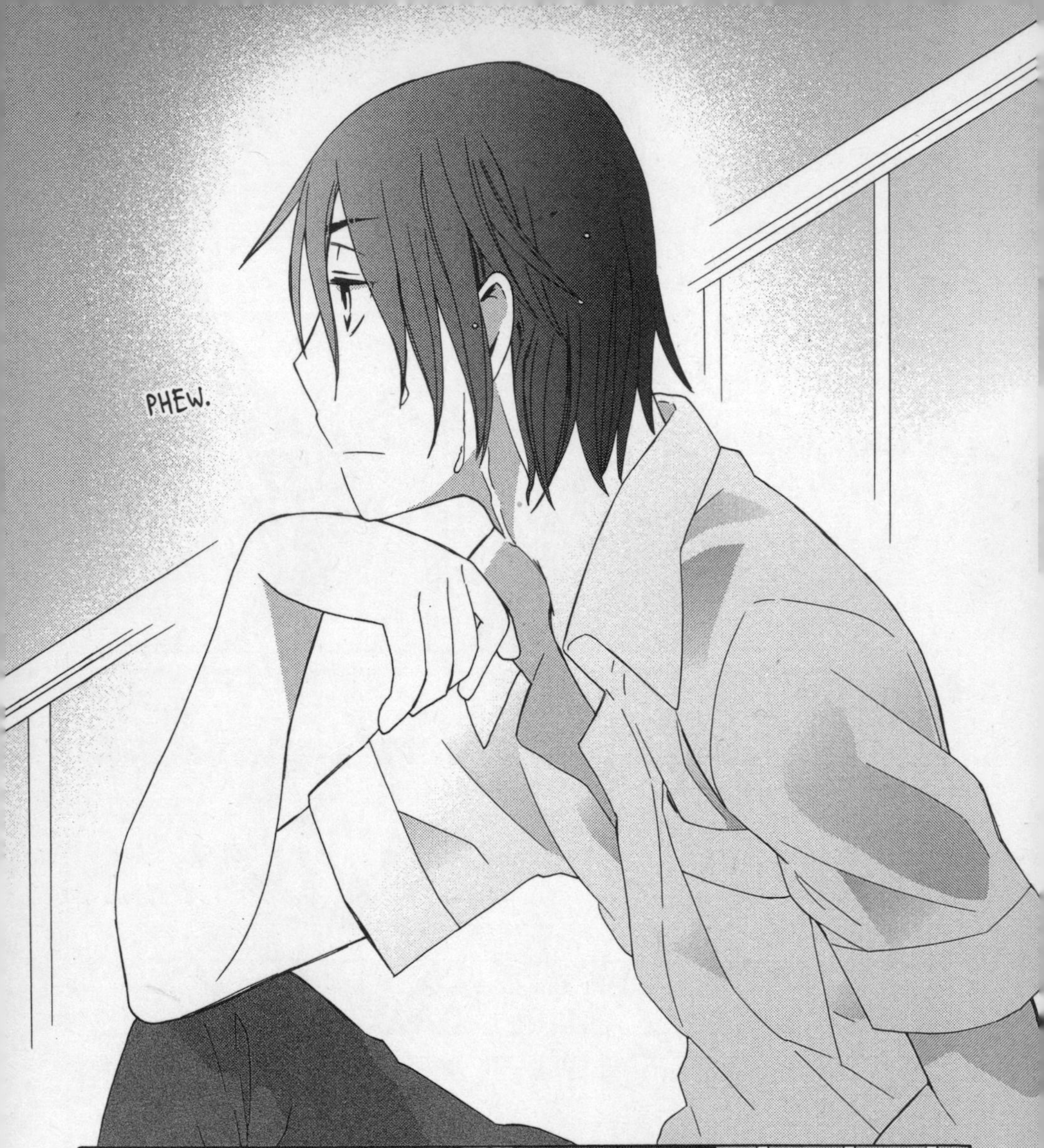
PHEW.
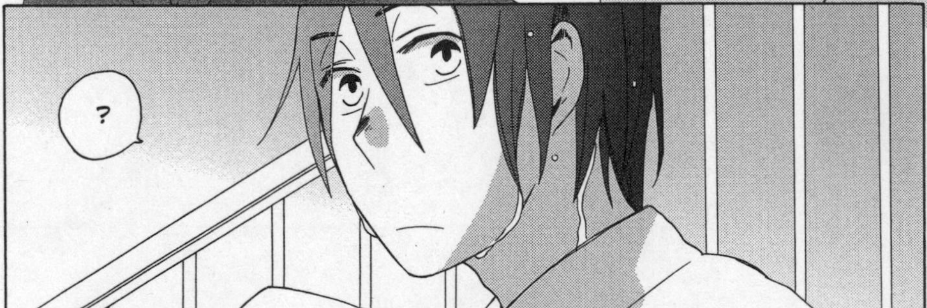
?

ZAAAAA
(FSHHH)

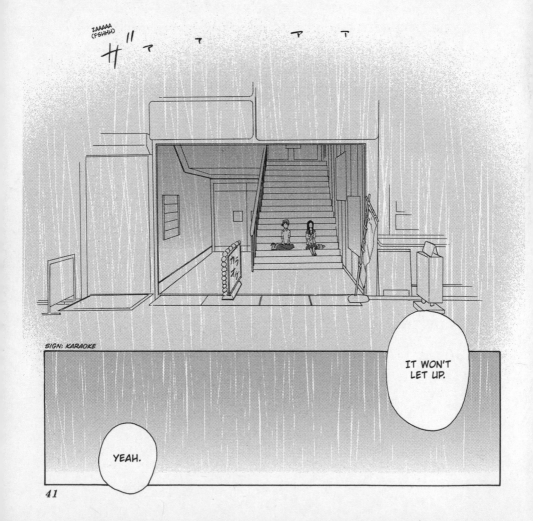

SIGN: KARAOKE

IT WON'T
LET UP.

YEAH.

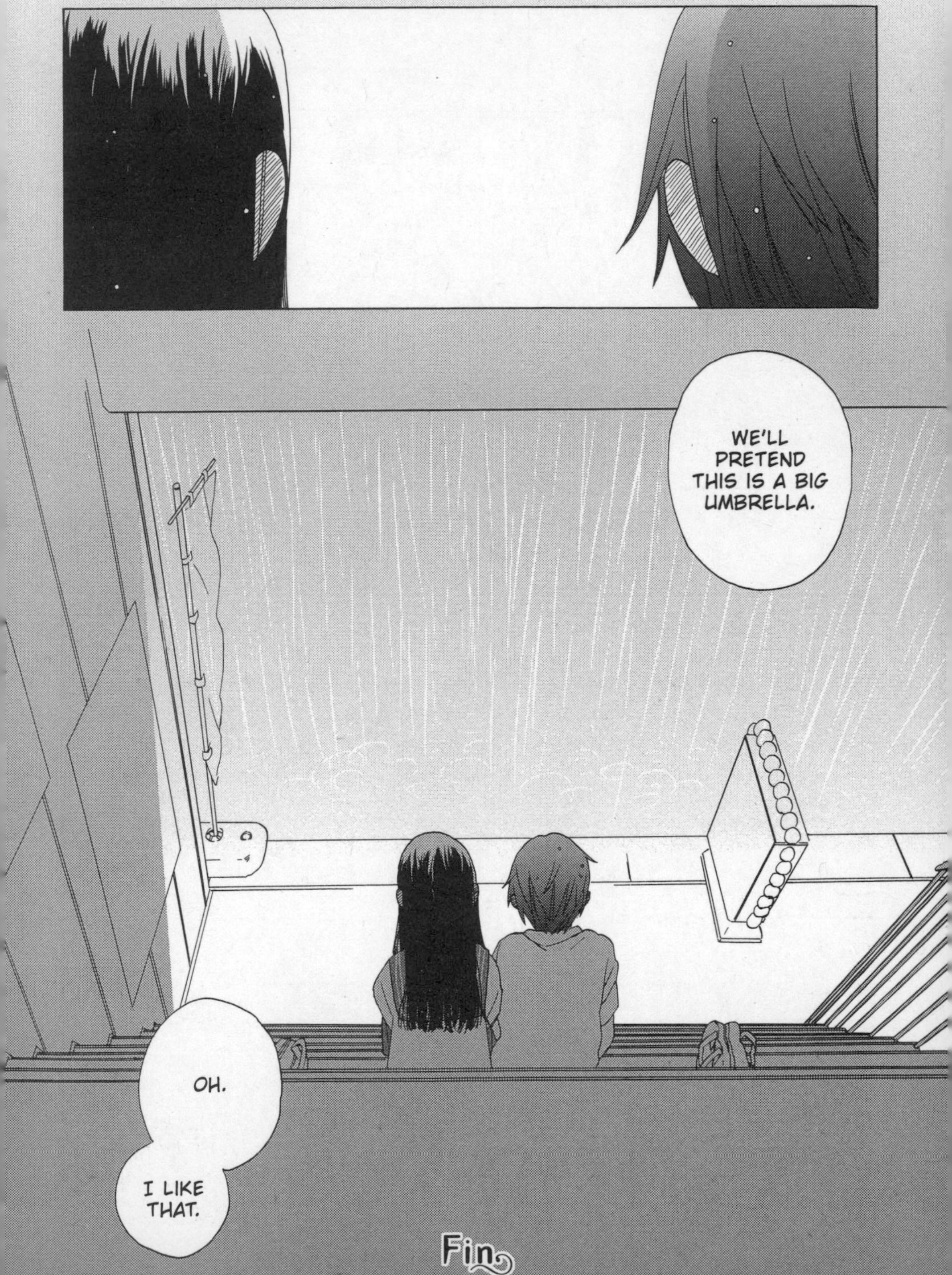
WE'LL PRETEND THIS IS A BIG UMBRELLA.
OH.
I LIKE THAT.
Fin

Love at Fourteen

[Intermission 7]

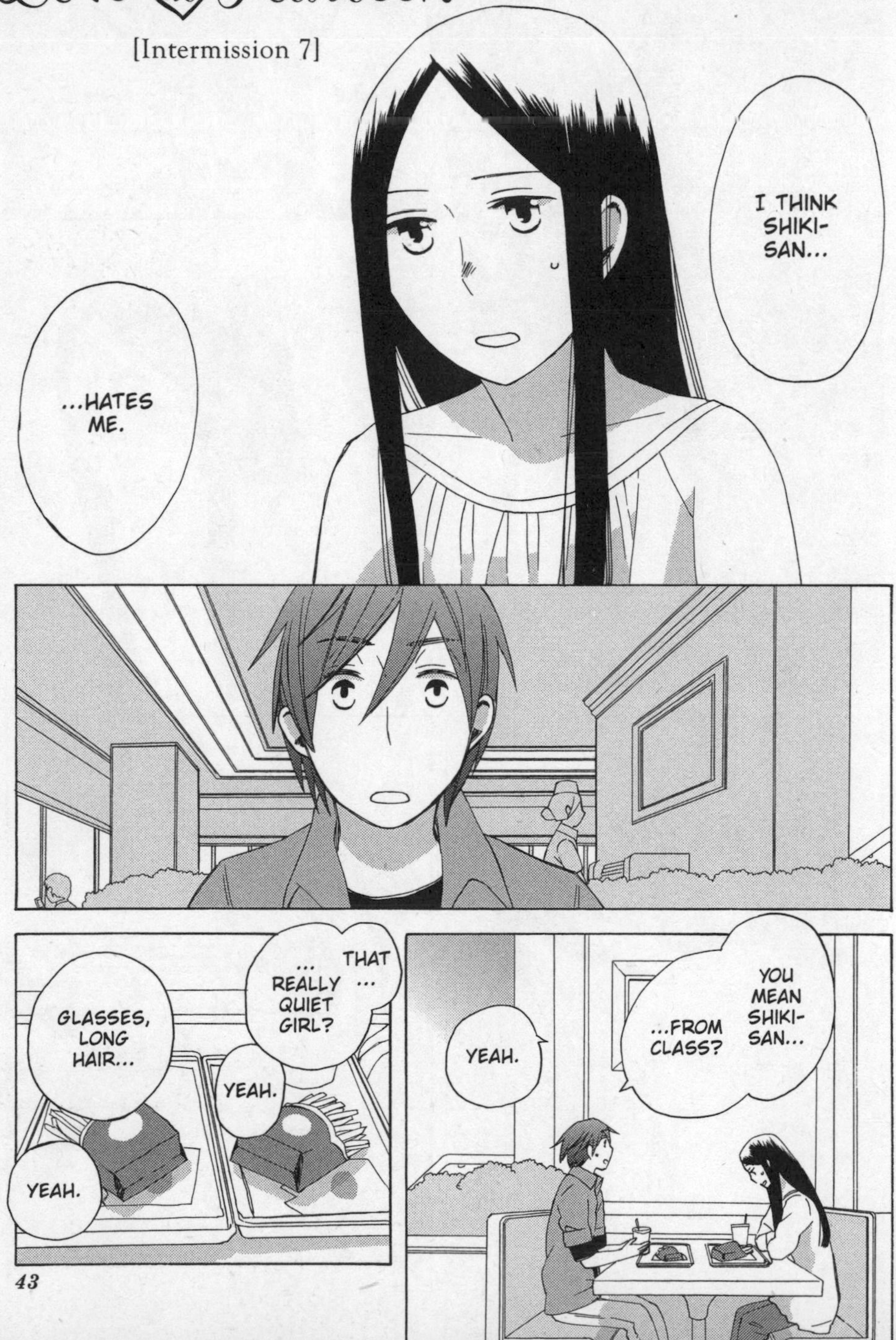

I THINK SHIKI-SAN...
...HATES ME.
YOU MEAN SHIKI-SAN...
...FROM CLASS?
YEAH.
THAT ... ... REALLY QUIET GIRL?
GLASSES, LONG HAIR...
YEAH.
YEAH.

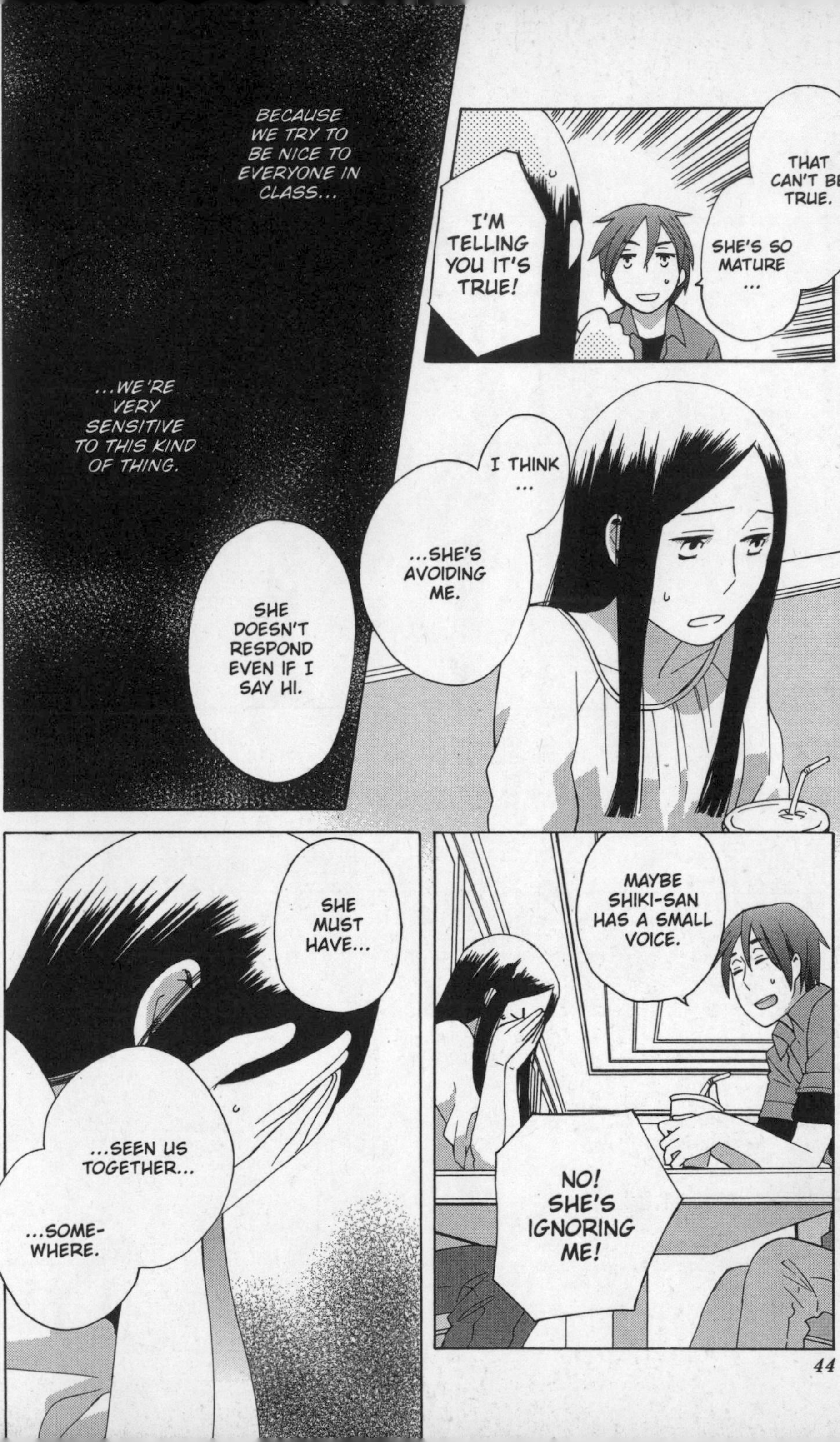
THAT CAN'T BE TRUE.
SHE'S SO MATURE ...
I'M TELLING YOU IT'S TRUE!
I THINK ...
...SHE'S AVOIDING ME.
SHE DOESN'T RESPOND EVEN IF I SAY HI.
BECAUSE WE TRY TO BE NICE TO EVERYONE IN CLASS...
...WE'RE VERY SENSITIVE TO THIS KIND OF THING.
MAYBE SHIKI-SAN HAS A SMALL VOICE.
NO! SHE'S IGNORING ME!
SHE MUST HAVE...
...SEEN US TOGETHER...
...SOME-WHERE.

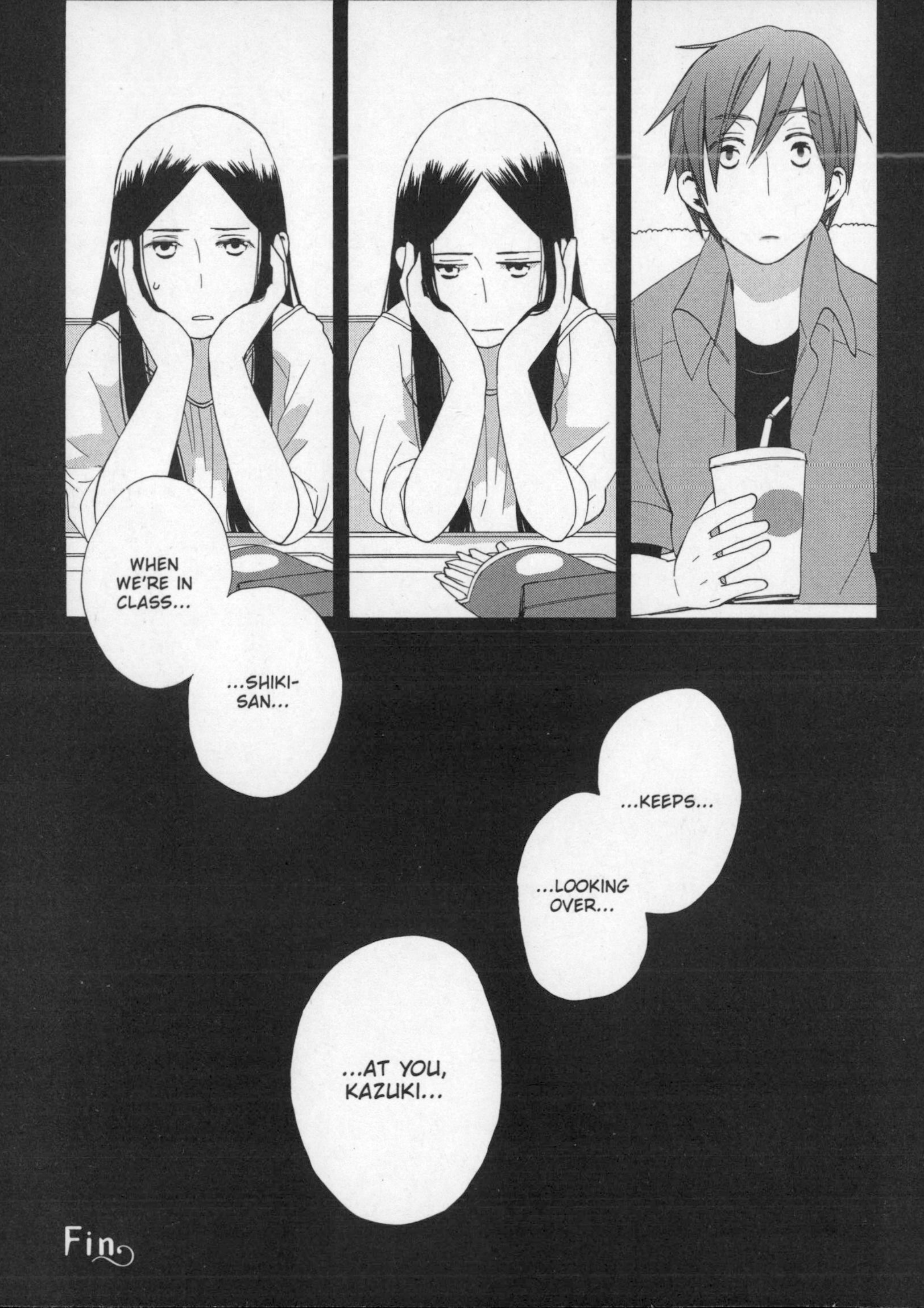
WHEN WE'RE IN CLASS...
...SHIKI-SAN...
...KEEPS...
...LOOKING OVER...
...AT YOU, KAZUKI...
Fin

Love at Fourteen

Fuka Mizutani

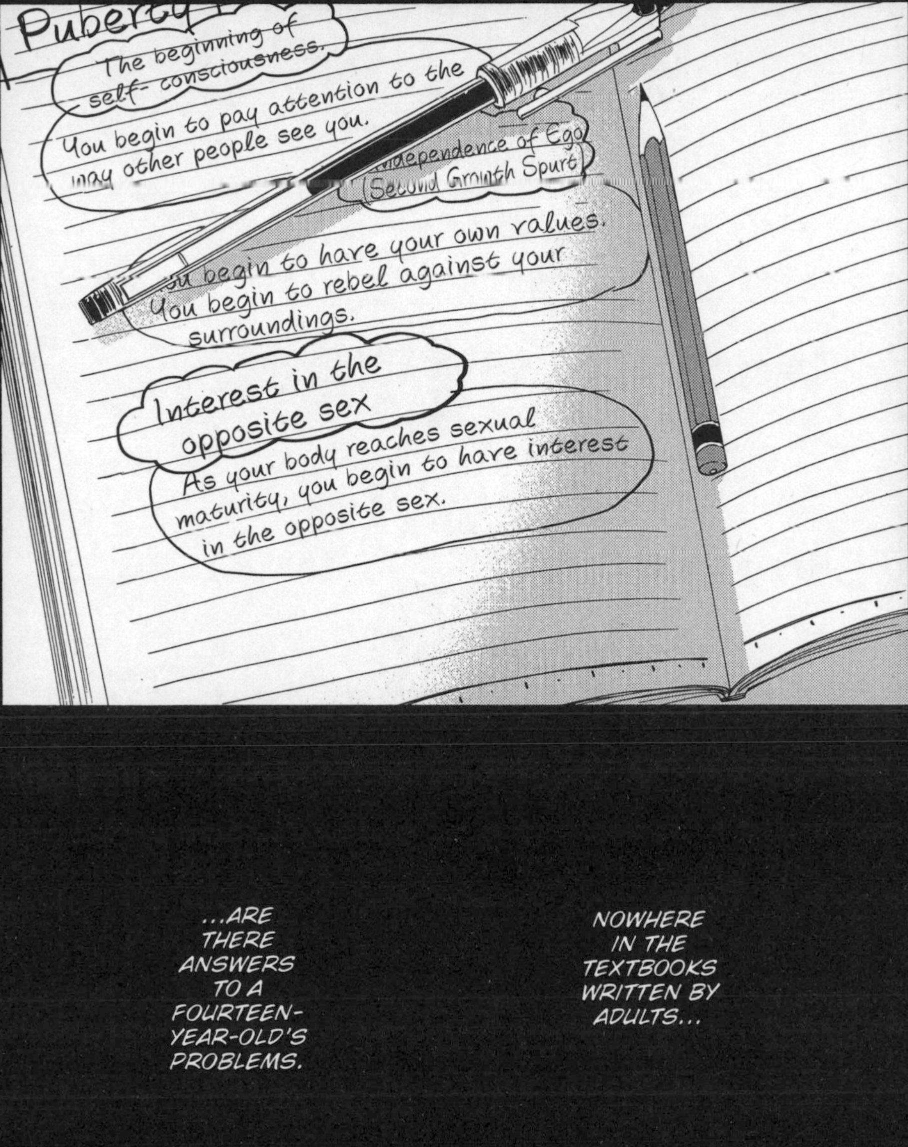
Puberty
The beginning of self-consciousness.
You begin to pay attention to the way other people see you.
ndependence of Ego (Second Growth Spurt)
ou begin to have your own values. You begin to rebel against your surroundings.
Interest in the opposite sex
As your body reaches sexual maturity, you begin to have interest in the opposite sex.
NOWHERE IN THE TEXTBOOKS WRITTEN BY ADULTS...
...ARE THERE ANSWERS TO A FOURTEEN-YEAR-OLD'S PROBLEMS.

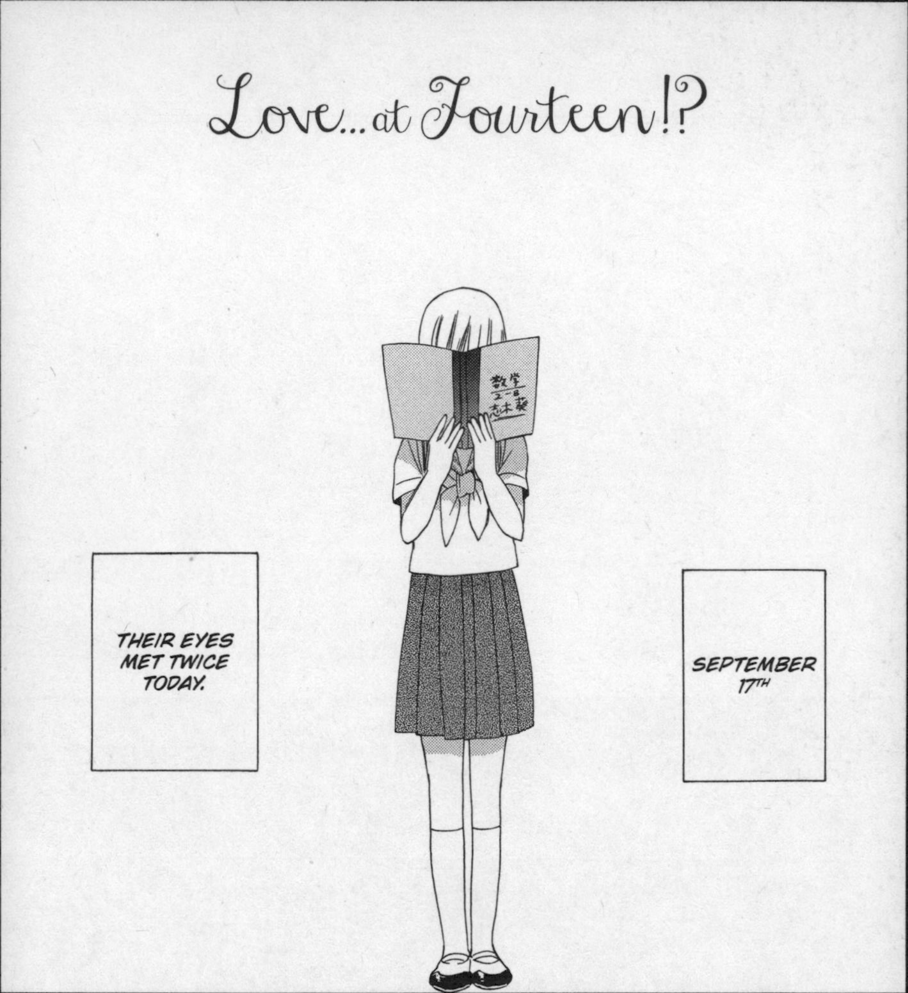
Love... at Fourteen!?
数学
2-B
志木 葵
SEPTEMBER 17TH
THEIR EYES MET TWICE TODAY.

BOOK: ALGEBRA 2-B AOI SHIKI

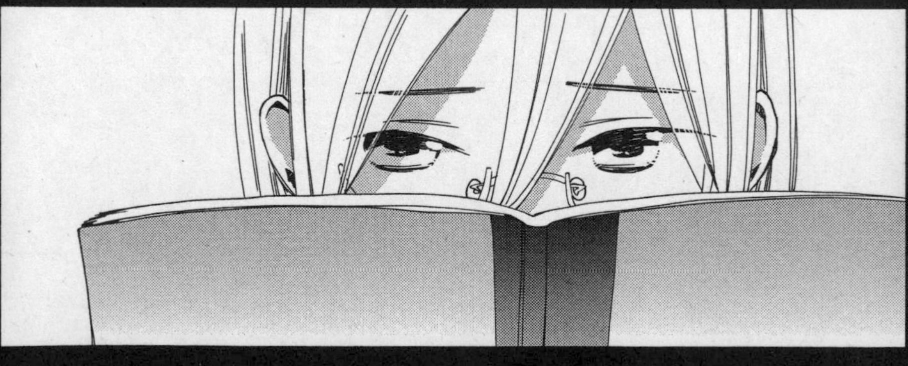

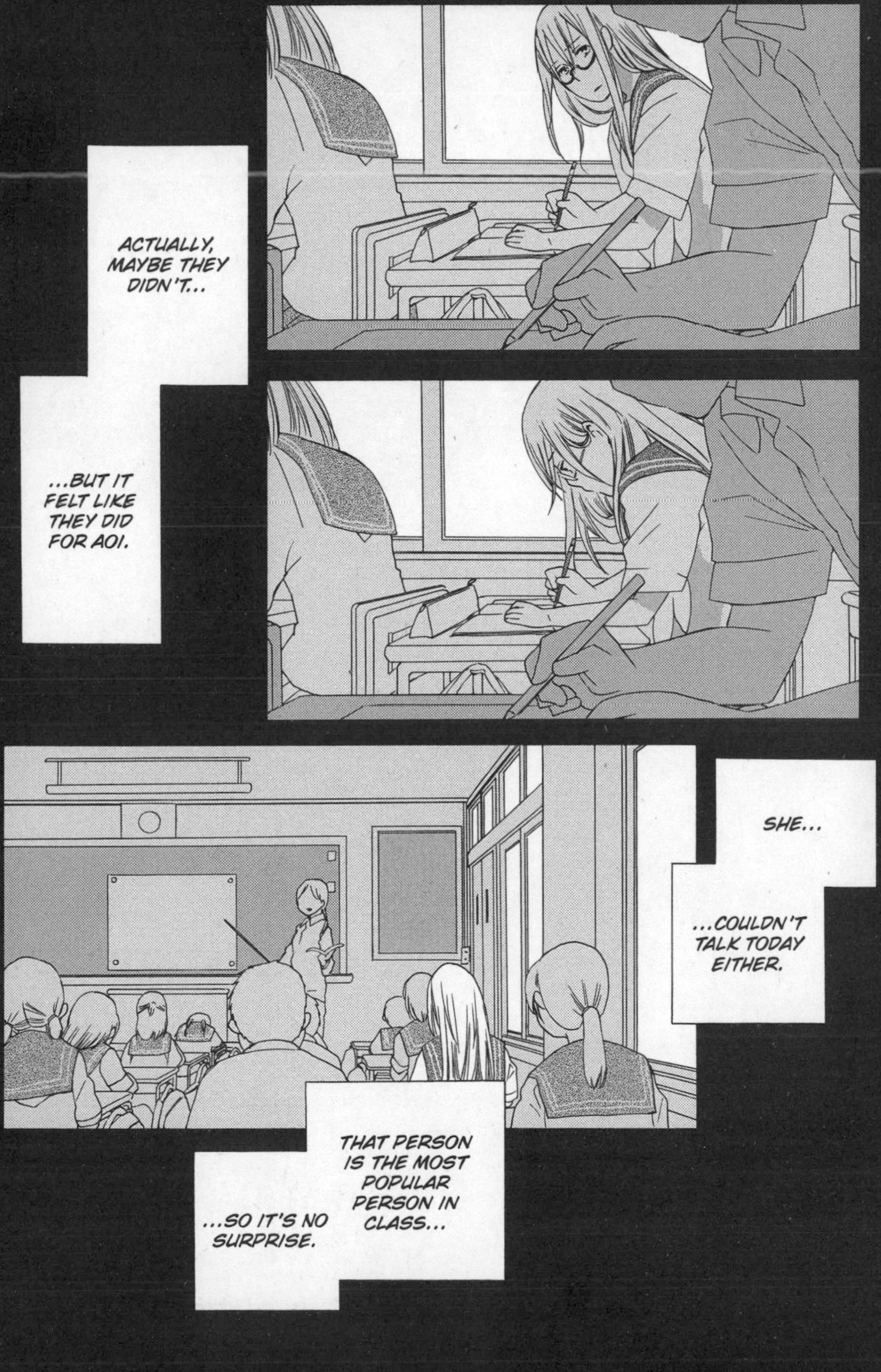
ACTUALLY, MAYBE THEY DIDN'T...
...BUT IT FELT LIKE THEY DID FOR AOI.
SHE...
...COULDN'T TALK TODAY EITHER.
THAT PERSON IS THE MOST POPULAR PERSON IN CLASS...
...SO IT'S NO SURPRISE.

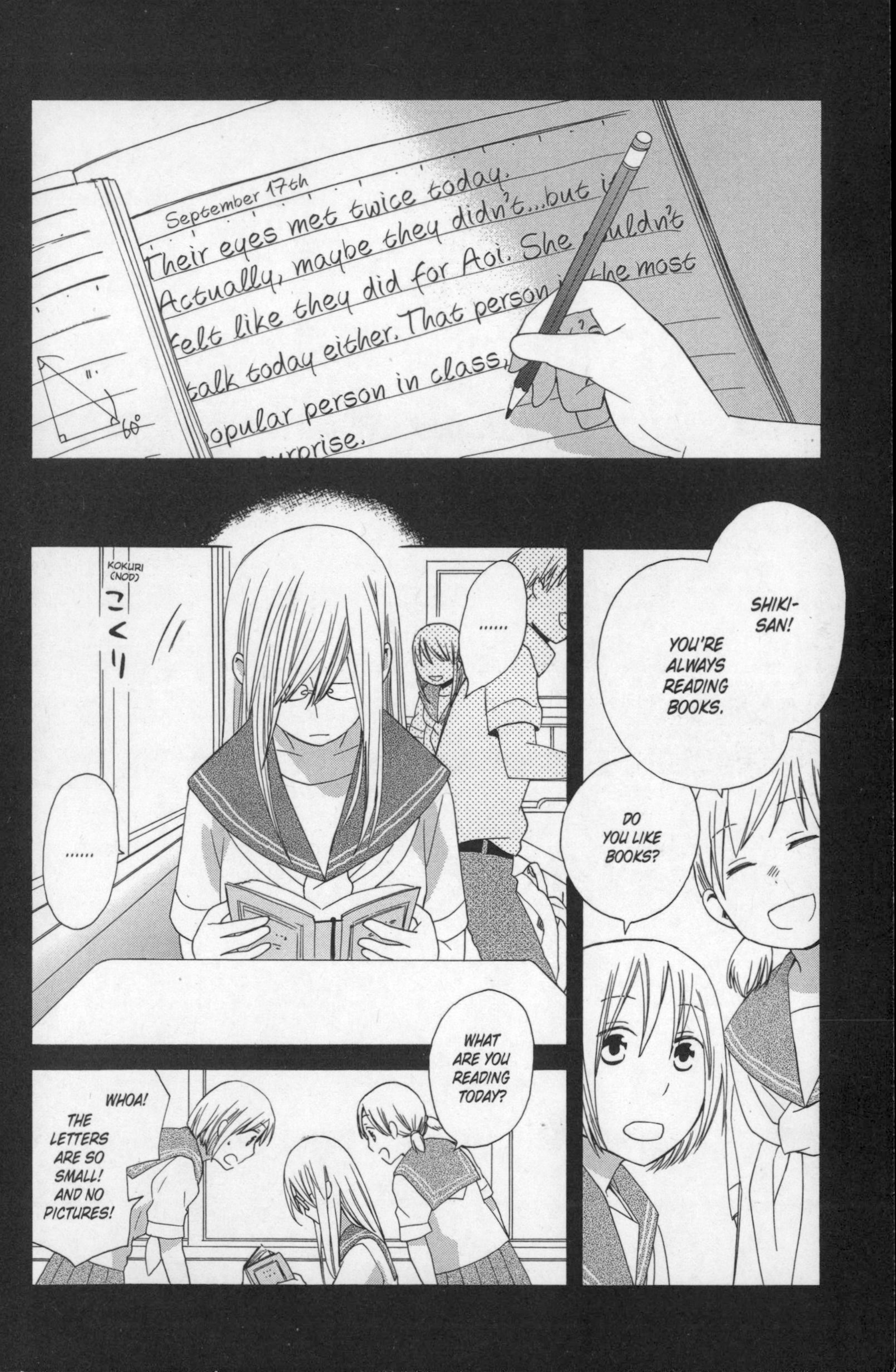
September 17th
Their eyes met twice today.
Actually, maybe they didn't...but i
felt like they did for Aoi. She
talk today either. That person
the most
popular person in class,
surprise.
SHIKI-SAN! YOU'RE ALWAYS READING BOOKS.
DO YOU LIKE BOOKS?
WHAT ARE YOU READING TODAY?
......
KOKURI (NOD)
こくり
......
WHOA! THE LETTERS ARE SO SMALL! AND NO PICTURES!

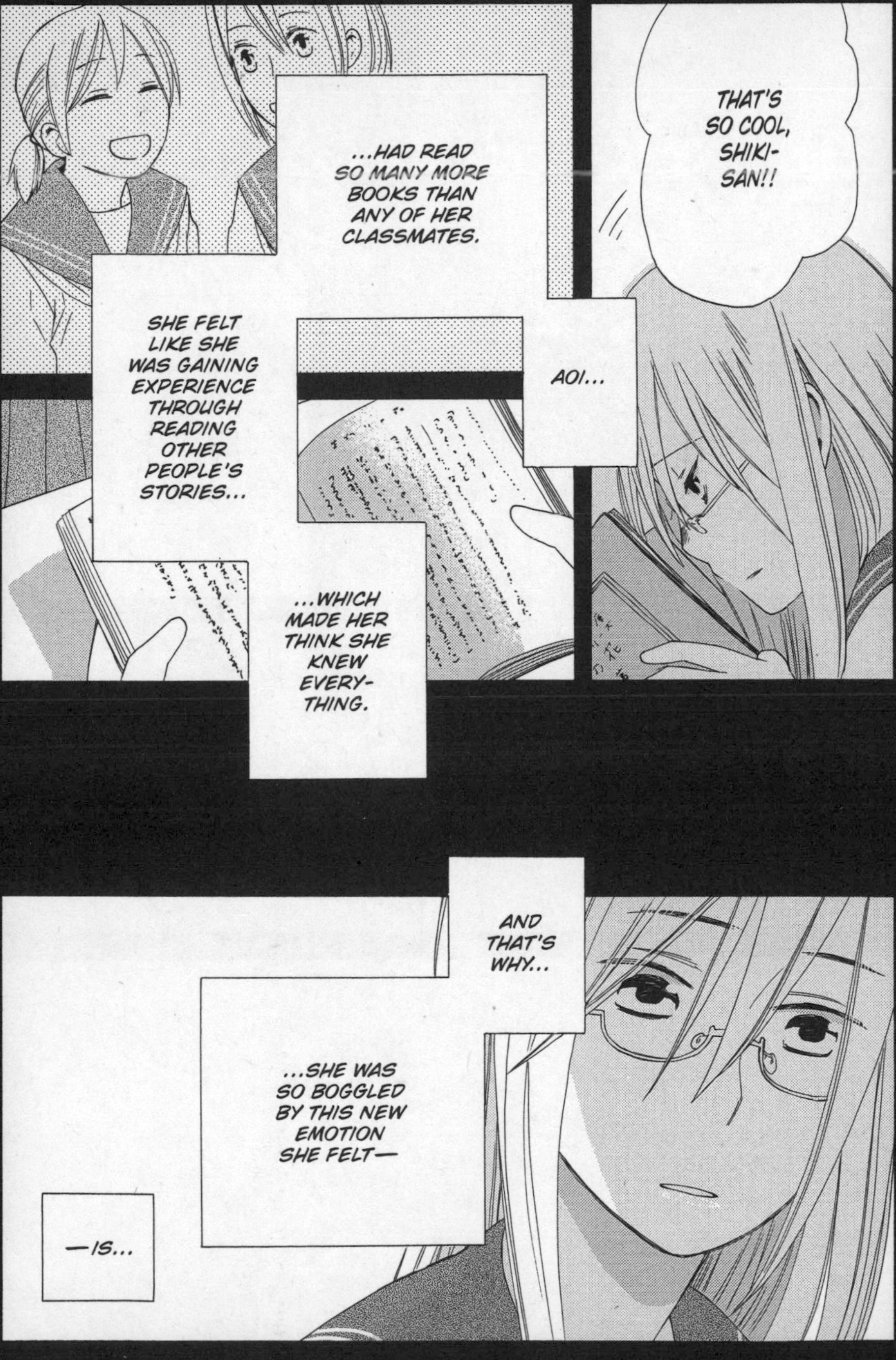
THAT'S SO COOL, SHIKI-SAN!!
AOI...
...HAD READ SO MANY MORE BOOKS THAN ANY OF HER CLASSMATES.
SHE FELT LIKE SHE WAS GAINING EXPERIENCE THROUGH READING OTHER PEOPLE'S STORIES...
...WHICH MADE HER THINK SHE KNEW EVERY-THING.
AND THAT'S WHY...
...SHE WAS SO BOGGLED BY THIS NEW EMOTION SHE FELT—
—IS...

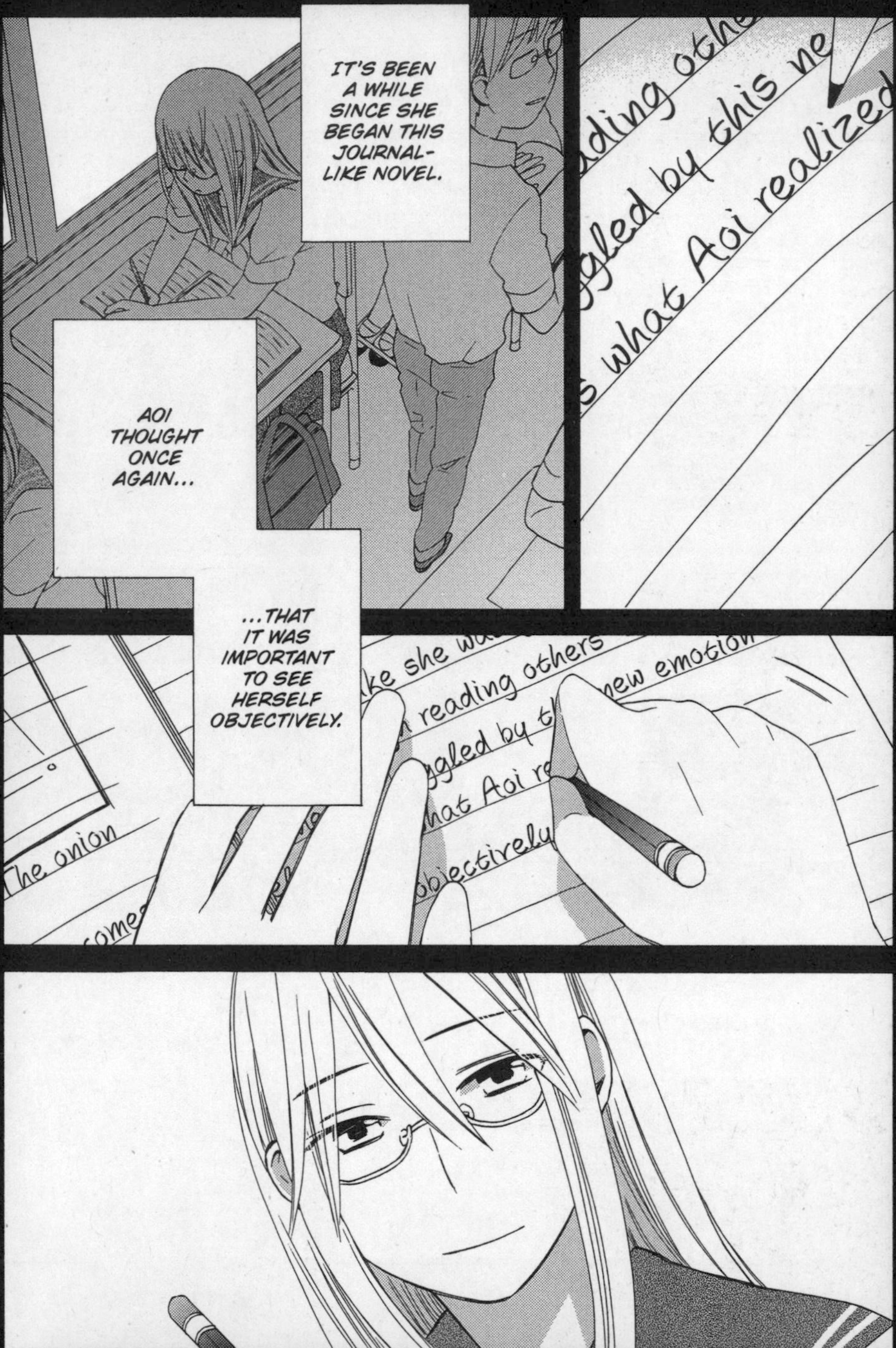
ading othe
ggled by this ne
s what Aoi realized
IT'S BEEN A WHILE SINCE SHE BEGAN THIS JOURNAL-LIKE NOVEL.
AOI THOUGHT ONCE AGAIN...
...THAT IT WAS IMPORTANT TO SEE HERSELF OBJECTIVELY.
ke she wa
reading others
new emotion
ggled by th
hat Aoi re
objectively
The onion
comes

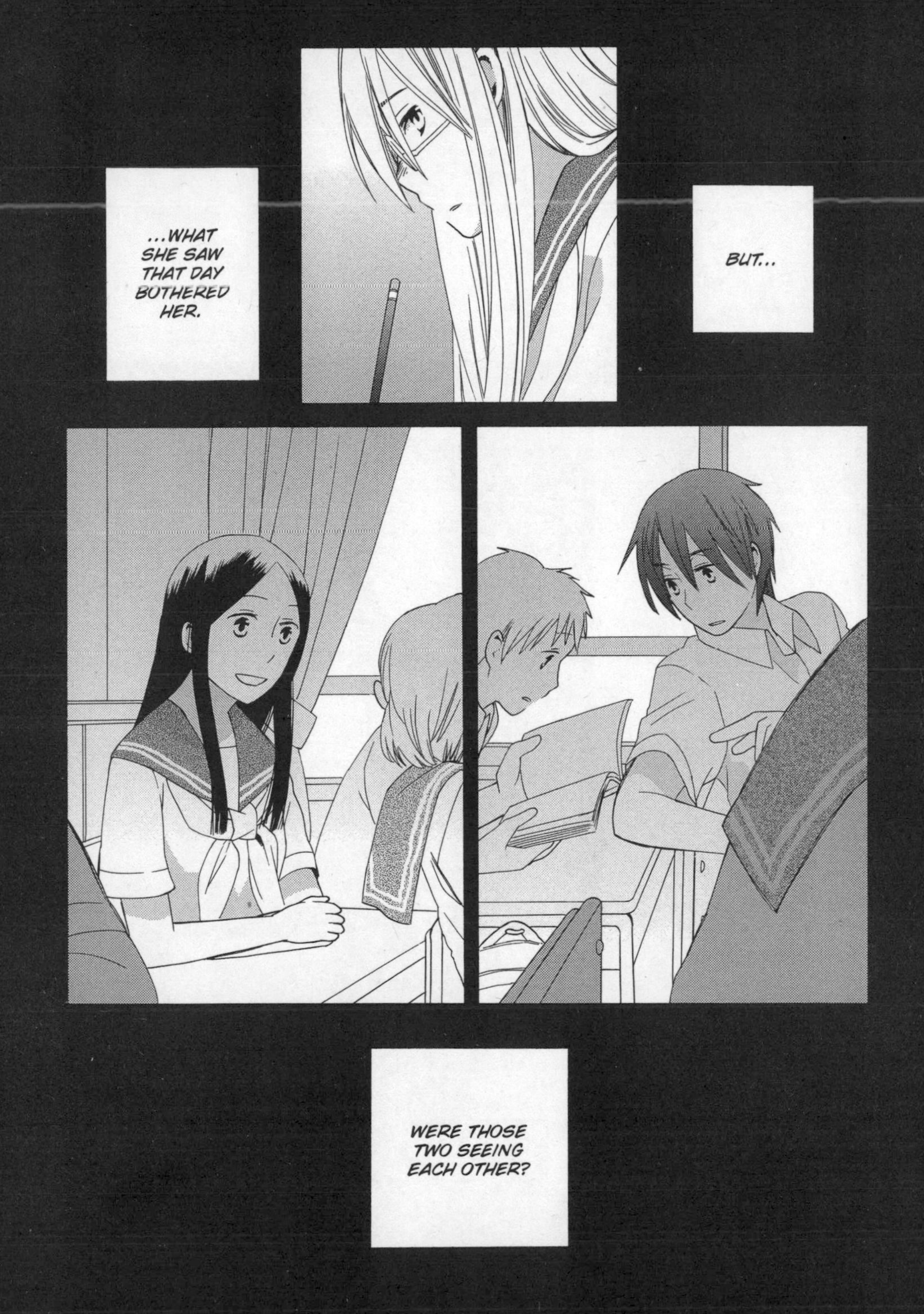
BUT...
...WHAT SHE SAW THAT DAY BOTHERED HER.
WERE THOSE TWO SEEING EACH OTHER?

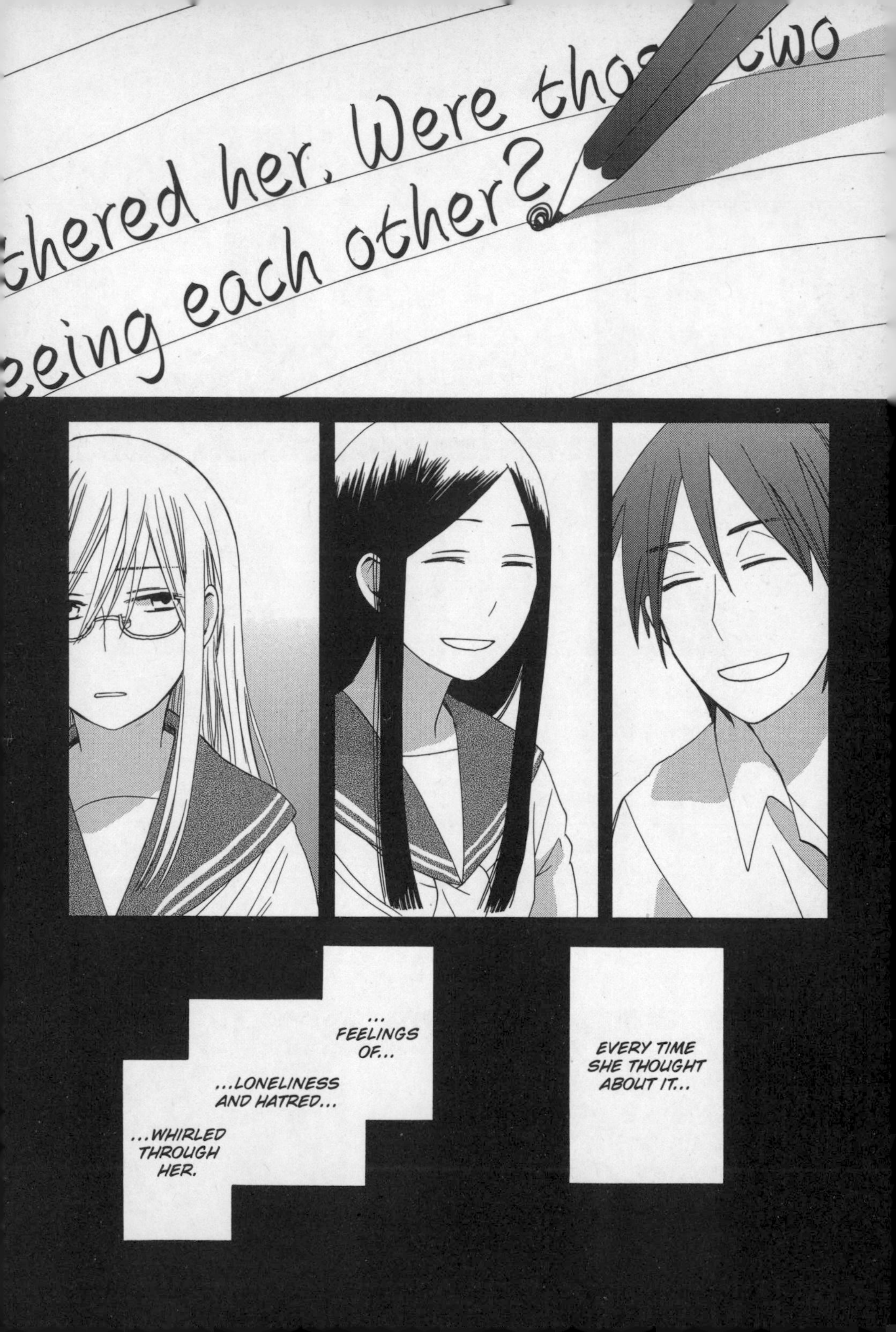
thered her, Were thos two
eeing each other?
EVERY TIME SHE THOUGHT ABOUT IT...
... FEELINGS OF...
...LONELINESS AND HATRED...
...WHIRLED THROUGH HER.

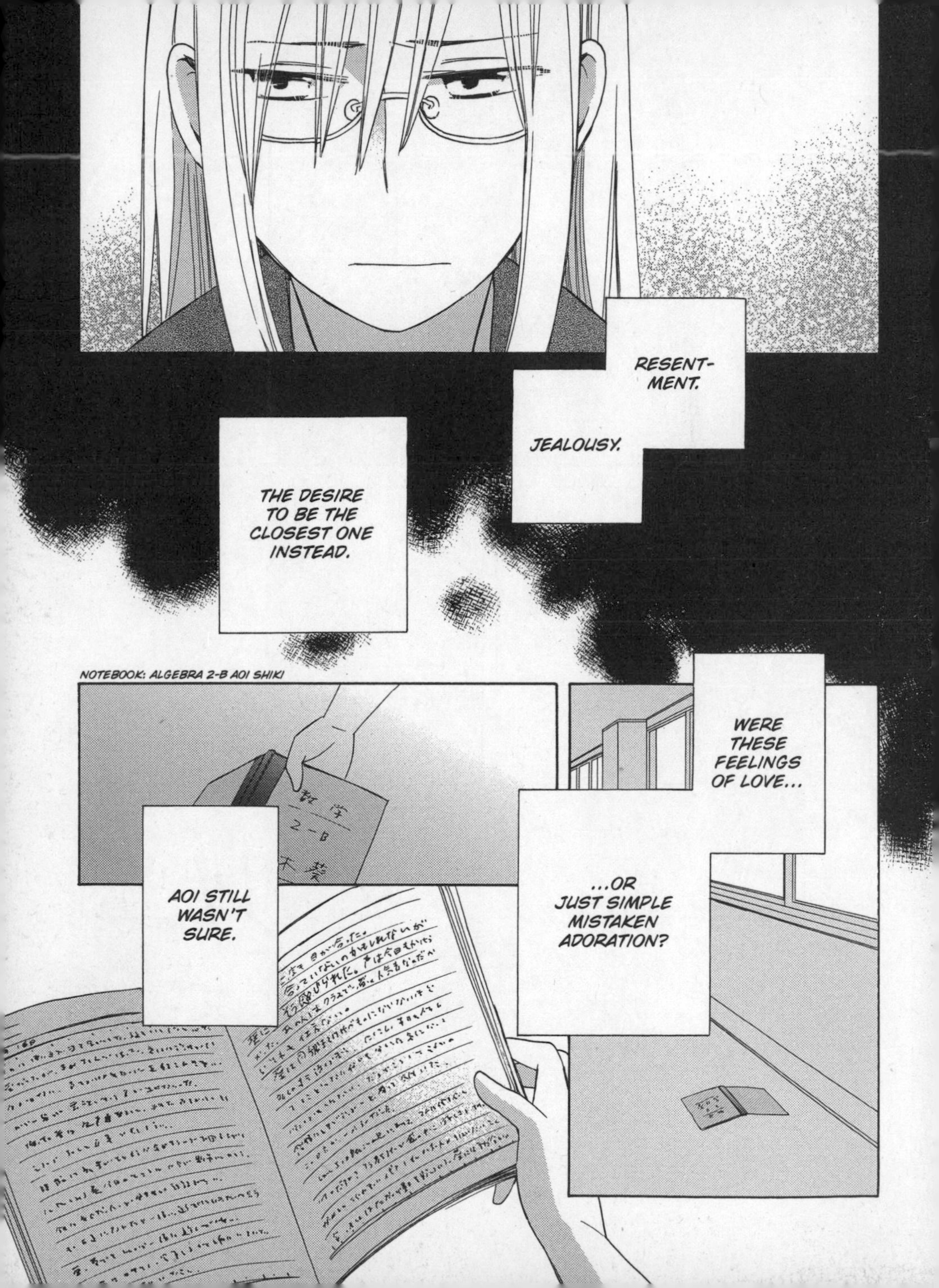
RESENT-MENT.
JEALOUSY.
THE DESIRE TO BE THE CLOSEST ONE INSTEAD.
NOTEBOOK: ALGEBRA 2-B AOI SHIKI
WERE THESE FEELINGS OF LOVE...
...OR JUST SIMPLE MISTAKEN ADORATION?
AOI STILL WASN'T SURE.

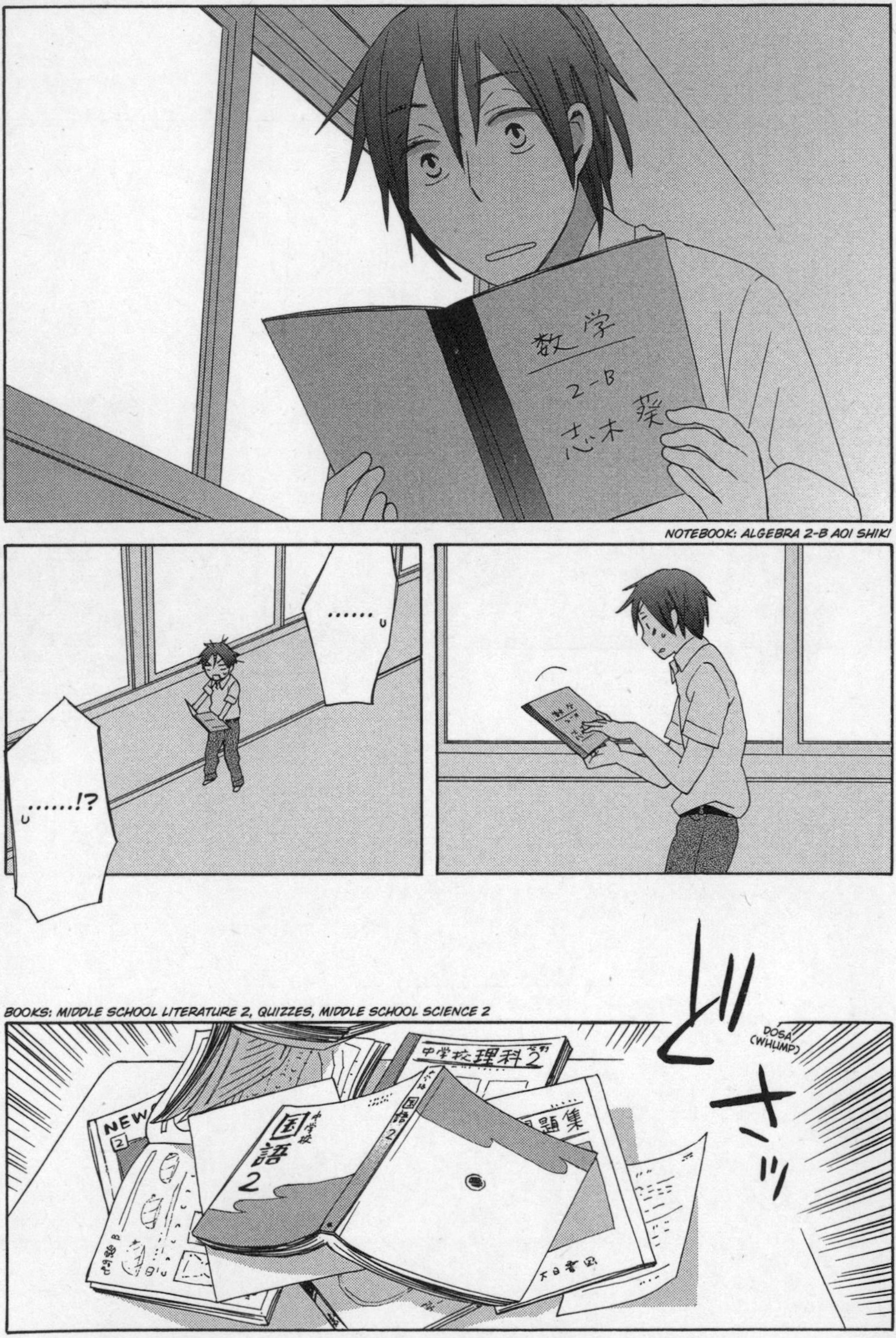
数学
2-B
志木葵
NOTEBOOK: ALGEBRA 2-B AOI SHIKI
......
......!?
BOOKS: MIDDLE SCHOOL LITERATURE 2, QUIZZES, MIDDLE SCHOOL SCIENCE 2
ドサッ
DOSA (WHUMP)
中学校理科2
中学校 国語 2
問題集

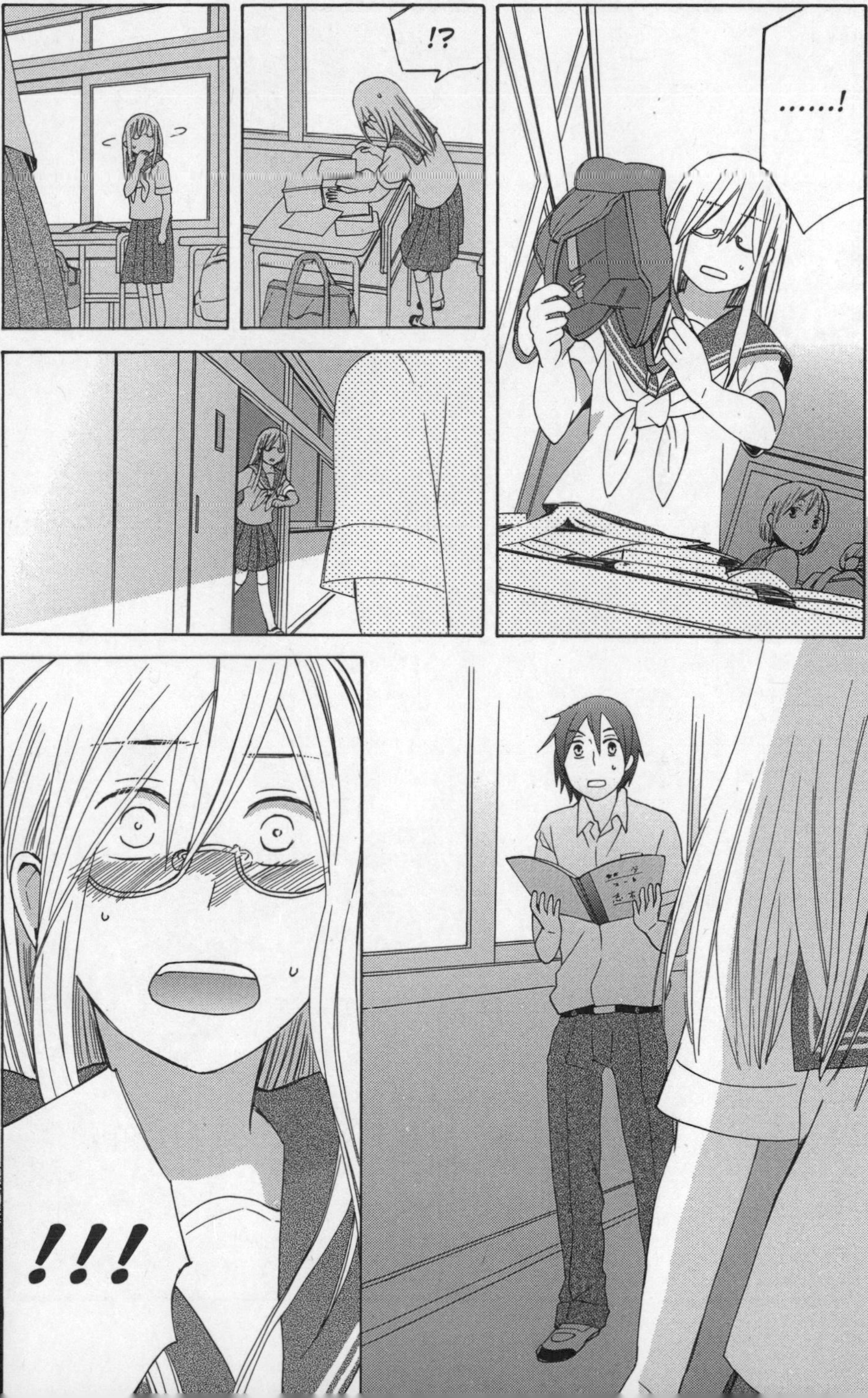
......!
!?
!!!

DEAR GOD, THIS WAS BAD.

AOI...

...WAS THROWN OFF.

TO HAVE IT READ...

...BY YOSHIKAWA-KUN OF ALL PEOPLE!!

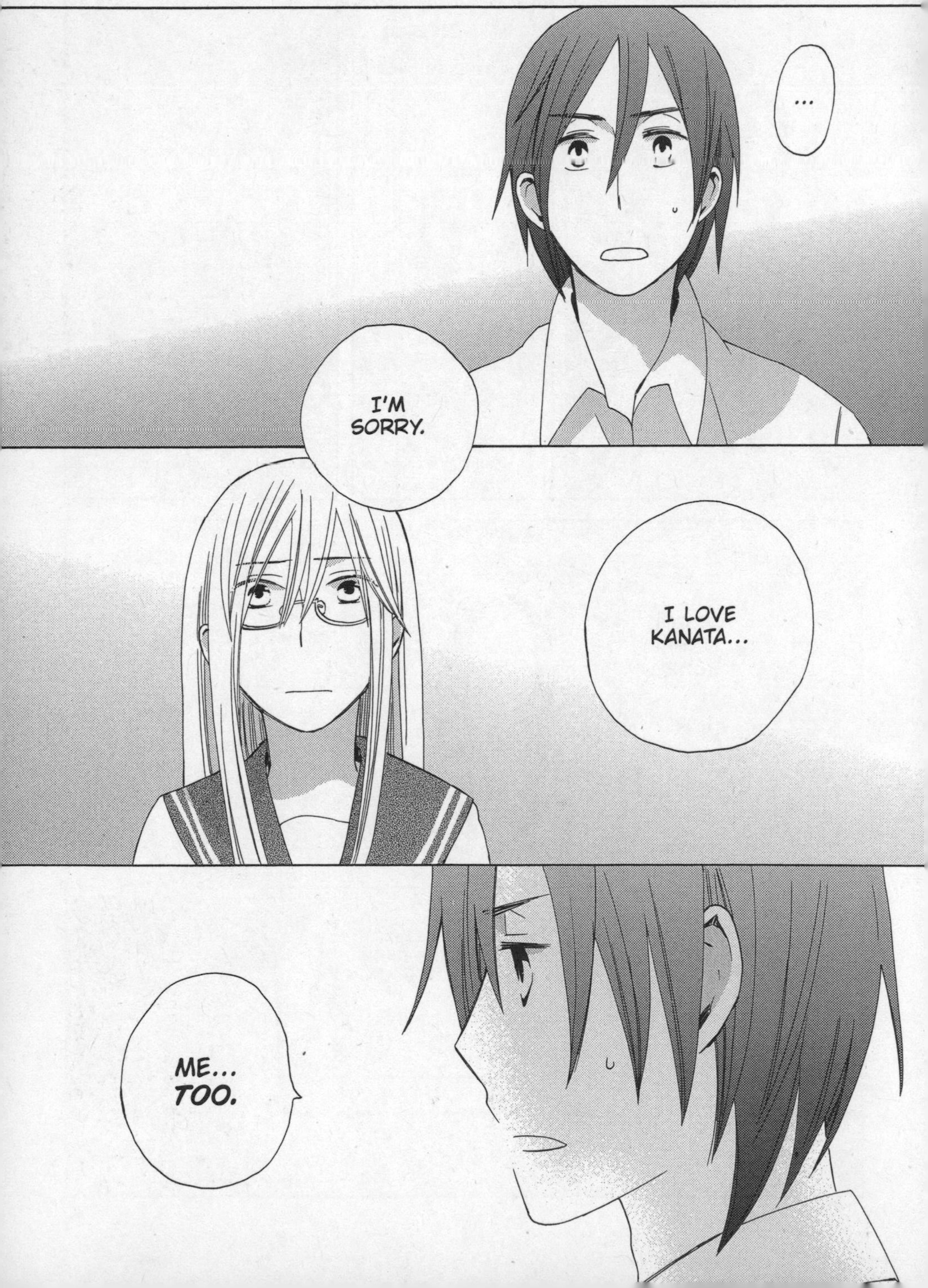
...
I'M SORRY.
I LOVE KANATA...
ME... *TOO.*

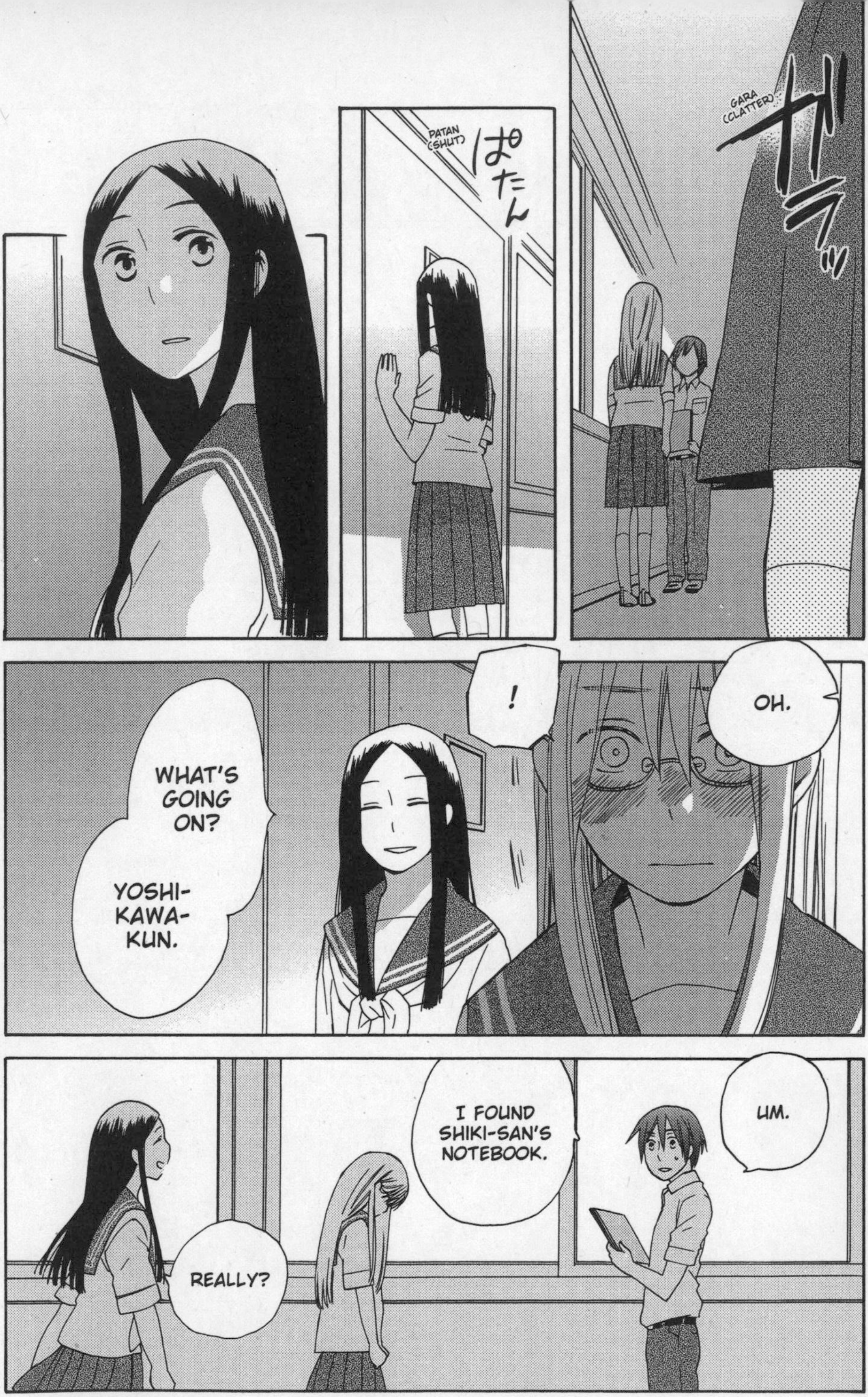
GARA (CLATTER)
ガラッ
PATAN (SHUT)
ぱたん
OH.
!
WHAT'S GOING ON?
YOSHI-KAWA-KUN.
UM.
I FOUND SHIKI-SAN'S NOTEBOOK.
REALLY?

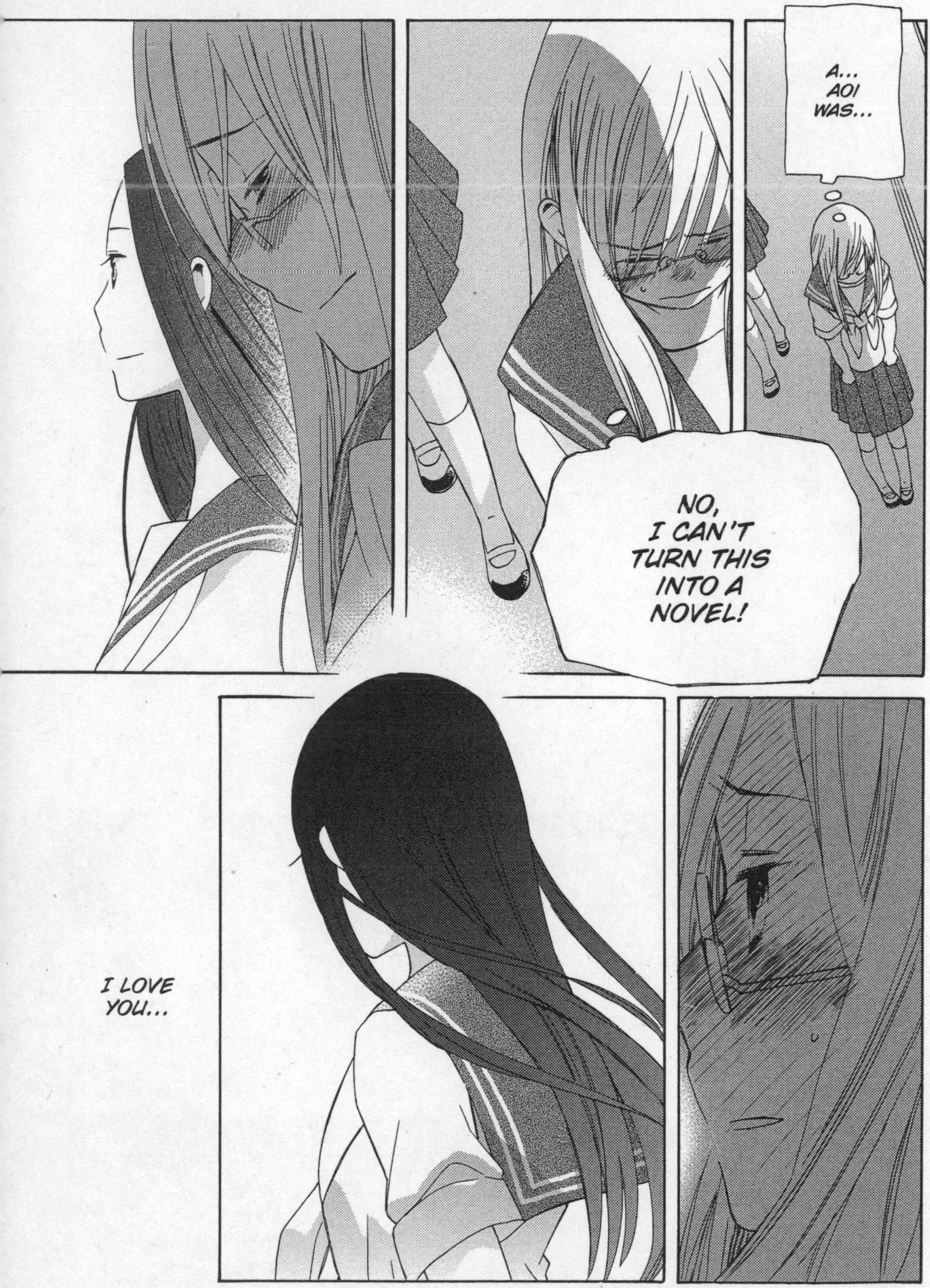
A... AOI WAS...
NO, I CAN'T TURN THIS INTO A NOVEL!
I LOVE YOU...

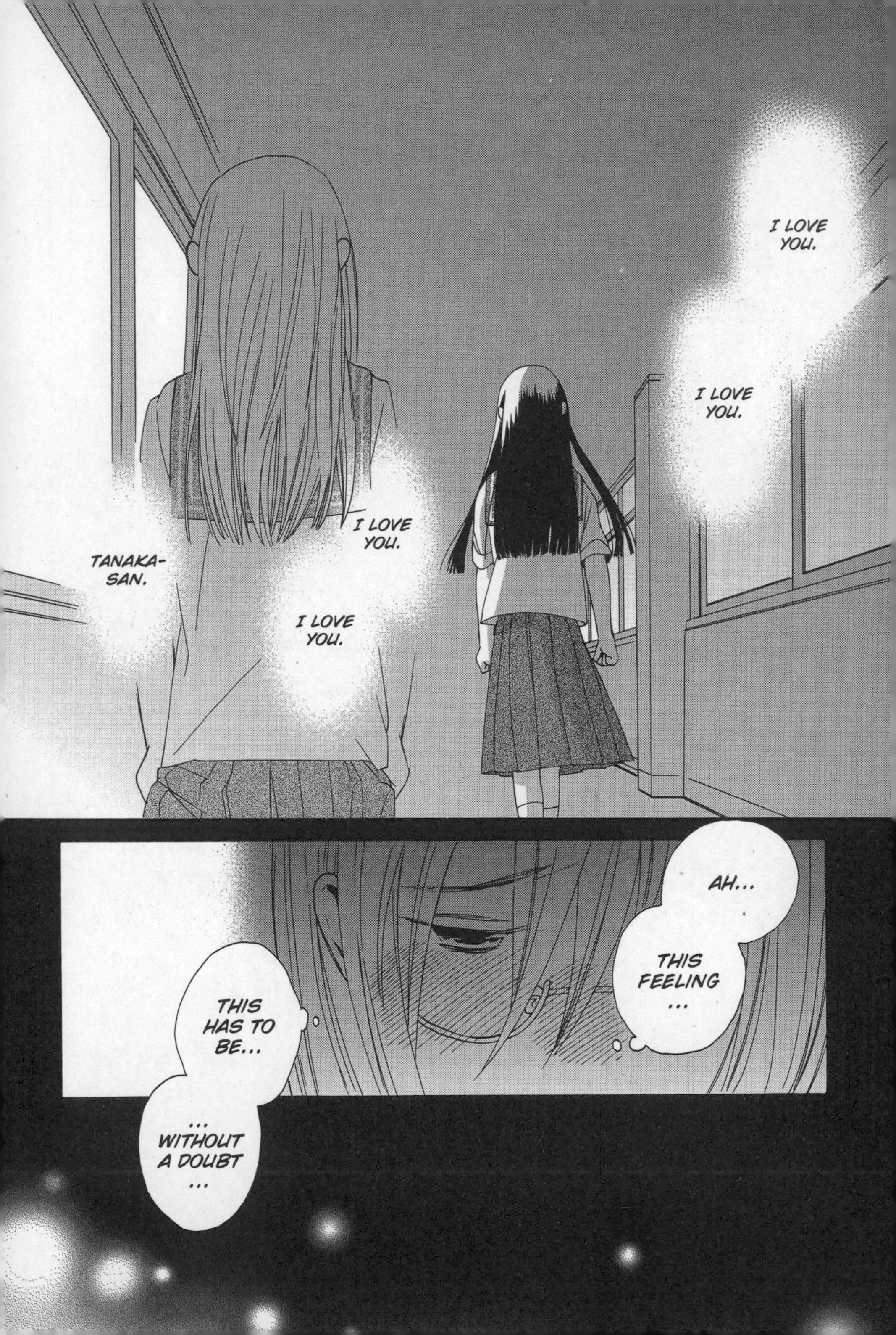
I LOVE YOU.
I LOVE YOU.
I LOVE YOU.
TANAKA-SAN.
I LOVE YOU.
AH...
THIS FEELING ...
THIS HAS TO BE...
... WITHOUT A DOUBT ...

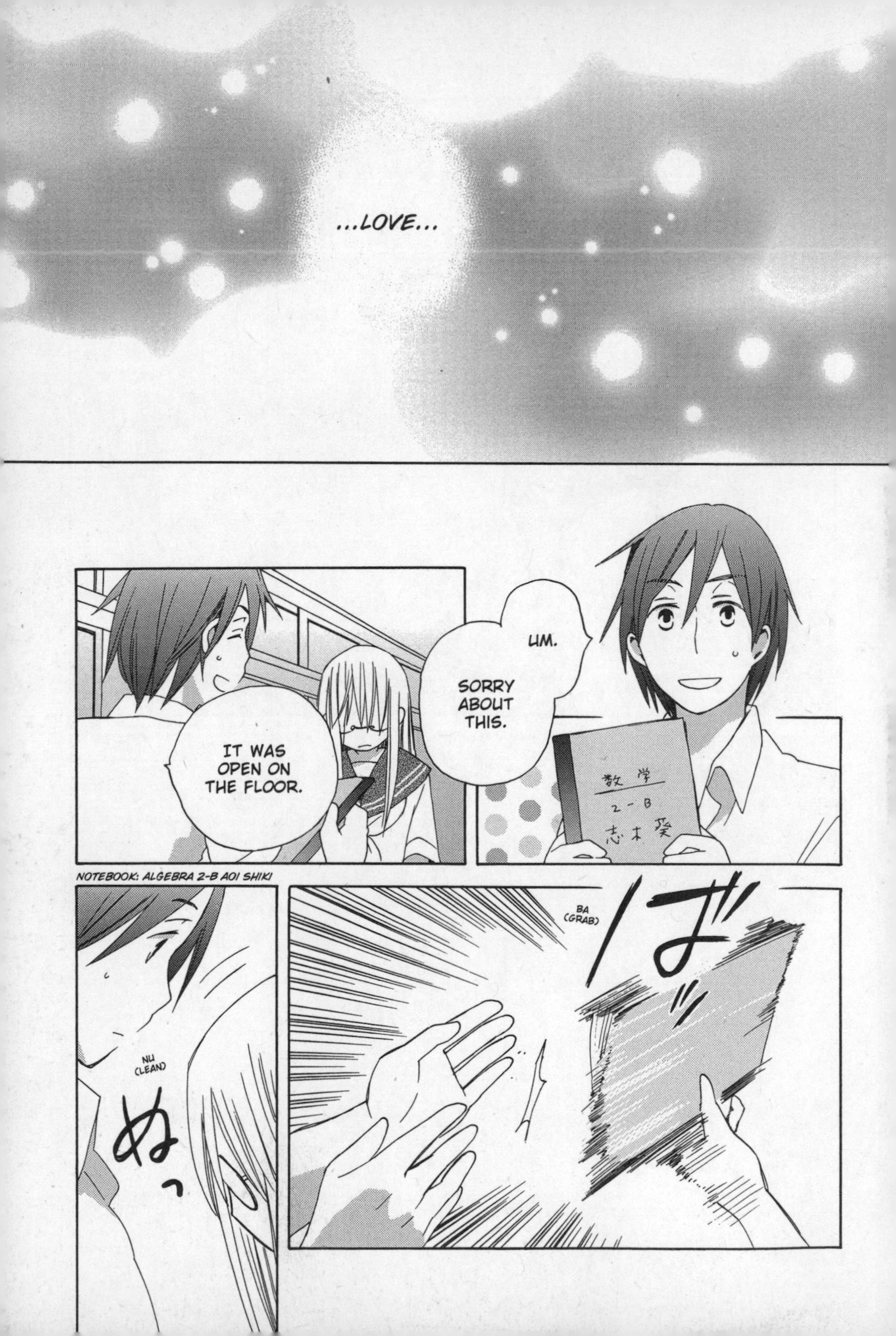
...LOVE...
UM.
SORRY ABOUT THIS.
数学 2-B 志木葵
IT WAS OPEN ON THE FLOOR.
NOTEBOOK: ALGEBRA 2-B AOI SHIKI
BA (GRAB)
NU (LEAN)

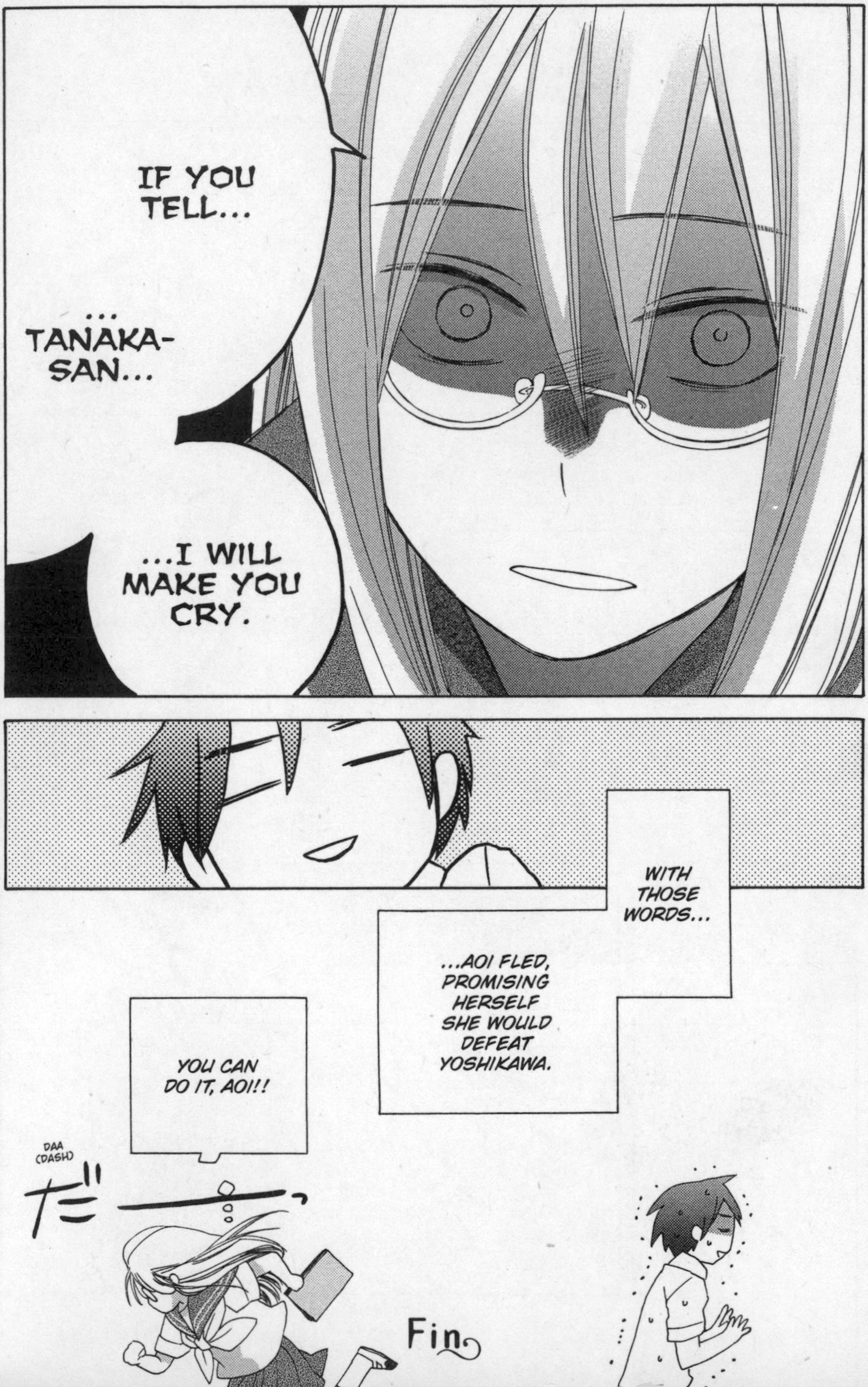
IF YOU TELL...
... TANAKA-SAN...
...I WILL MAKE YOU CRY.
WITH THOSE WORDS...
...AOI FLED, PROMISING HERSELF SHE WOULD DEFEAT YOSHIKAWA.
YOU CAN DO IT, AOI!!
DAA (DASH)
Fin

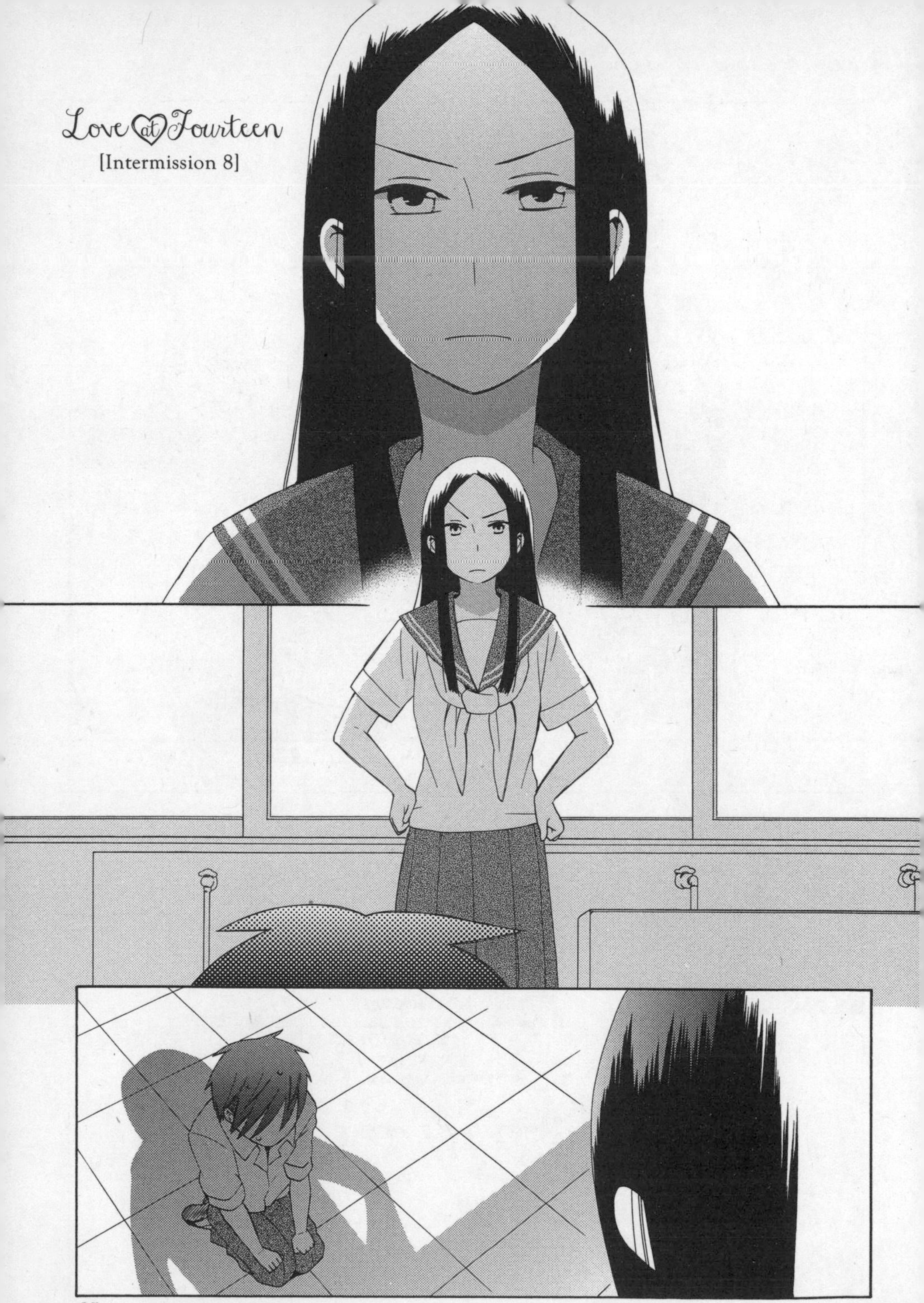
Love at Fourteen
[Intermission 8]

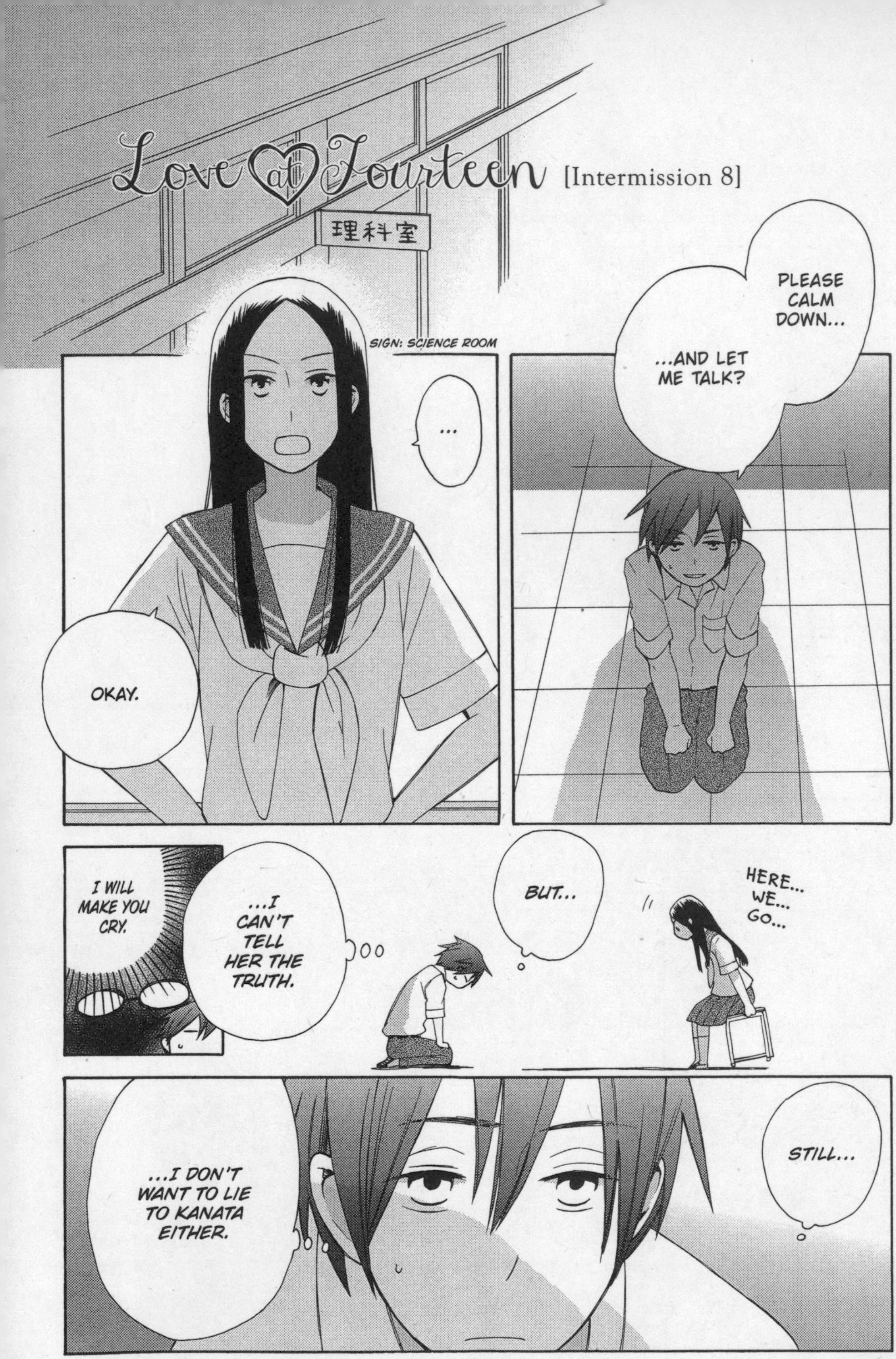
Love at Fourteen [Intermission 8]
理科室
SIGN: SCIENCE ROOM
PLEASE CALM DOWN...
...AND LET ME TALK?
...
OKAY.
HERE... WE... GO...
BUT...
...I CAN'T TELL HER THE TRUTH.
I WILL MAKE YOU CRY.
STILL...
...I DON'T WANT TO LIE TO KANATA EITHER.

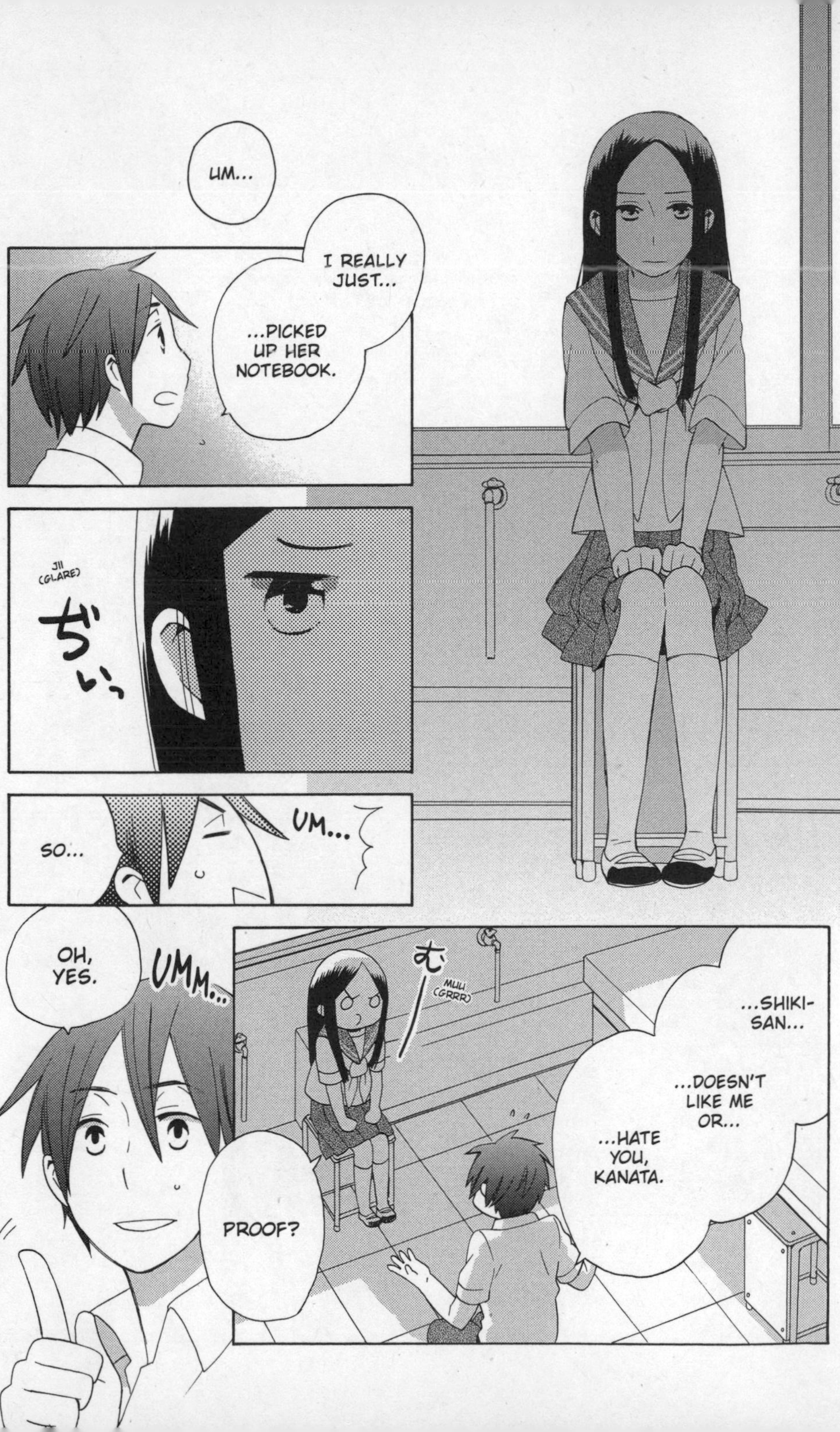
UM...
I REALLY JUST...
...PICKED UP HER NOTEBOOK.
JII (GLARE)
UM...
SO...
...SHIKI-SAN...
...DOESN'T LIKE ME OR...
...HATE YOU, KANATA.
MUU (GRRR)
PROOF?
OH, YES.
UMM...

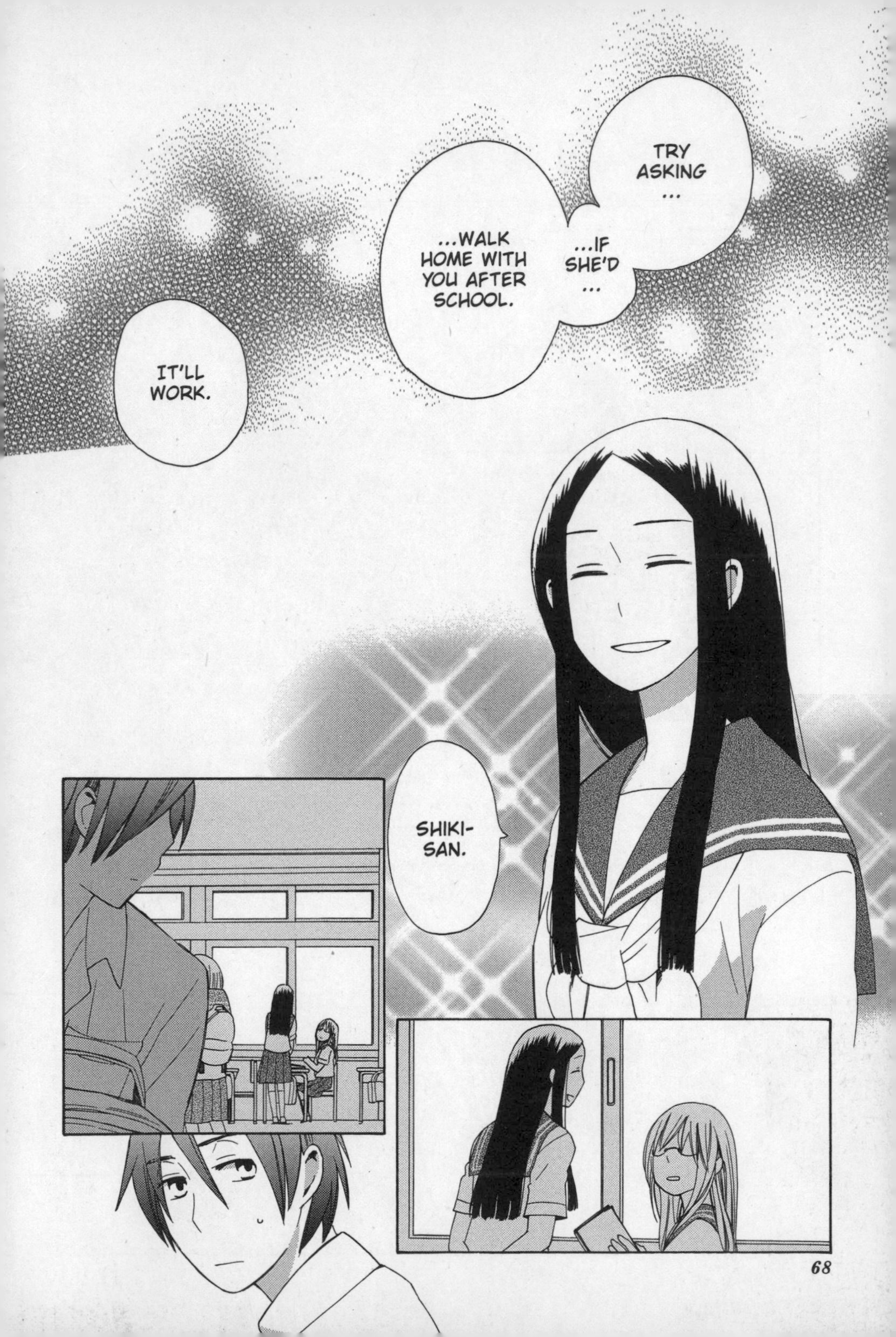
TRY ASKING...
...IF SHE'D...
...WALK HOME WITH YOU AFTER SCHOOL.
IT'LL WORK.
SHIKI-SAN.

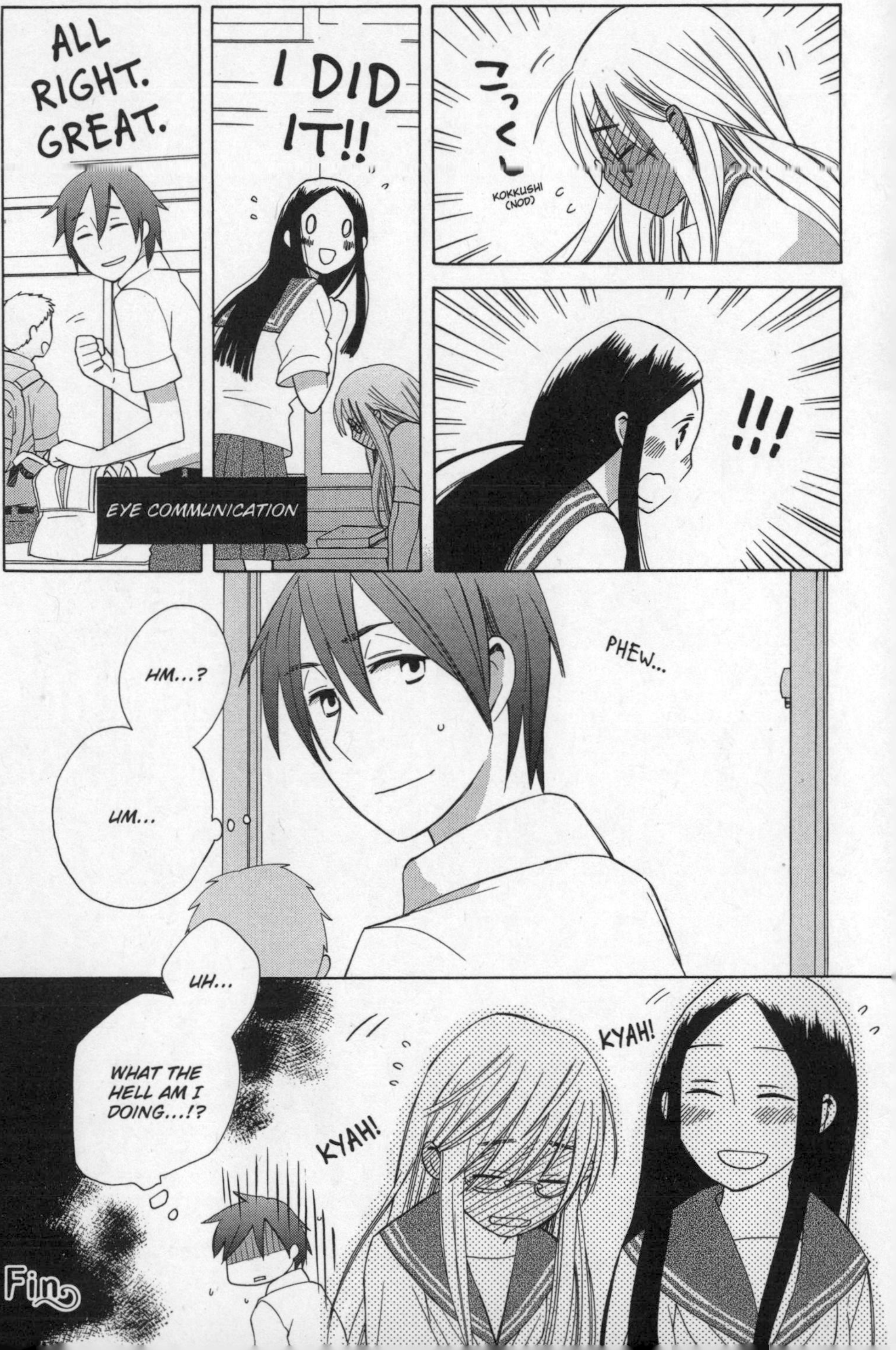
こっくし
KOKKUSHI (NOD)
!!!
I DID IT!!
ALL RIGHT. GREAT.
EYE COMMUNICATION
PHEW...
HM...?
UM...
UH...
KYAH!
KYAH!
WHAT THE HELL AM I DOING...!?
Fin

Love at Fourteen

Fuka Mizutani

Love at Fourteen

[Chapter 8]

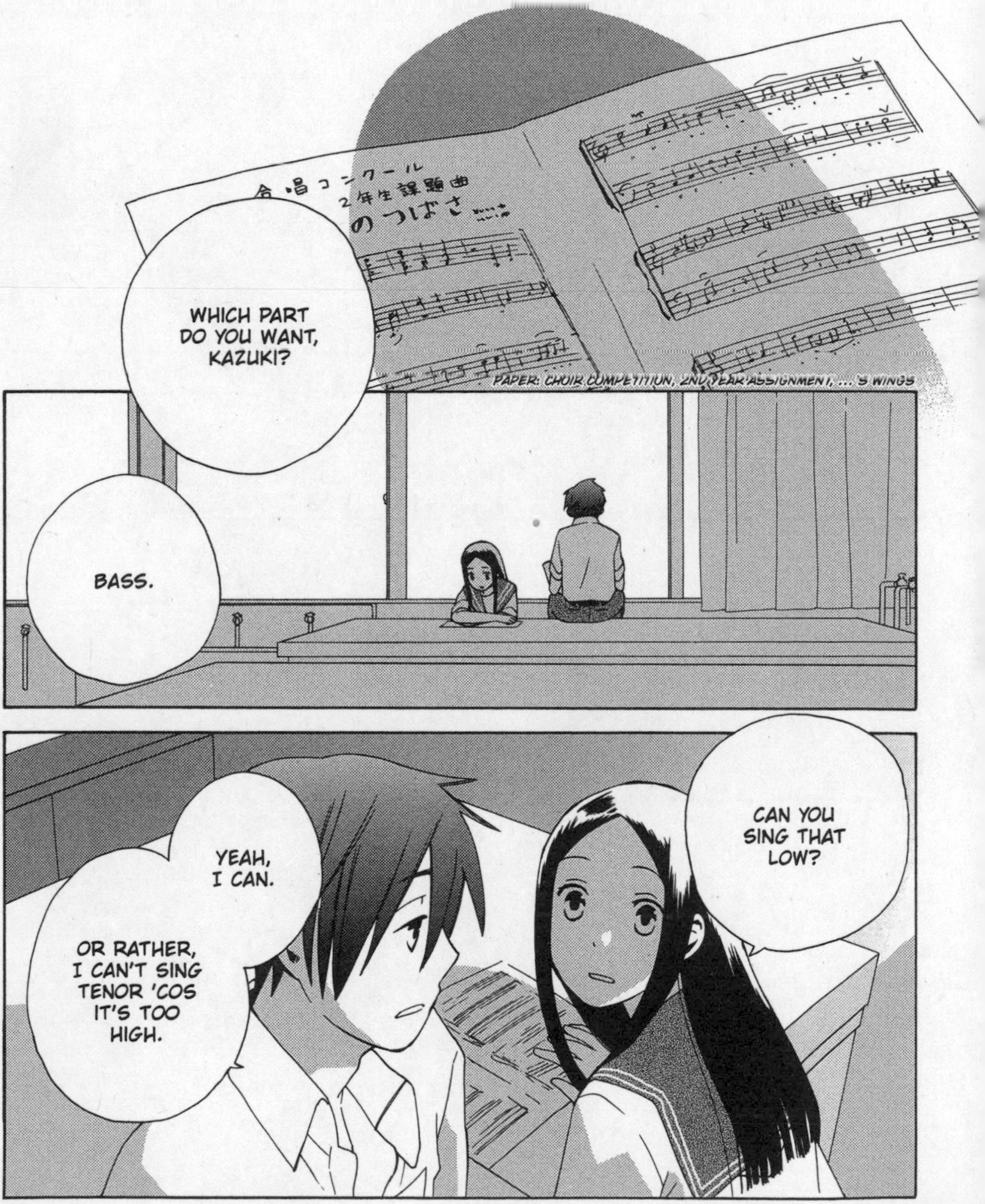

合唱コンクール
2年生課題曲
のつばさ
WHICH PART DO YOU WANT, KAZUKI?
PAPER: CHOIR COMPETITION, 2ND YEAR ASSIGNMENT, ... 'S WINGS
BASS.
CAN YOU SING THAT LOW?
YEAH, I CAN.
OR RATHER, I CAN'T SING TENOR 'COS IT'S TOO HIGH.

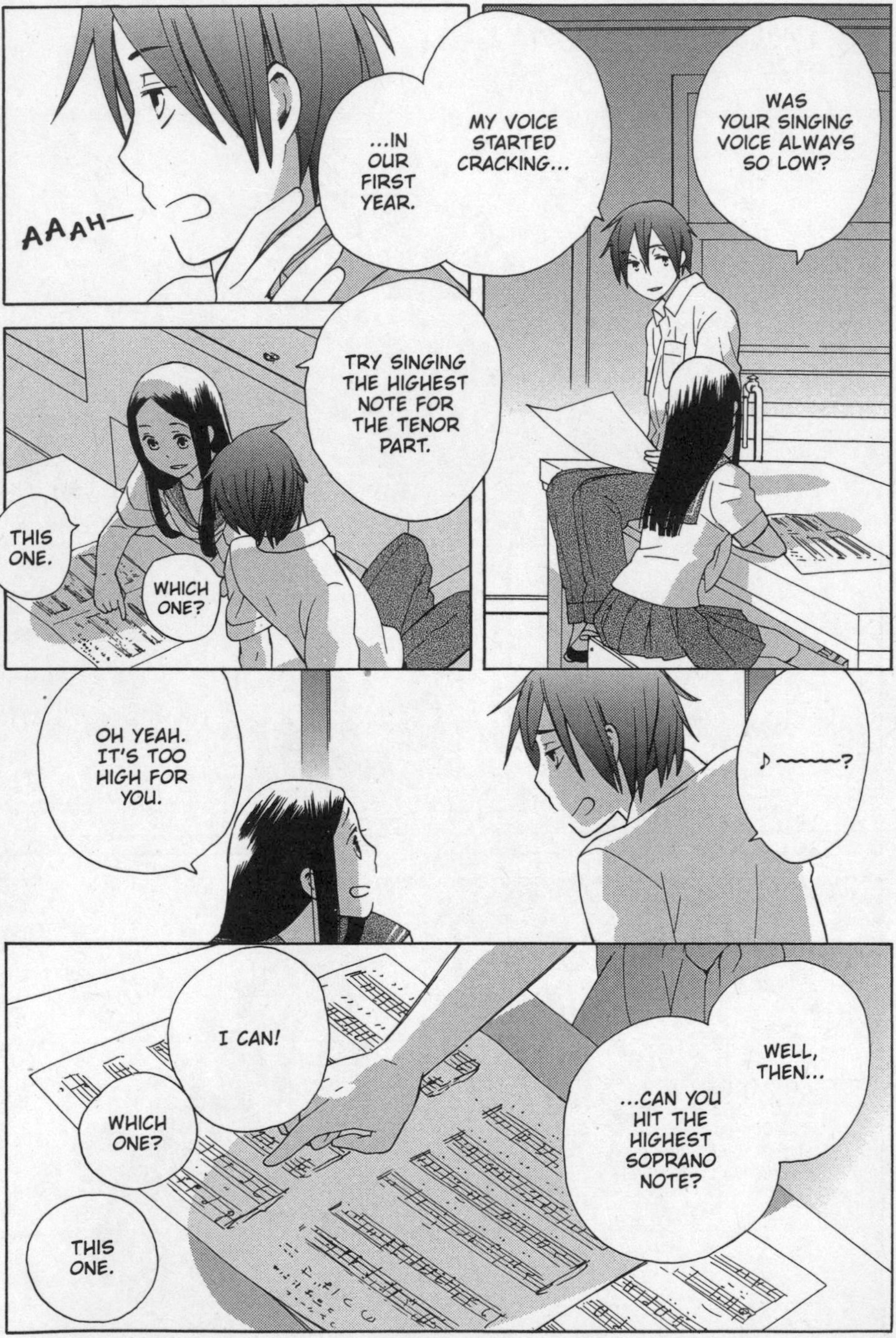

WAS YOUR SINGING VOICE ALWAYS SO LOW?
MY VOICE STARTED CRACKING...
...IN OUR FIRST YEAR.
AAAH—
TRY SINGING THE HIGHEST NOTE FOR THE TENOR PART.
WHICH ONE?
THIS ONE.
♪ ~~~~~~?
OH YEAH. IT'S TOO HIGH FOR YOU.
WELL, THEN...
...CAN YOU HIT THE HIGHEST SOPRANO NOTE?
I CAN!
WHICH ONE?
THIS ONE.

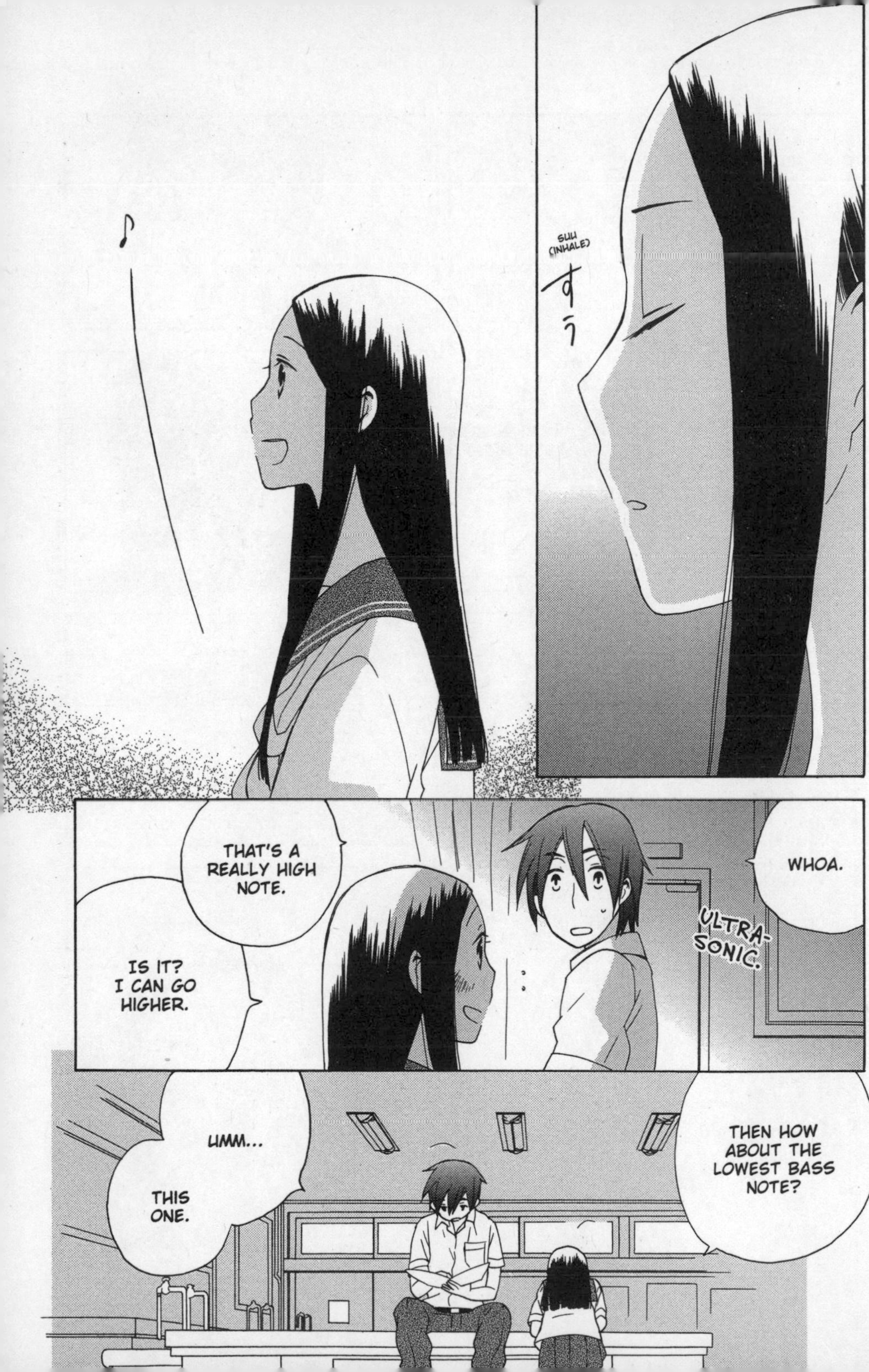
SUU (INHALE)
すぅ
♪
WHOA.
ULTRA-SONIC.
THAT'S A REALLY HIGH NOTE.
IS IT? I CAN GO HIGHER.
THEN HOW ABOUT THE LOWEST BASS NOTE?
UMM...
THIS ONE.

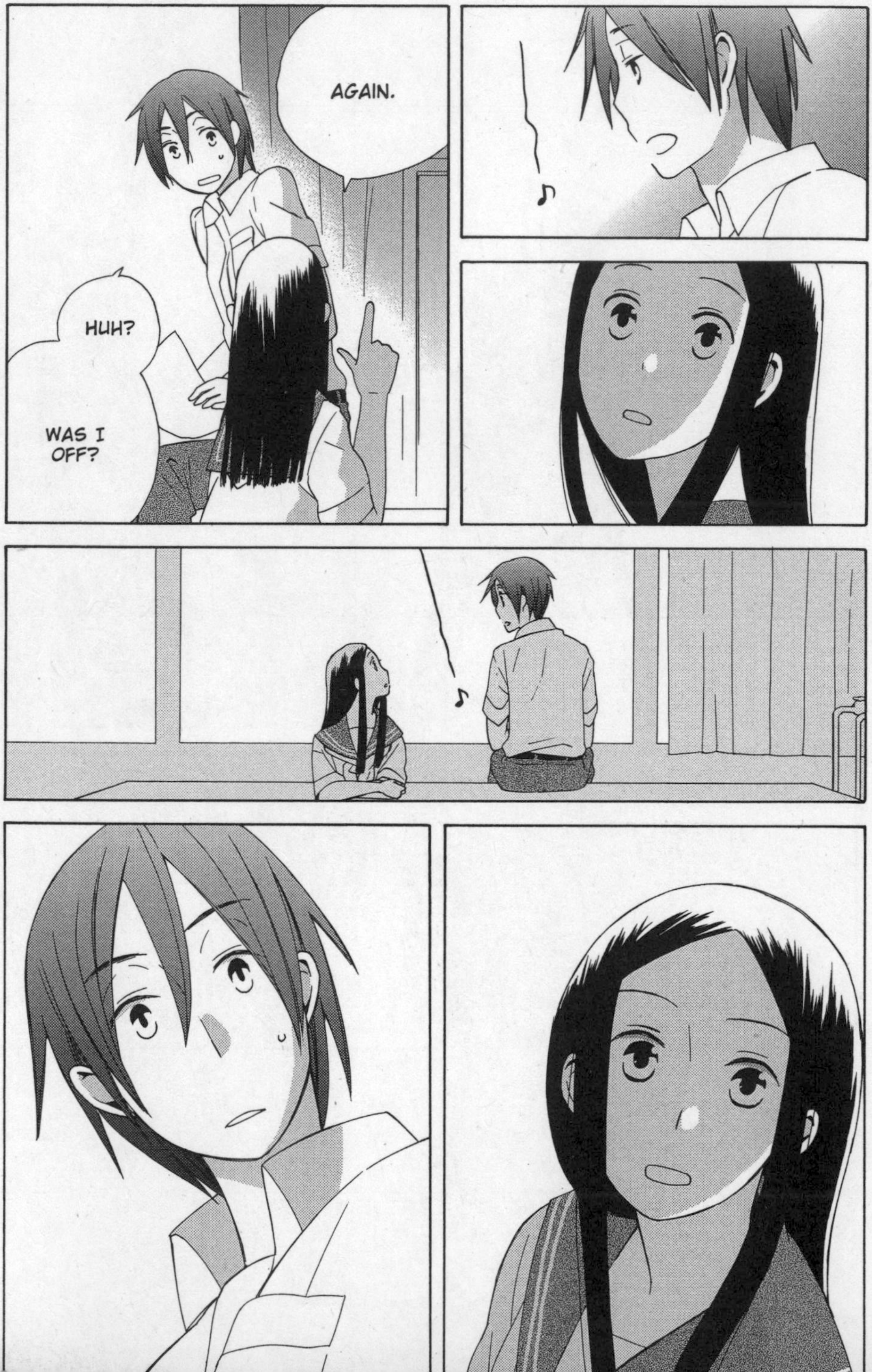
AGAIN.
HUH?
WAS I OFF?

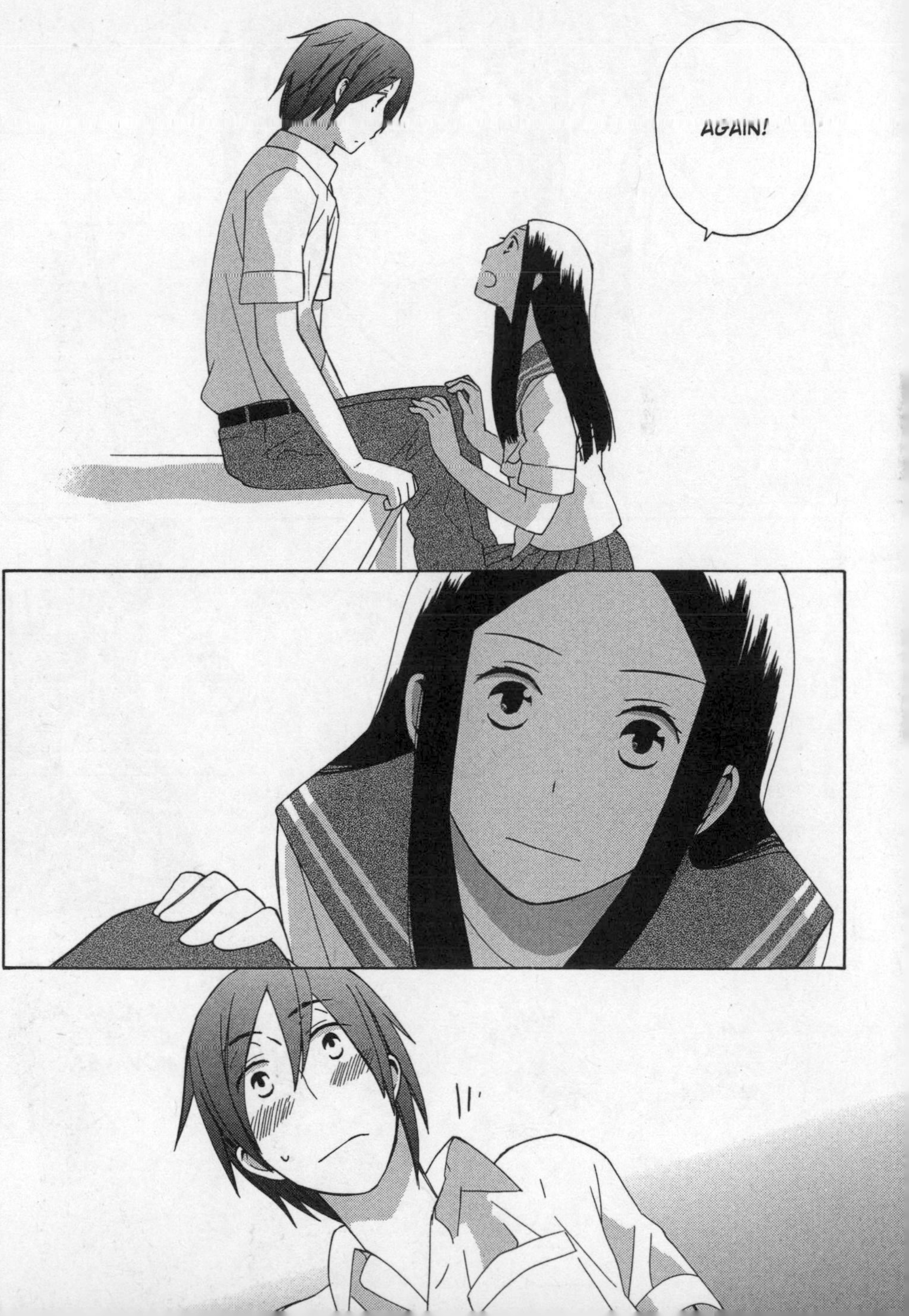
AGAIN!

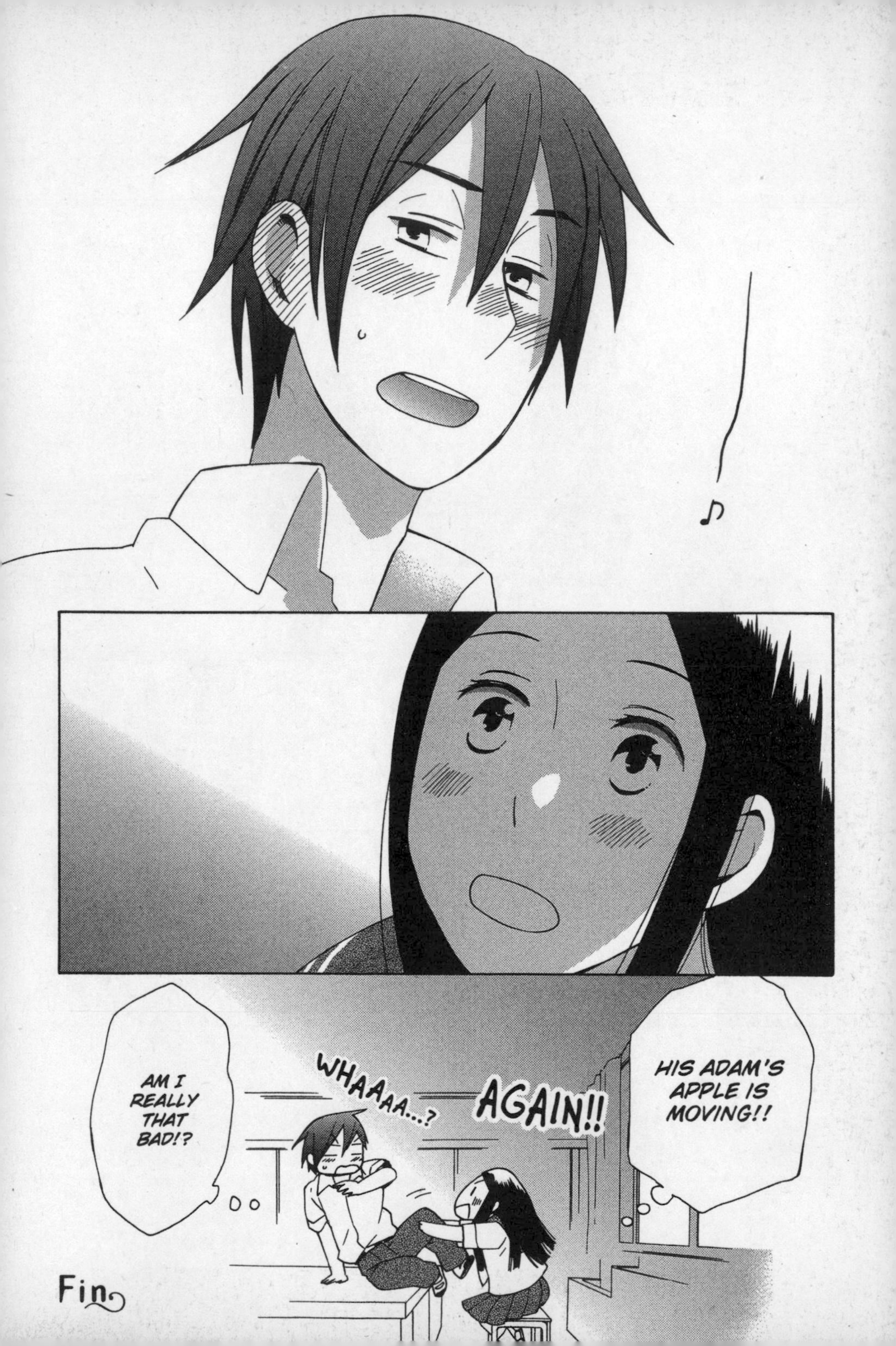
HIS ADAM'S APPLE IS MOVING!!
AGAIN!!
WHAAAA...?
AM I REALLY THAT BAD!?
Fin

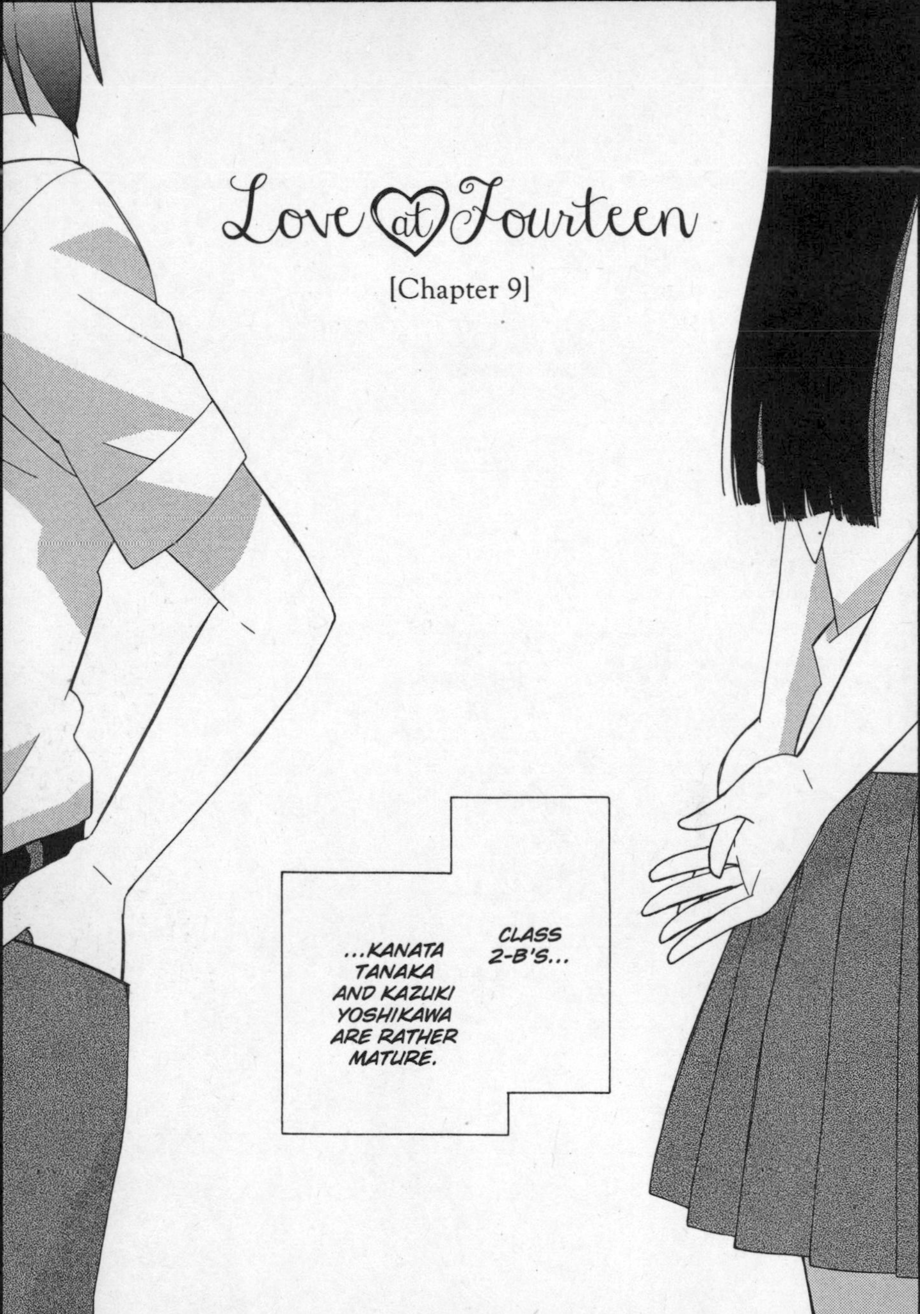
Love at Fourteen
[Chapter 9]
CLASS 2-B'S...
...KANATA TANAKA AND KAZUKI YOSHIKAWA ARE RATHER MATURE.

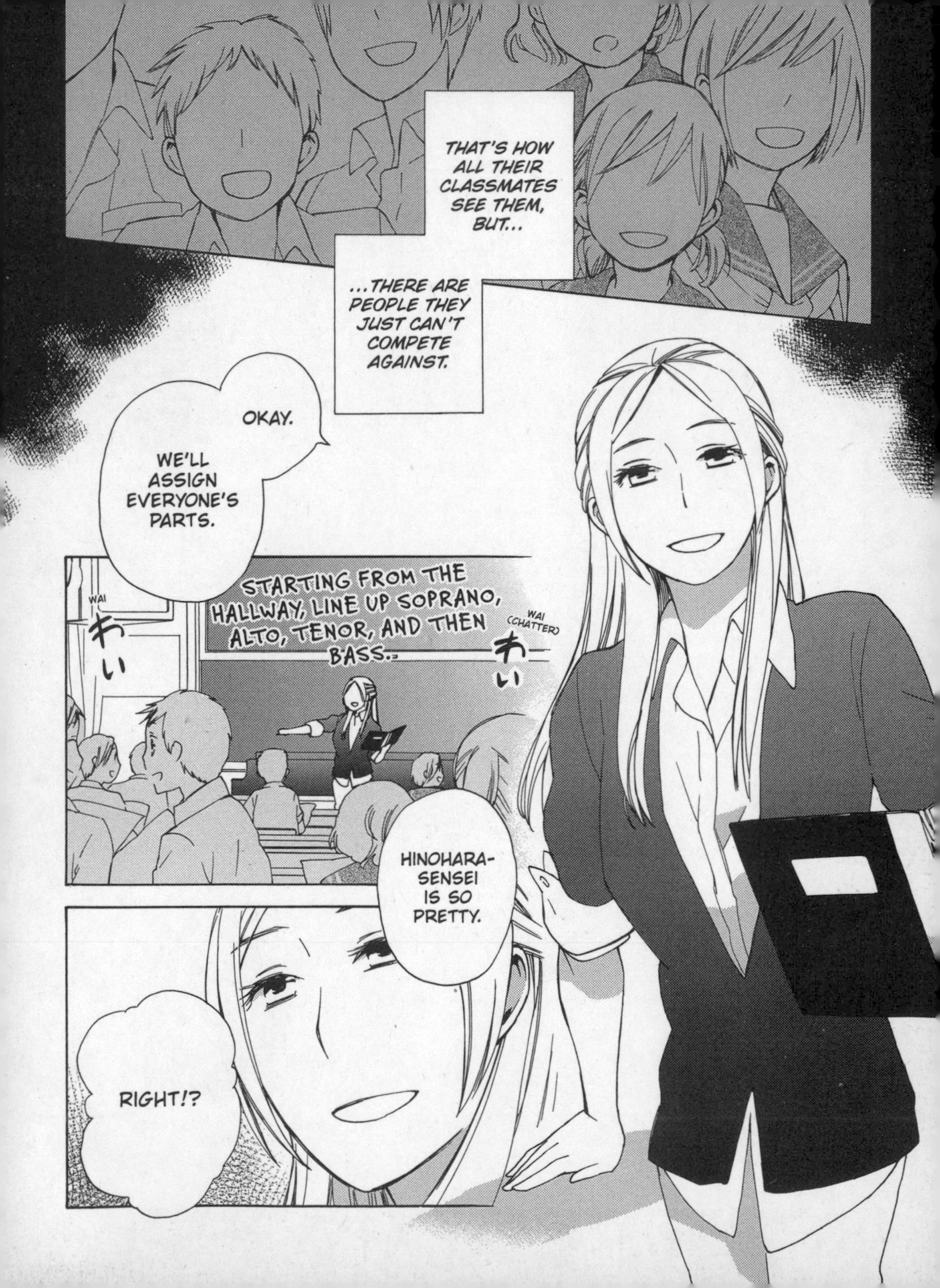
THAT'S HOW ALL THEIR CLASSMATES SEE THEM, BUT...
...THERE ARE PEOPLE THEY JUST CAN'T COMPETE AGAINST.
OKAY.
WE'LL ASSIGN EVERYONE'S PARTS.
HINOHARA-SENSEI IS SO PRETTY.
STARTING FROM THE HALLWAY, LINE UP SOPRANO, ALTO, TENOR, AND THEN BASS.
わい
WAI (CHATTER)
わい
WAI
RIGHT!?

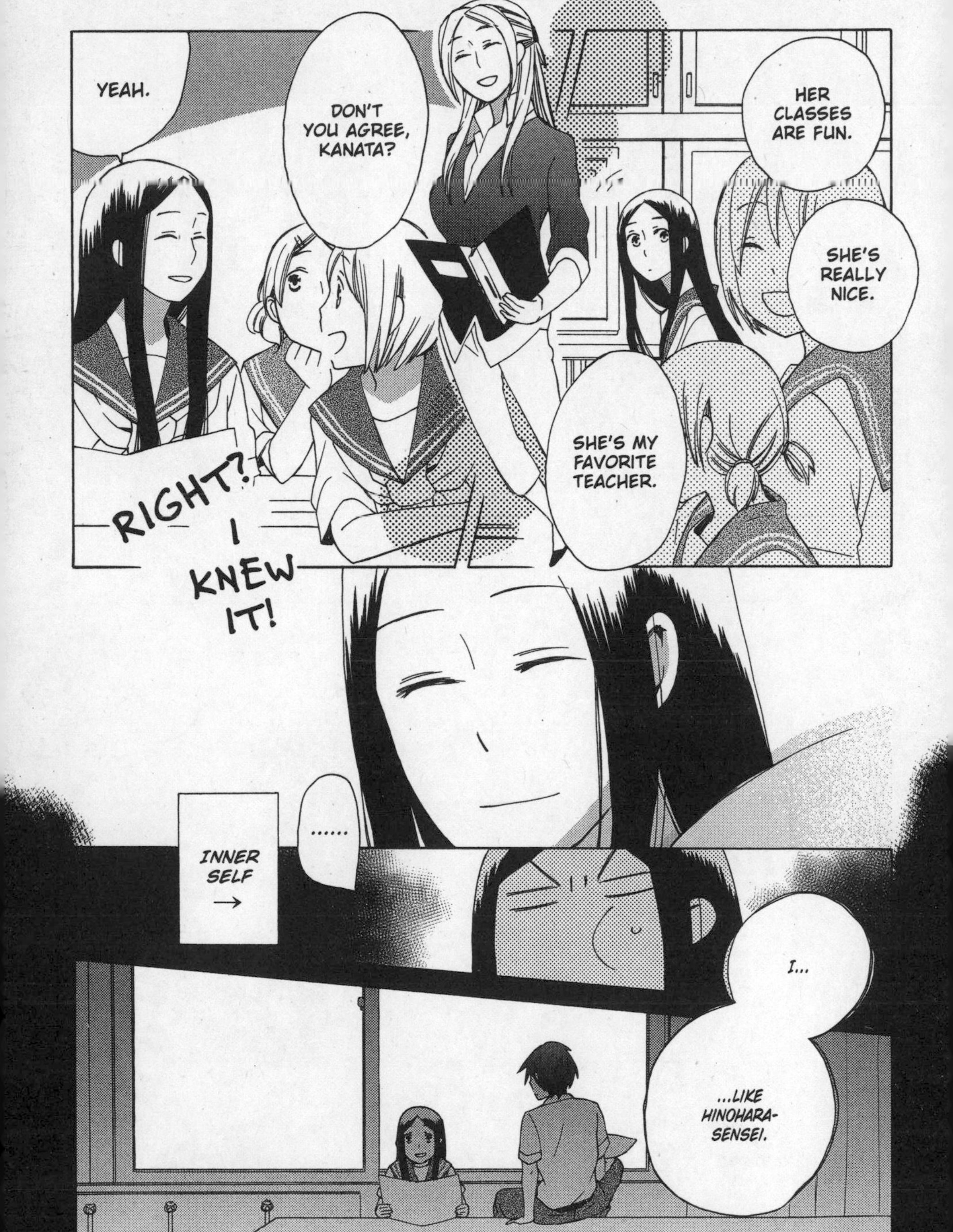
HER CLASSES ARE FUN.
SHE'S REALLY NICE.
SHE'S MY FAVORITE TEACHER.
DON'T YOU AGREE, KANATA?
YEAH.
RIGHT? I KNEW IT!
......
INNER SELF →
I...
...LIKE HINOHARA-SENSEI.

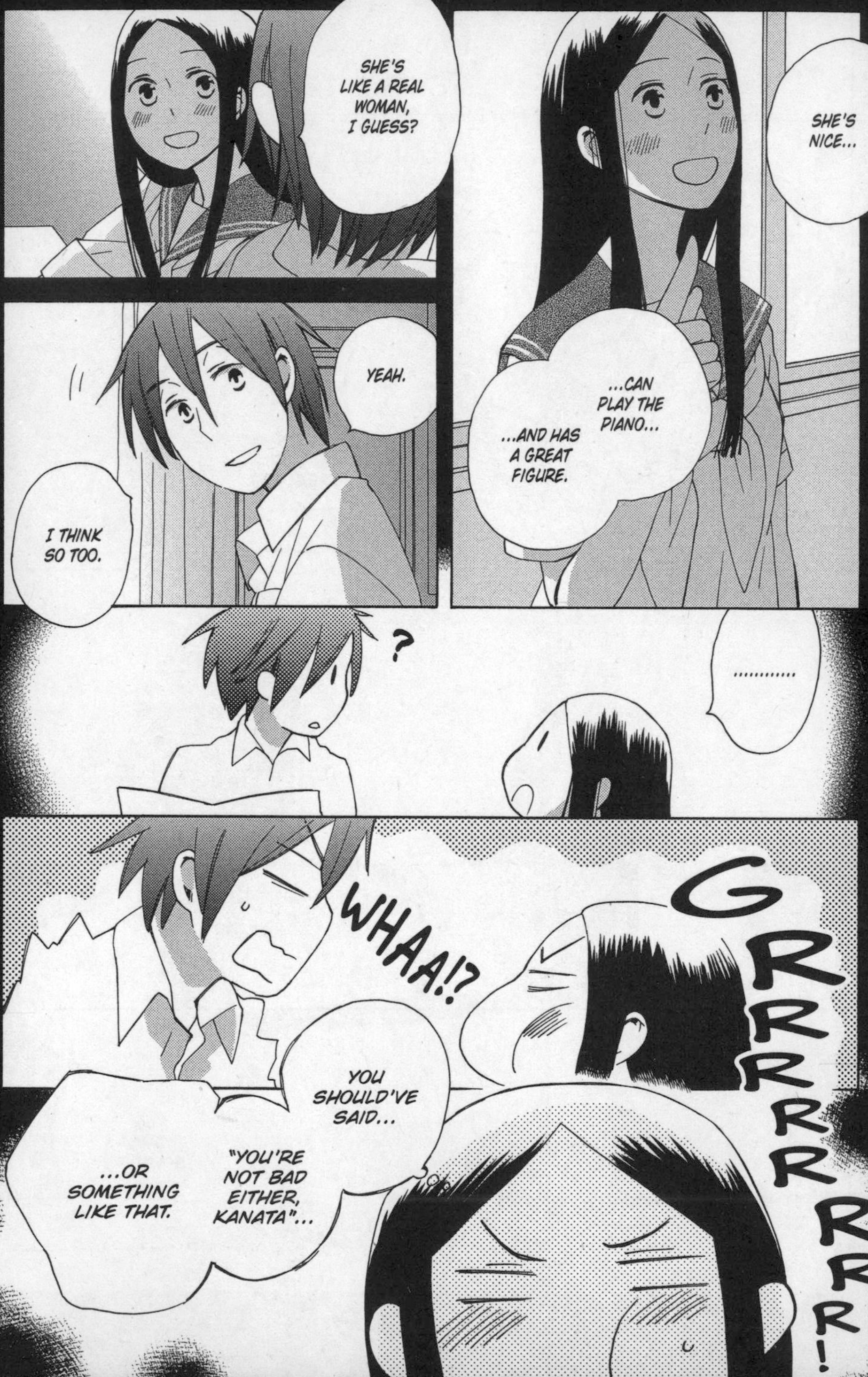
SHE'S NICE...
...CAN PLAY THE PIANO...
...AND HAS A GREAT FIGURE.
SHE'S LIKE A REAL WOMAN, I GUESS?
YEAH.
I THINK SO TOO.
....
?
GRRRRRRRRR!
WHAA!?
YOU SHOULD'VE SAID...
"YOU'RE NOT BAD EITHER, KANATA"...
...OR SOMETHING LIKE THAT.

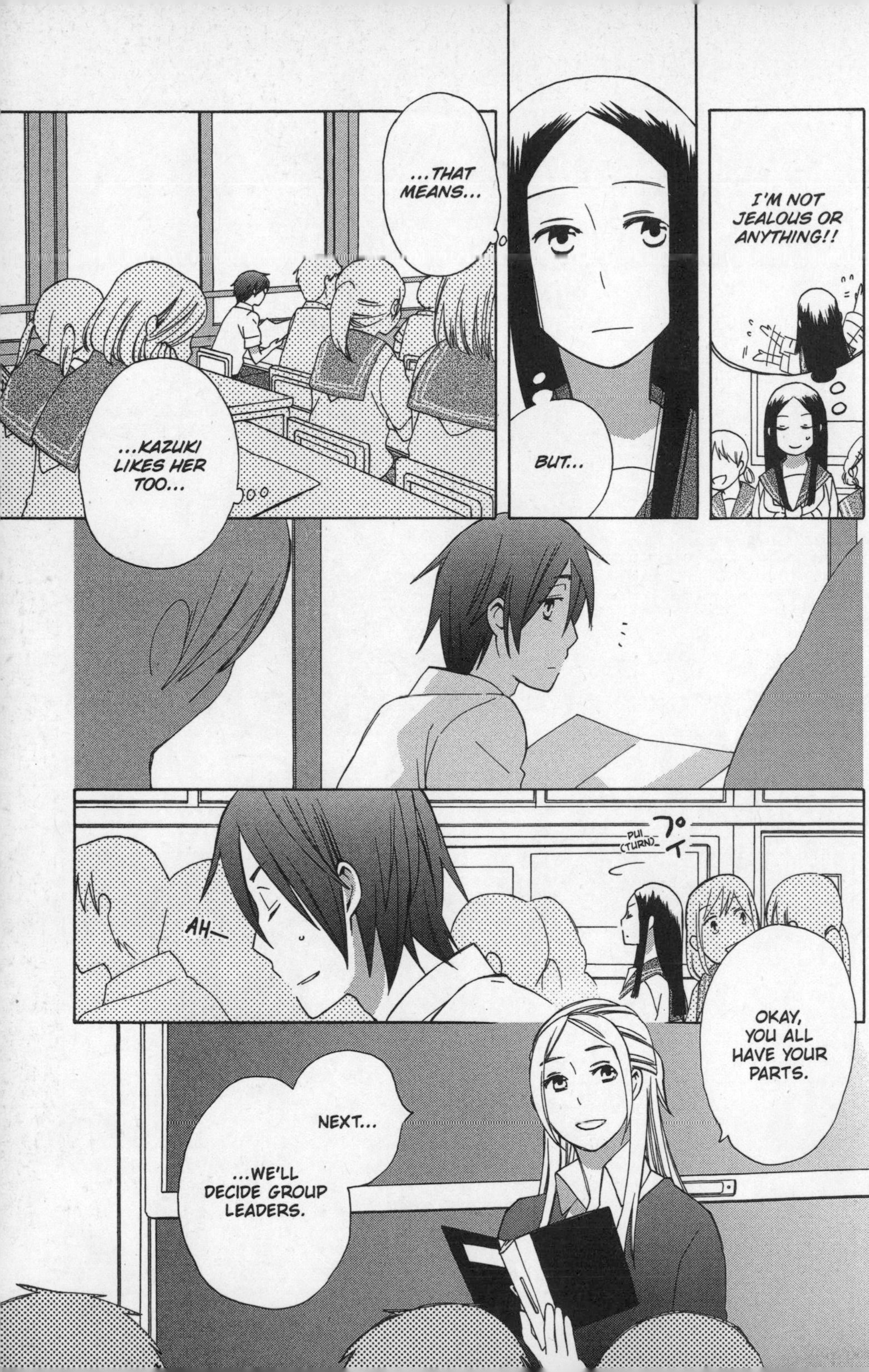
I'M NOT JEALOUS OR ANYTHING!!
BUT...
...THAT MEANS...
...KAZUKI LIKES HER TOO...
PUI (TURN)
AH—
OKAY, YOU ALL HAVE YOUR PARTS.
NEXT...
...WE'LL DECIDE GROUP LEADERS.

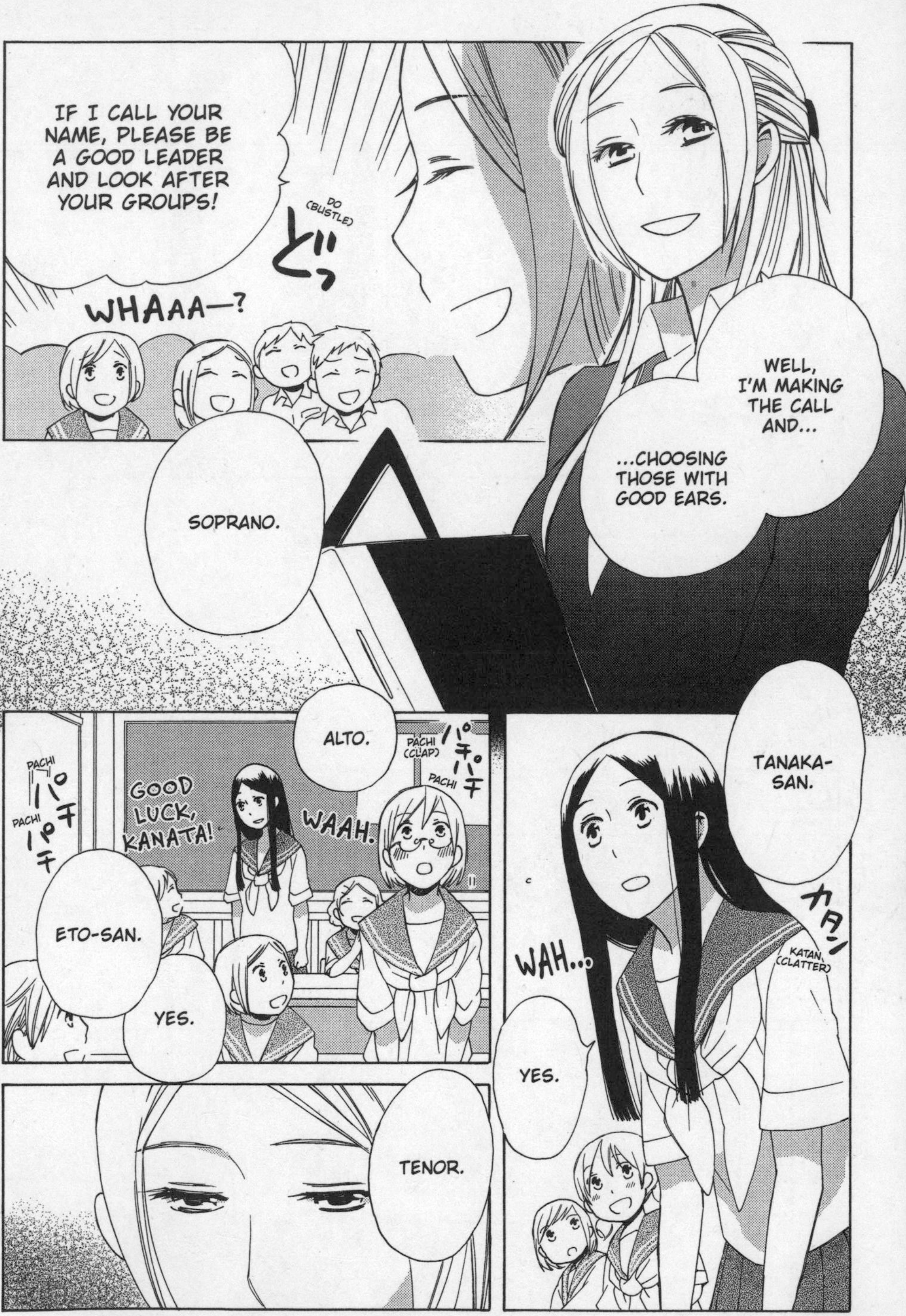

IF I CALL YOUR NAME, PLEASE BE A GOOD LEADER AND LOOK AFTER YOUR GROUPS!
どっ
DO (BUSTLE)
WHAAA—?
WELL, I'M MAKING THE CALL AND...
...CHOOSING THOSE WITH GOOD EARS.
SOPRANO.
TANAKA-SAN.
カタン
KATAN (CLATTER)
WAH...
YES.
ALTO.
パチパチ
PACHI (CLAP) PACHI
パチパチ
PACHI PACHI
GOOD LUCK, KANATA!
WAAH.
ETO-SAN.
YES.
TENOR.

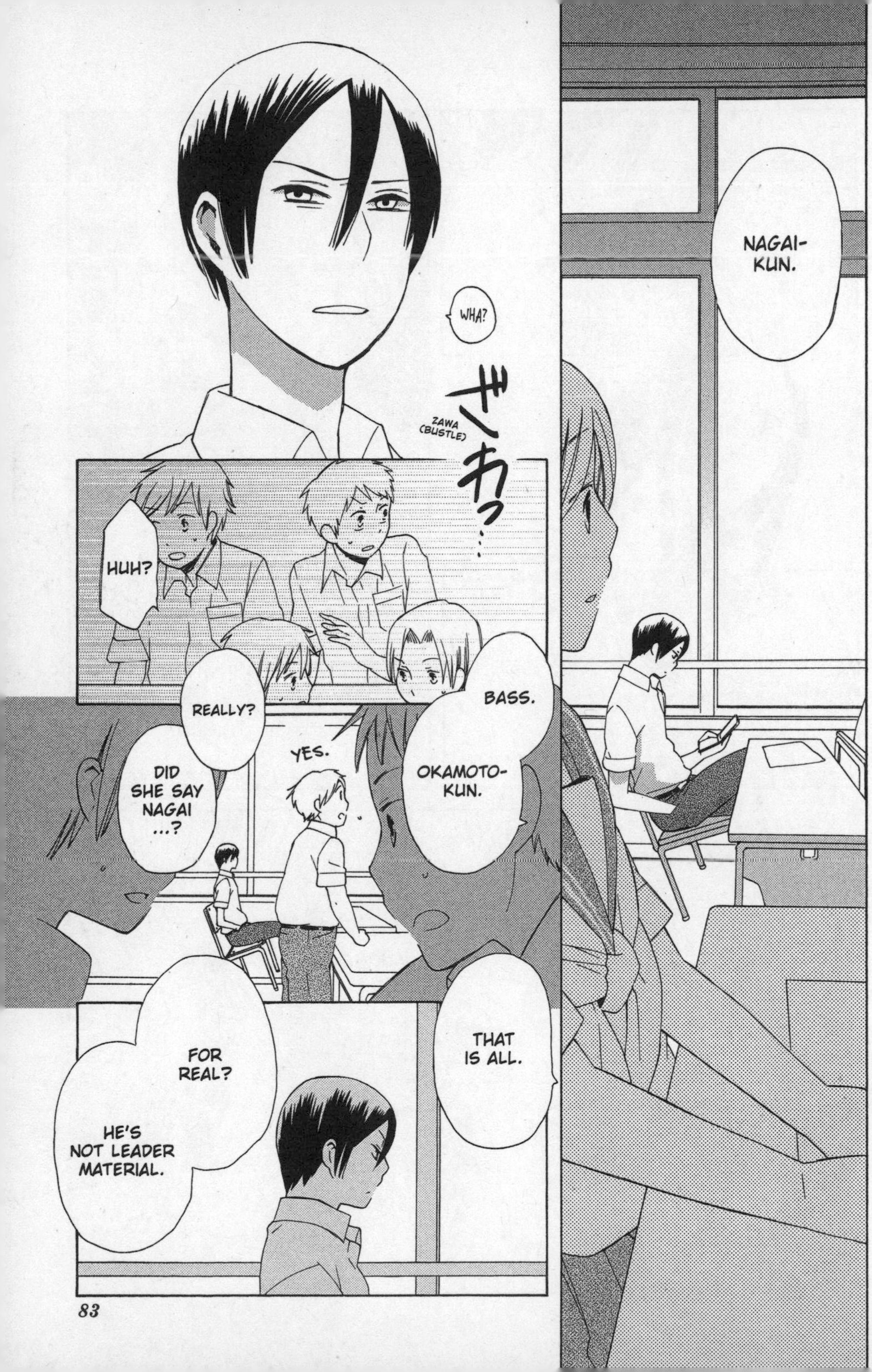
NAGAI-KUN.
WHA?
ZAWA (BUSTLE)
HUH?
REALLY?
BASS.
OKAMOTO-KUN.
YES.
DID SHE SAY NAGAI ...?
THAT IS ALL.
FOR REAL?
HE'S NOT LEADER MATERIAL.

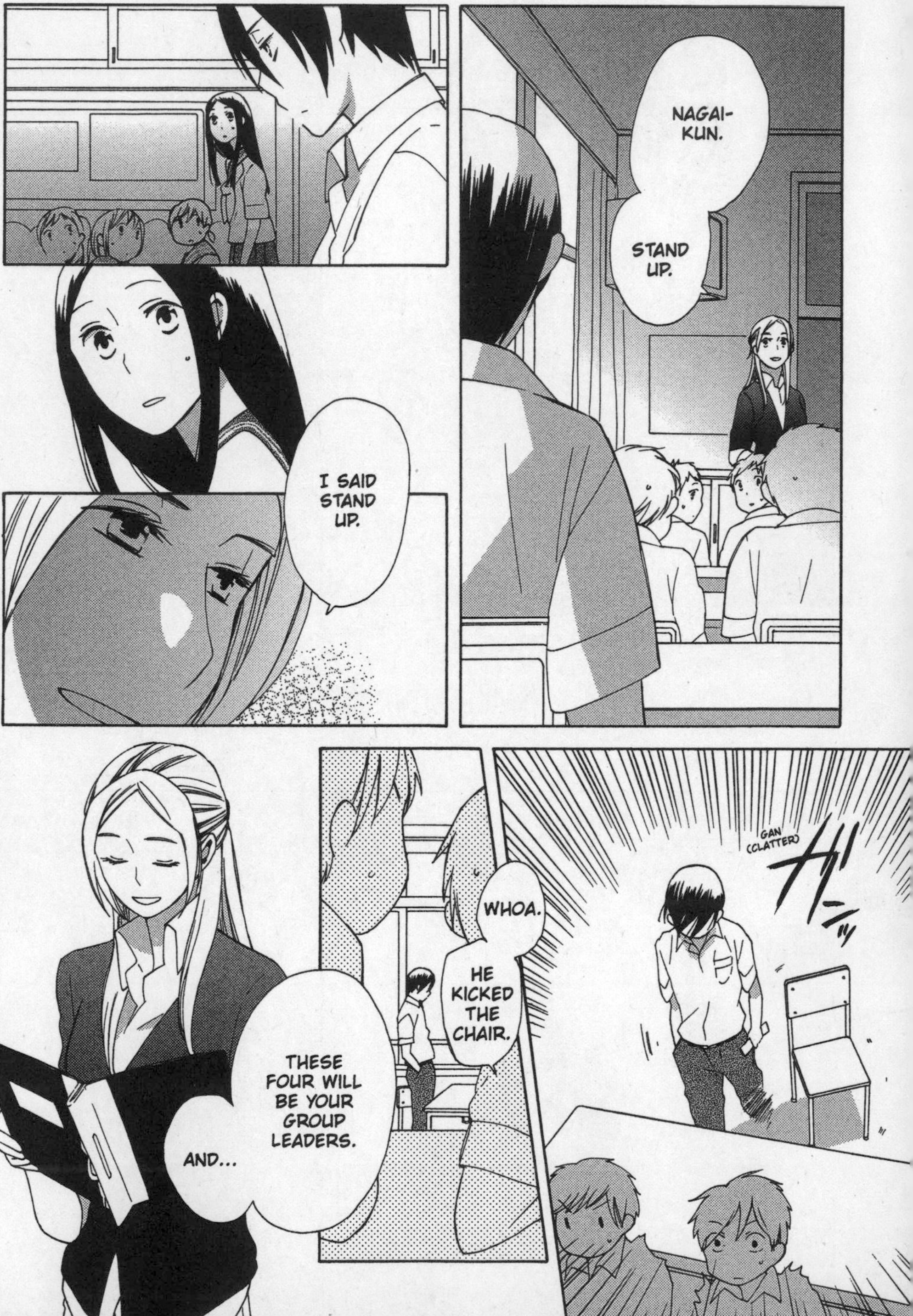
NAGAI-KUN.
STAND UP.
I SAID STAND UP.
GAN (CLATTER)
WHOA.
HE KICKED THE CHAIR.
THESE FOUR WILL BE YOUR GROUP LEADERS.
AND...

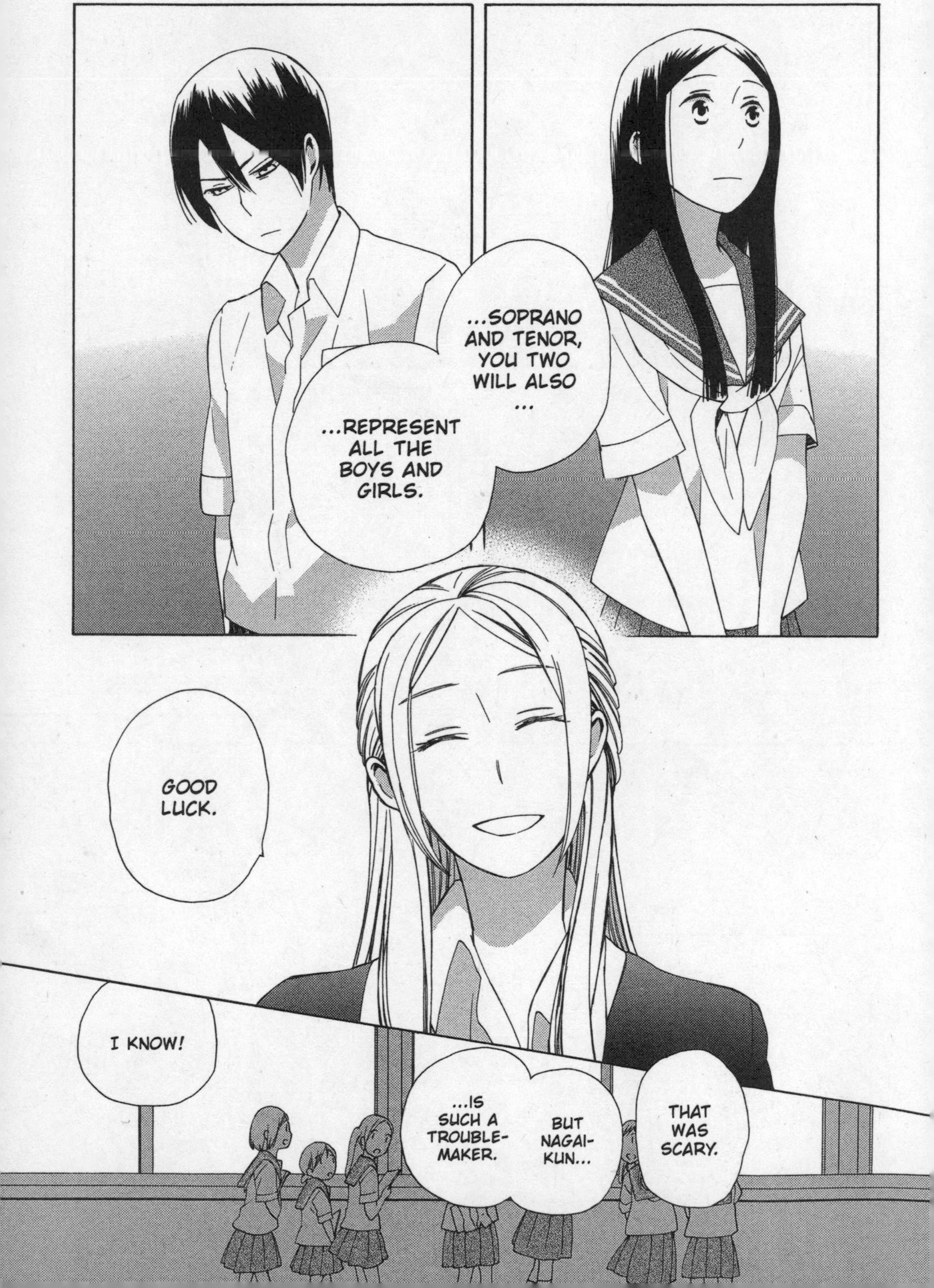
...SOPRANO AND TENOR, YOU TWO WILL ALSO ...
...REPRESENT ALL THE BOYS AND GIRLS.
GOOD LUCK.
THAT WAS SCARY.
BUT NAGAI-KUN...
...IS SUCH A TROUBLE-MAKER.
I KNOW!

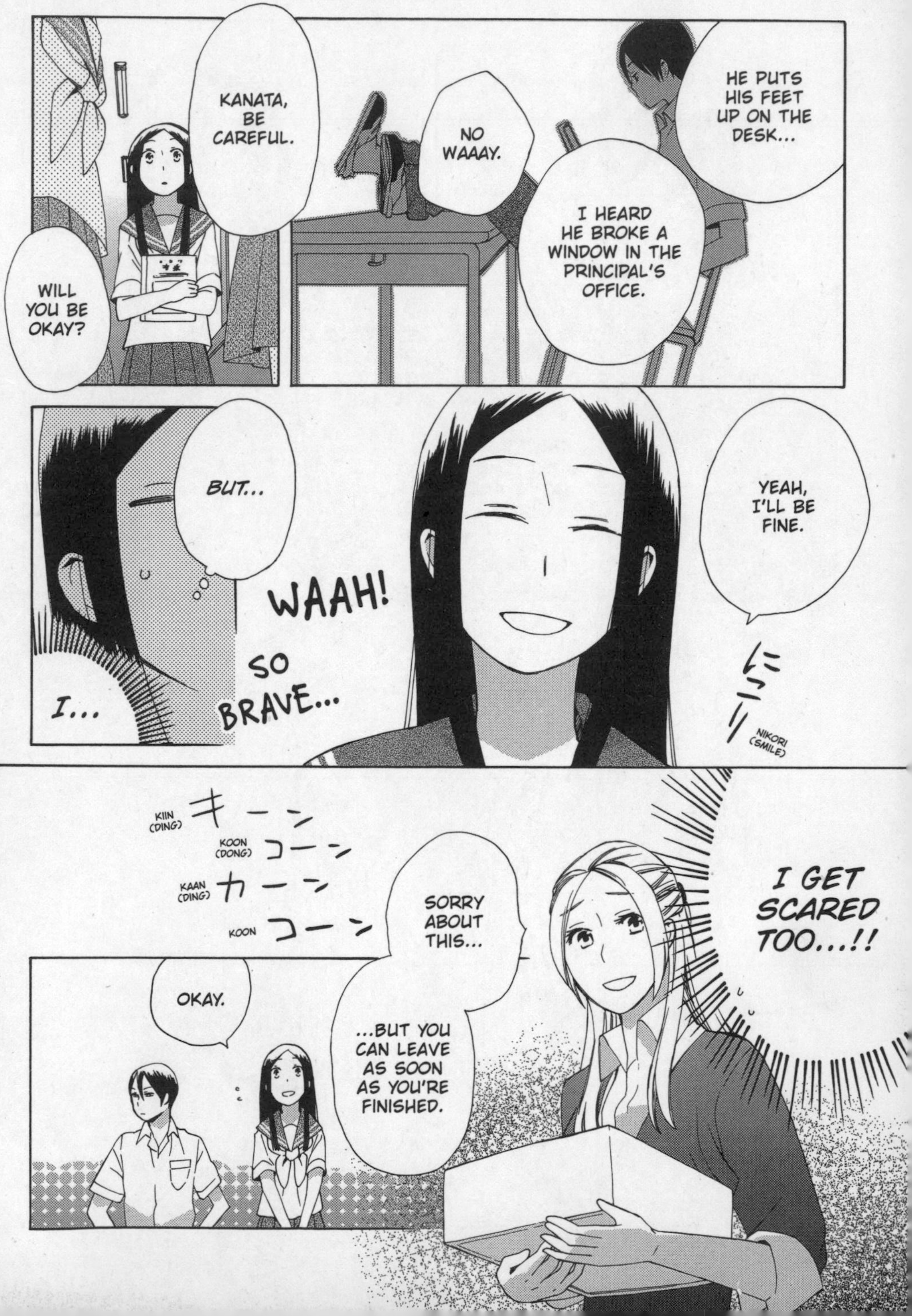

HE PUTS HIS FEET UP ON THE DESK...
NO WAAAY.
I HEARD HE BROKE A WINDOW IN THE PRINCIPAL'S OFFICE.
KANATA, BE CAREFUL.
WILL YOU BE OKAY?
YEAH, I'LL BE FINE.
にこり
NIKORI (SMILE)
BUT...
WAAH!
SO BRAVE...
I...
I GET SCARED TOO...!!
キーン
KIIN (DING)
コーン
KOON (DONG)
カーン
KAAN (DING)
コーン
KOON
SORRY ABOUT THIS...
...BUT YOU CAN LEAVE AS SOON AS YOU'RE FINISHED.
OKAY.

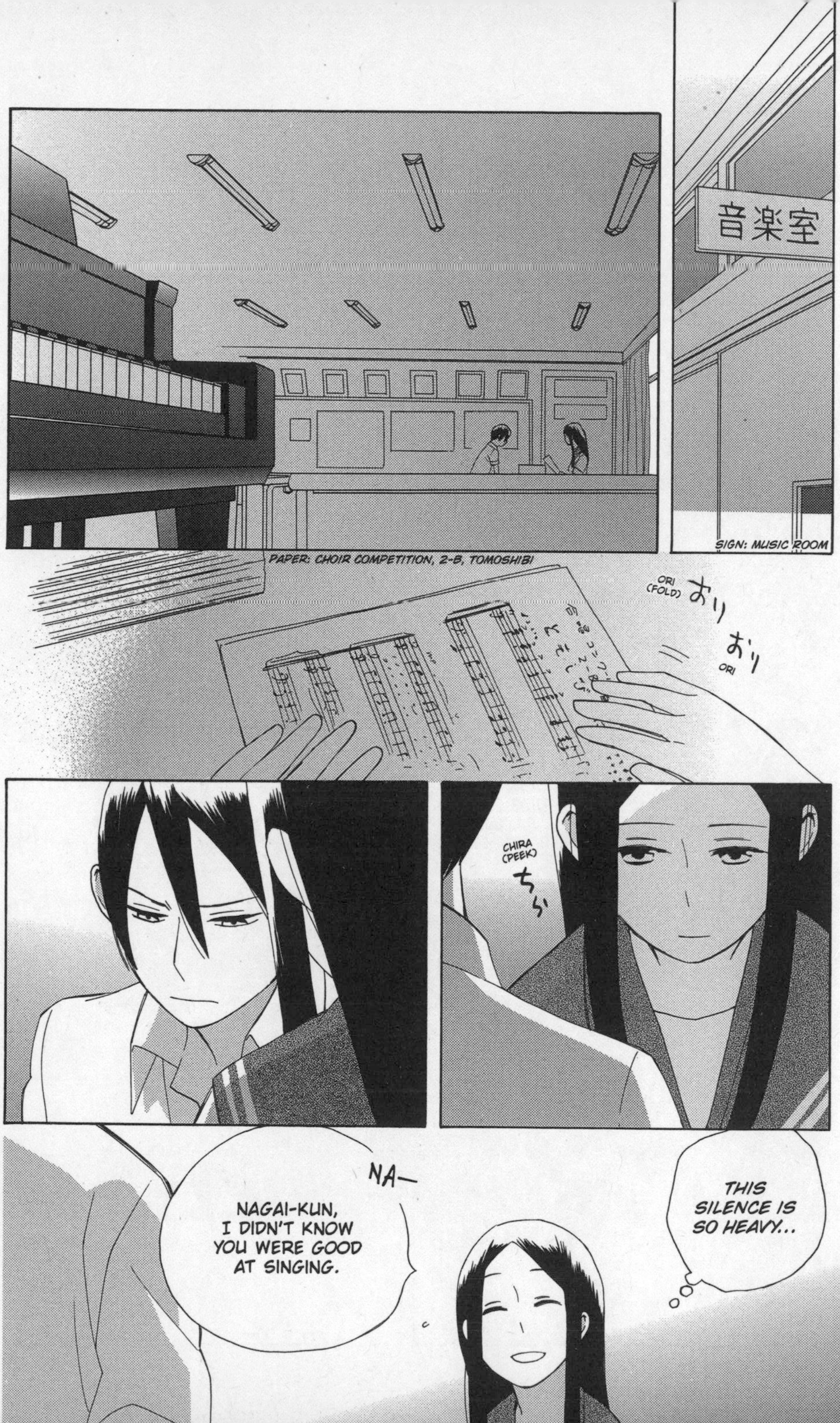
音楽室
SIGN: MUSIC ROOM
PAPER: CHOIR COMPETITION, 2-B, TOMOSHIBI
ORI (FOLD) おり
おり ORI
CHIRA (PEEK) ちら
THIS SILENCE IS SO HEAVY...
NA—
NAGAI-KUN, I DIDN'T KNOW YOU WERE GOOD AT SINGING.

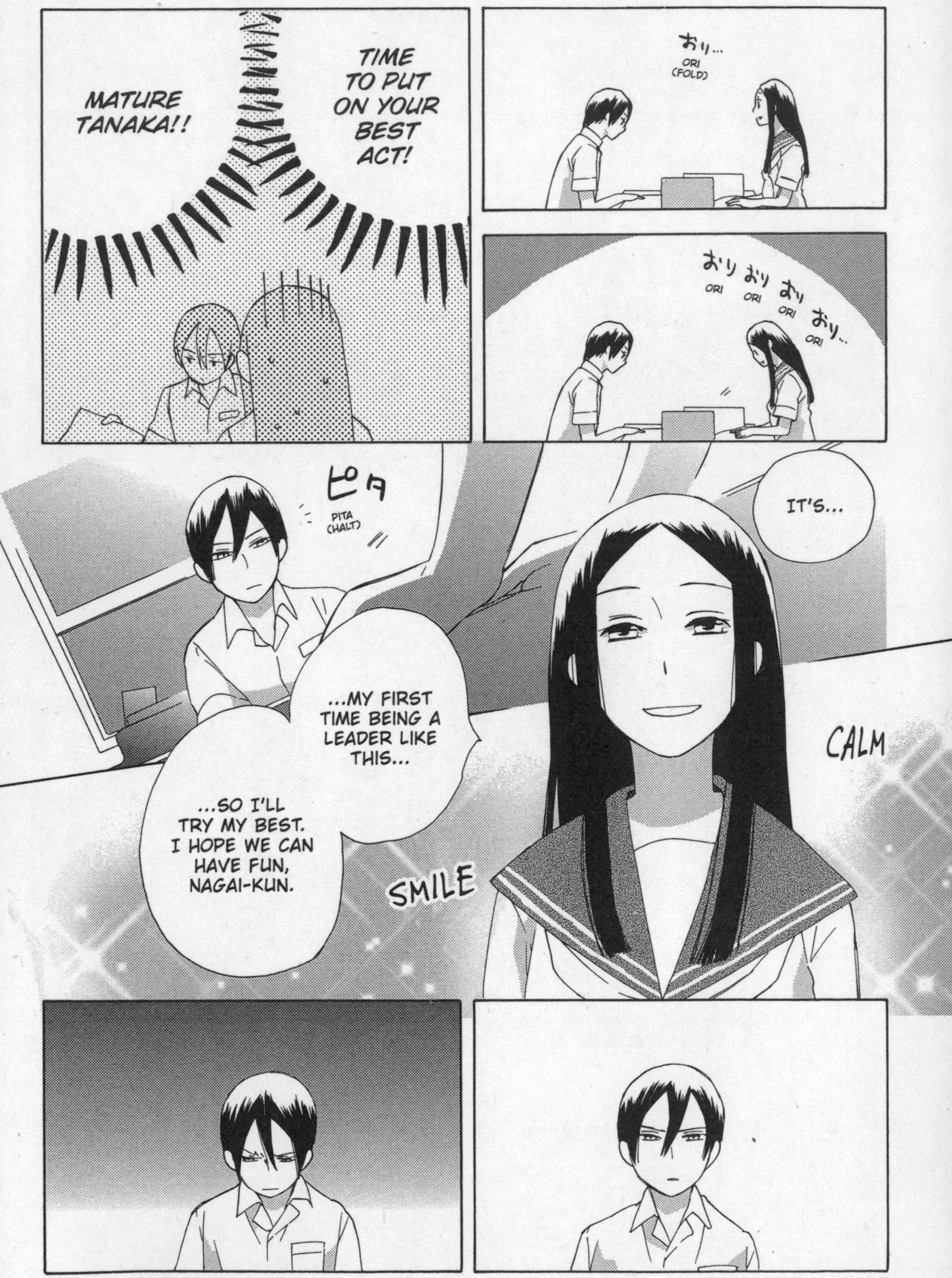

おり…
ORI (FOLD)
おり おり おり おり…
ORI ORI ORI ORI
TIME TO PUT ON YOUR BEST ACT!
MATURE TANAKA!!
IT'S...
ピタ
PITA (HALT)
...MY FIRST TIME BEING A LEADER LIKE THIS...
CALM
...SO I'LL TRY MY BEST. I HOPE WE CAN HAVE FUN, NAGAI-KUN.
SMILE

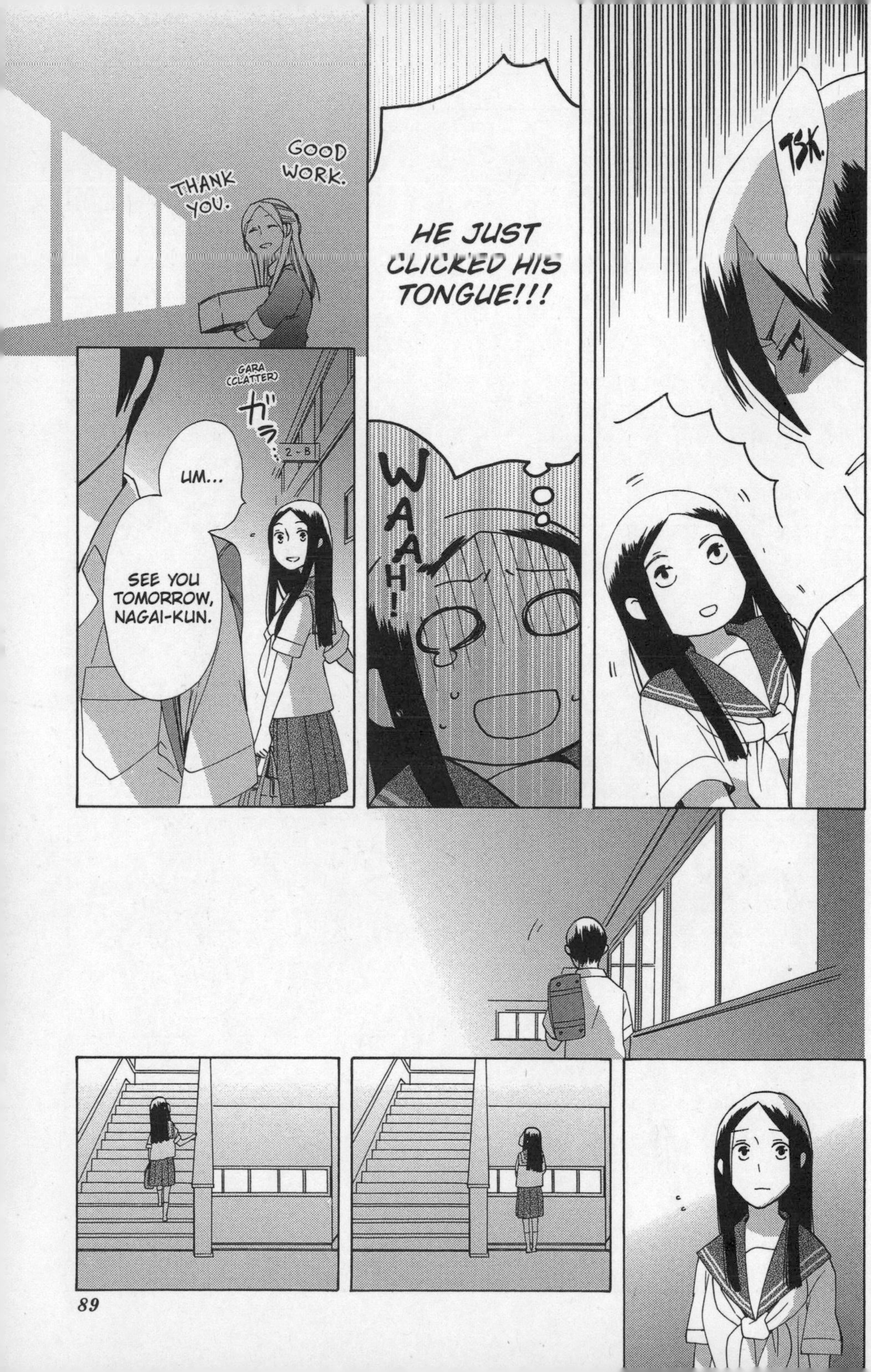
TSK.
HE JUST CLICKED HIS TONGUE!!!
WAAH!
GOOD WORK.
THANK YOU.
GARA (CLATTER)
ガラ
2-B
UM...
SEE YOU TOMORROW, NAGAI-KUN.

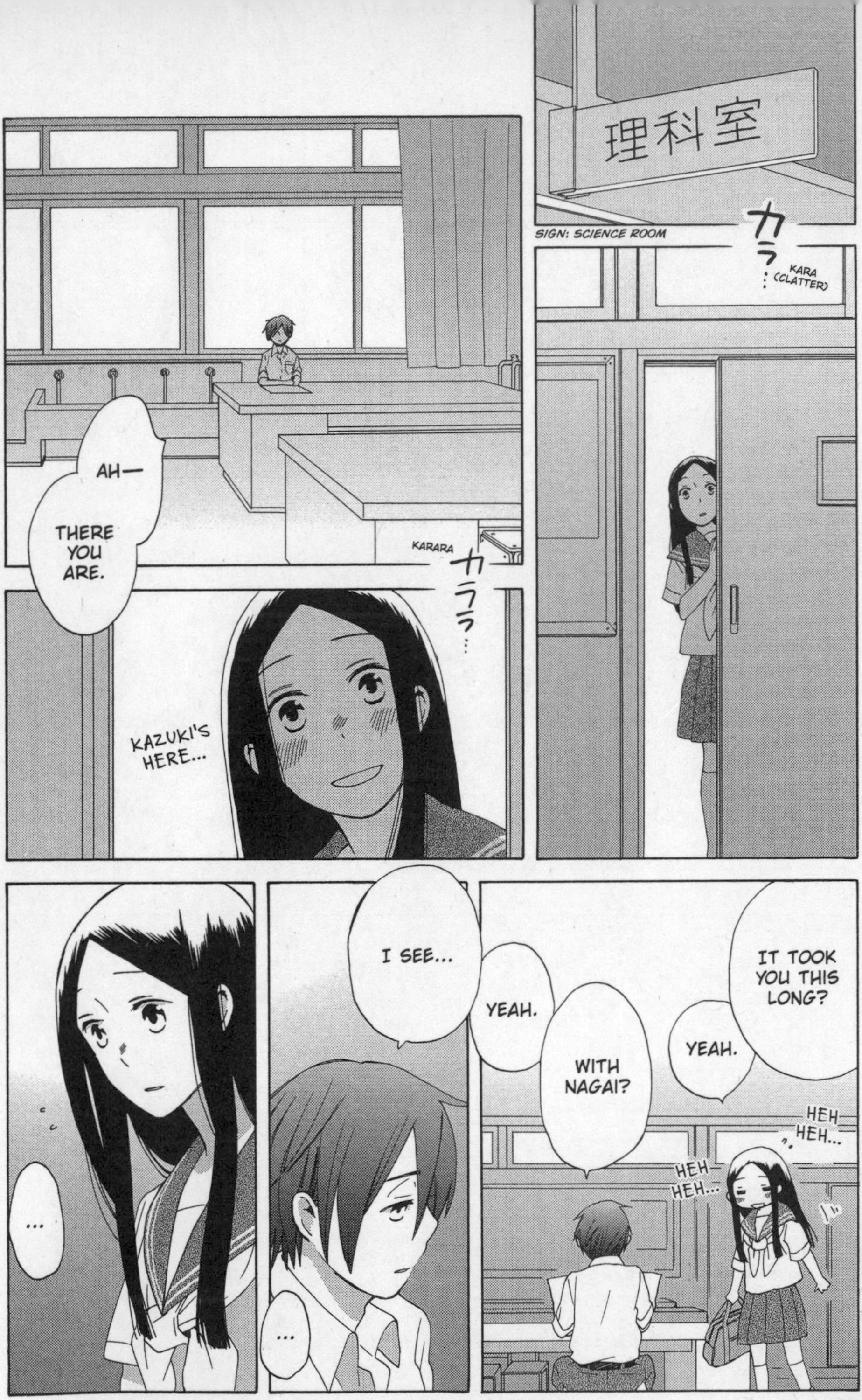
理科室
SIGN: SCIENCE ROOM
カラ…
KARA (CLATTER)
AH—
THERE YOU ARE.
カララ…
KARARA
KAZUKI'S HERE...
IT TOOK YOU THIS LONG?
YEAH.
WITH NAGAI?
YEAH.
HEH HEH...
HEH HEH...
I SEE...
...
...

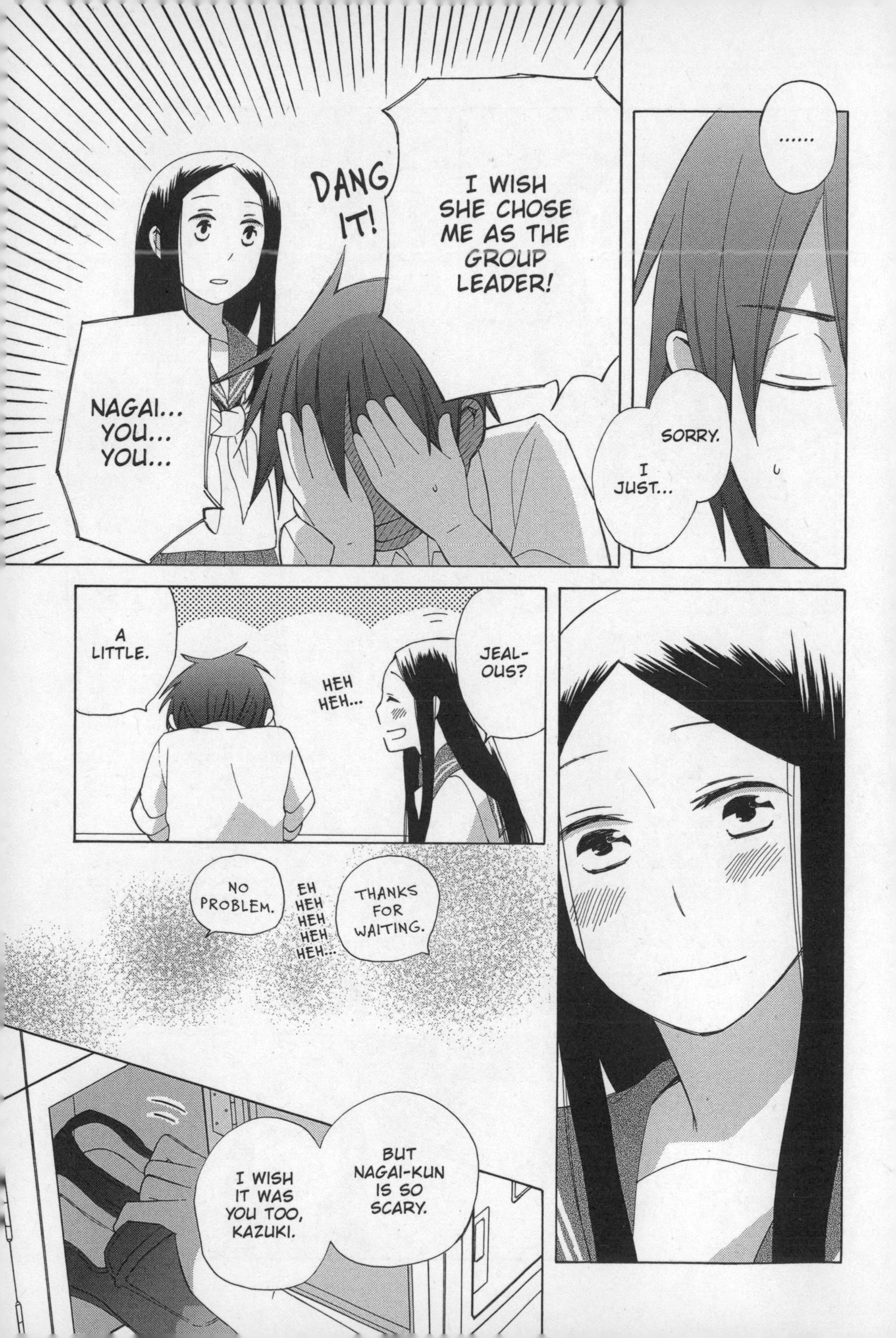
......
SORRY. I JUST...
DANG IT!
I WISH SHE CHOSE ME AS THE GROUP LEADER!
NAGAI... YOU... YOU...
JEAL-OUS?
HEH HEH...
A LITTLE.
THANKS FOR WAITING.
EH HEH HEH HEH HEH...
NO PROBLEM.
BUT NAGAI-KUN IS SO SCARY.
I WISH IT WAS YOU TOO, KAZUKI.

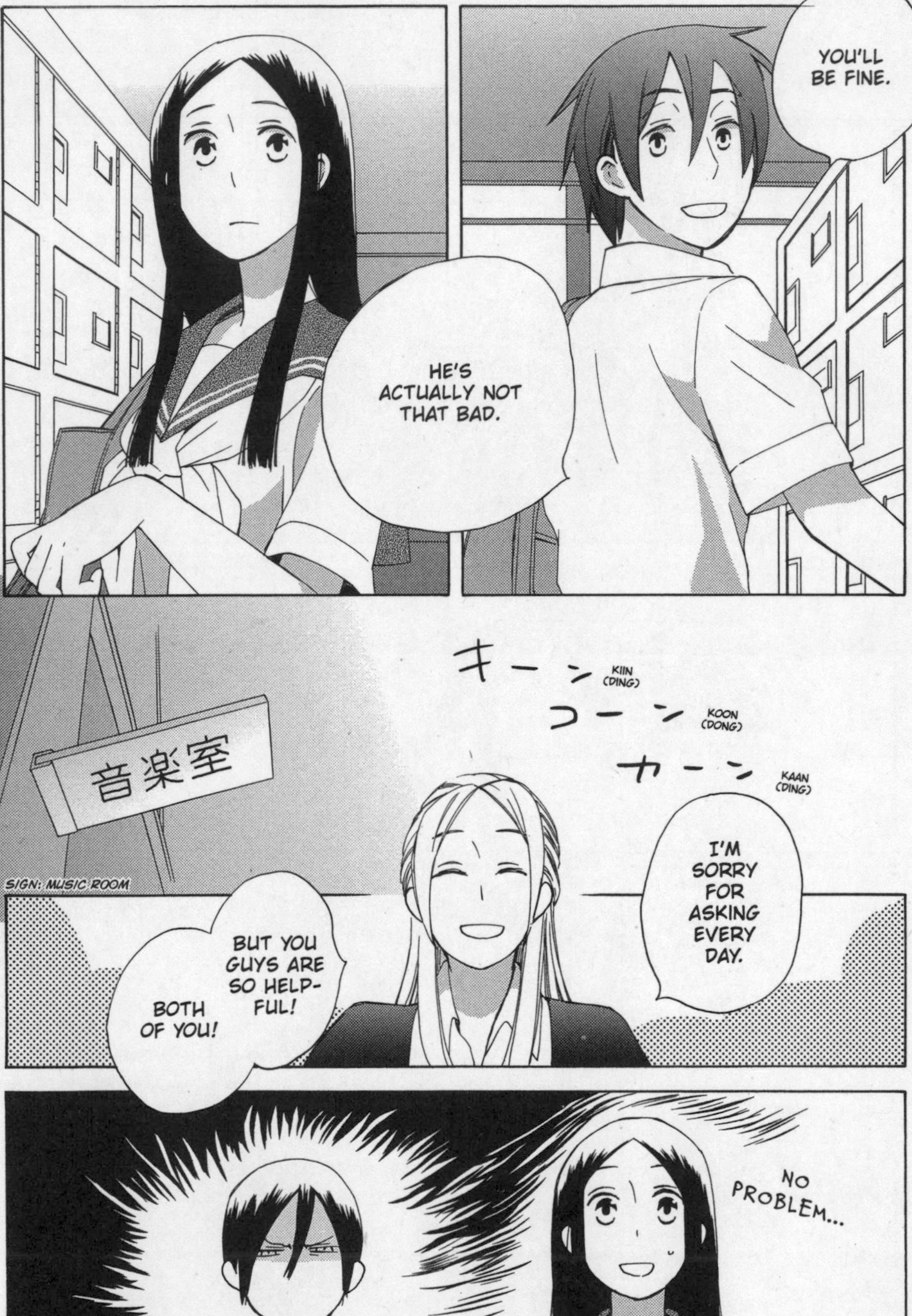
YOU'LL BE FINE.
HE'S ACTUALLY NOT THAT BAD.
キーン KIIN (DING)
コーン KOON (DONG)
カーン KAAN (DING)
音楽室
SIGN: MUSIC ROOM
I'M SORRY FOR ASKING EVERY DAY.
BUT YOU GUYS ARE SO HELPFUL!
BOTH OF YOU!
NO PROBLEM...

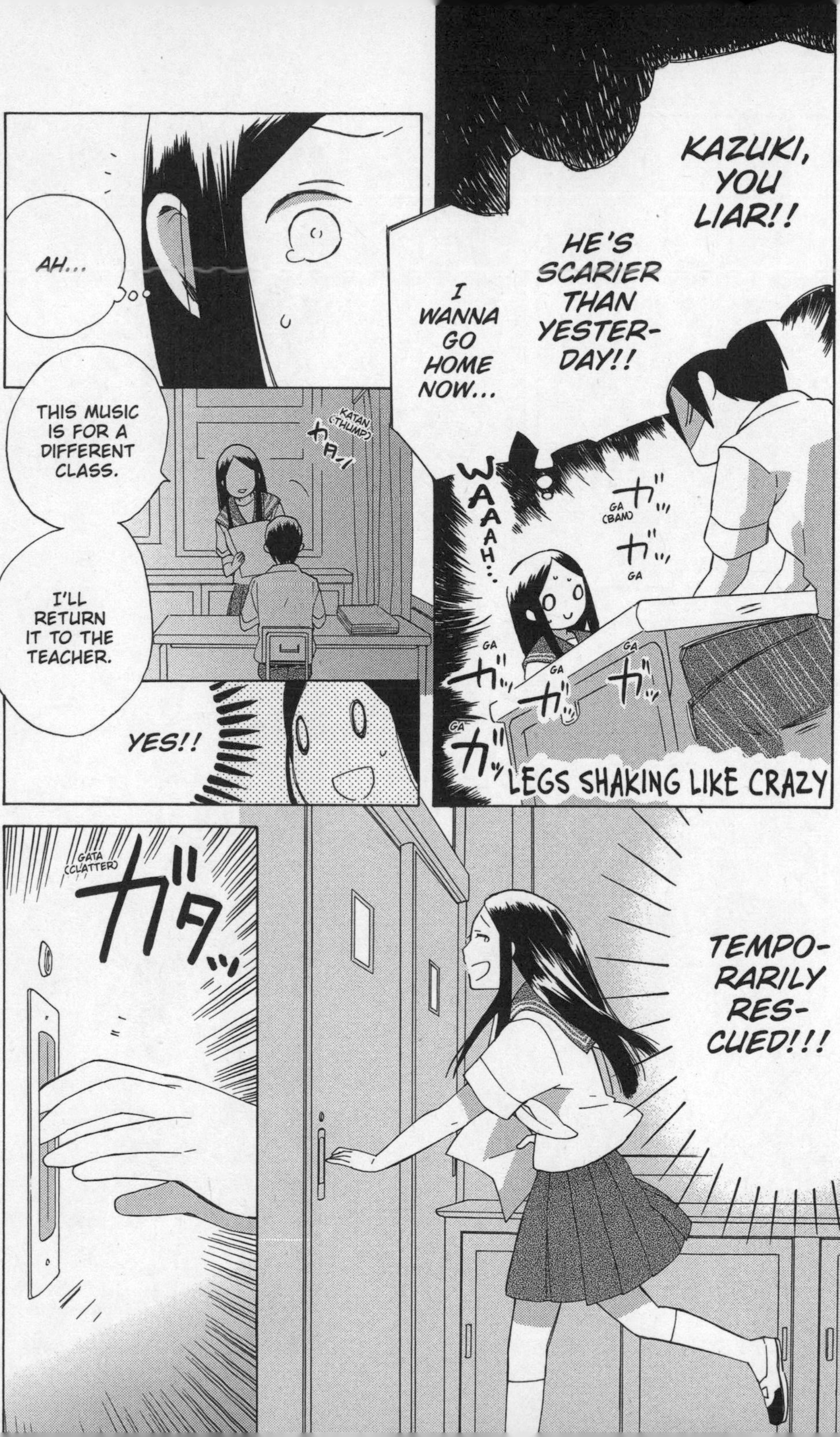
KAZUKI, YOU LIAR!!
HE'S SCARIER THAN YESTER-DAY!!
I WANNA GO HOME NOW...
WAAAAH...
GA (BAM)
GA
GA
GA
GA
GA
LEGS SHAKING LIKE CRAZY
AH...
THIS MUSIC IS FOR A DIFFERENT CLASS.
KATAN (THUMP)
I'LL RETURN IT TO THE TEACHER.
YES!!
TEMPO-RARILY RES-CUED!!!
GATA (CLATTER)

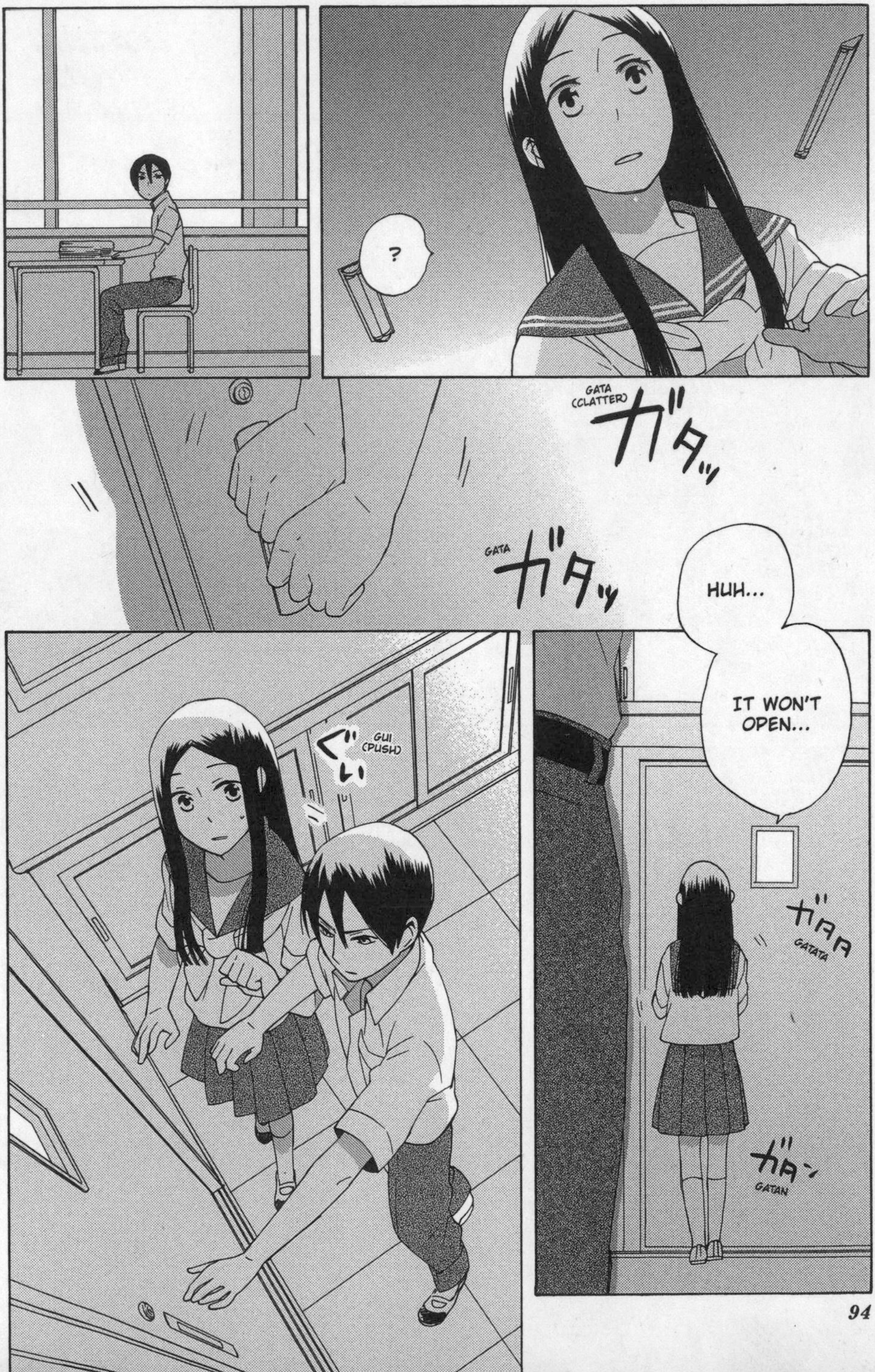
?
ガタッ
GATA (CLATTER)
ガタッ
GATA
HUH...
IT WON'T OPEN...
ガタタ
GATATA
ガタン
GATAN
ぐい
GUI (PUSH)

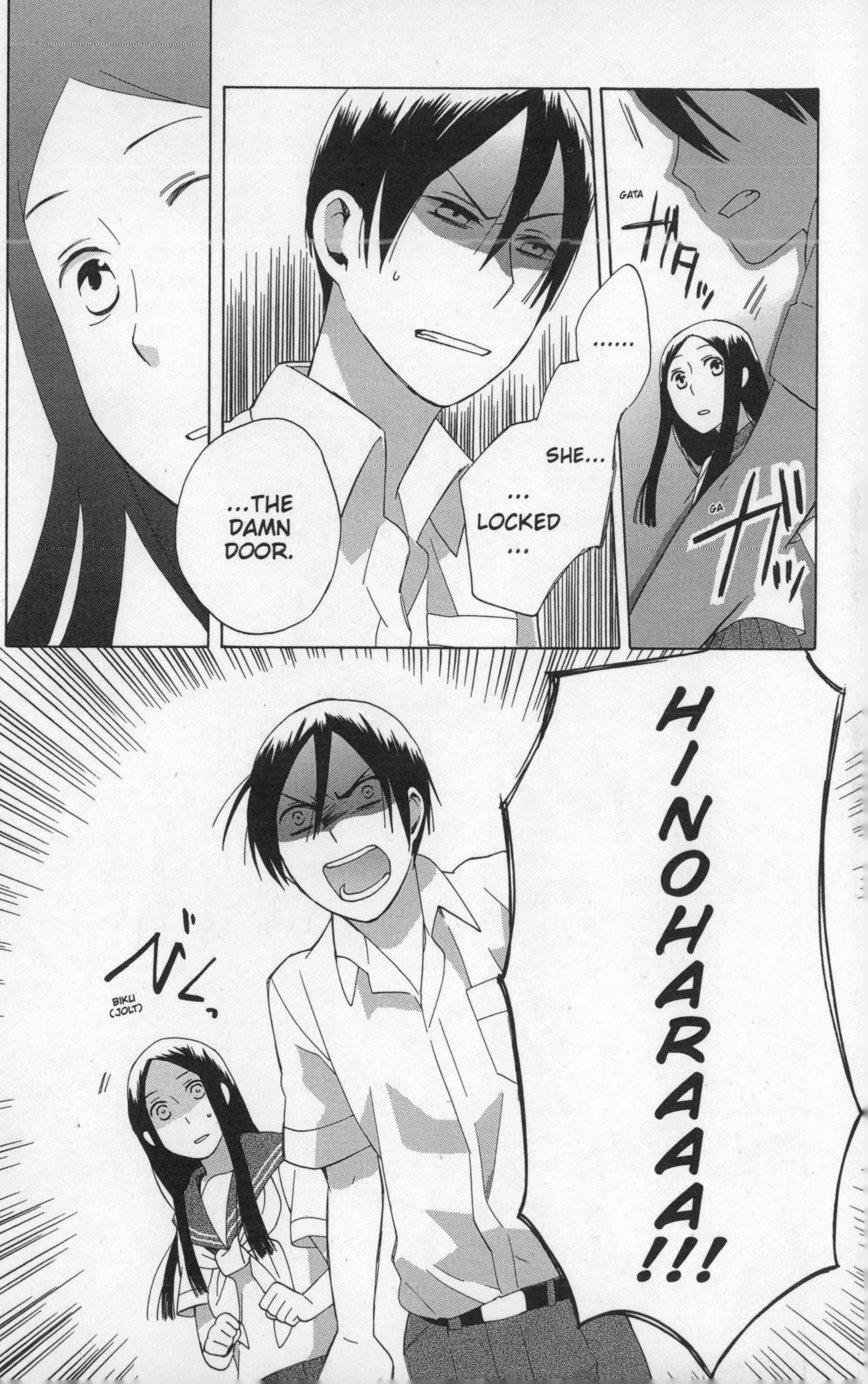
GATA
......
GA
SHE...
... LOCKED ...
...THE DAMN DOOR.
HINOHARAAA!!!
BIKU (JOLT)

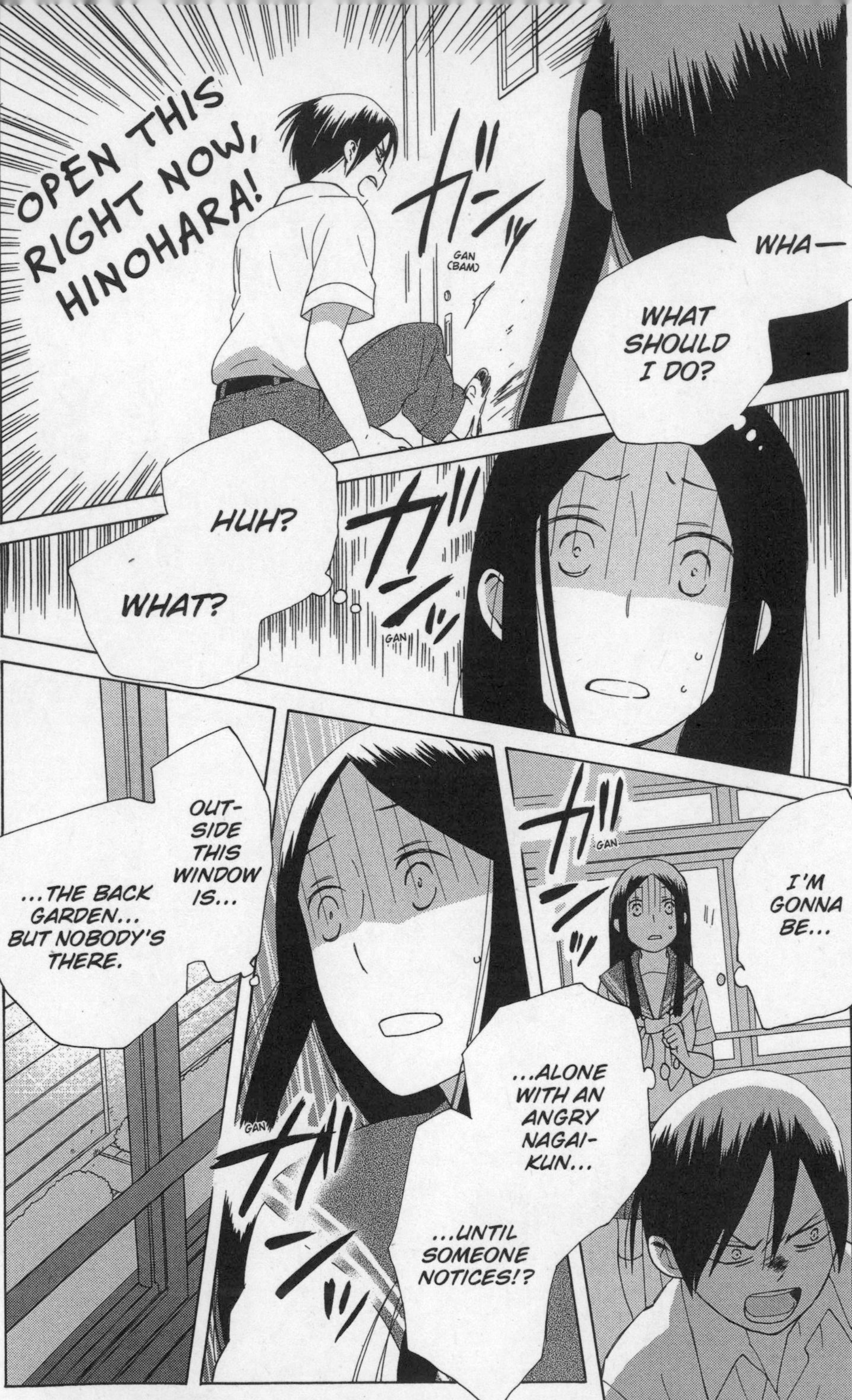
WHA—
WHAT SHOULD I DO?
OPEN THIS RIGHT NOW, HINOHARA!
GAN (BAM)
HUH?
WHAT?
GAN
GAN
I'M GONNA BE...
OUT-SIDE THIS WINDOW IS...
...THE BACK GARDEN... BUT NOBODY'S THERE.
GAN
...ALONE WITH AN ANGRY NAGAI-KUN...
...UNTIL SOMEONE NOTICES!?

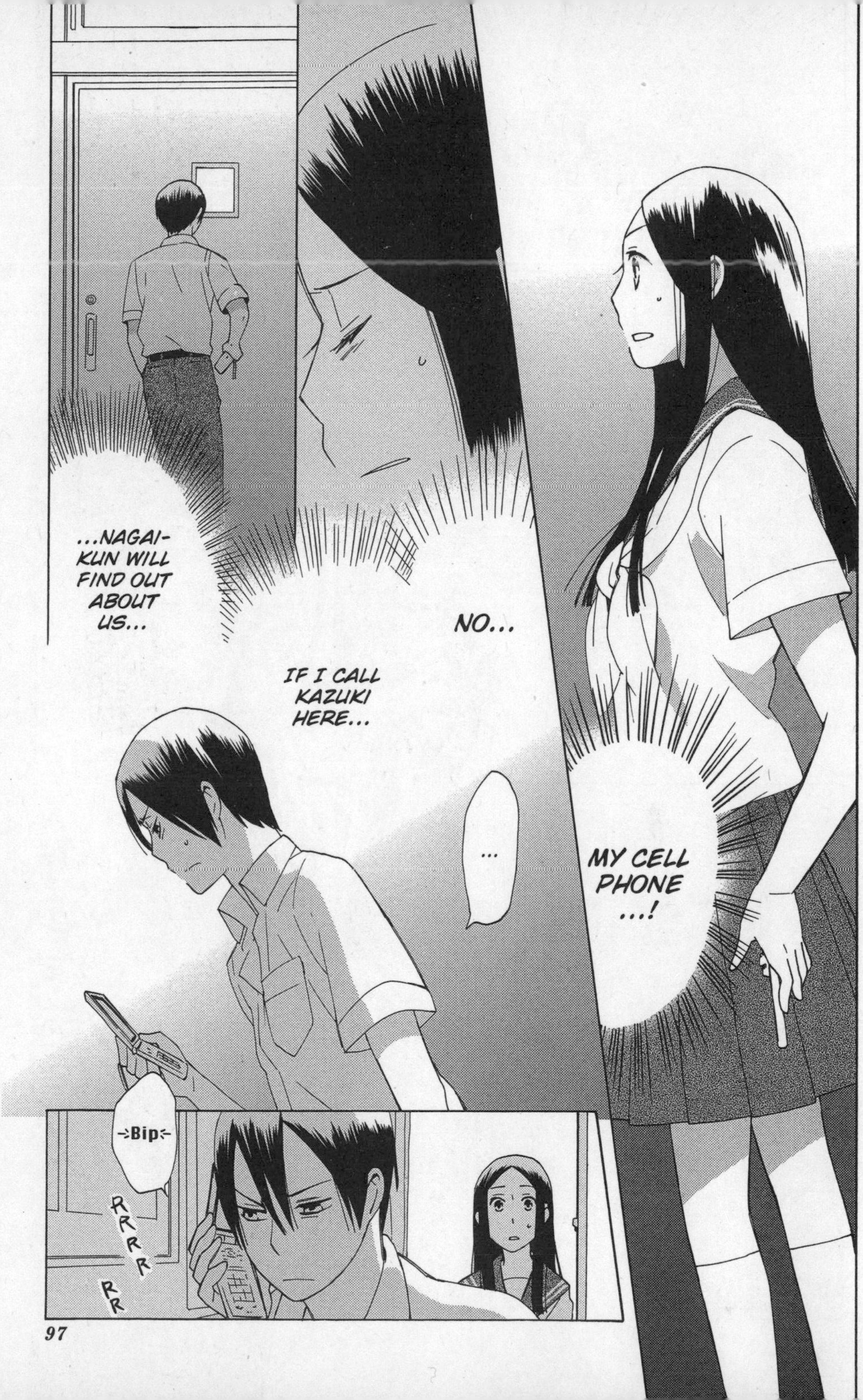
...NAGAI-KUN WILL FIND OUT ABOUT US...
NO...
IF I CALL KAZUKI HERE...
...
MY CELL PHONE ...!
Bip
RRRR
RR

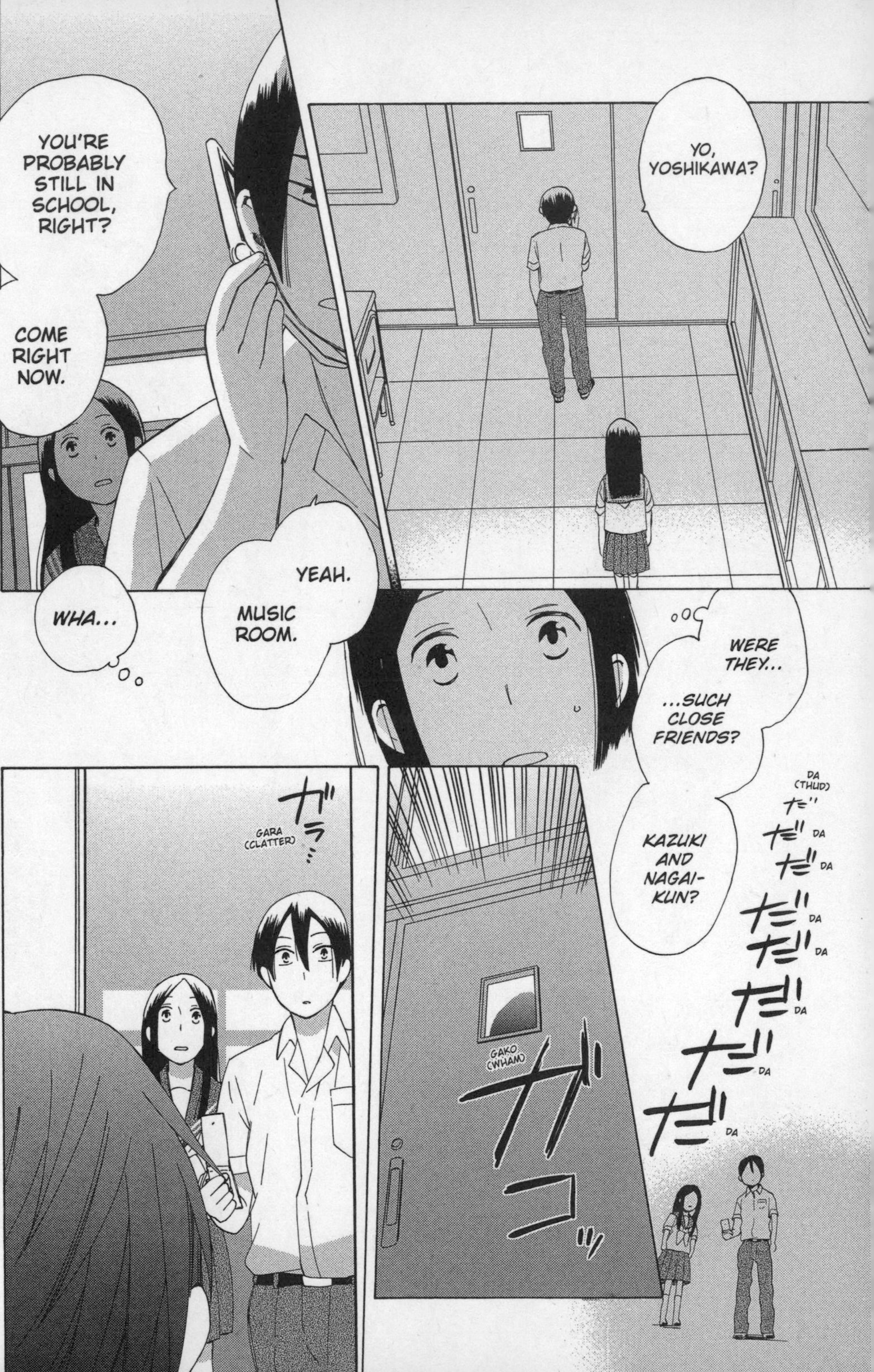
YO, YOSHIKAWA?
YOU'RE PROBABLY STILL IN SCHOOL, RIGHT?
COME RIGHT NOW.
YEAH.
MUSIC ROOM.
WHA...
WERE THEY...
...SUCH CLOSE FRIENDS?
KAZUKI AND NAGAI-KUN?
DA (THUD)
だだだだだだだだだ
DA DA DA DA DA DA DA DA
GAKO (WHAM)
ガコッ
GARA (CLATTER)
ガラ…

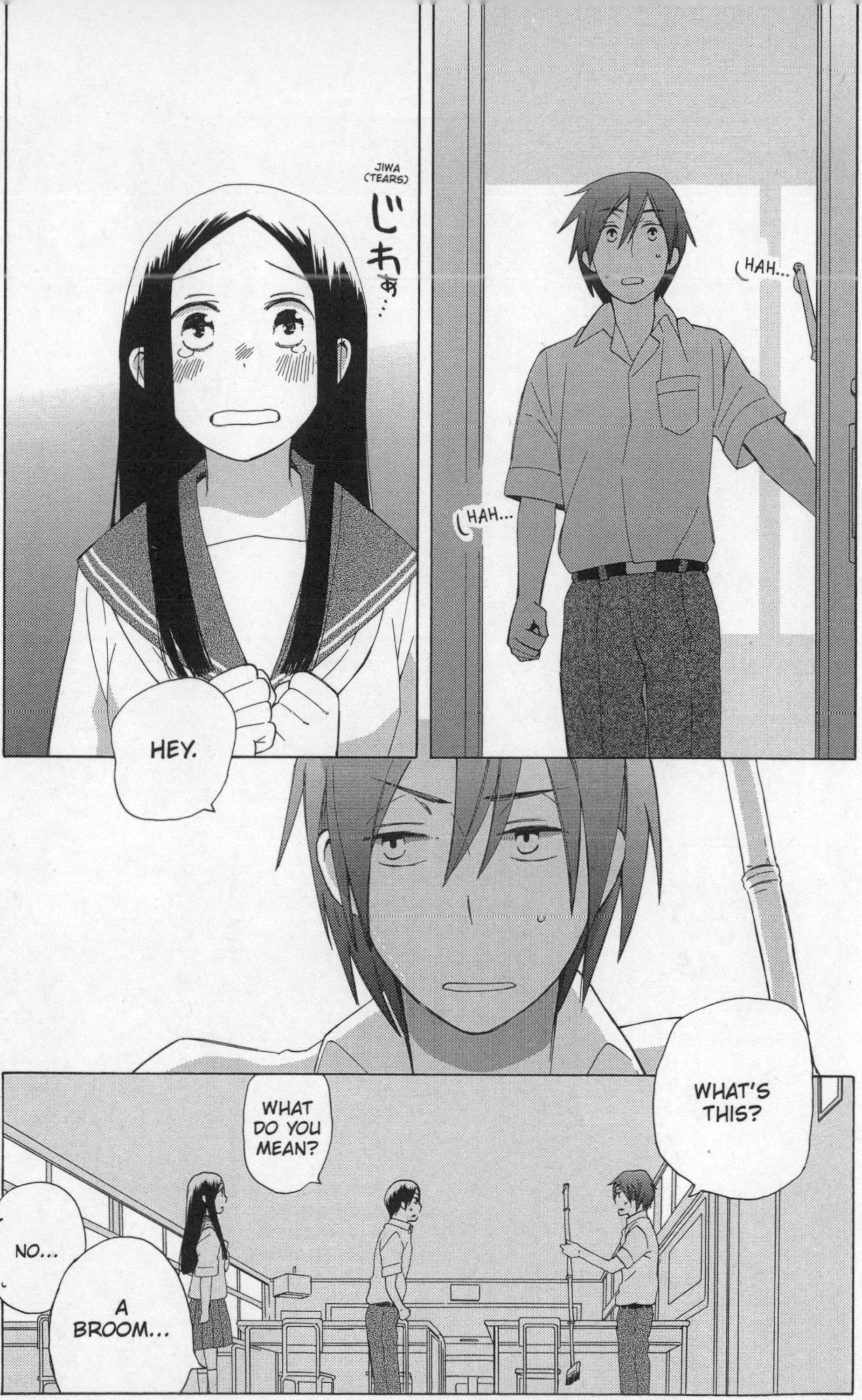
HAH...
HAH...
JIWA (TEARS)
じわぁ…
HEY.
WHAT'S THIS?
WHAT DO YOU MEAN?
NO...
A BROOM...

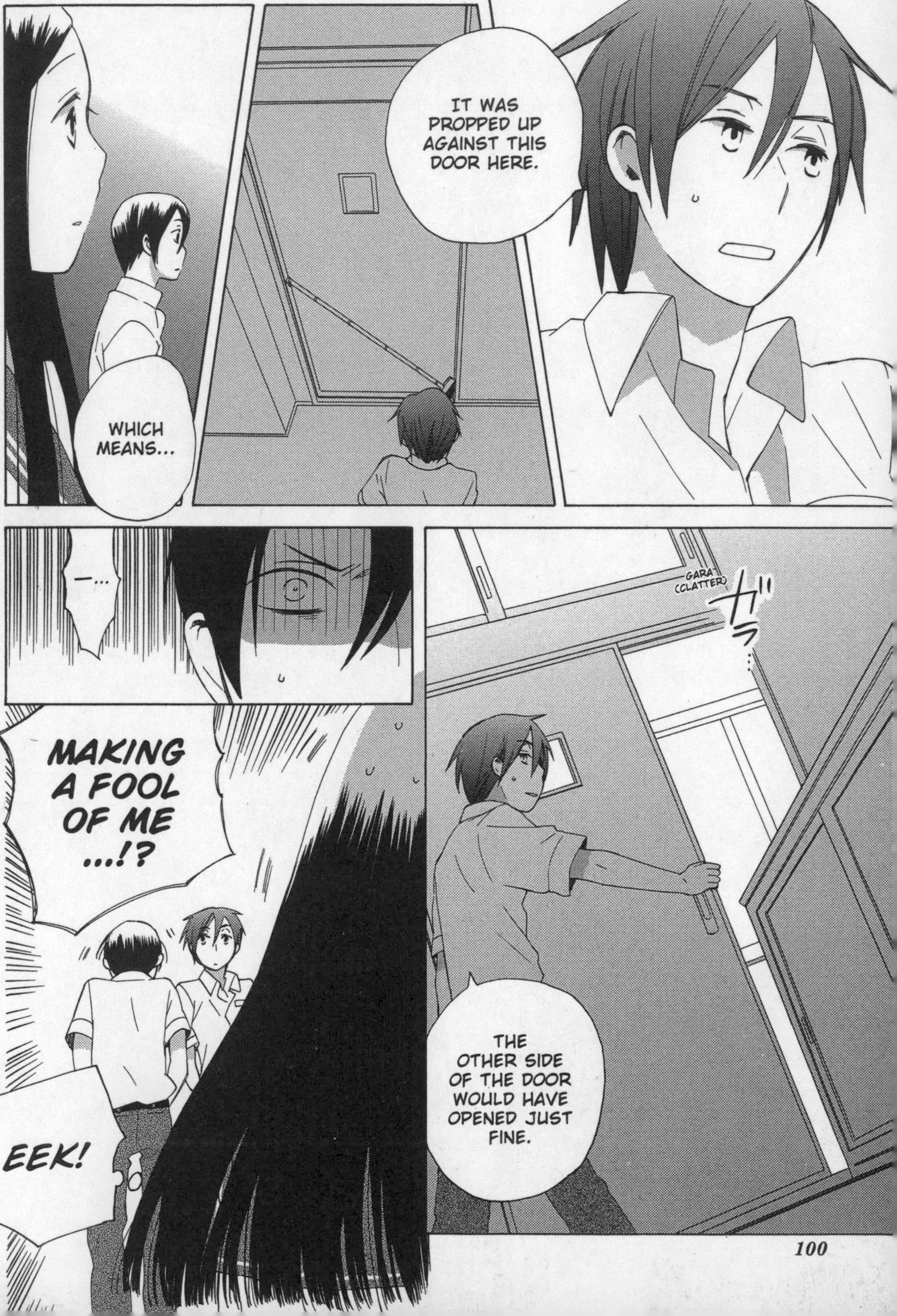
IT WAS PROPPED UP AGAINST THIS DOOR HERE.
WHICH MEANS...
GARA (CLATTER)
THE OTHER SIDE OF THE DOOR WOULD HAVE OPENED JUST FINE.
—...
MAKING A FOOL OF ME ...!?
EEK!

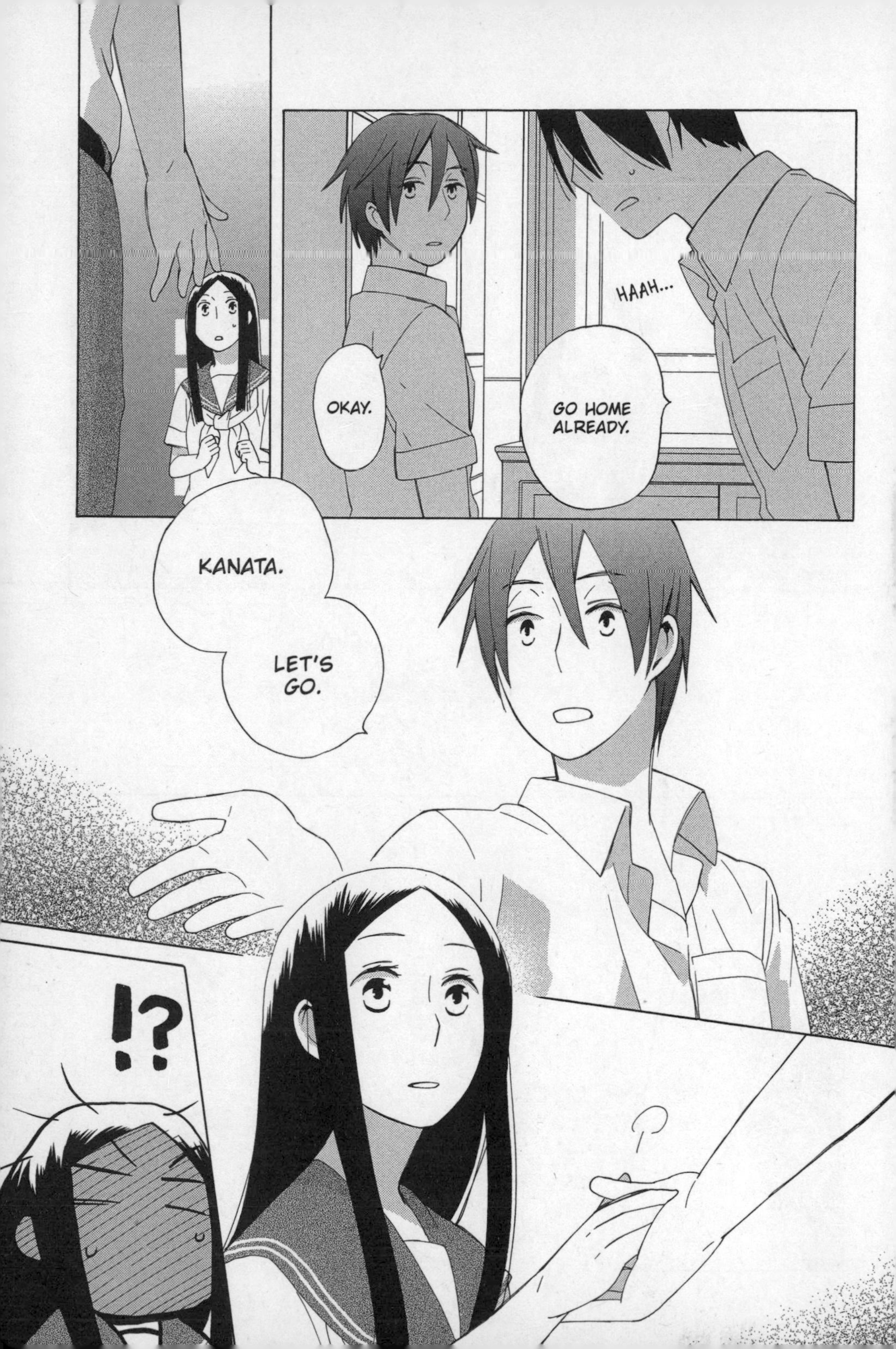
HAAH...
GO HOME ALREADY.
OKAY.
KANATA.
LET'S GO.
!?

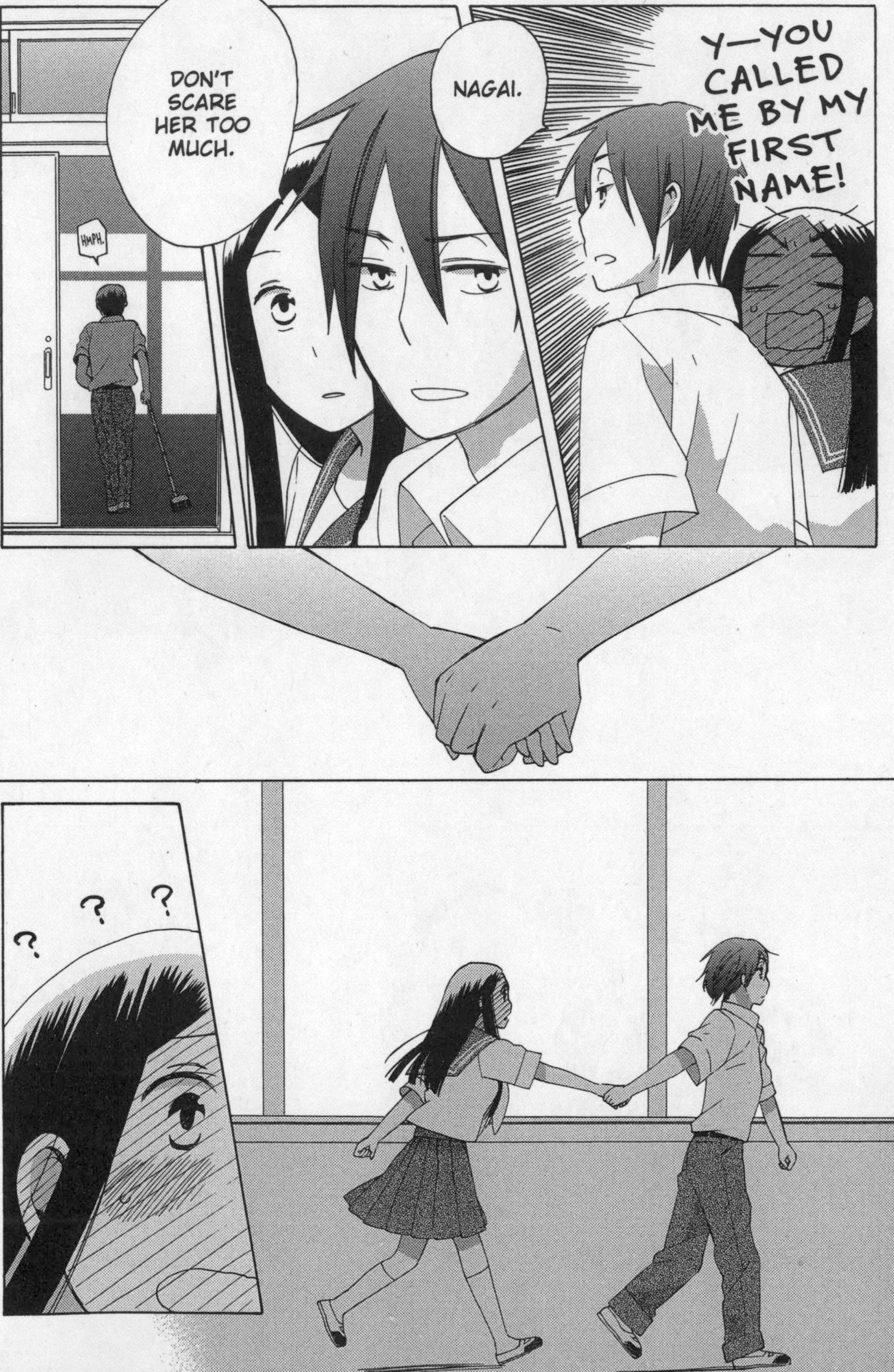
Y—YOU CALLED ME BY MY FIRST NAME!
NAGAI.
DON'T SCARE HER TOO MUCH.
HMPH.
? ? ?

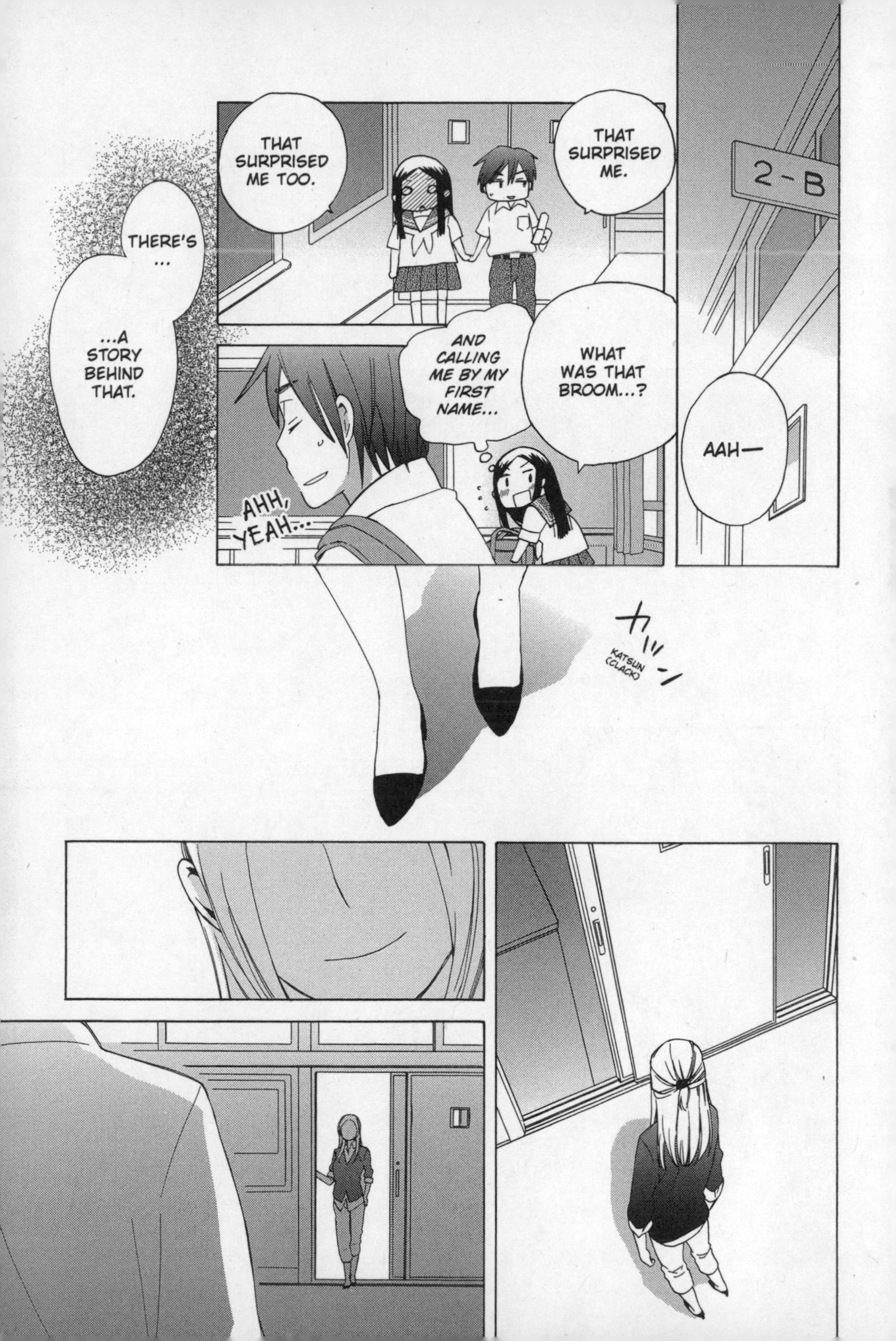
2-B
AAH—
THAT SURPRISED ME.
THAT SURPRISED ME TOO.
WHAT WAS THAT BROOM...?
AND CALLING ME BY MY FIRST NAME...
AHH, YEAH...
THERE'S...
...A STORY BEHIND THAT.
カツン
KATSUN (CLACK)

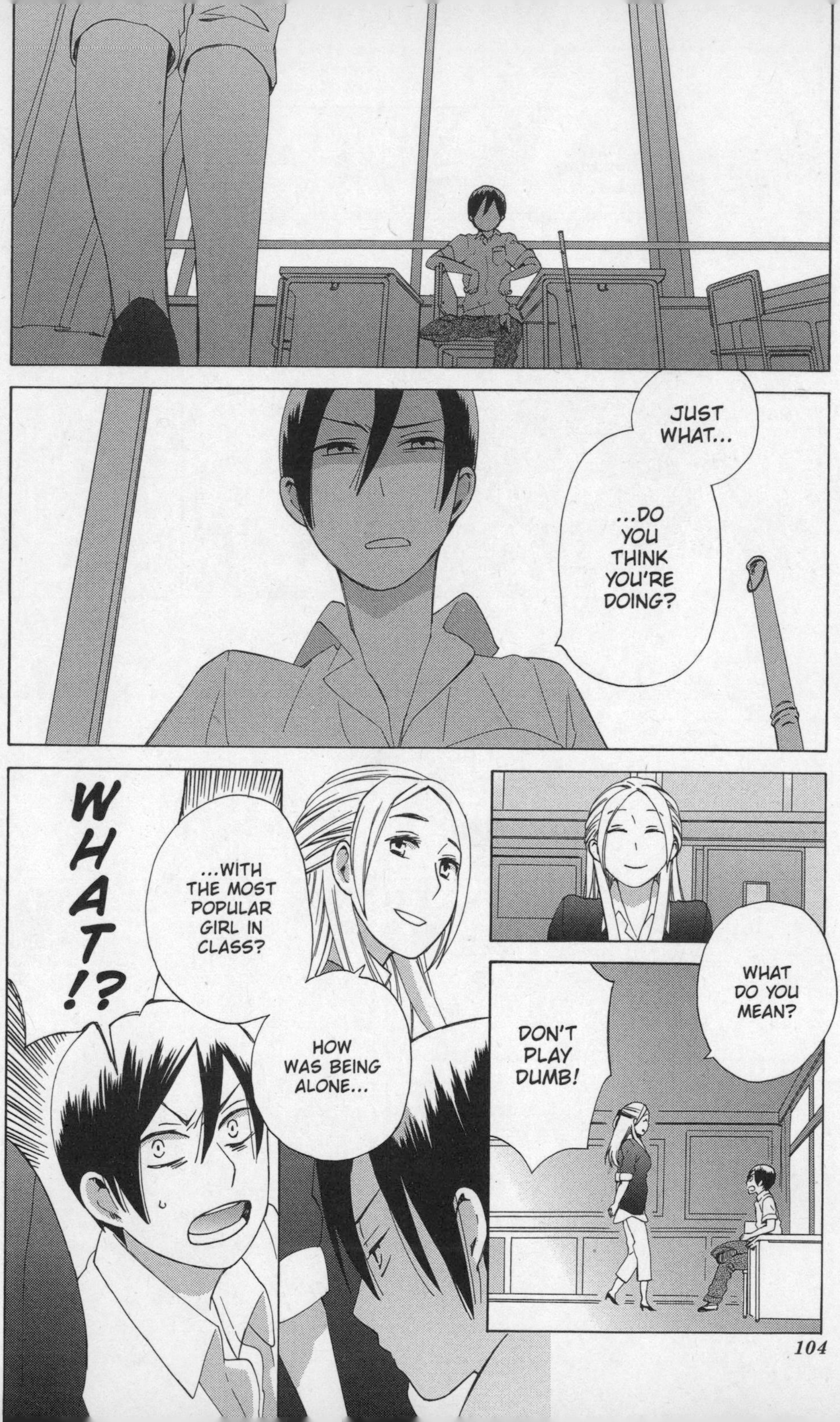
JUST WHAT...
...DO YOU THINK YOU'RE DOING?
WHAT DO YOU MEAN?
DON'T PLAY DUMB!
HOW WAS BEING ALONE...
...WITH THE MOST POPULAR GIRL IN CLASS?
WHAT!?

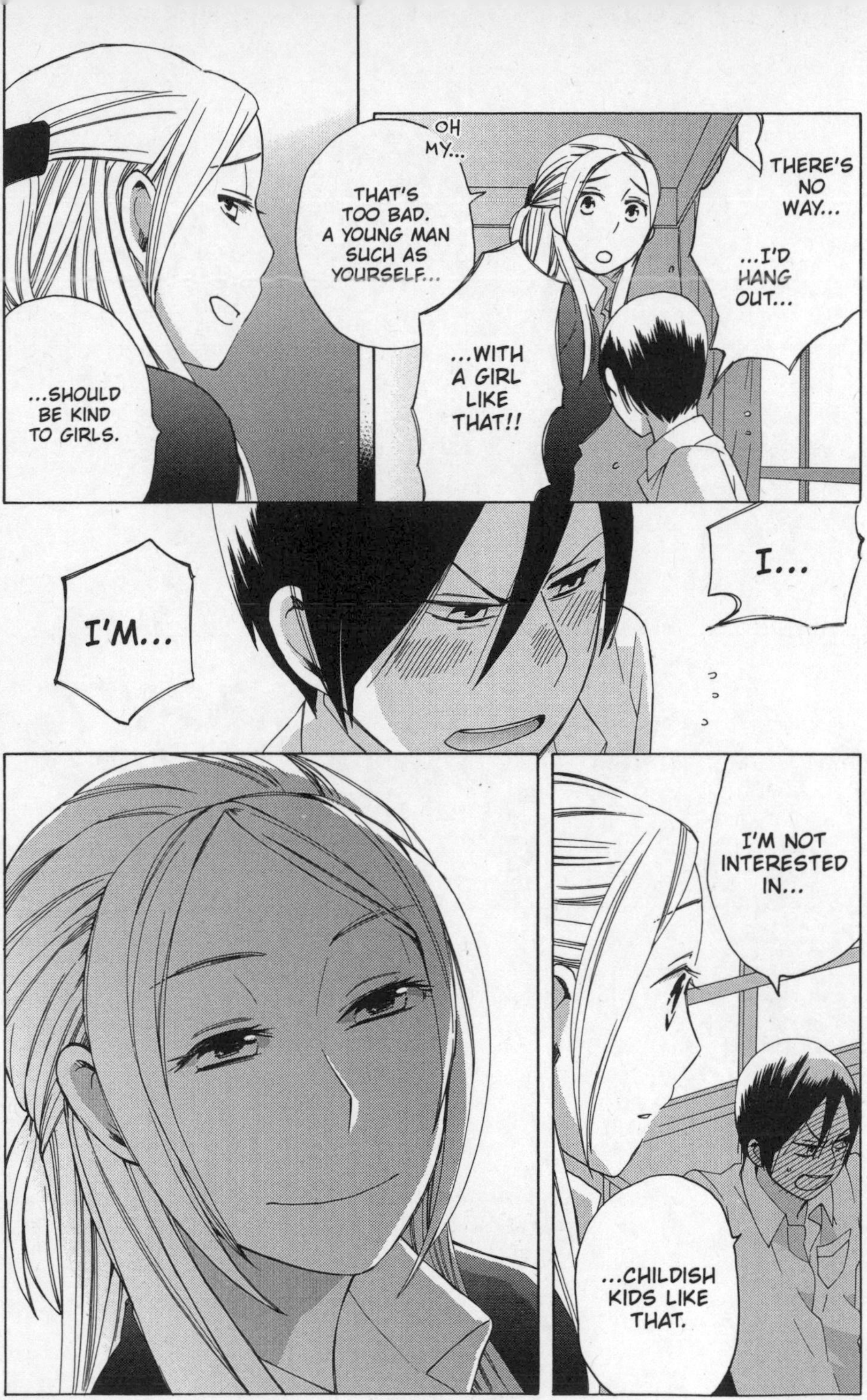
THERE'S NO WAY...
...I'D HANG OUT...
...WITH A GIRL LIKE THAT!!
OH MY...
THAT'S TOO BAD. A YOUNG MAN SUCH AS YOURSELF...
...SHOULD BE KIND TO GIRLS.
I...
I'M...
I'M NOT INTERESTED IN...
...CHILDISH KIDS LIKE THAT.

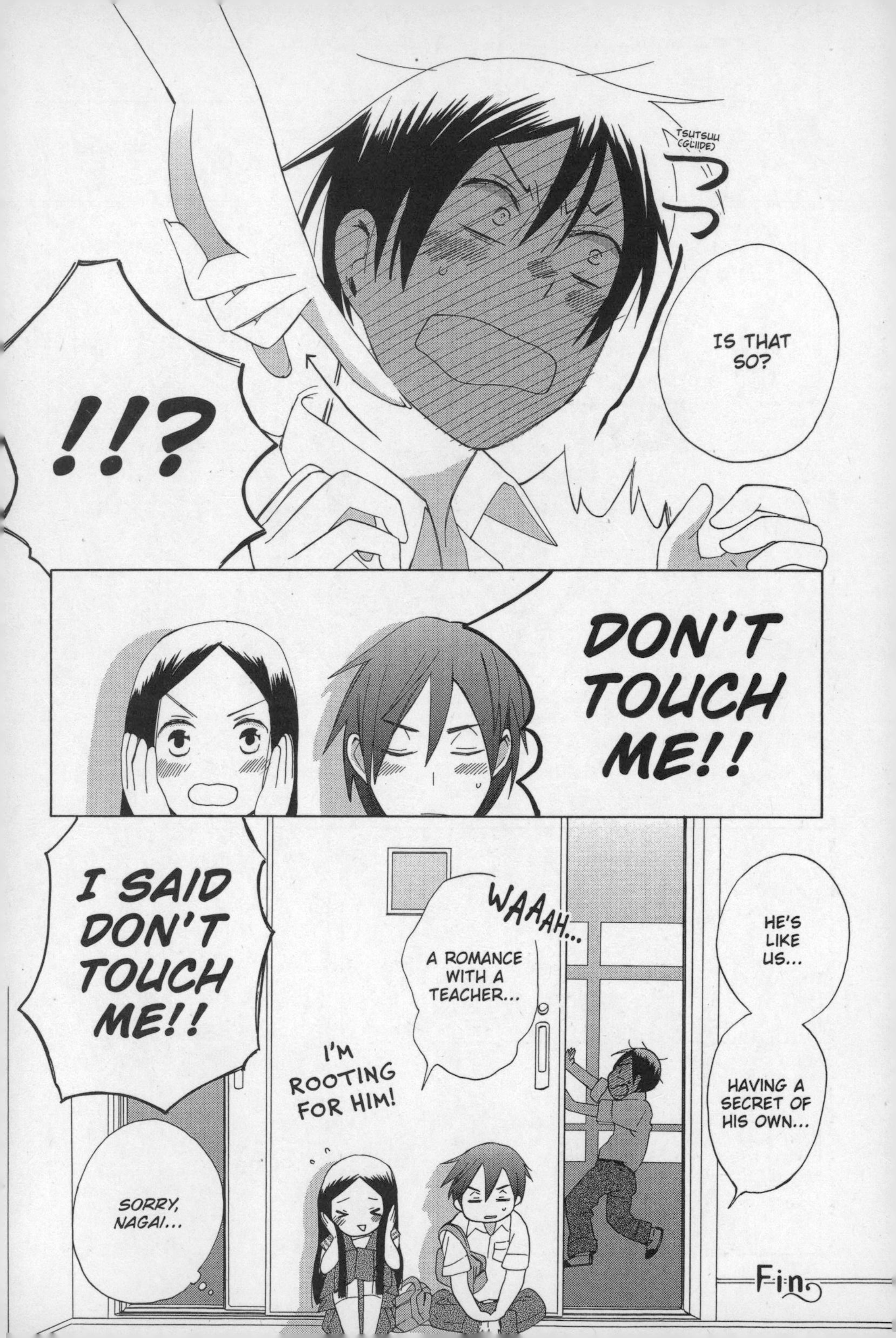
TSUTSUU (GLIIDE)
IS THAT SO?
!!?
DON'T TOUCH ME!!
HE'S LIKE US...
HAVING A SECRET OF HIS OWN...
WAAAH...
A ROMANCE WITH A TEACHER...
I'M ROOTING FOR HIM!
I SAID DON'T TOUCH ME!!
SORRY, NAGAI...
Fin

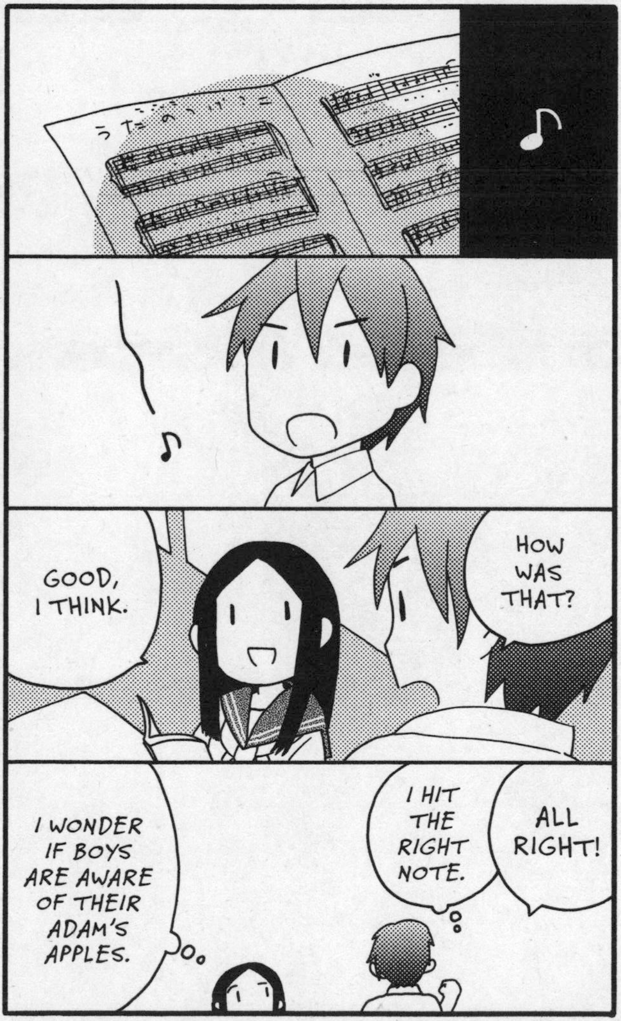
HOW WAS THAT?
GOOD, I THINK.
ALL RIGHT!
I HIT THE RIGHT NOTE.
I WONDER IF BOYS ARE AWARE OF THEIR ADAM'S APPLES.

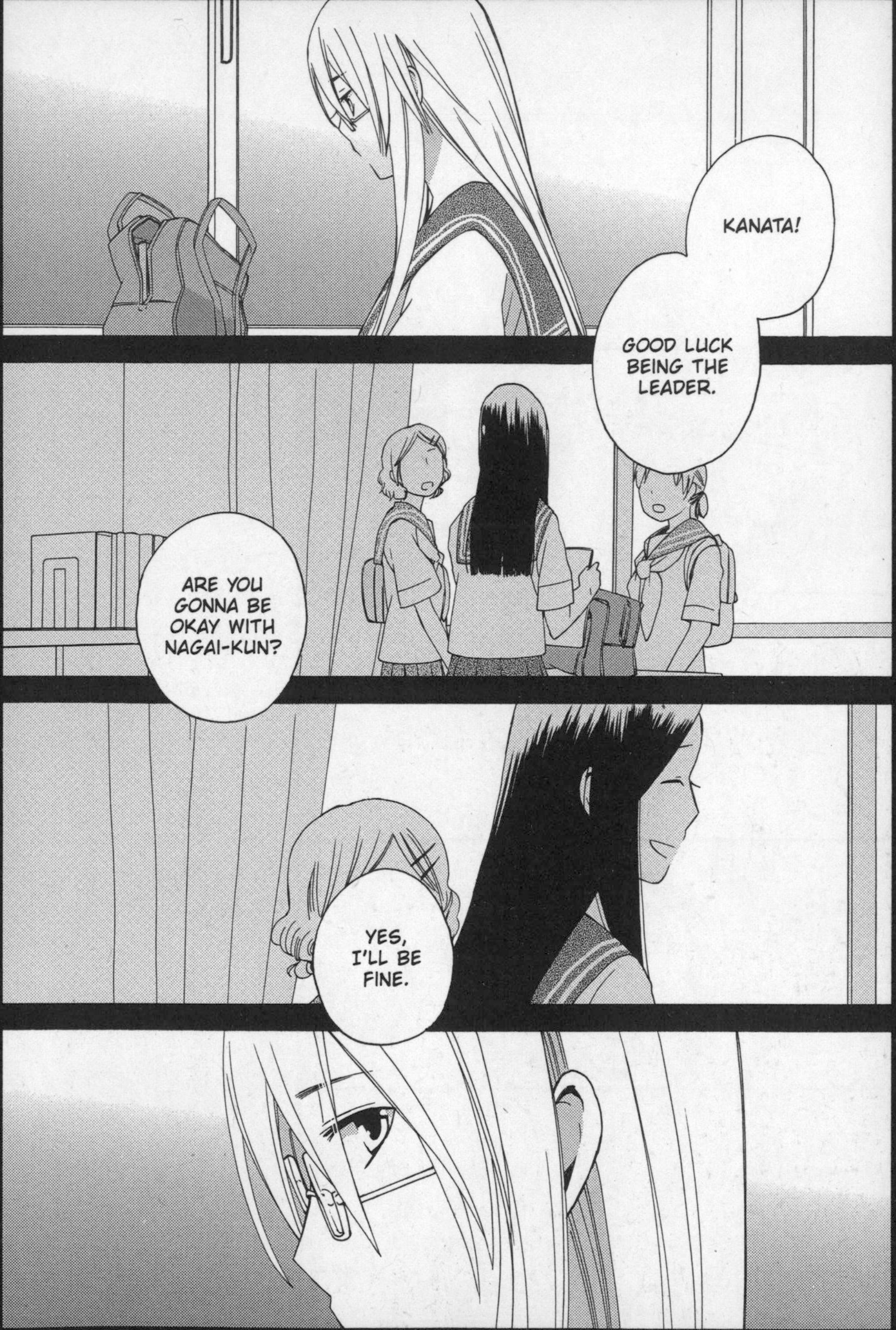
KANATA!
GOOD LUCK BEING THE LEADER.
ARE YOU GONNA BE OKAY WITH NAGAI-KUN?
YES, I'LL BE FINE.

OH, DEAR GOD!

music
Oh, dear God!
Why is my voice low!?

WHY IS MY VOICE LOW!?

Love at Fourteen

[Intermission 9]

AOI WAS GRIEVING.

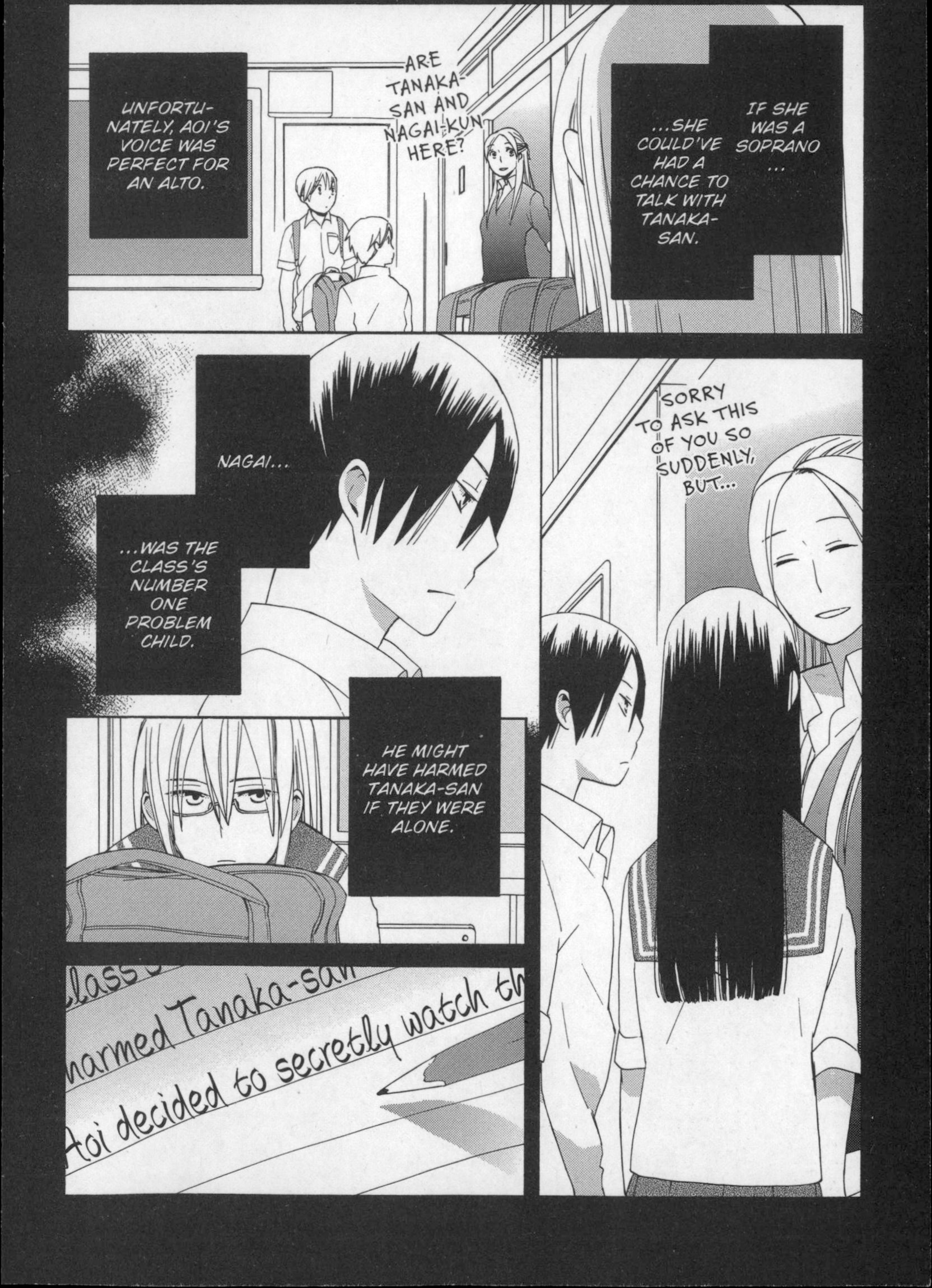
IF SHE WAS A SOPRANO...
...SHE COULD'VE HAD A CHANCE TO TALK WITH TANAKA-SAN.
ARE TANAKA-SAN AND NAGAI-KUN HERE?
UNFORTUNATELY, AOI'S VOICE WAS PERFECT FOR AN ALTO.
SORRY TO ASK THIS OF YOU SO SUDDENLY, BUT...
NAGAI...
...WAS THE CLASS'S NUMBER ONE PROBLEM CHILD.
HE MIGHT HAVE HARMED TANAKA-SAN IF THEY WERE ALONE.
class
Tanaka-san
harmed Tanaka-san
Aoi decided to secretly watch th

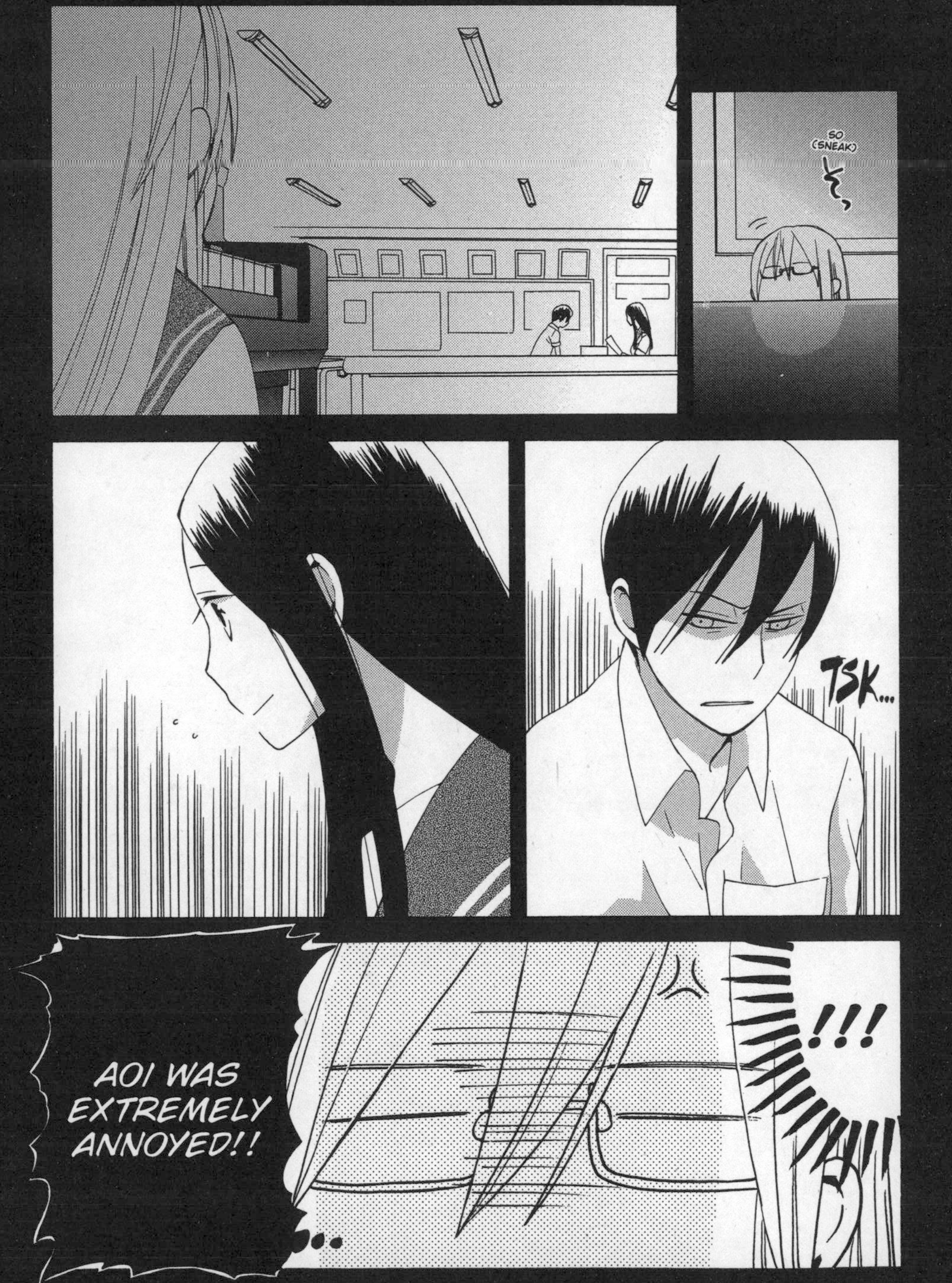
SO (SNEAK)
TSK...
!!!
AOI WAS EXTREMELY ANNOYED!!

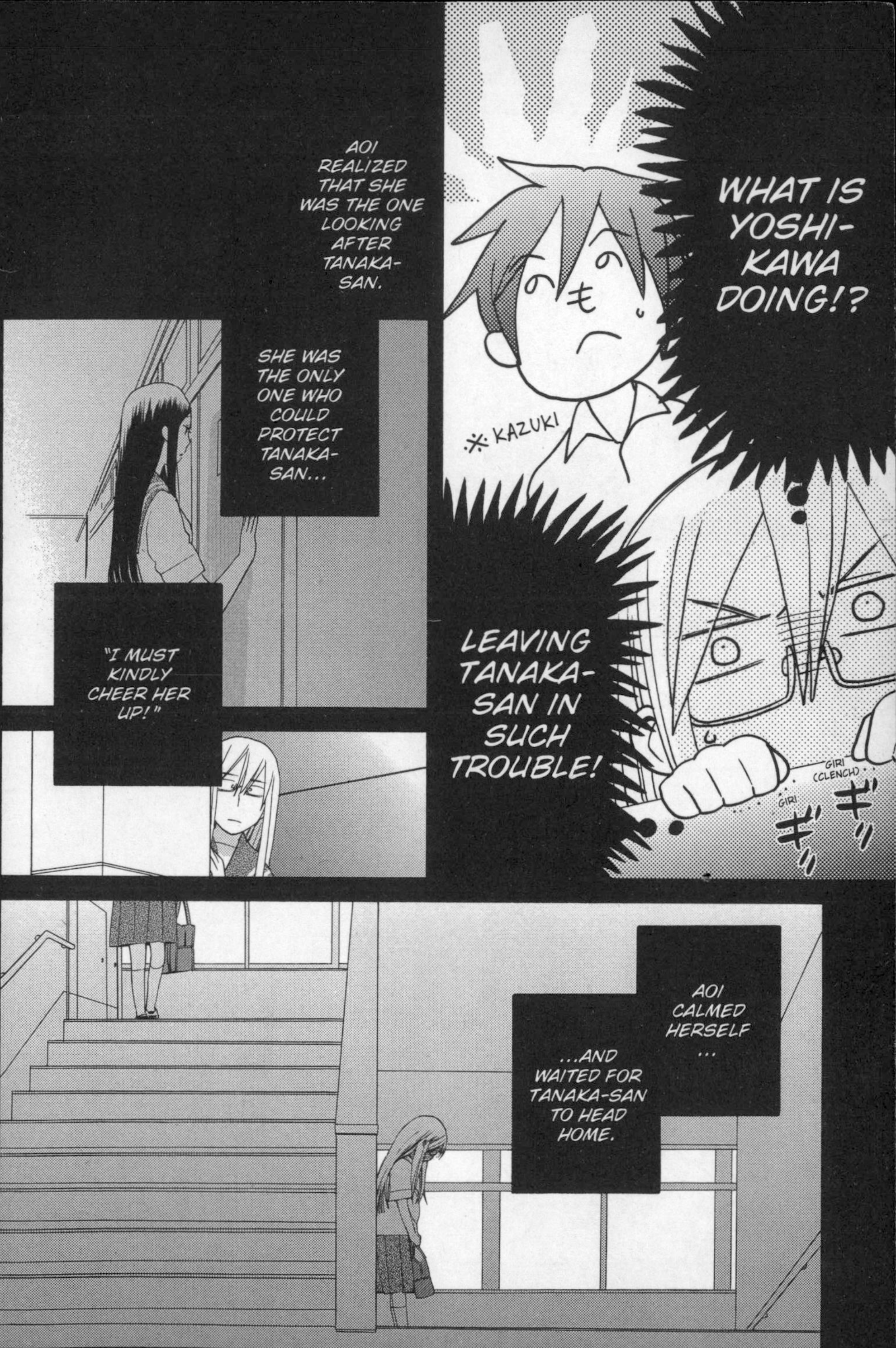
WHAT IS YOSHI-KAWA DOING!?
※ KAZUKI
LEAVING TANAKA-SAN IN SUCH TROUBLE!
GIRI (CLENCH)
GIRI
AOI REALIZED THAT SHE WAS THE ONE LOOKING AFTER TANAKA-SAN.
SHE WAS THE ONLY ONE WHO COULD PROTECT TANAKA-SAN...
"I MUST KINDLY CHEER HER UP!"
AOI CALMED HERSELF...
...AND WAITED FOR TANAKA-SAN TO HEAD HOME.

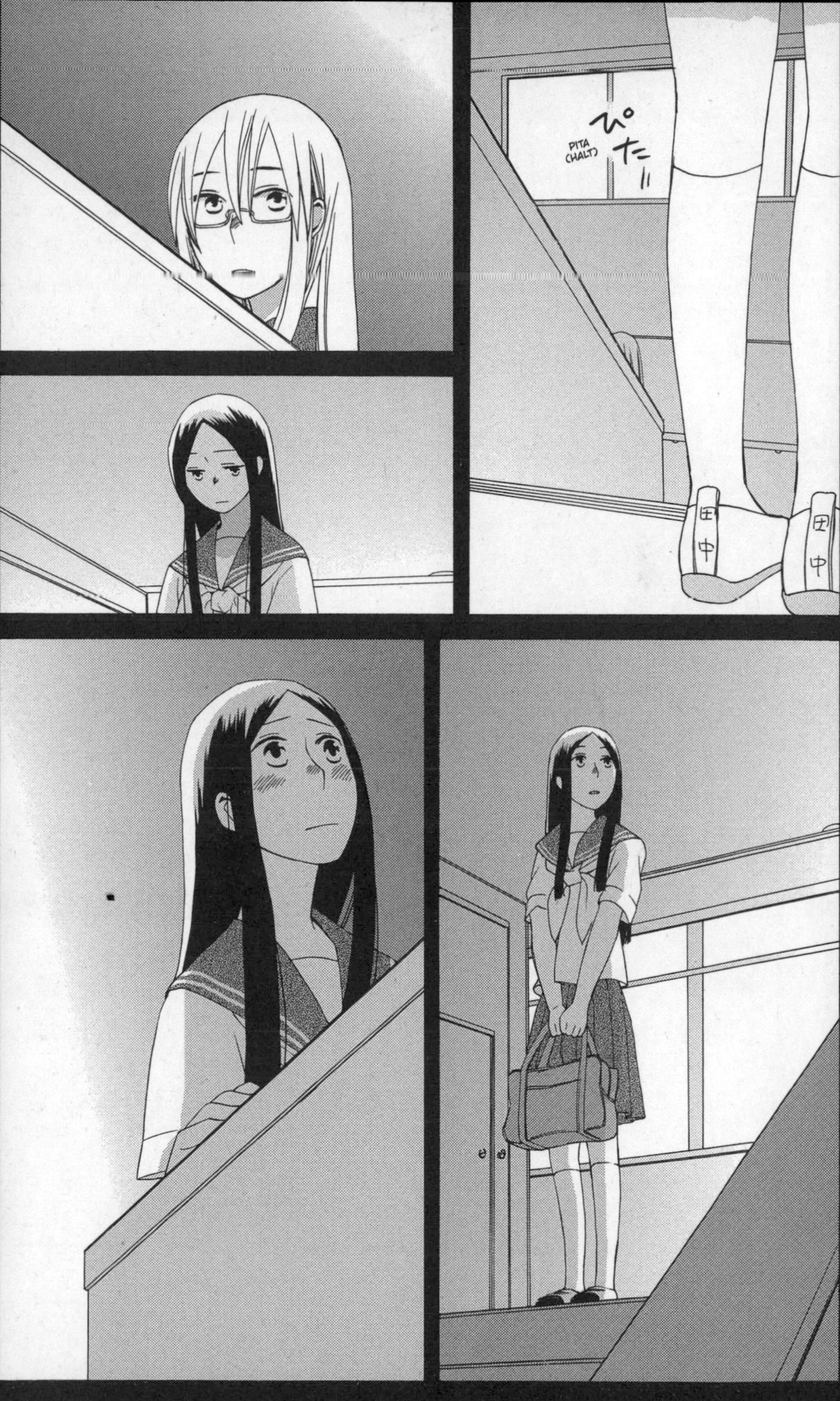
ぴた
PITA (HALT)
田中
田中

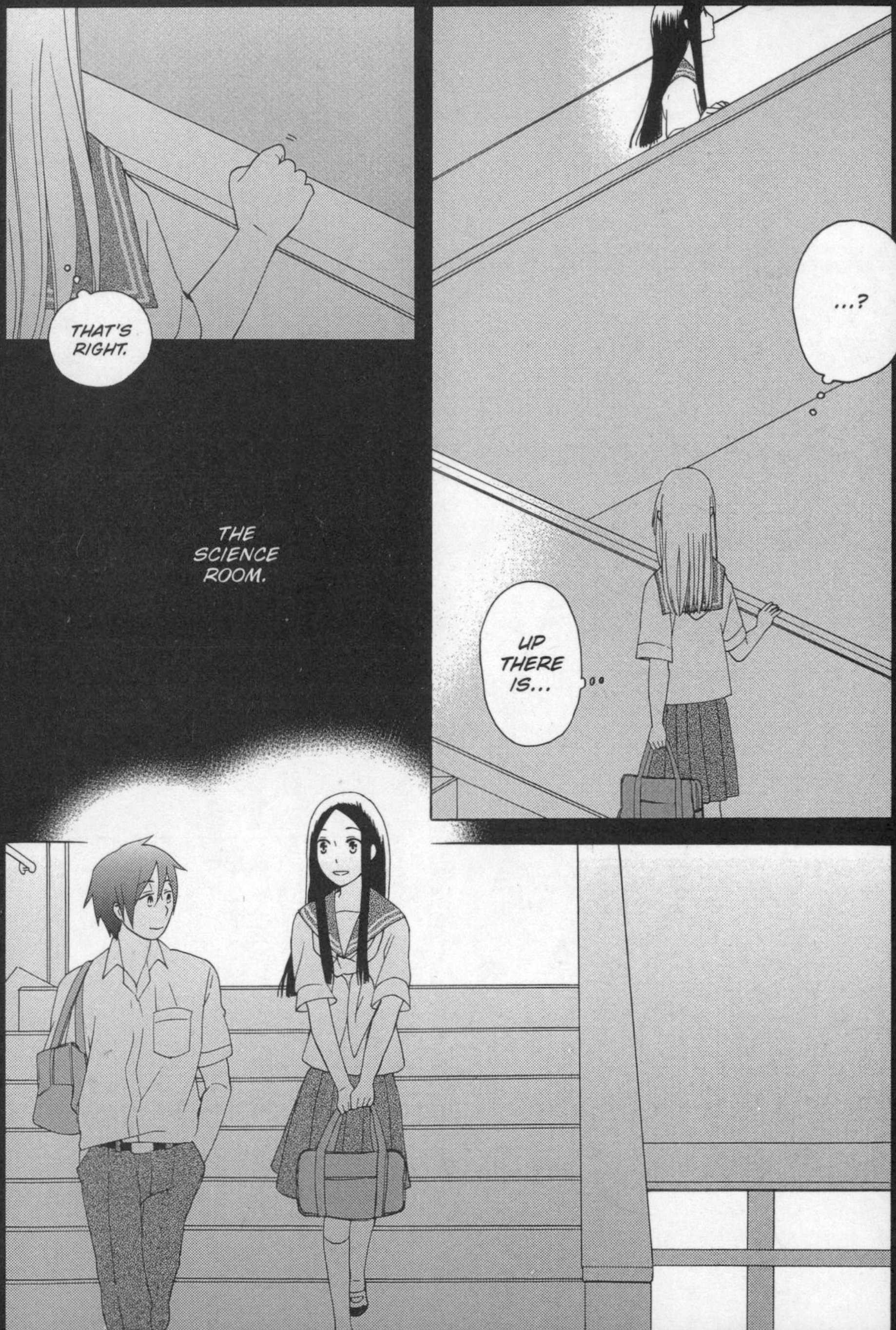
...?
UP THERE IS...
THAT'S RIGHT.
THE SCIENCE ROOM.

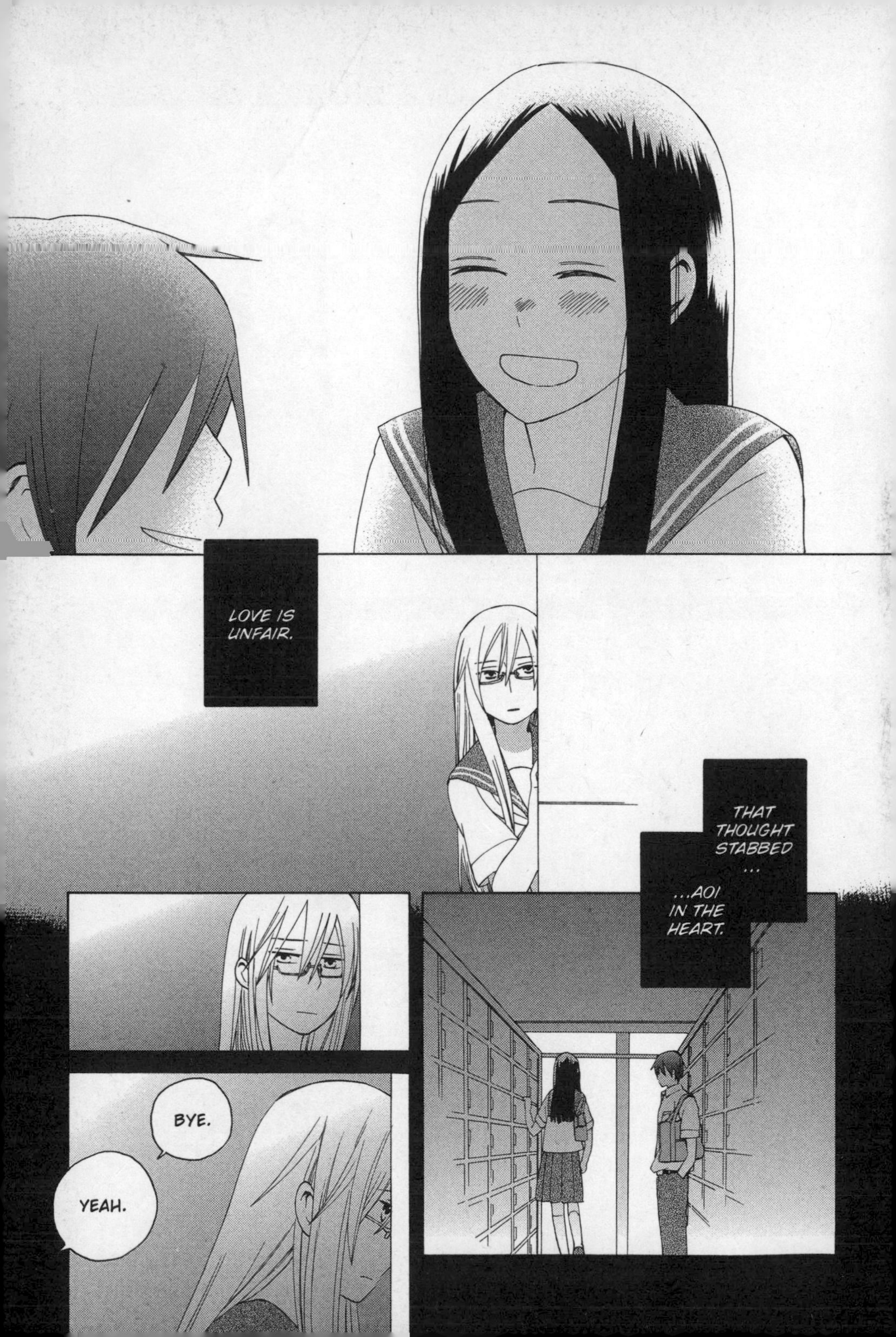
LOVE IS UNFAIR.
THAT THOUGHT STABBED ...
...AOI IN THE HEART.
BYE.
YEAH.

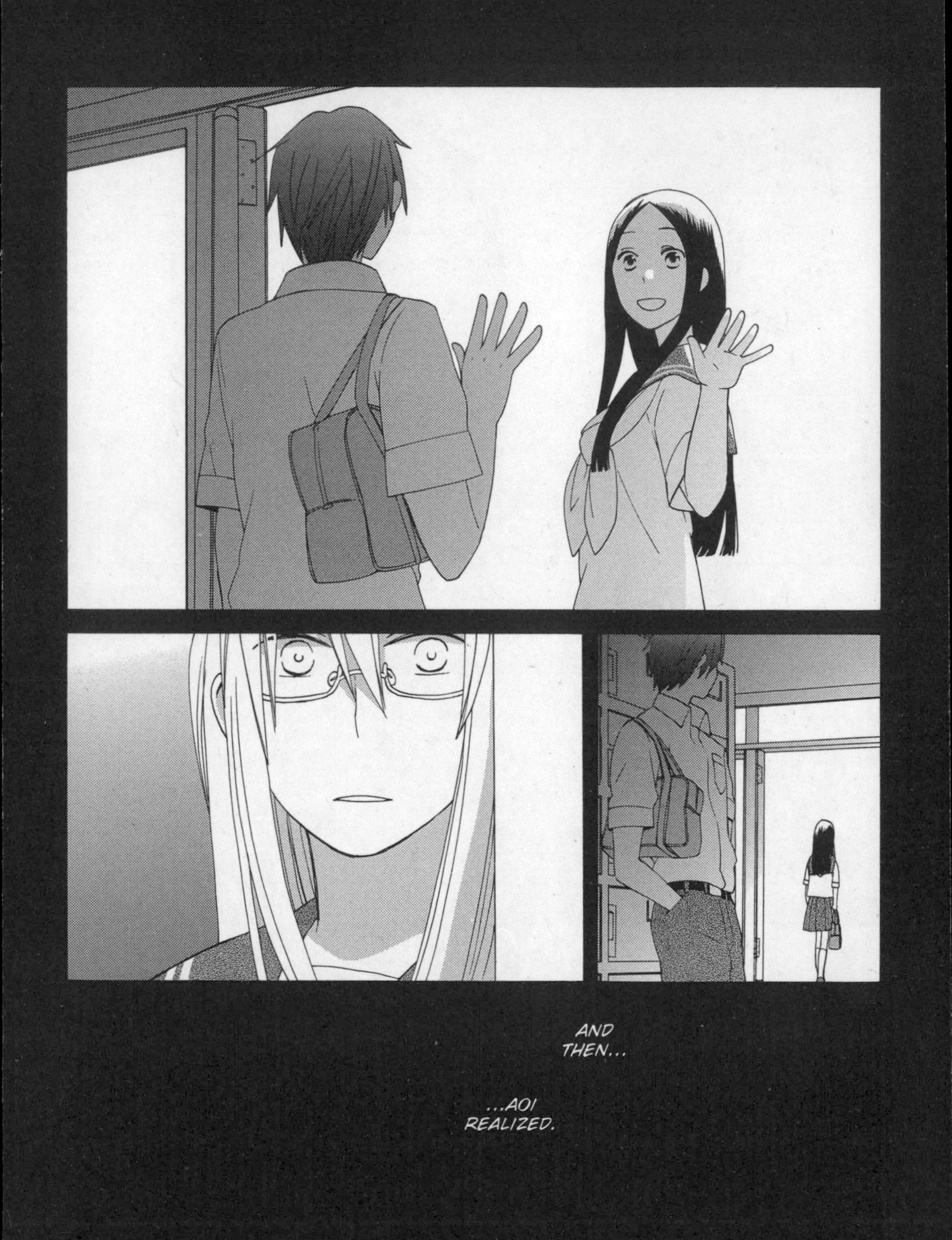

AND THEN...

...AOI REALIZED.

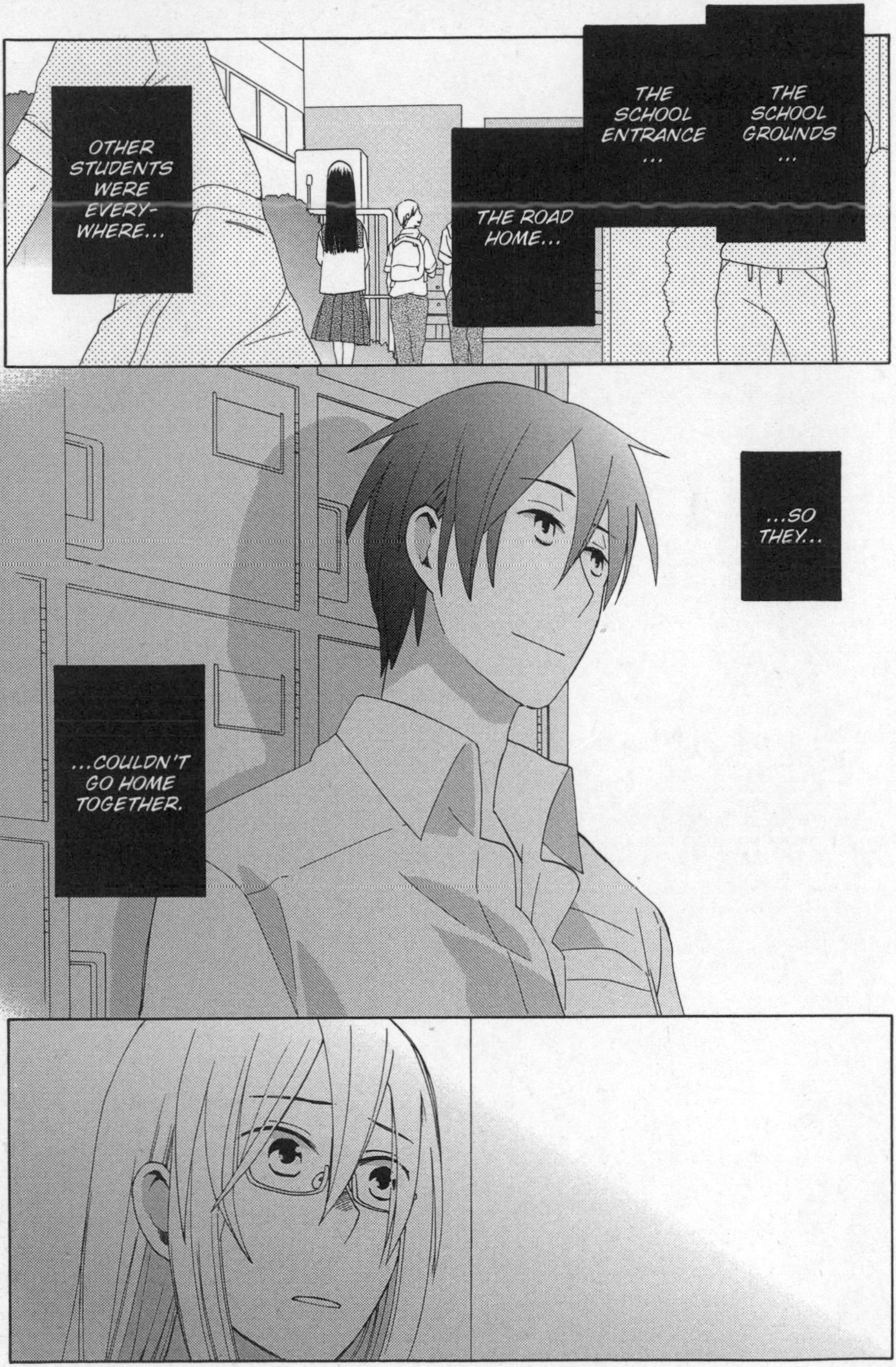
THE SCHOOL GROUNDS...
THE SCHOOL ENTRANCE...
THE ROAD HOME...
OTHER STUDENTS WERE EVERY-WHERE...
...SO THEY...
...COULDN'T GO HOME TOGETHER.

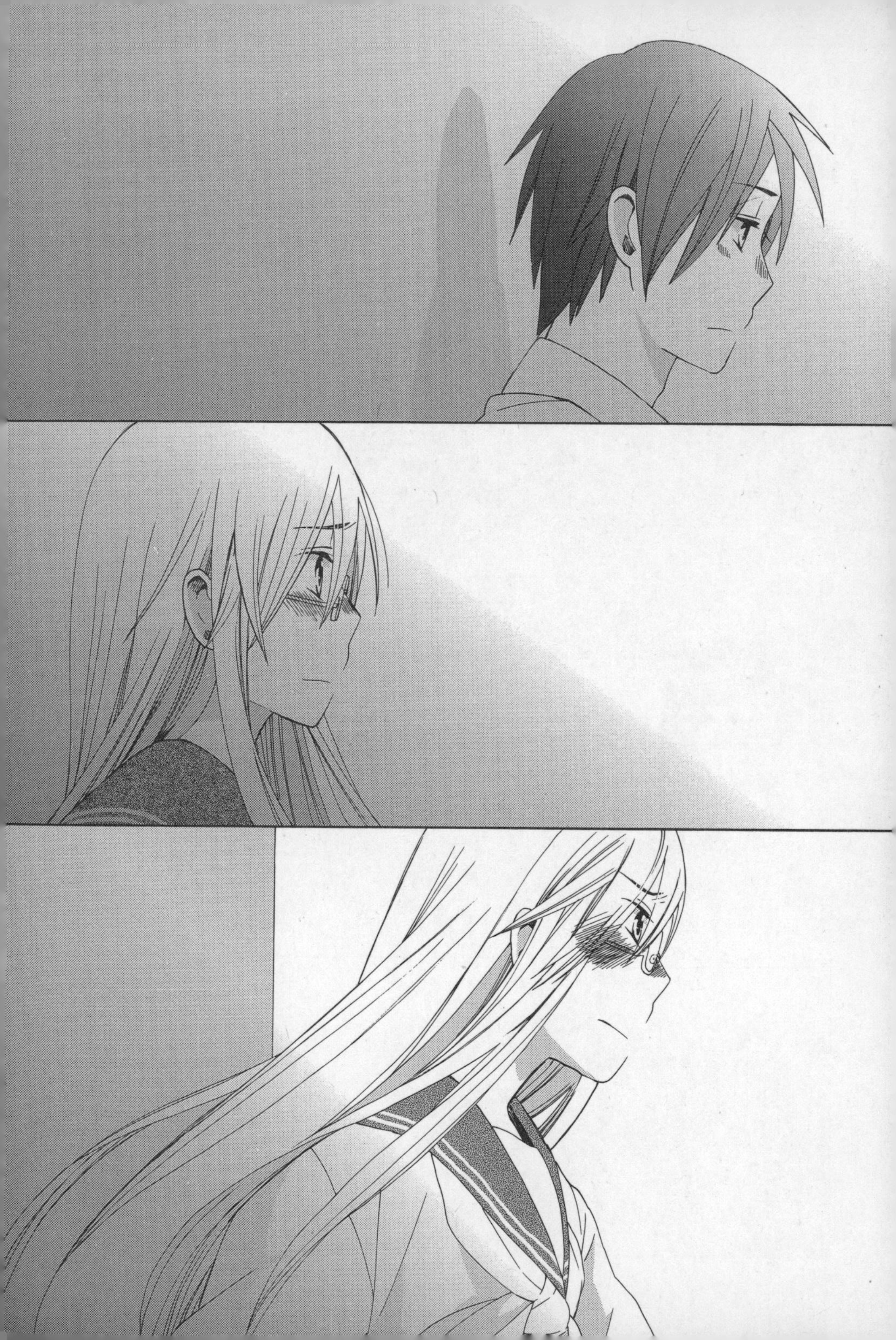

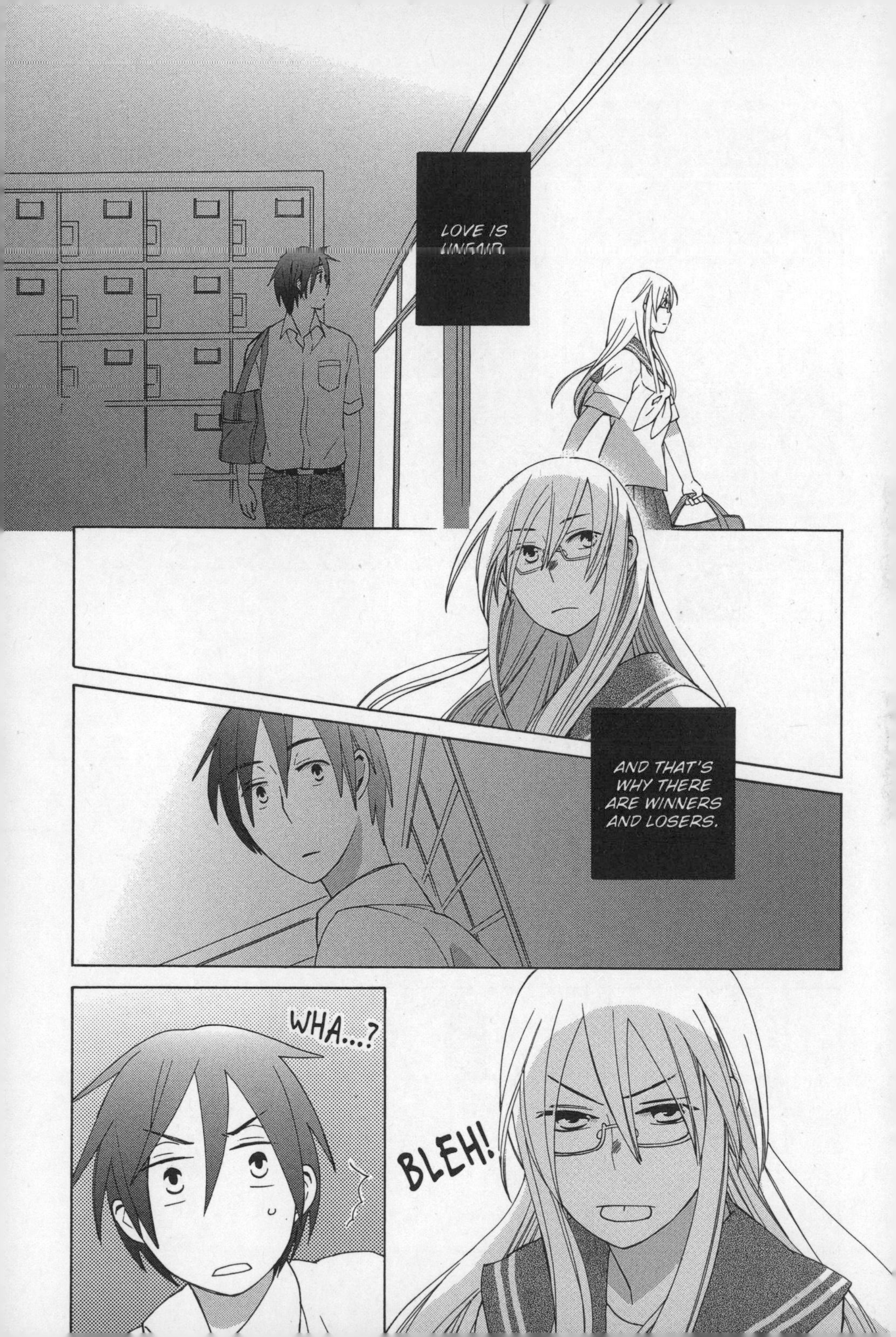
LOVE IS UNFAIR.
AND THAT'S WHY THERE ARE WINNERS AND LOSERS.
BLEH!
WHA...?

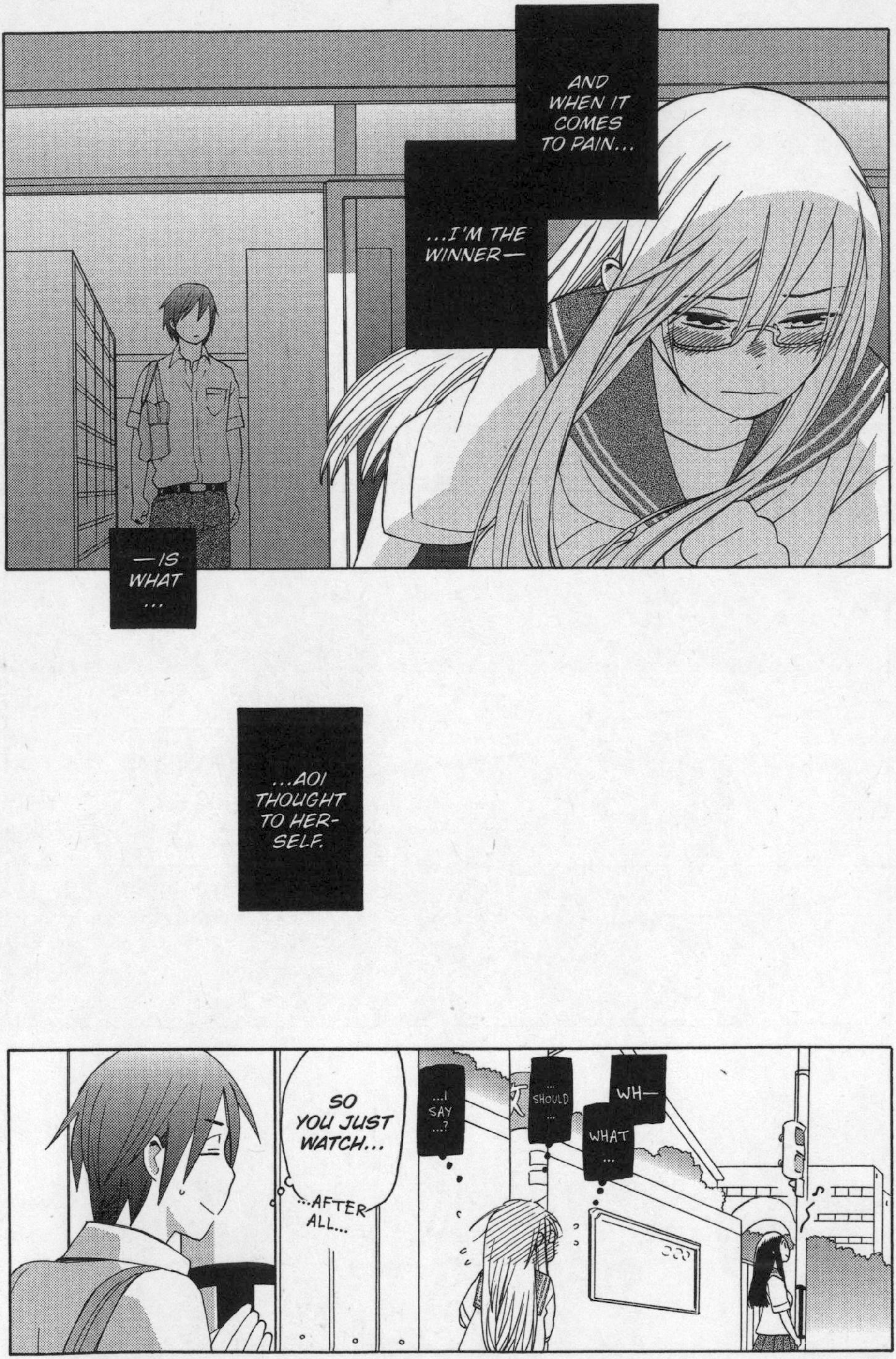
AND WHEN IT COMES TO PAIN...
...I'M THE WINNER—
—IS WHAT...
...AOI THOUGHT TO HER-SELF.
WH—
WHAT...
...SHOULD...
...I SAY...?
SO YOU JUST WATCH...
...AFTER ALL...

Fin

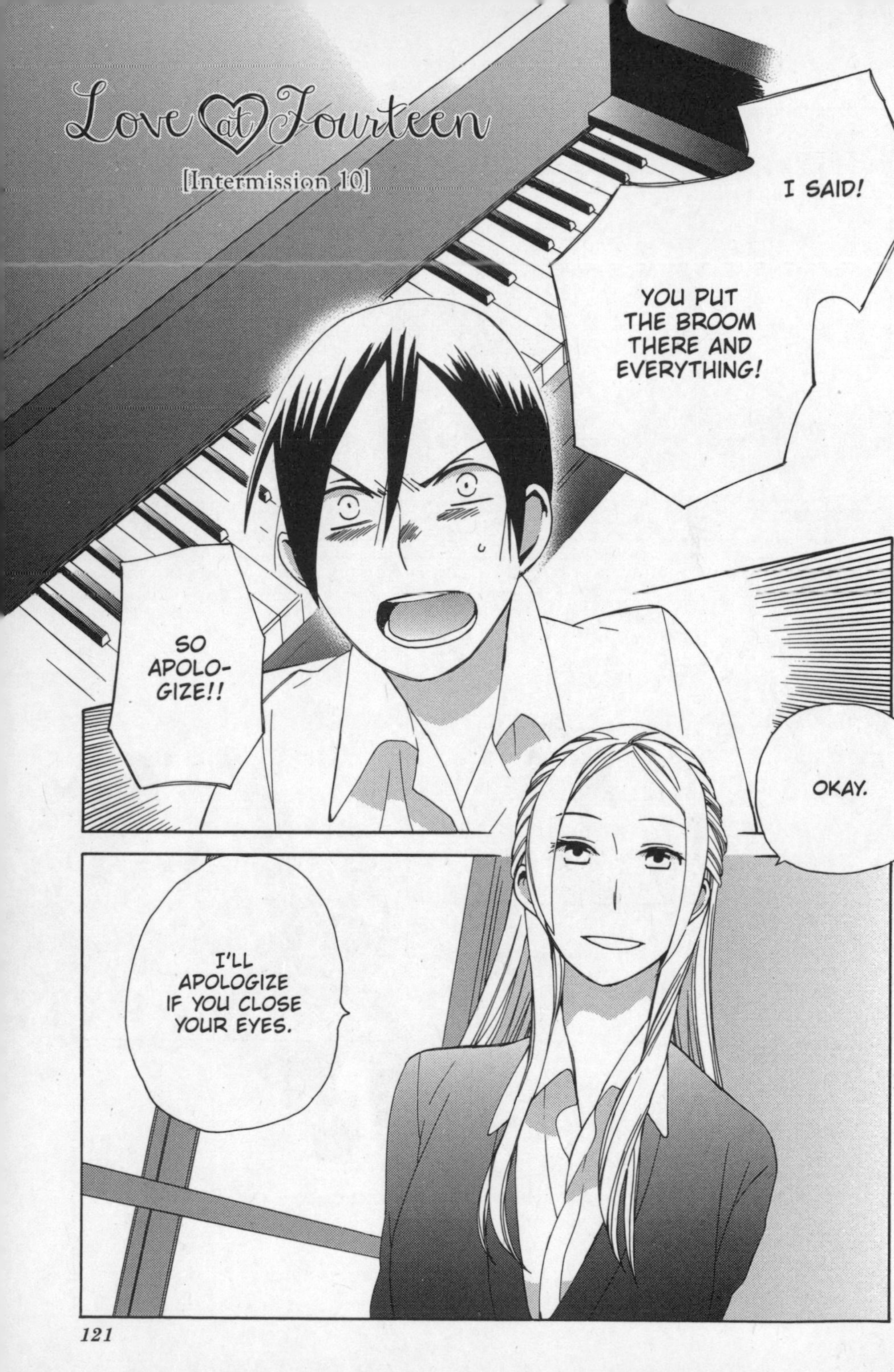
Love at Fourteen
[Intermission 10]
I SAID!
YOU PUT THE BROOM THERE AND EVERYTHING!
SO APOLOGIZE!!
OKAY.
I'LL APOLOGIZE IF YOU CLOSE YOUR EYES.

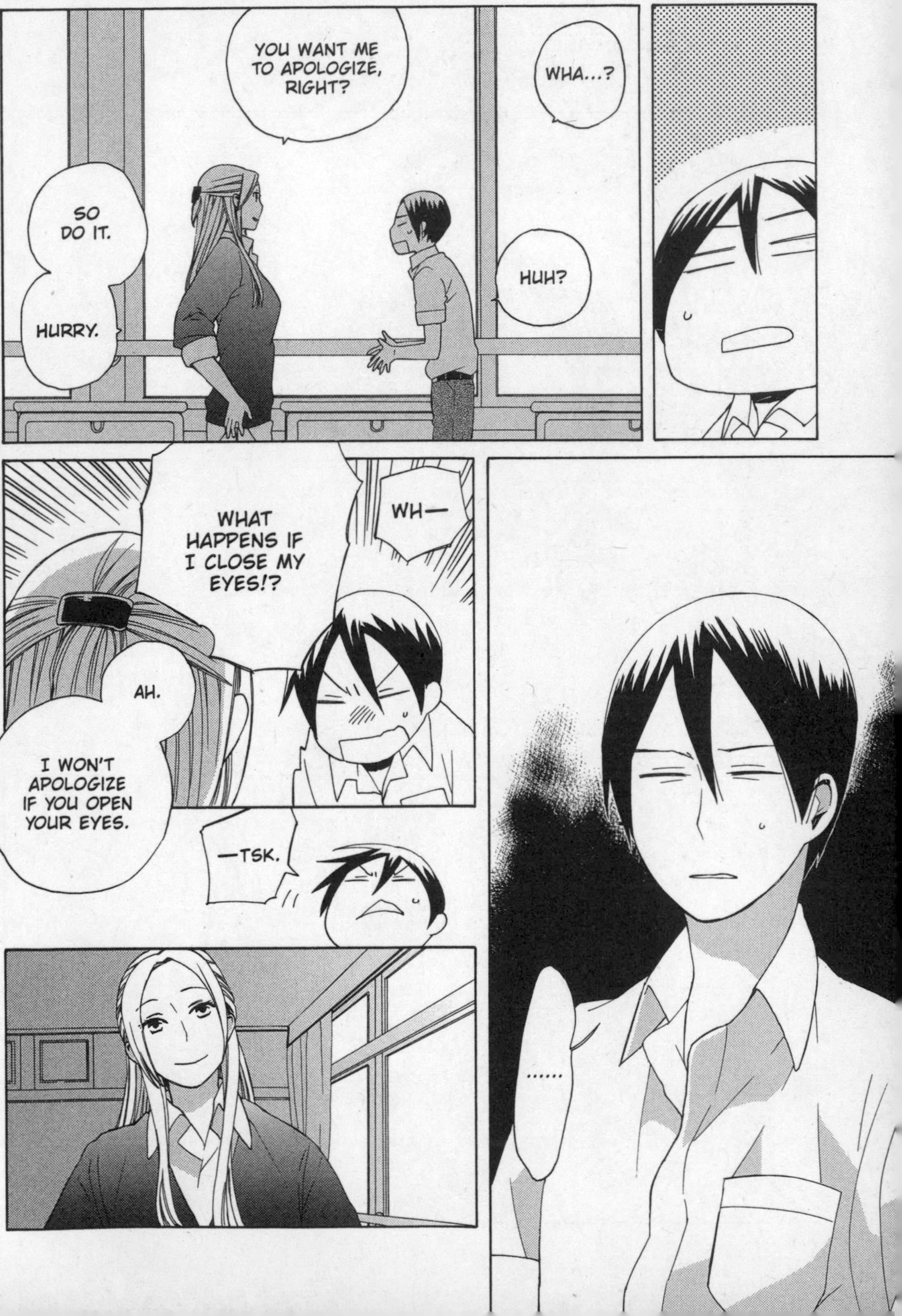
YOU WANT ME TO APOLOGIZE, RIGHT?
WHA...?
SO DO IT.
HURRY.
HUH?
......
WH—
WHAT HAPPENS IF I CLOSE MY EYES!?
AH.
I WON'T APOLOGIZE IF YOU OPEN YOUR EYES.
—TSK.

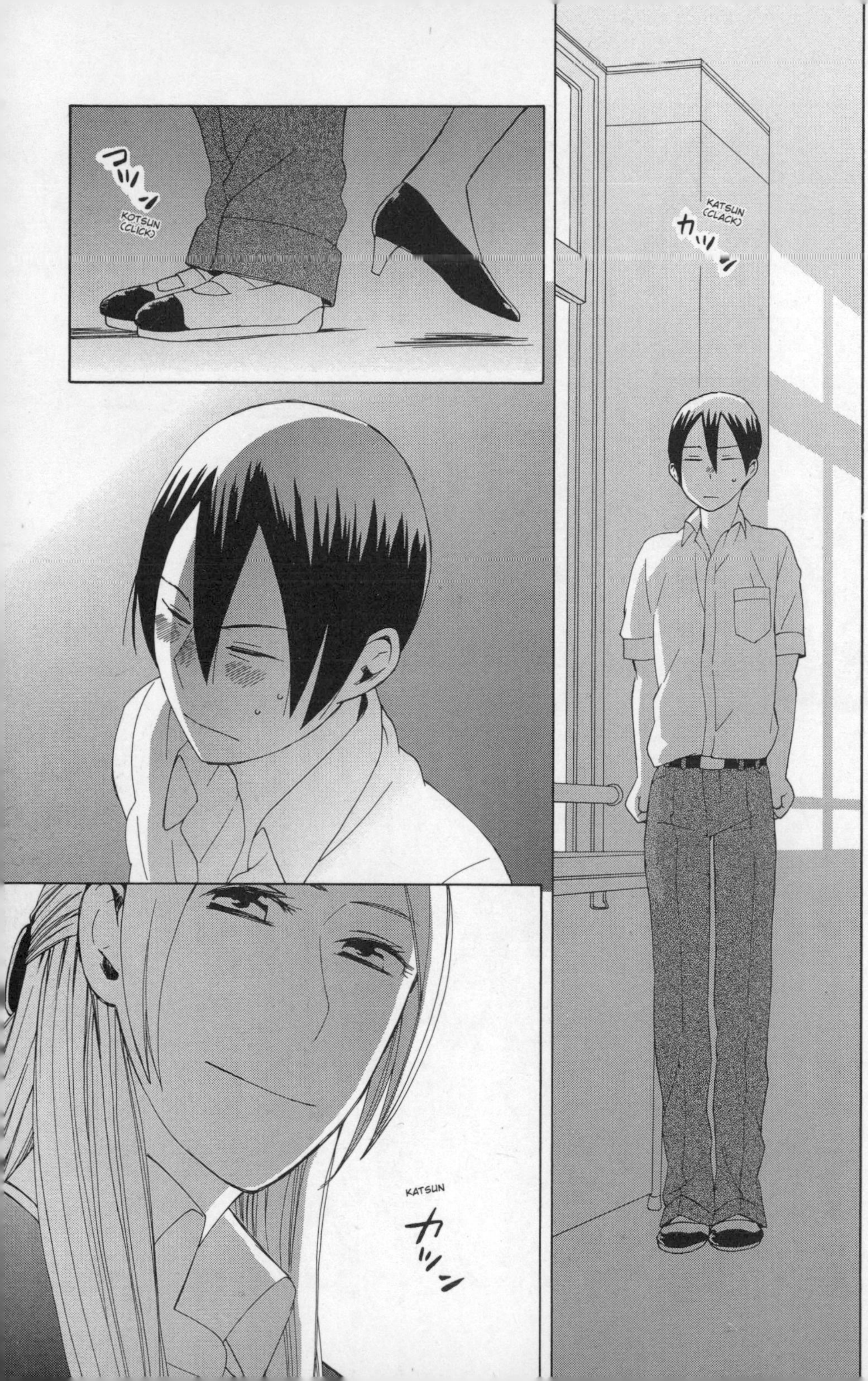
KATSUN (CLACK)
カツン
コツン
KOTSUN (CLICK)
KATSUN
カツン

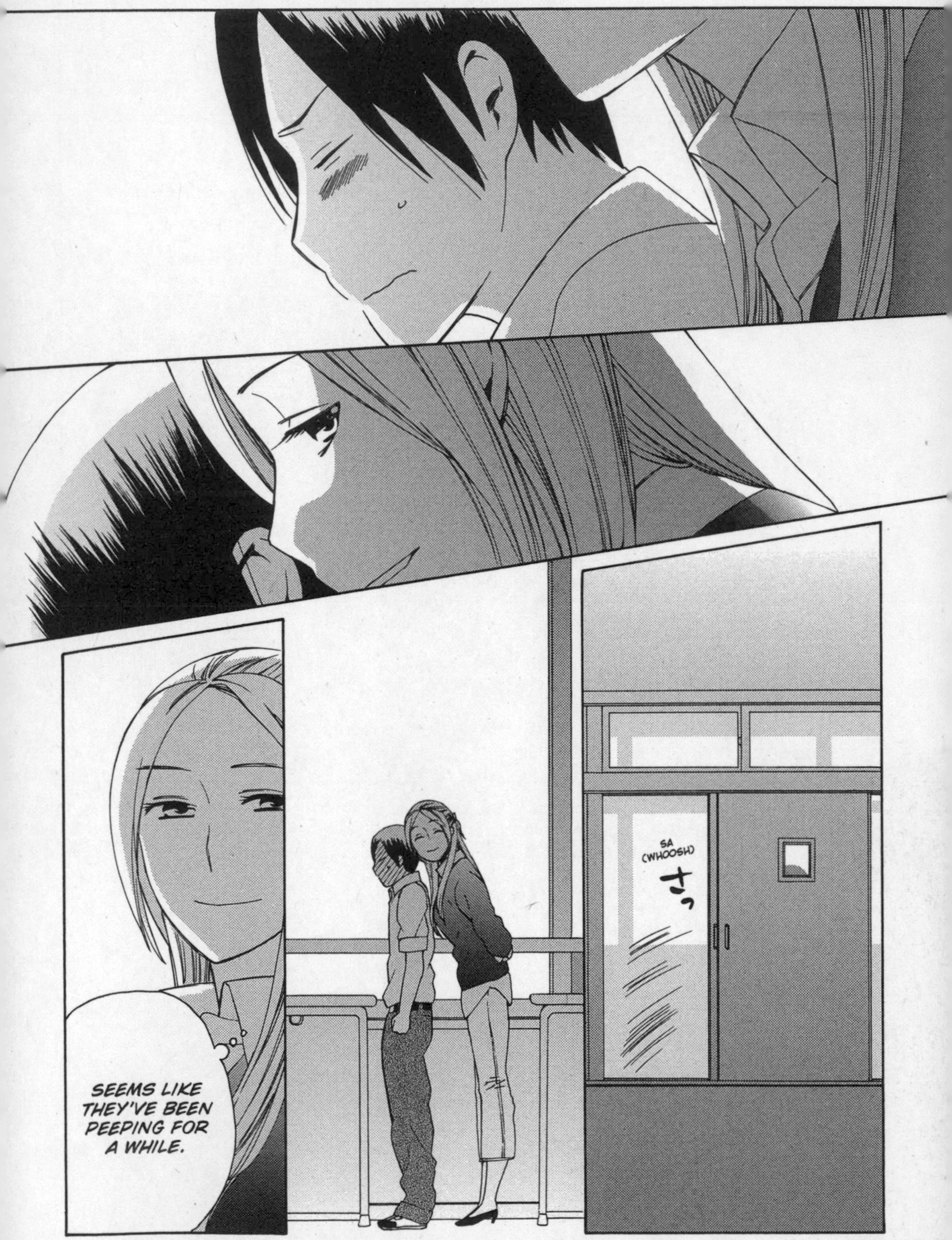
SA (WHOOSH)
さっ
SEEMS LIKE THEY'VE BEEN PEEPING FOR A WHILE.

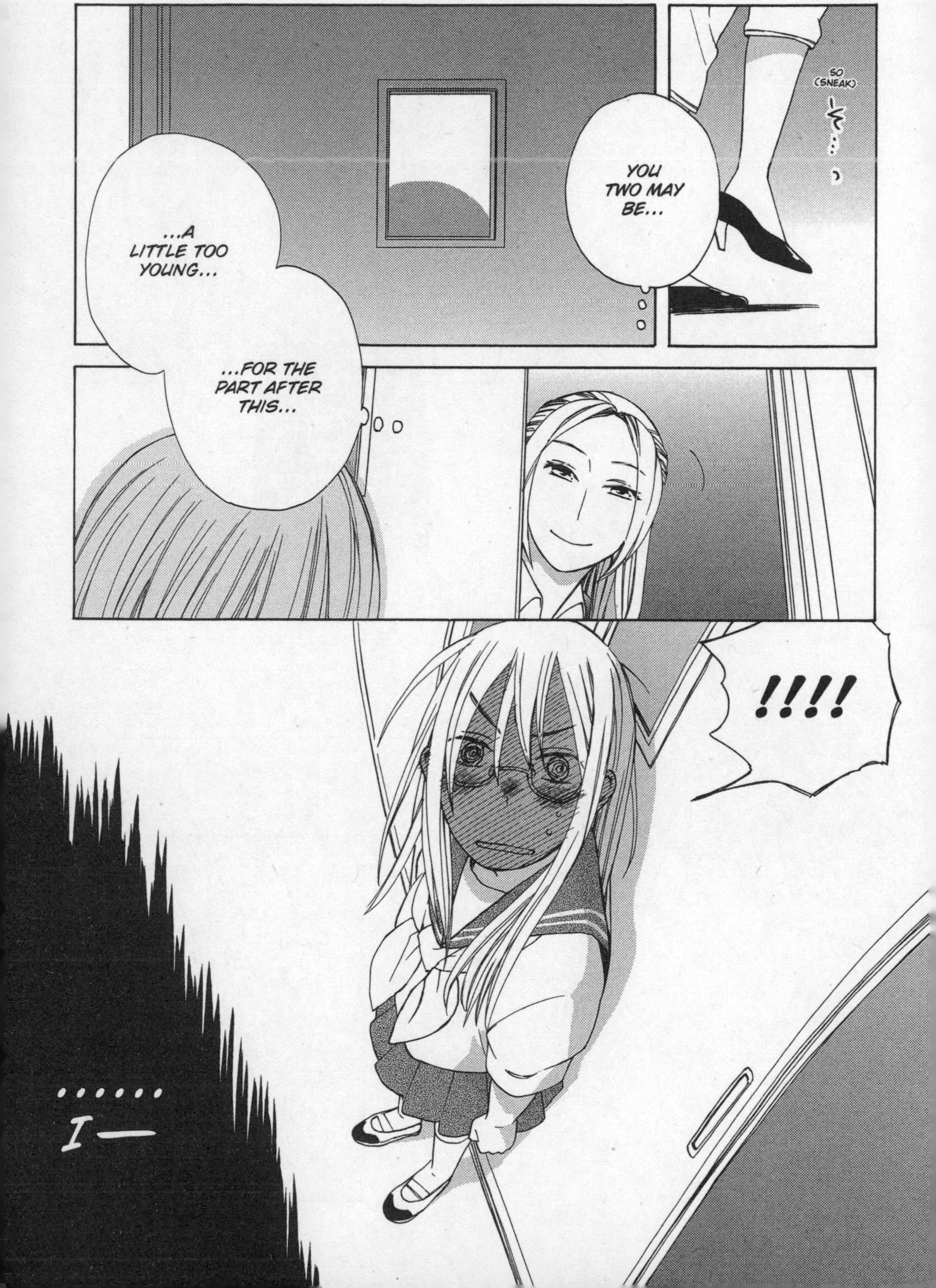
SO (SNEAK)
YOU TWO MAY BE...
...A LITTLE TOO YOUNG...
...FOR THE PART AFTER THIS...
!!!!
......
I—

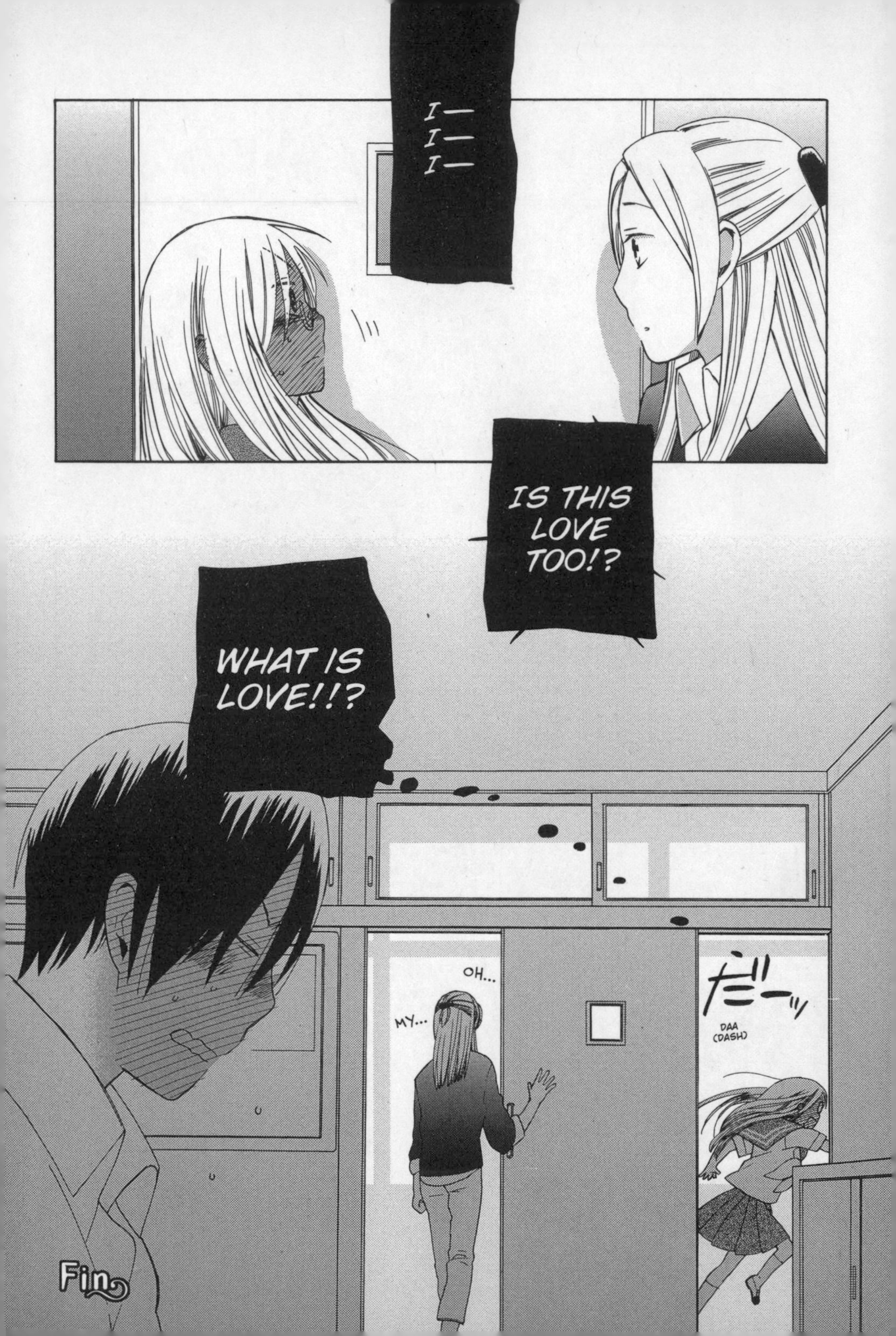
I—
I—
I—
IS THIS LOVE TOO!?
WHAT IS LOVE!!?
だーッ
DAA (DASH)
OH...
MY...
Fin

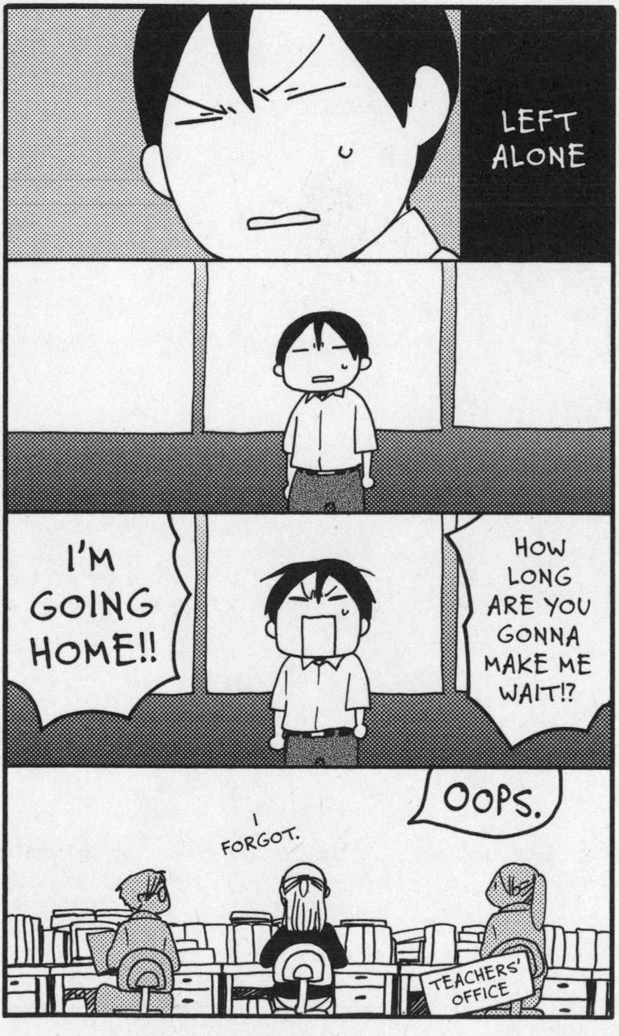
LEFT ALONE
HOW LONG ARE YOU GONNA MAKE ME WAIT!?
I'M GOING HOME!!
OOPS.
I FORGOT.
TEACHERS' OFFICE

Love at Fourteen

Fuka Mizutani

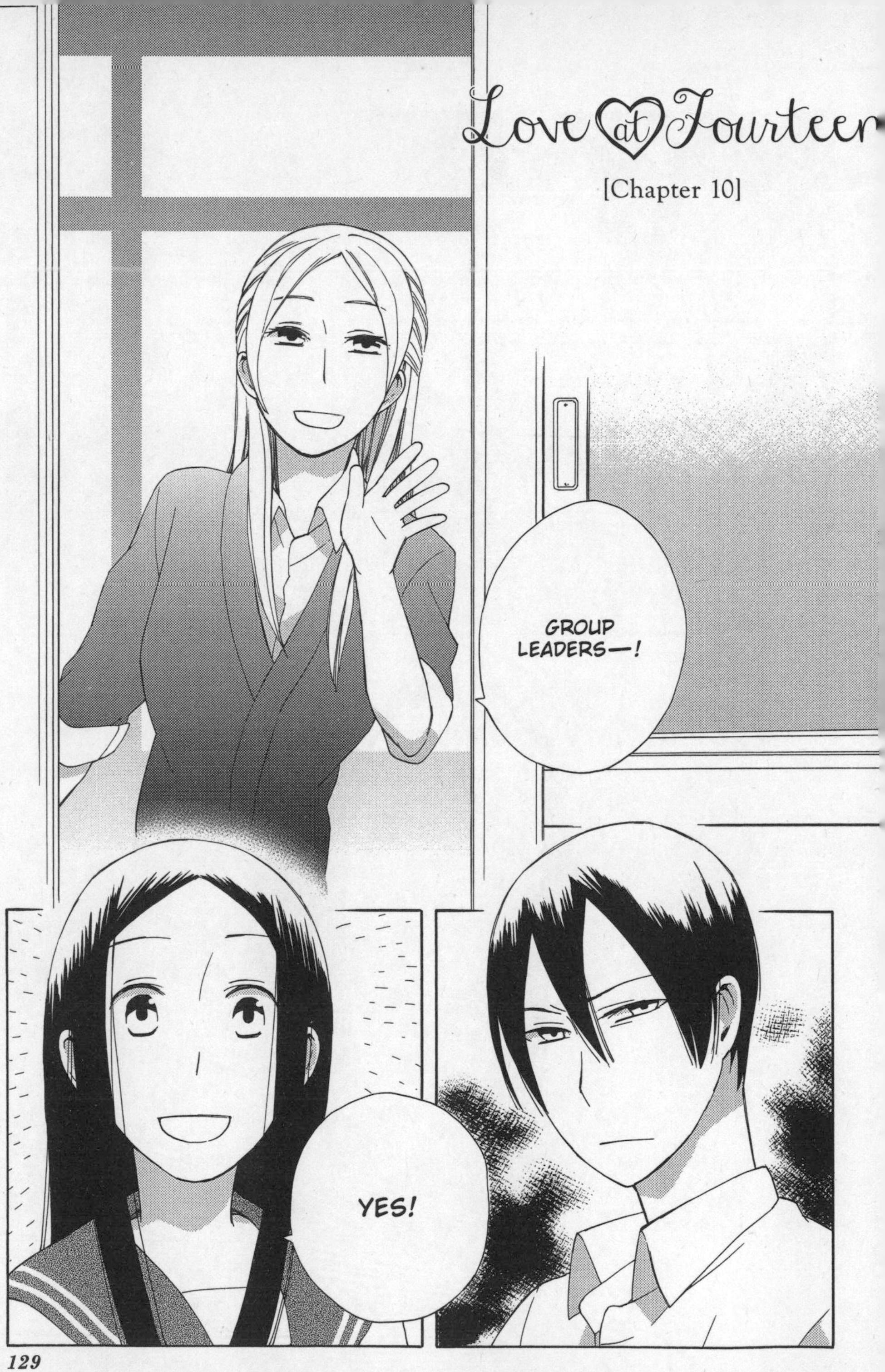
Love at Fourteen
[Chapter 10]
GROUP LEADERS—!
YES!

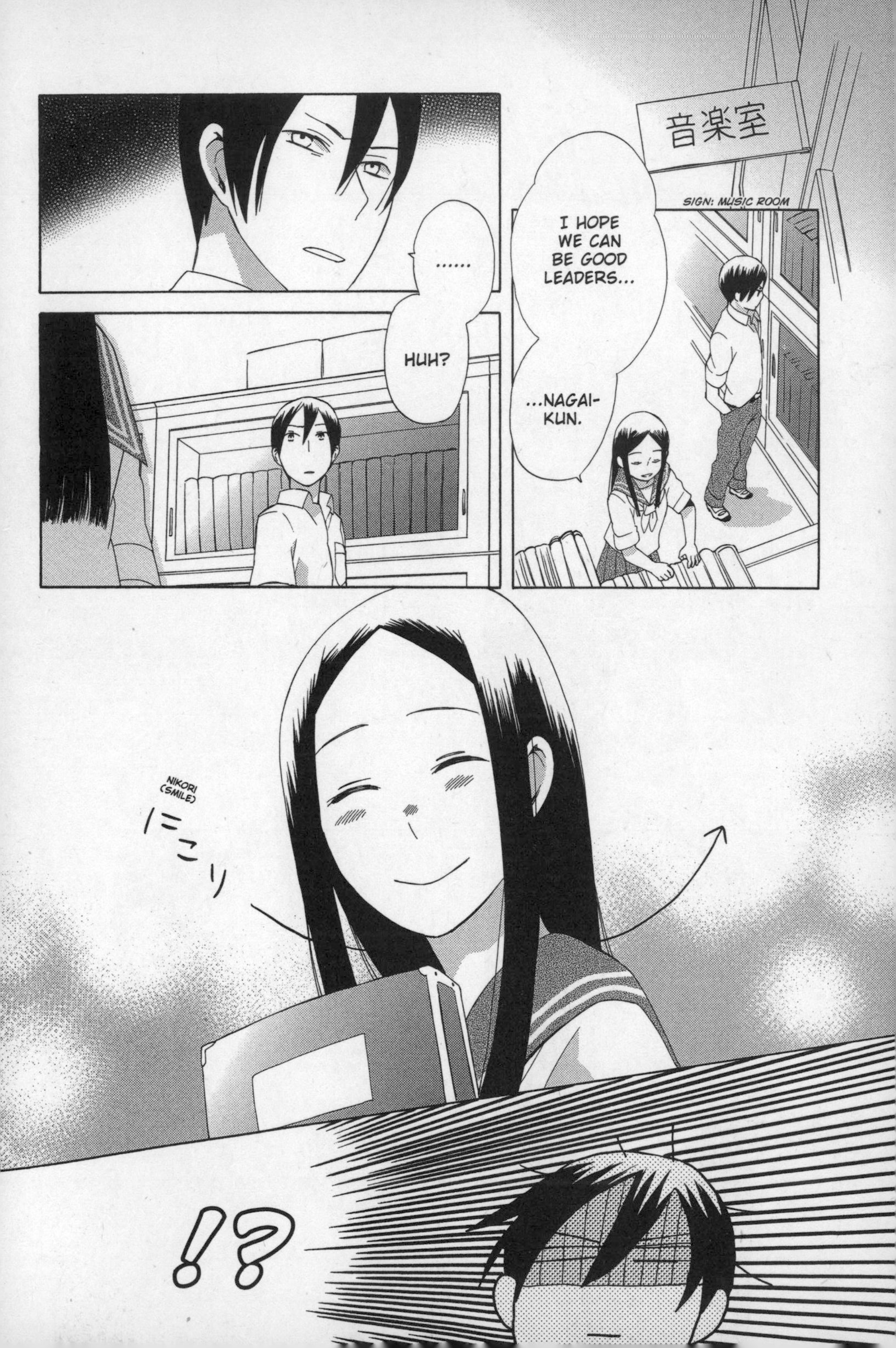

音楽室
SIGN: MUSIC ROOM
I HOPE WE CAN BE GOOD LEADERS...
...NAGAI-KUN.
......
HUH?
NIKORI (SMILE)
にこり
!?

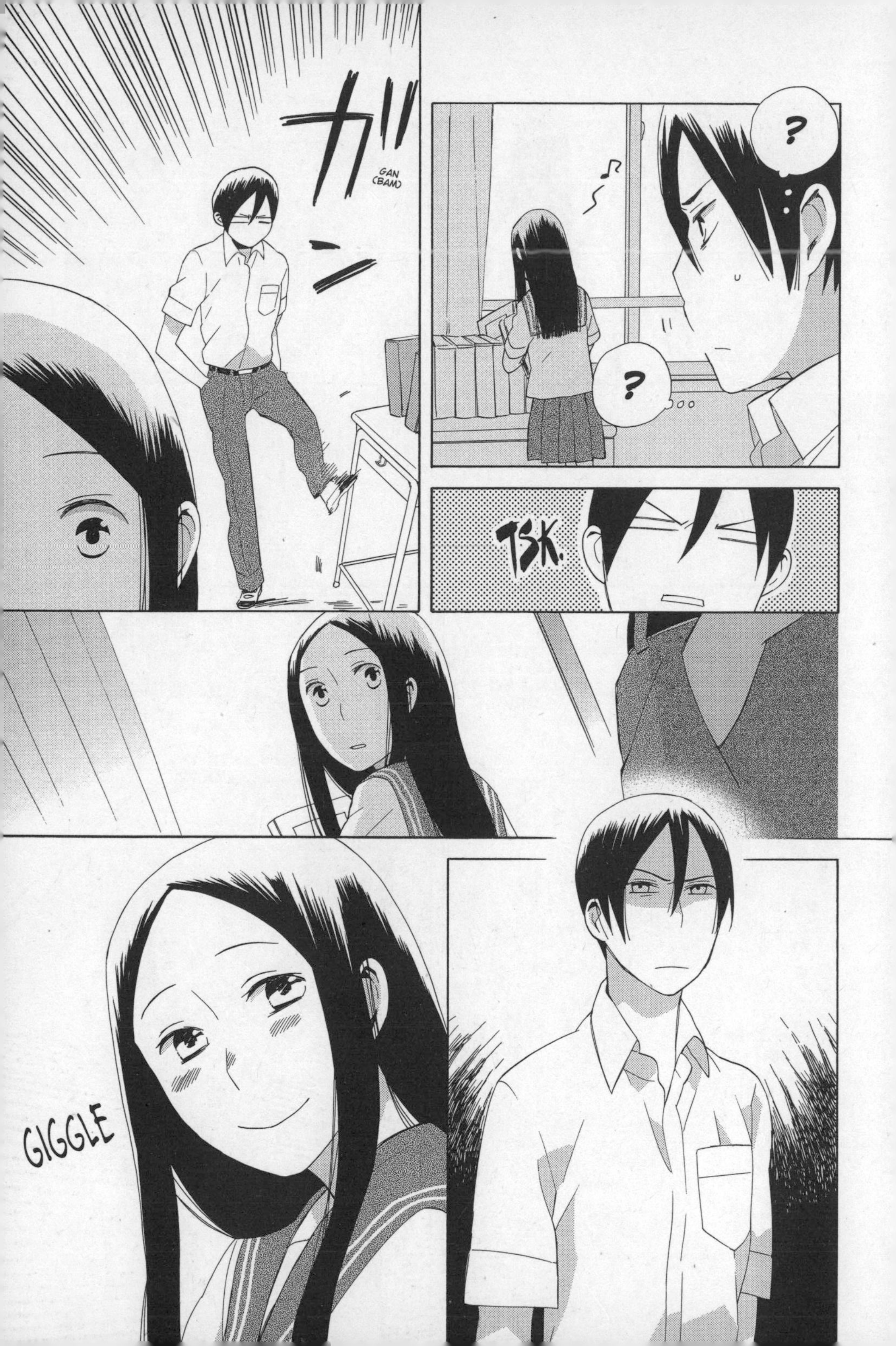
?
?
TSK.
GAN (BAM)
GIGGLE

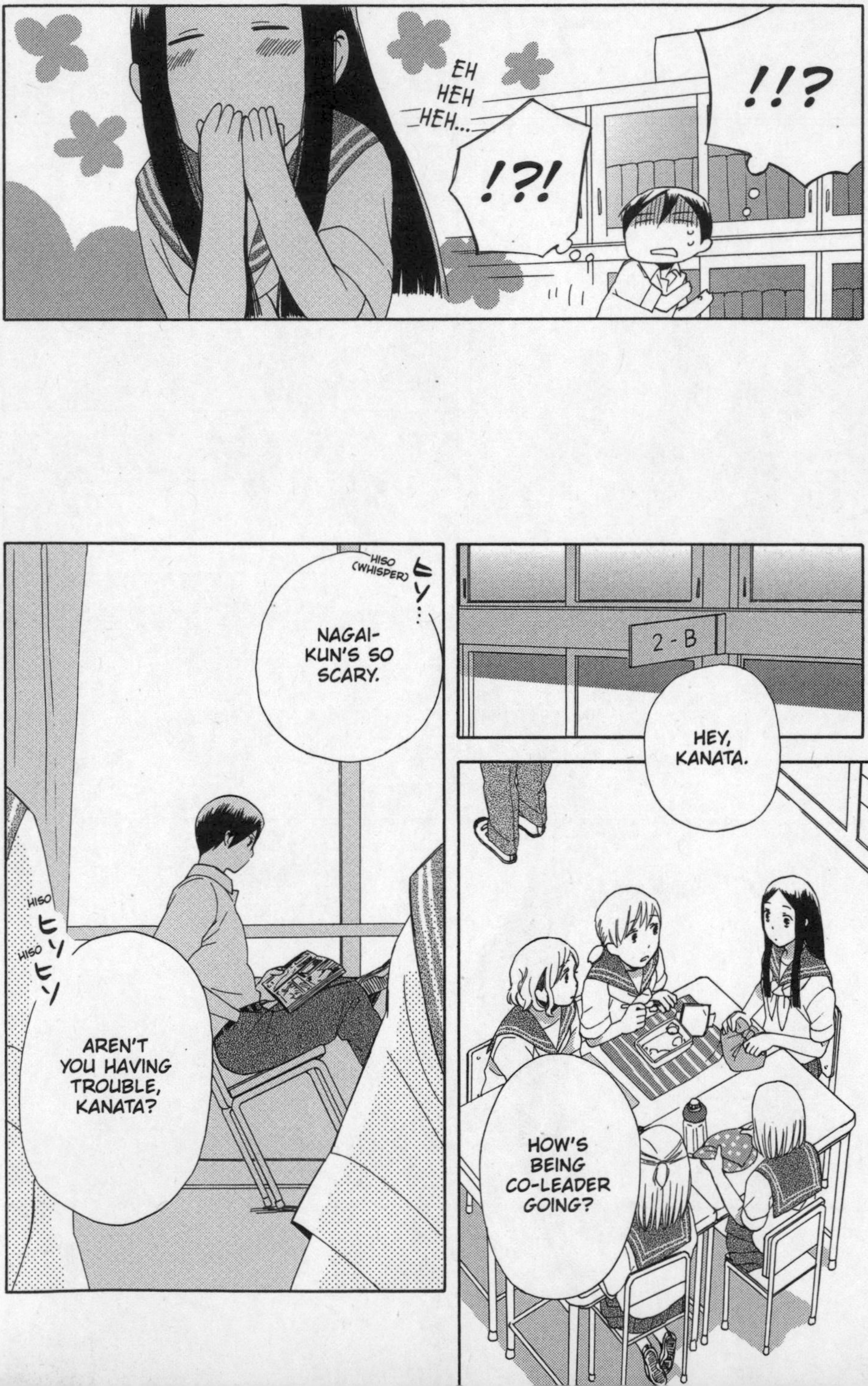
!!?
EH HEH HEH...
!?!
2-B
HEY, KANATA.
HOW'S BEING CO-LEADER GOING?
HISO (WHISPER) ヒソ…
NAGAI-KUN'S SO SCARY.
HISO ヒソ HISO ヒソ
AREN'T YOU HAVING TROUBLE, KANATA?

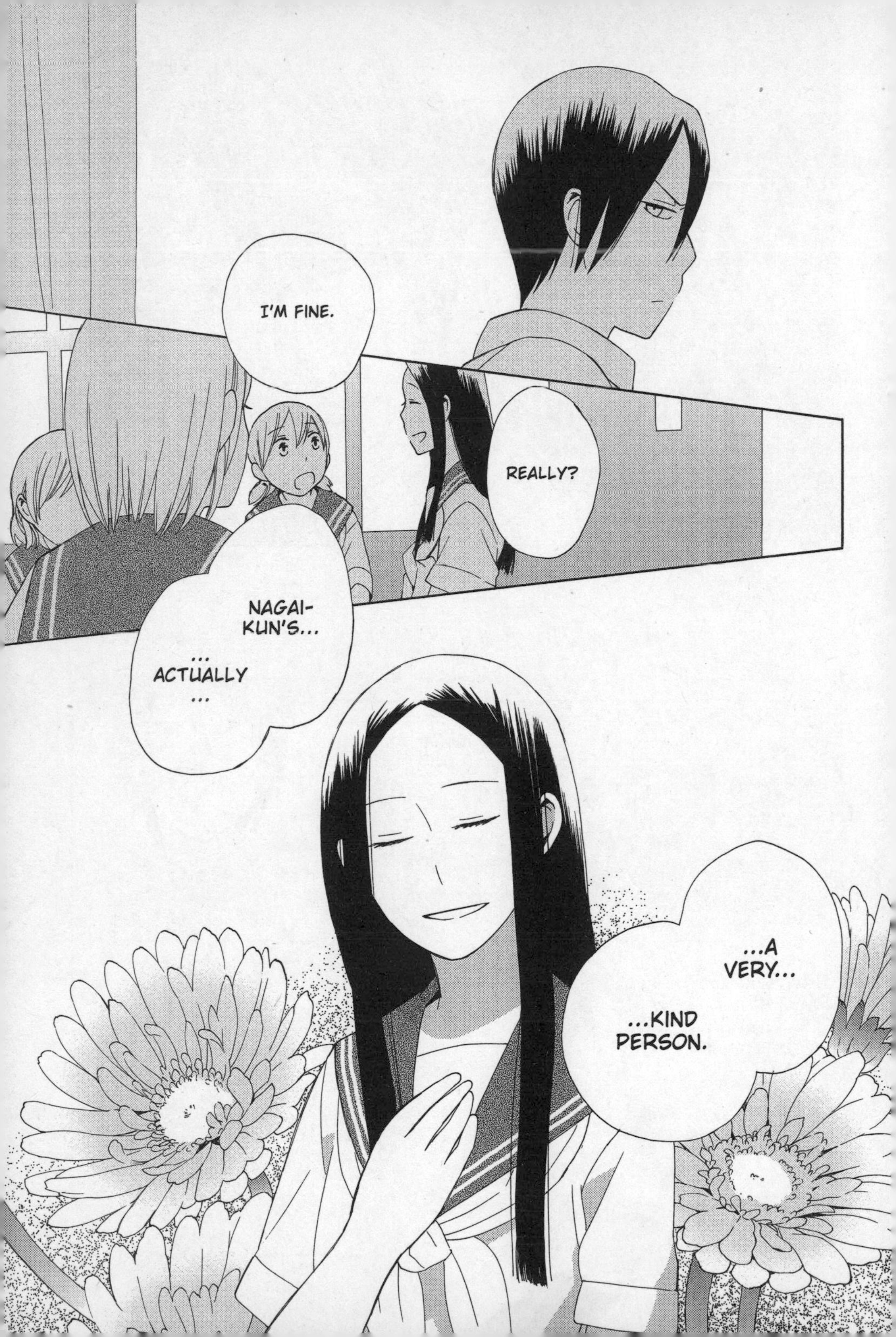
I'M FINE.
REALLY?
NAGAI-KUN'S... ...ACTUALLY...
...A VERY... ...KIND PERSON.

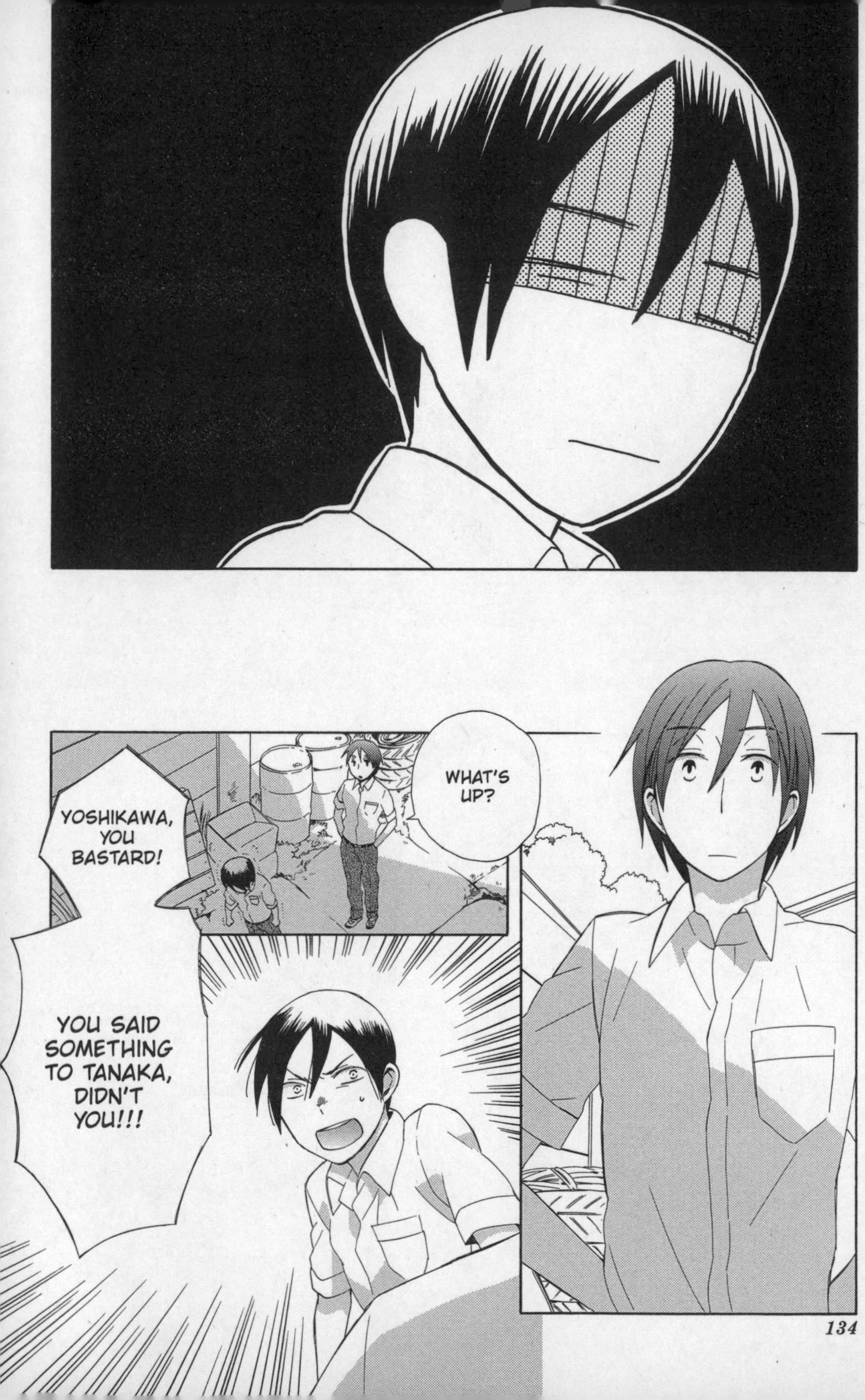
WHAT'S UP?
YOSHIKAWA, YOU BASTARD!
YOU SAID SOMETHING TO TANAKA, DIDN'T YOU!!!

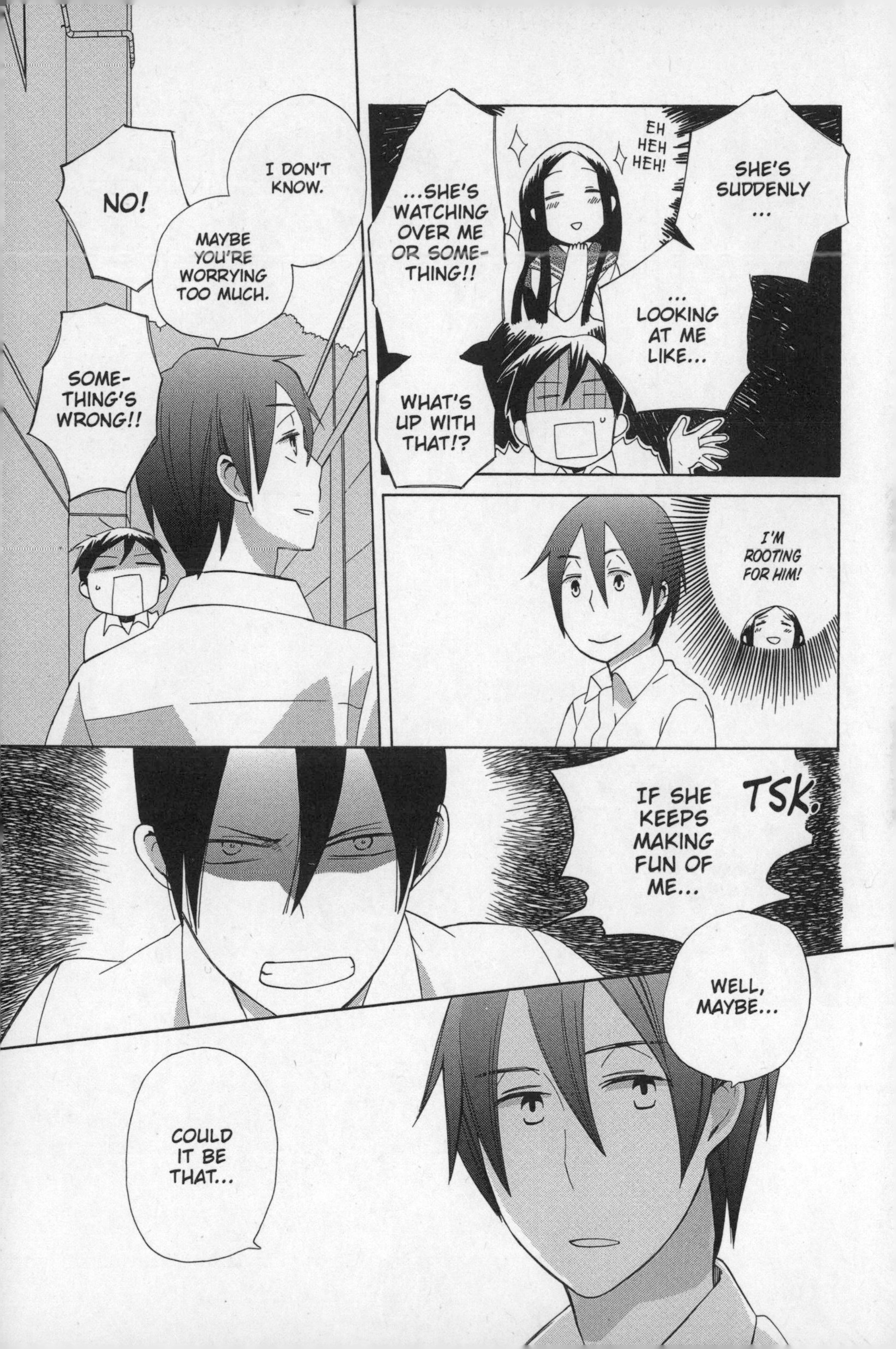
SHE'S SUDDENLY ...
EH HEH HEH!
... LOOKING AT ME LIKE...
...SHE'S WATCHING OVER ME OR SOME-THING!!
WHAT'S UP WITH THAT!?
I'M ROOTING FOR HIM!
I DON'T KNOW.
NO!
MAYBE YOU'RE WORRYING TOO MUCH.
SOME-THING'S WRONG!!
TSK.
IF SHE KEEPS MAKING FUN OF ME...
WELL, MAYBE...
COULD IT BE THAT...

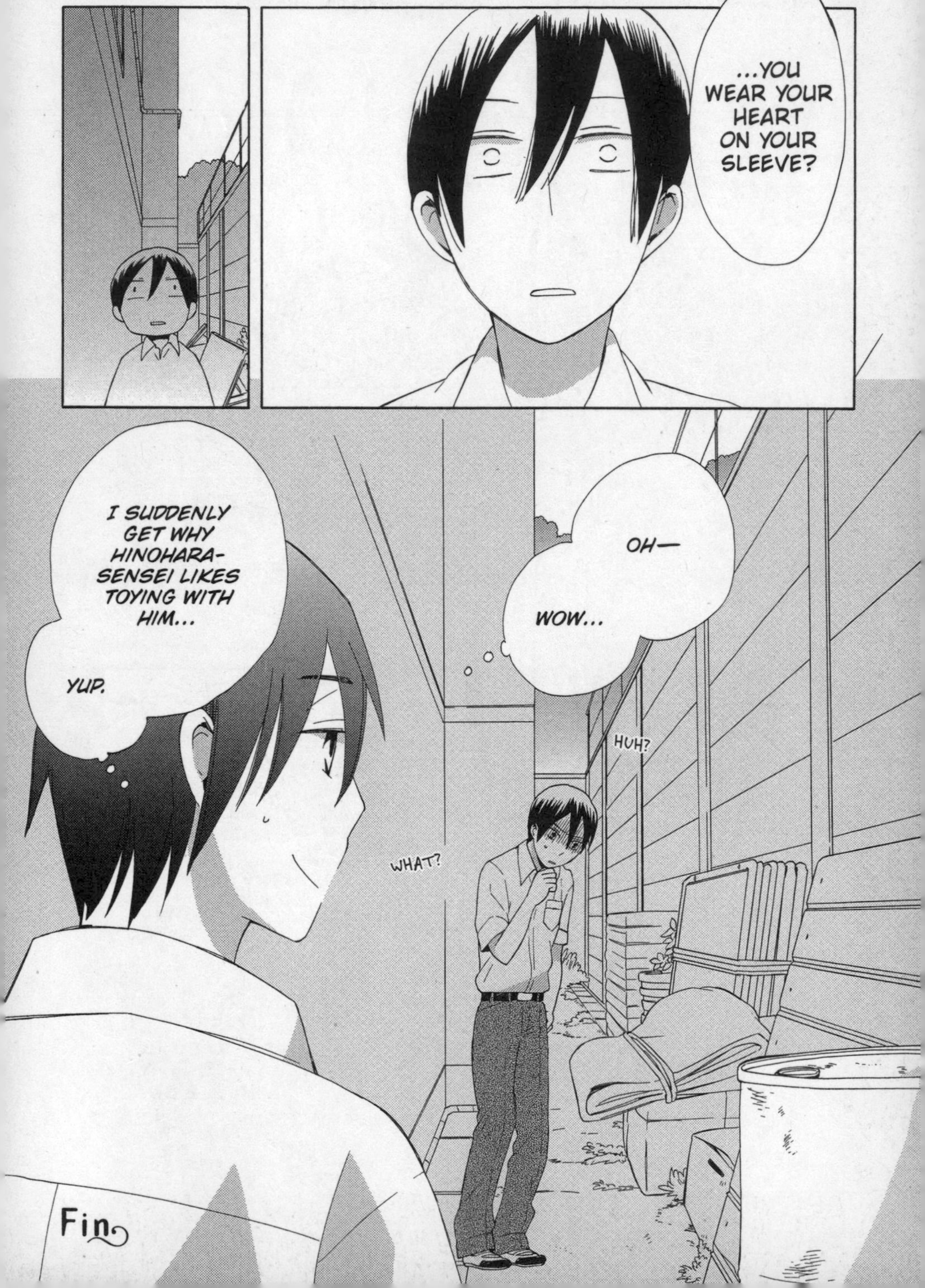
...YOU WEAR YOUR HEART ON YOUR SLEEVE?
OH— WOW...
I SUDDENLY GET WHY HINOHARA-SENSEI LIKES TOYING WITH HIM...
YUP.
HUH?
WHAT?
Fin

Love at Fourteen

[Chapter 11]

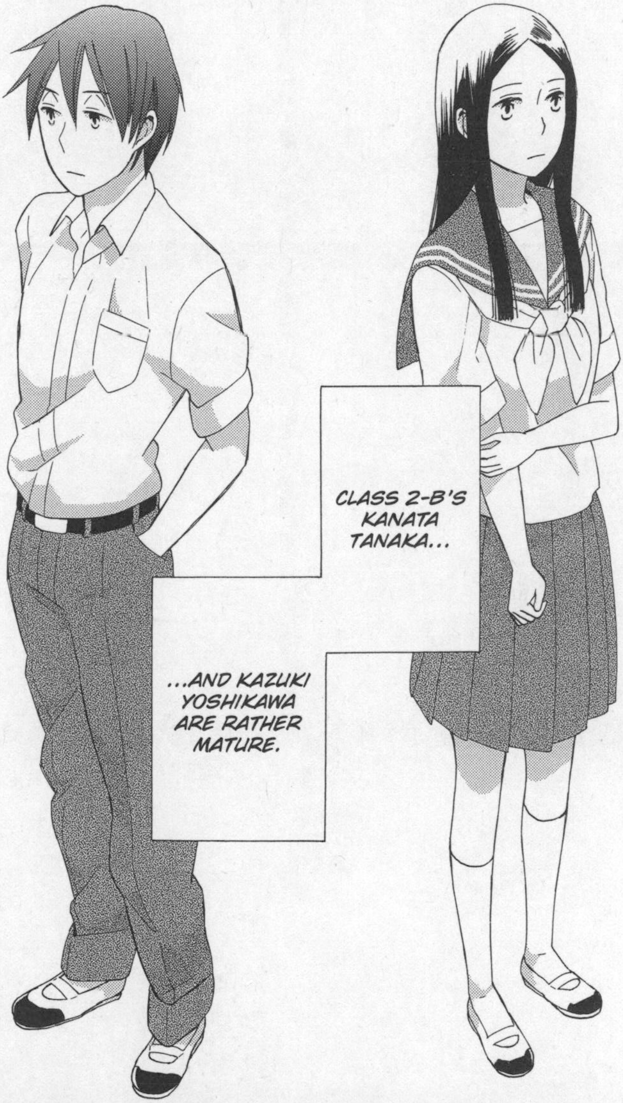
CLASS 2-B'S KANATA TANAKA...
...AND KAZUKI YOSHIKAWA ARE RATHER MATURE.

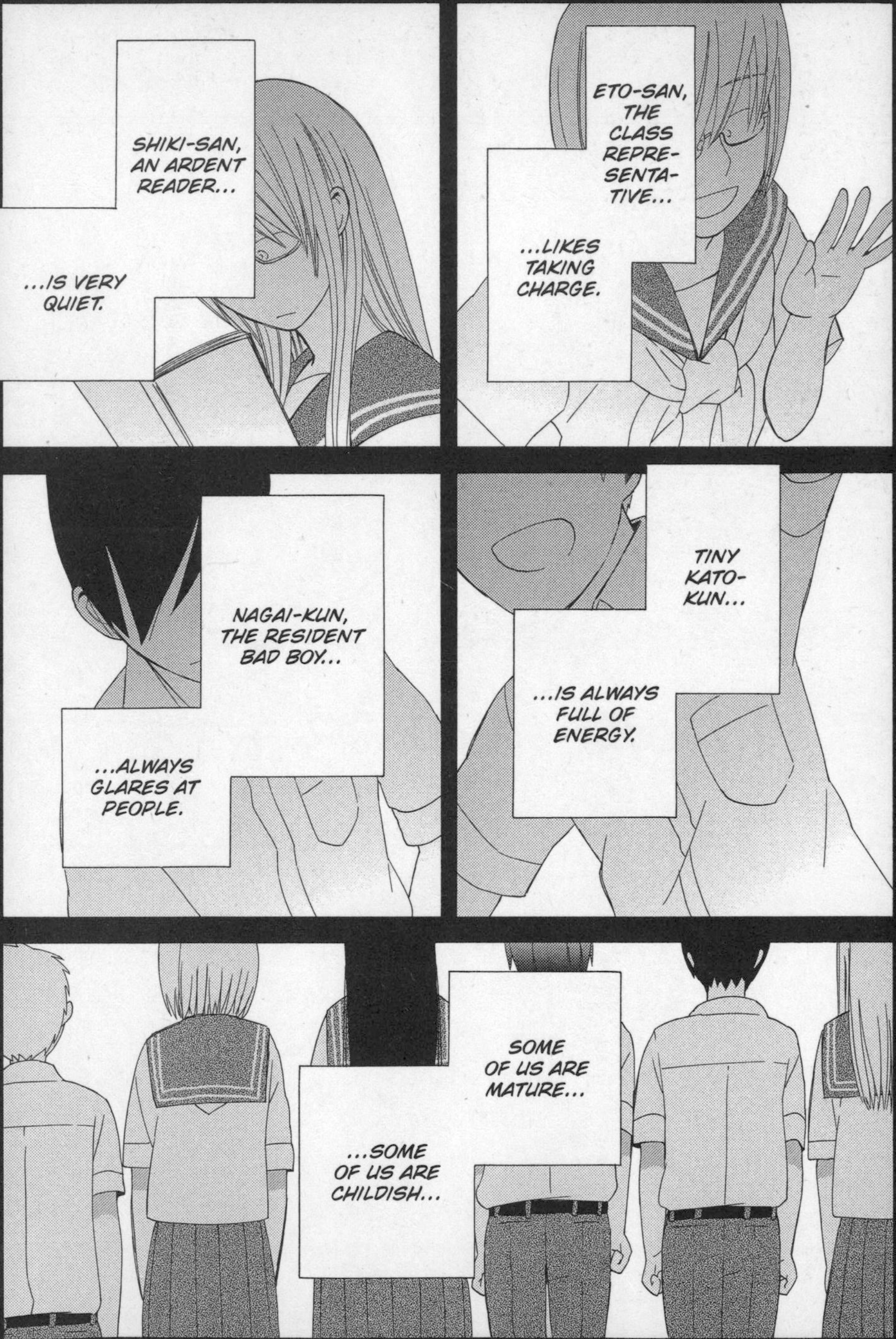
ETO-SAN, THE CLASS REPRESENTATIVE...
...LIKES TAKING CHARGE.
SHIKI-SAN, AN ARDENT READER...
...IS VERY QUIET.
TINY KATO-KUN...
...IS ALWAYS FULL OF ENERGY.
NAGAI-KUN, THE RESIDENT BAD BOY...
...ALWAYS GLARES AT PEOPLE.
SOME OF US ARE MATURE...
...SOME OF US ARE CHILDISH...

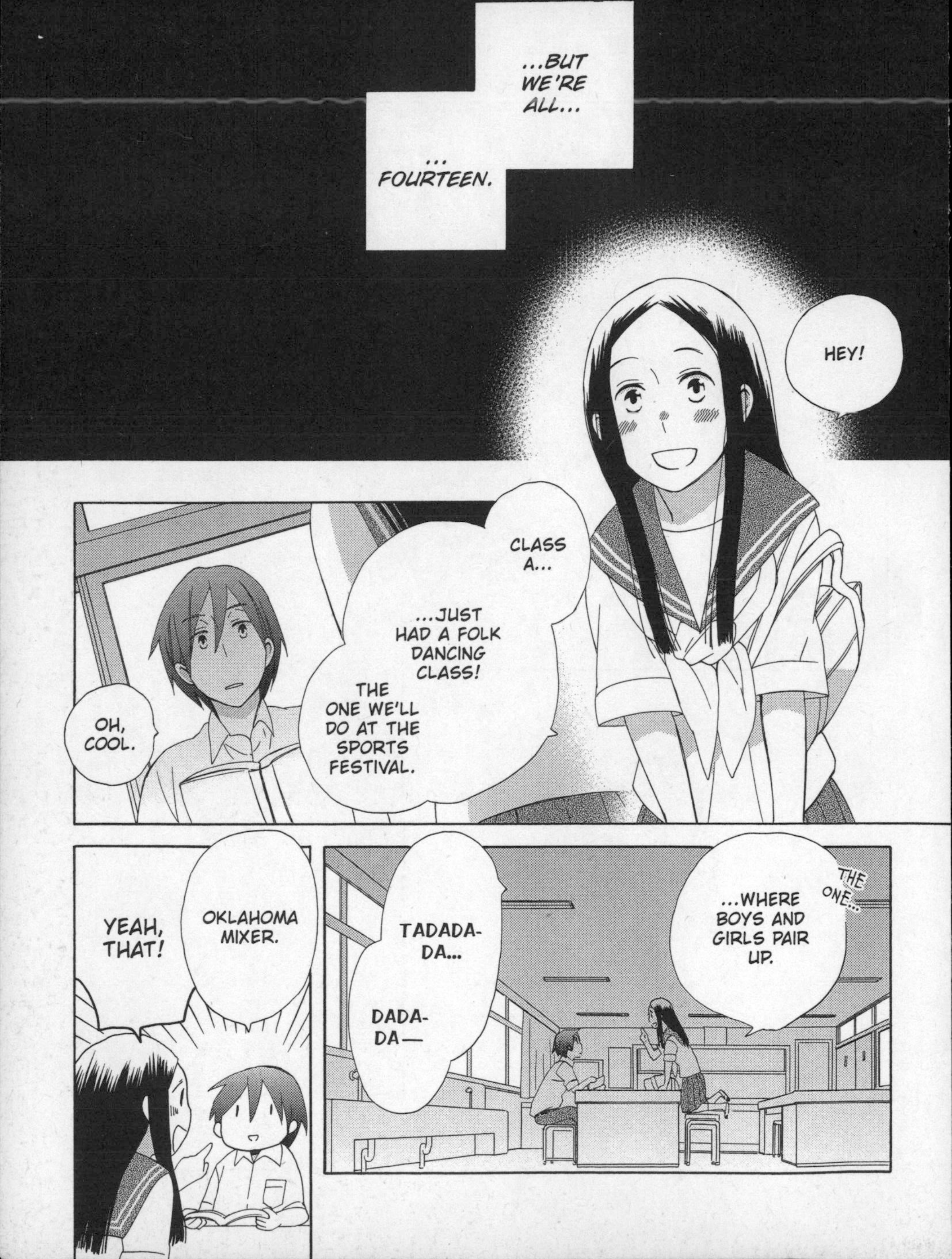
...BUT WE'RE ALL...
...FOURTEEN.
HEY!
CLASS A...
...JUST HAD A FOLK DANCING CLASS!
THE ONE WE'LL DO AT THE SPORTS FESTIVAL.
OH, COOL.
THE ONE...
...WHERE BOYS AND GIRLS PAIR UP.
TADADA-DA...
DADADA—
OKLAHOMA MIXER.
YEAH, THAT!

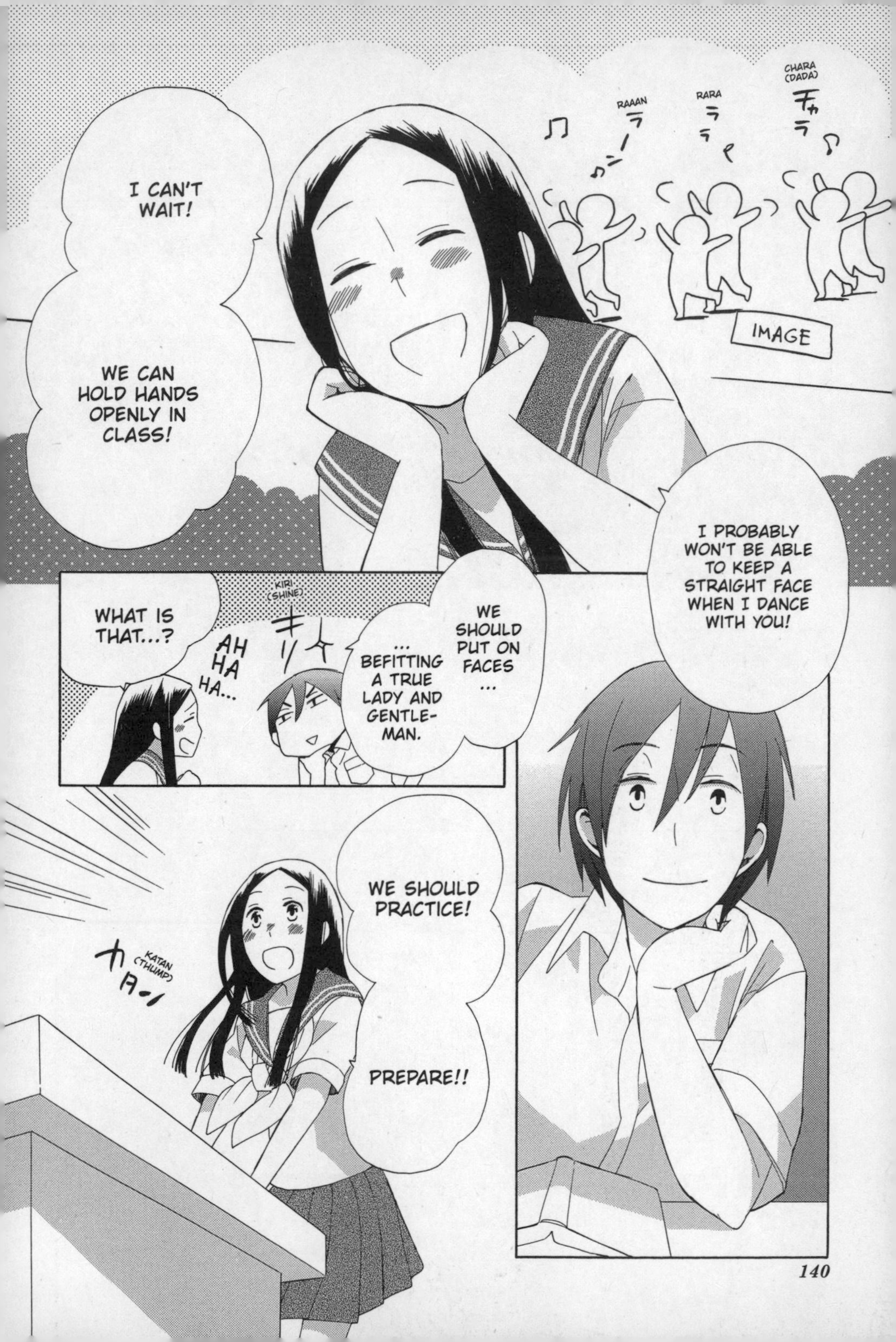
CHARA (DADA)
RARA
RAAAN
IMAGE
I CAN'T WAIT!
WE CAN HOLD HANDS OPENLY IN CLASS!
I PROBABLY WON'T BE ABLE TO KEEP A STRAIGHT FACE WHEN I DANCE WITH YOU!
WE SHOULD PUT ON FACES...
...BEFITTING A TRUE LADY AND GENTLE-MAN.
KIRI (SHINE)
AH HA HA...
WHAT IS THAT...?
WE SHOULD PRACTICE!
PREPARE!!
KATAN (THUMP)

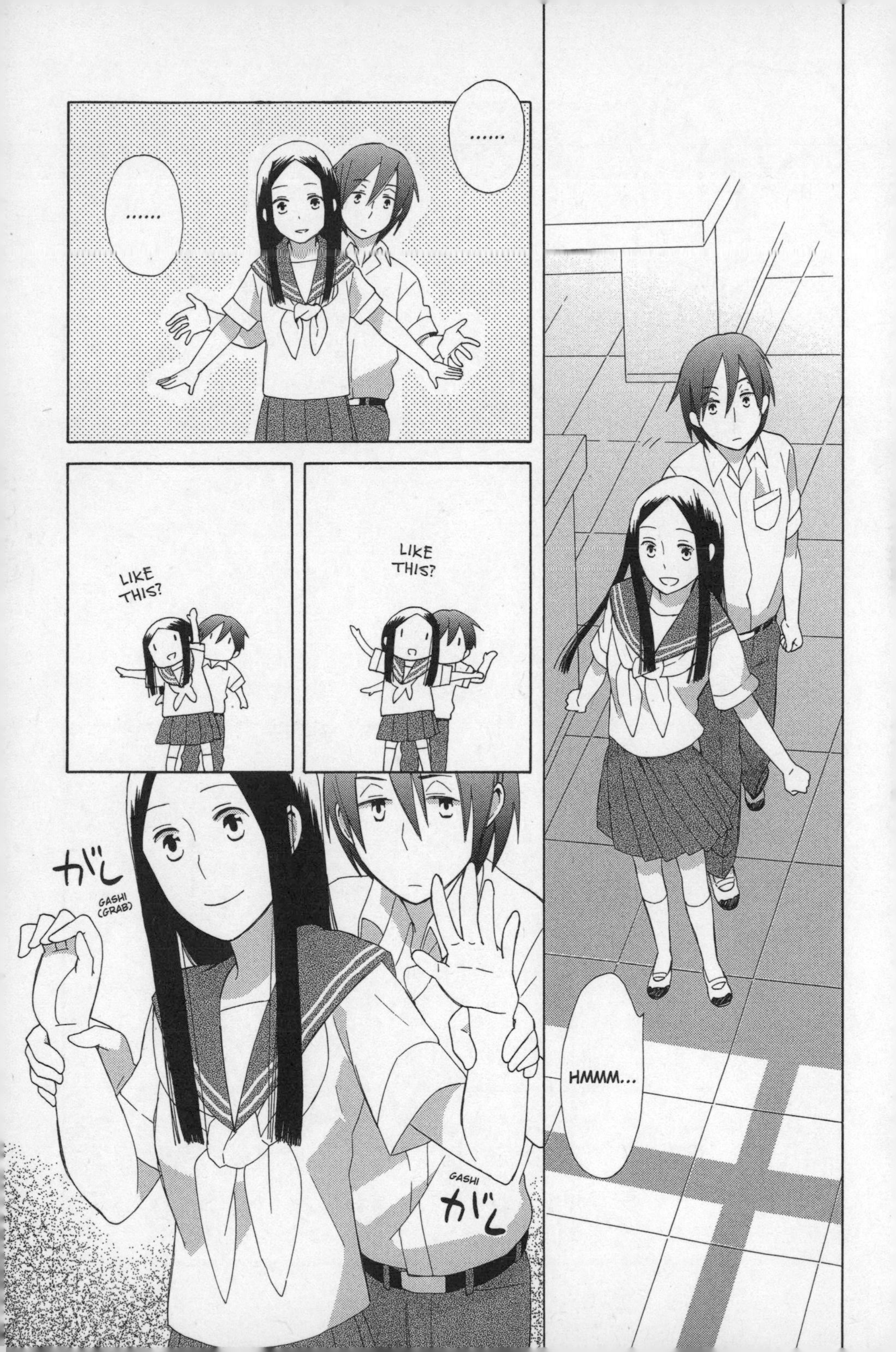
HMMM...
......
......
LIKE THIS?
LIKE THIS?
がし
GASHI (GRAB)
GASHI
がし

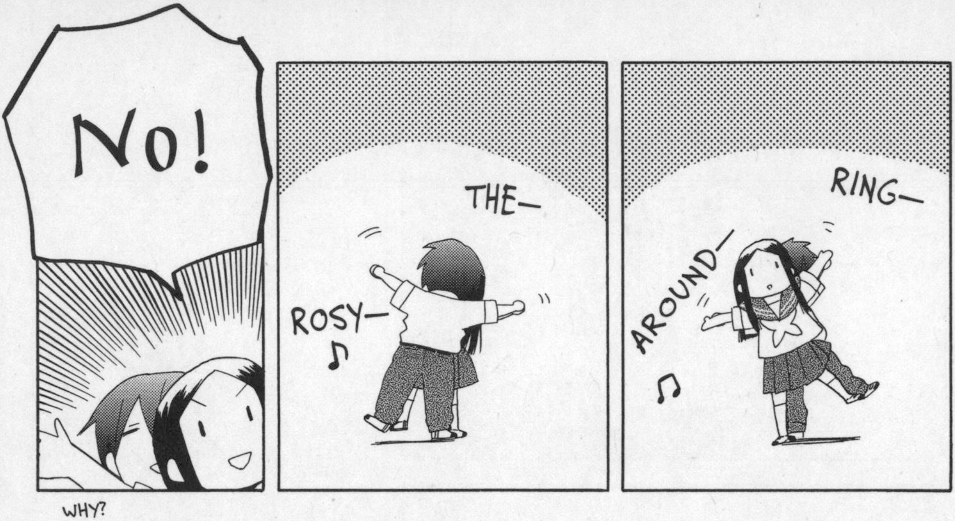
RING—
AROUND—
♪
THE—
ROSY—
♪
No!
WHY?

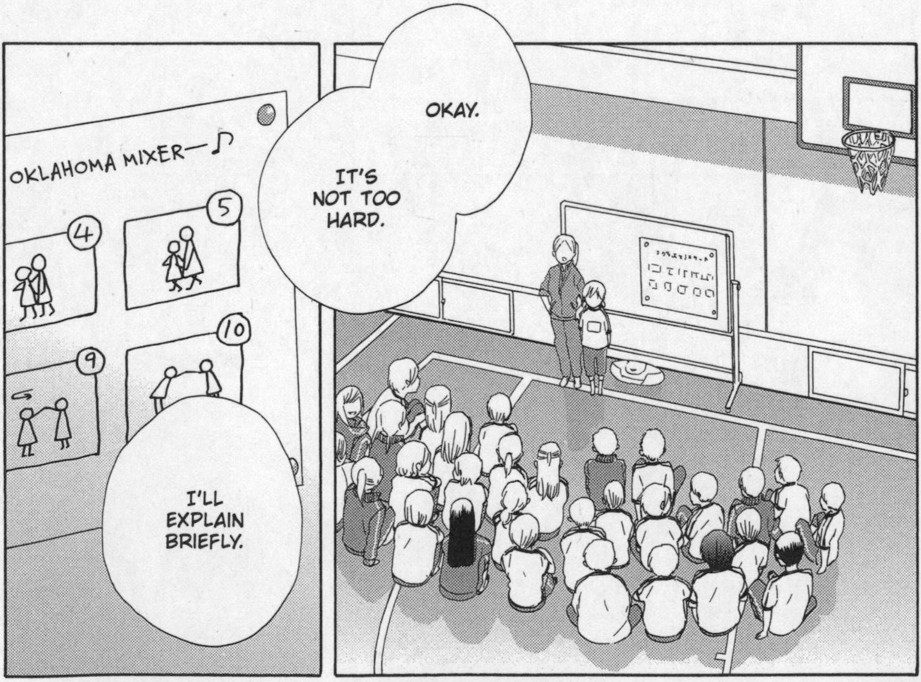
OKAY.
IT'S NOT TOO HARD.
OKLAHOMA MIXER—♪
4
5
9
10
I'LL EXPLAIN BRIEFLY.

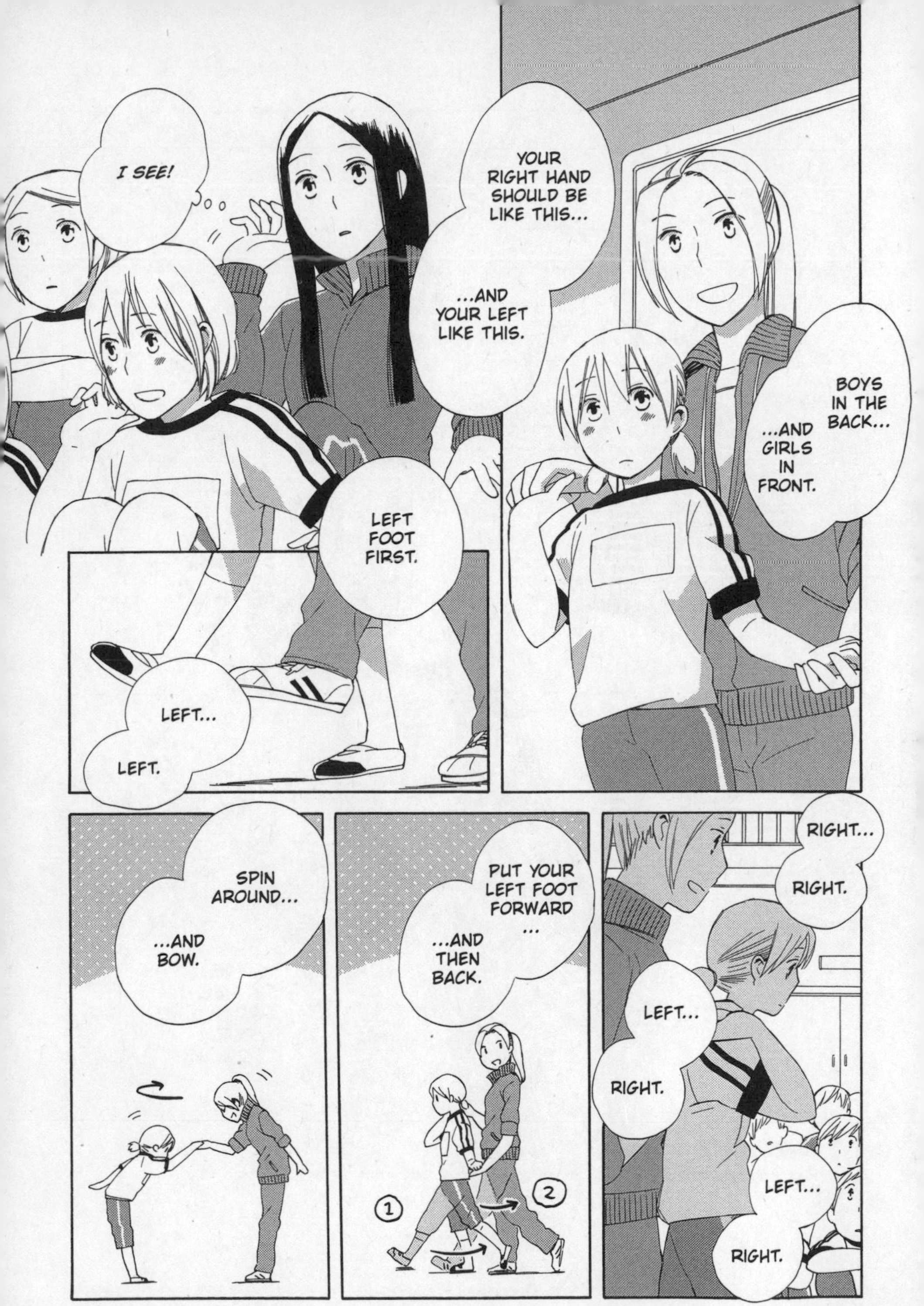
BOYS IN THE BACK...
...AND GIRLS IN FRONT.
YOUR RIGHT HAND SHOULD BE LIKE THIS...
...AND YOUR LEFT LIKE THIS.
I SEE!
LEFT FOOT FIRST.
LEFT...
LEFT.
RIGHT...
RIGHT.
LEFT...
RIGHT.
LEFT...
RIGHT.
PUT YOUR LEFT FOOT FORWARD ...
...AND THEN BACK.
1
2
SPIN AROUND...
...AND BOW.

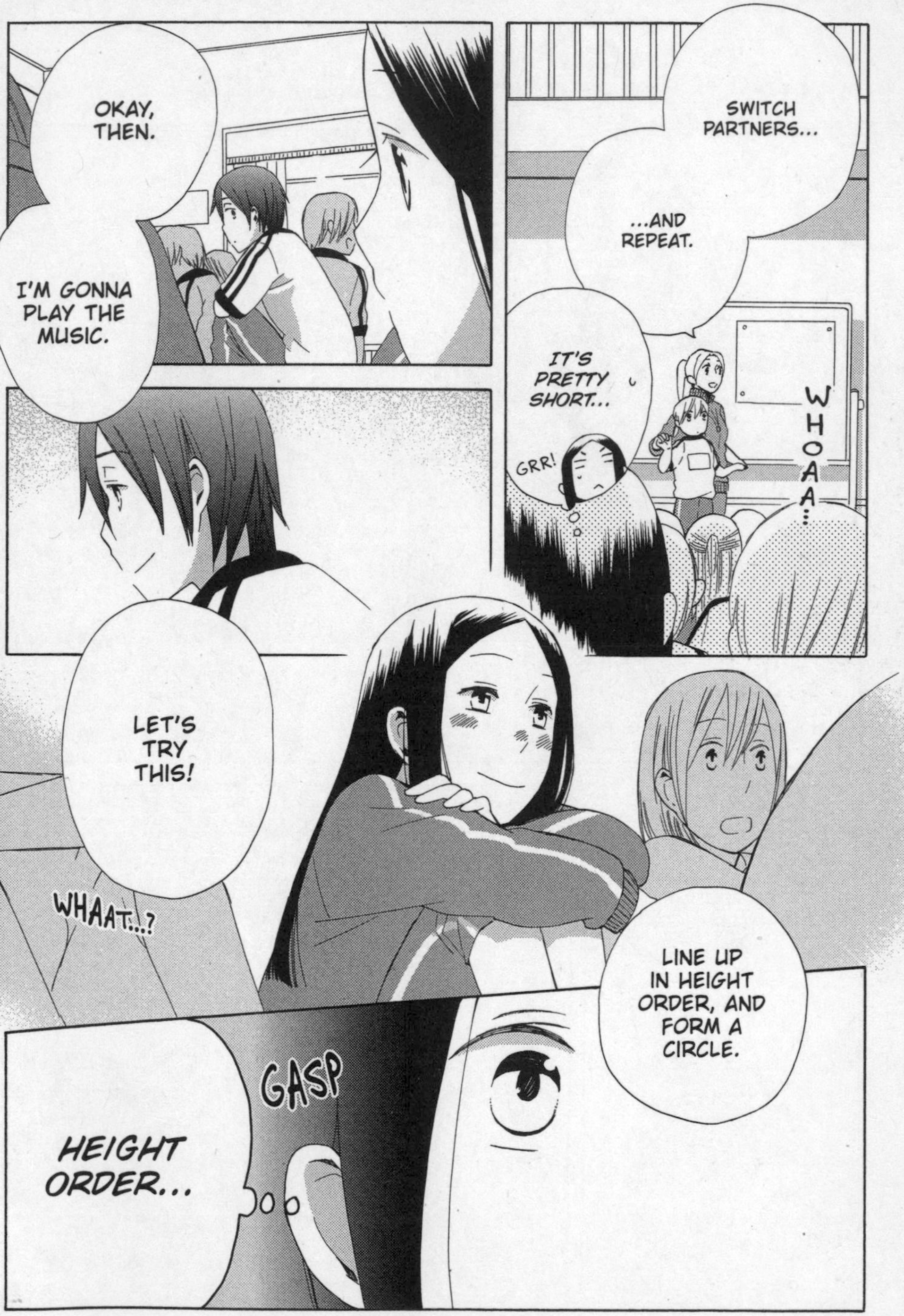

SWITCH PARTNERS...
...AND REPEAT.
IT'S PRETTY SHORT...
GRR!
WHOAA...
OKAY, THEN.
I'M GONNA PLAY THE MUSIC.
LET'S TRY THIS!
LINE UP IN HEIGHT ORDER, AND FORM A CIRCLE.
WHAAT...?
GASP
HEIGHT ORDER...

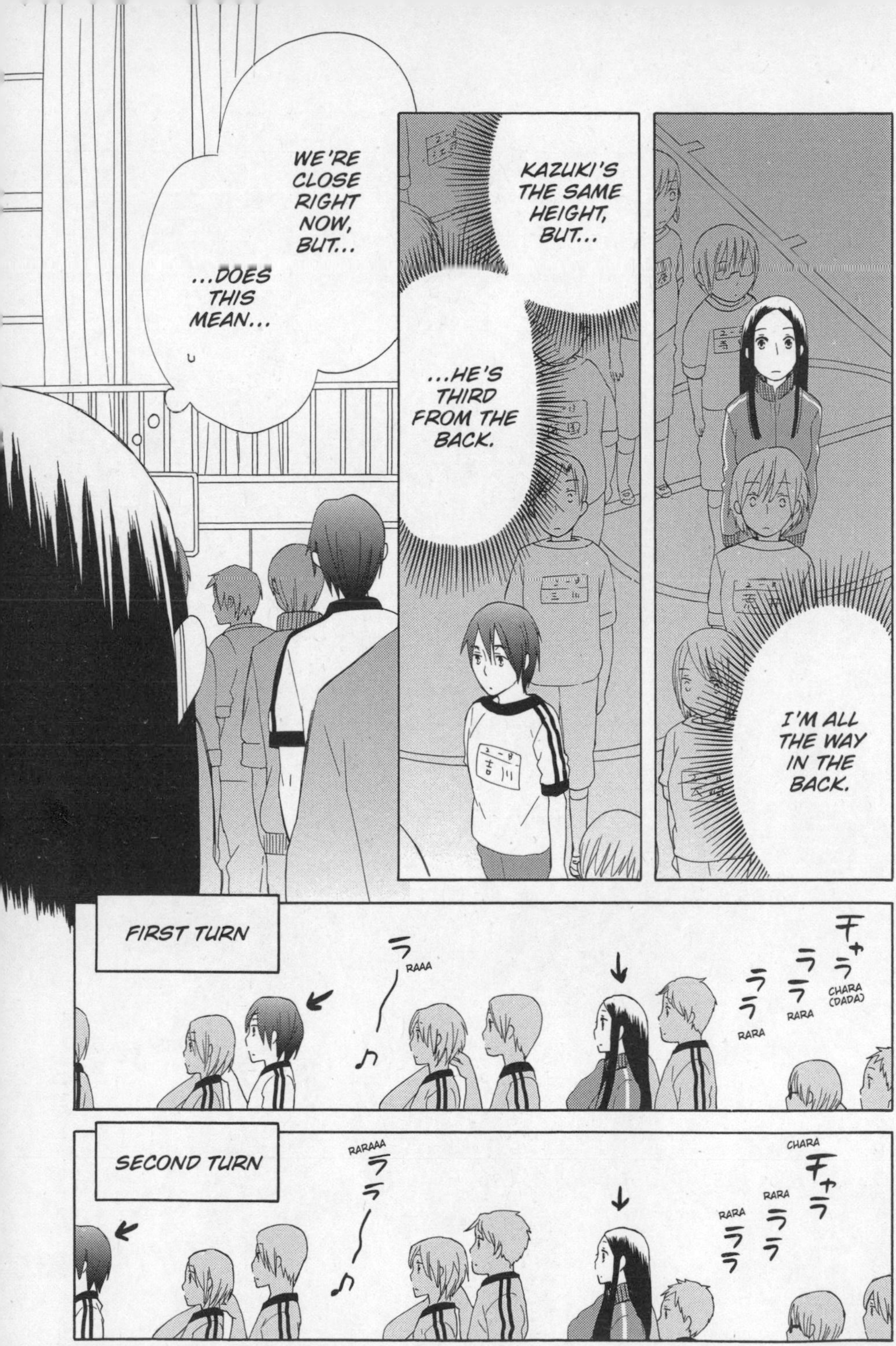
I'M ALL THE WAY IN THE BACK.
KAZUKI'S THE SAME HEIGHT, BUT...
...HE'S THIRD FROM THE BACK.
WE'RE CLOSE RIGHT NOW, BUT...
...DOES THIS MEAN...
FIRST TURN
チャラ
CHARA (DADA)
ララ
RARA
ララ
RARA
ラ
RAAA
SECOND TURN
チャラ
CHARA
ララ
RARA
ララ
RARA
ララ
RARAAA

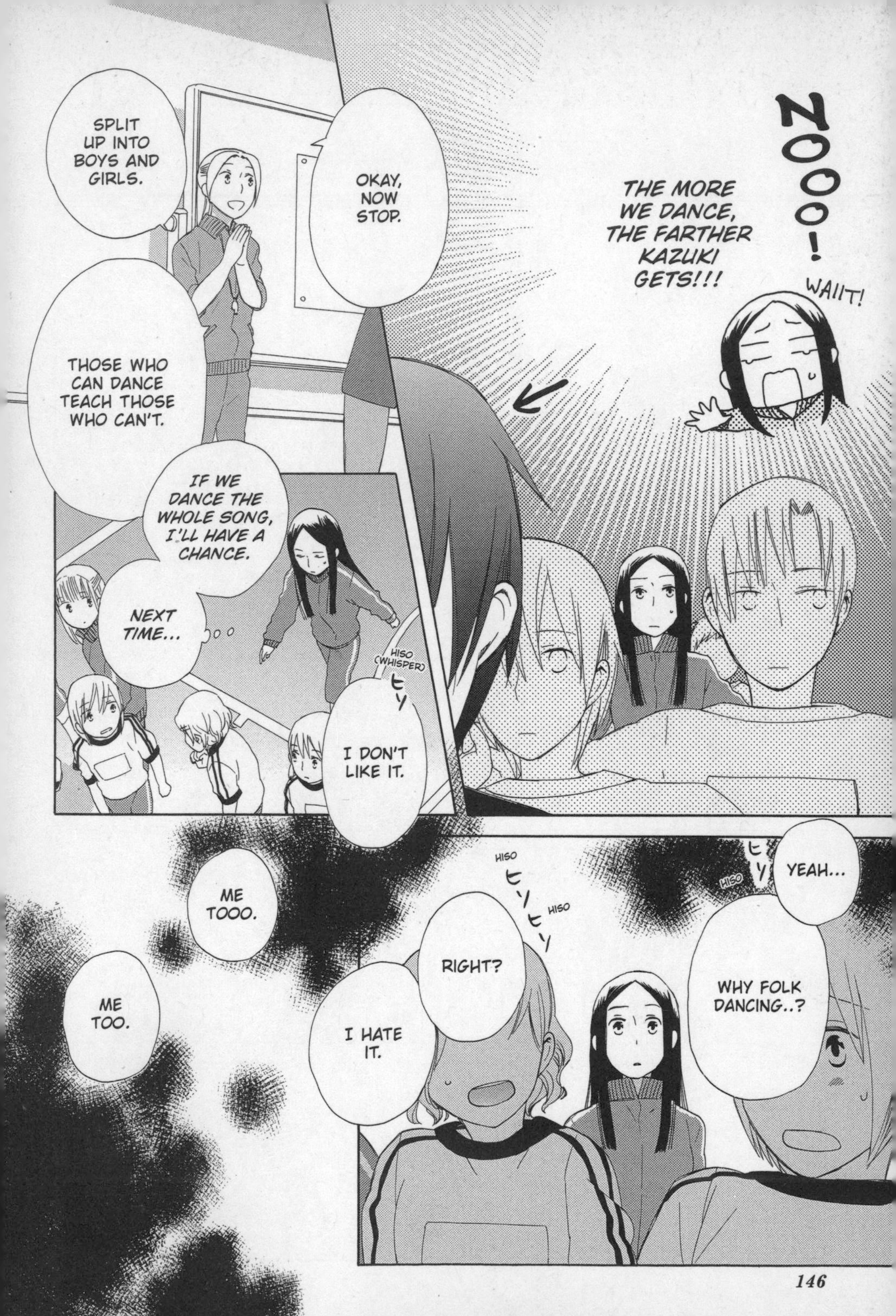
NOOO!
THE MORE WE DANCE, THE FARTHER KAZUKI GETS!!!
WAIIT!
OKAY, NOW STOP.
SPLIT UP INTO BOYS AND GIRLS.
THOSE WHO CAN DANCE TEACH THOSE WHO CAN'T.
HISO (WHISPER)
ヒソ
I DON'T LIKE IT.
IF WE DANCE THE WHOLE SONG, I'LL HAVE A CHANCE.
NEXT TIME...
ヒソ
HISO
YEAH...
WHY FOLK DANCING..?
HISO
ヒソヒソ
HISO
RIGHT?
I HATE IT.
ME TOOO.
ME TOO.

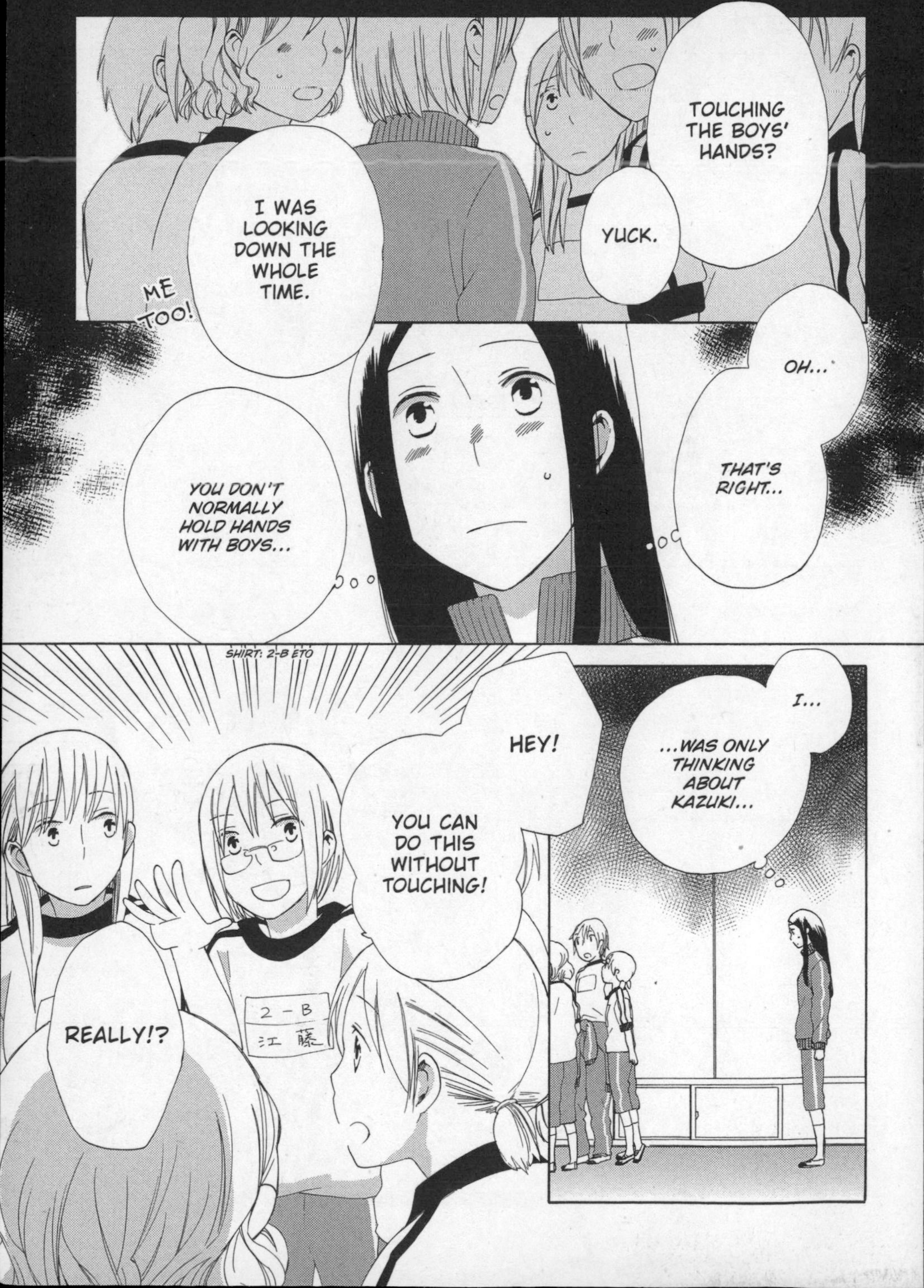
TOUCHING THE BOYS' HANDS?
YUCK.
I WAS LOOKING DOWN THE WHOLE TIME.
ME TOO!
OH...
THAT'S RIGHT...
YOU DON'T NORMALLY HOLD HANDS WITH BOYS...
I...
...WAS ONLY THINKING ABOUT KAZUKI...
HEY!
YOU CAN DO THIS WITHOUT TOUCHING!
SHIRT: 2-B ETO
2-B 江藤
REALLY!?

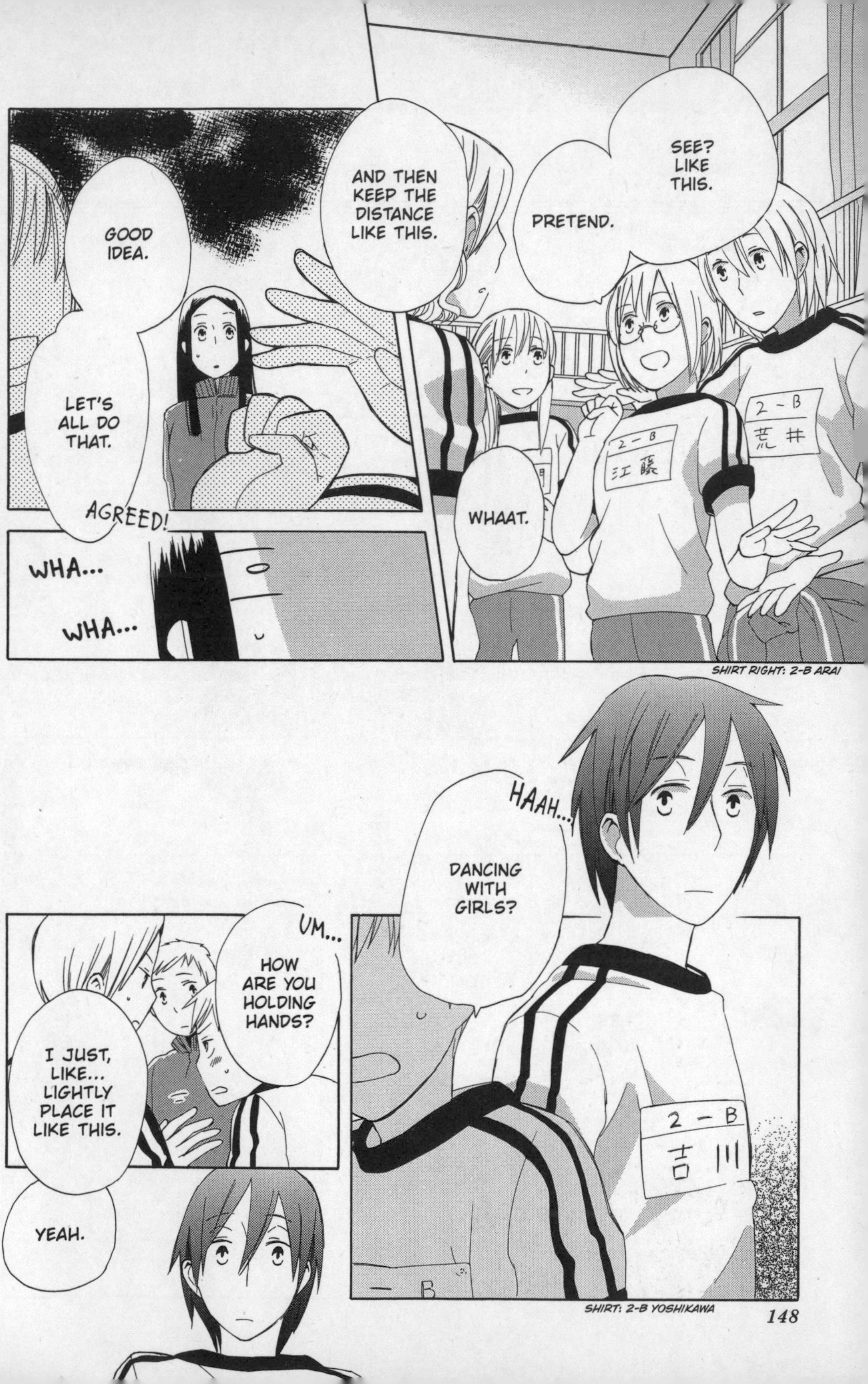
SEE? LIKE THIS.
PRETEND.
AND THEN KEEP THE DISTANCE LIKE THIS.
2-B 荒井
2-B 江藤
WHAAT.
GOOD IDEA.
LET'S ALL DO THAT.
AGREED!
WHA...
WHA...
HAAH...
DANCING WITH GIRLS?
2-B 吉川
UM...
HOW ARE YOU HOLDING HANDS?
I JUST, LIKE... LIGHTLY PLACE IT LIKE THIS.
YEAH.

SHIRT RIGHT: 2-B ARAI

SHIRT: 2-B YOSHIKAWA

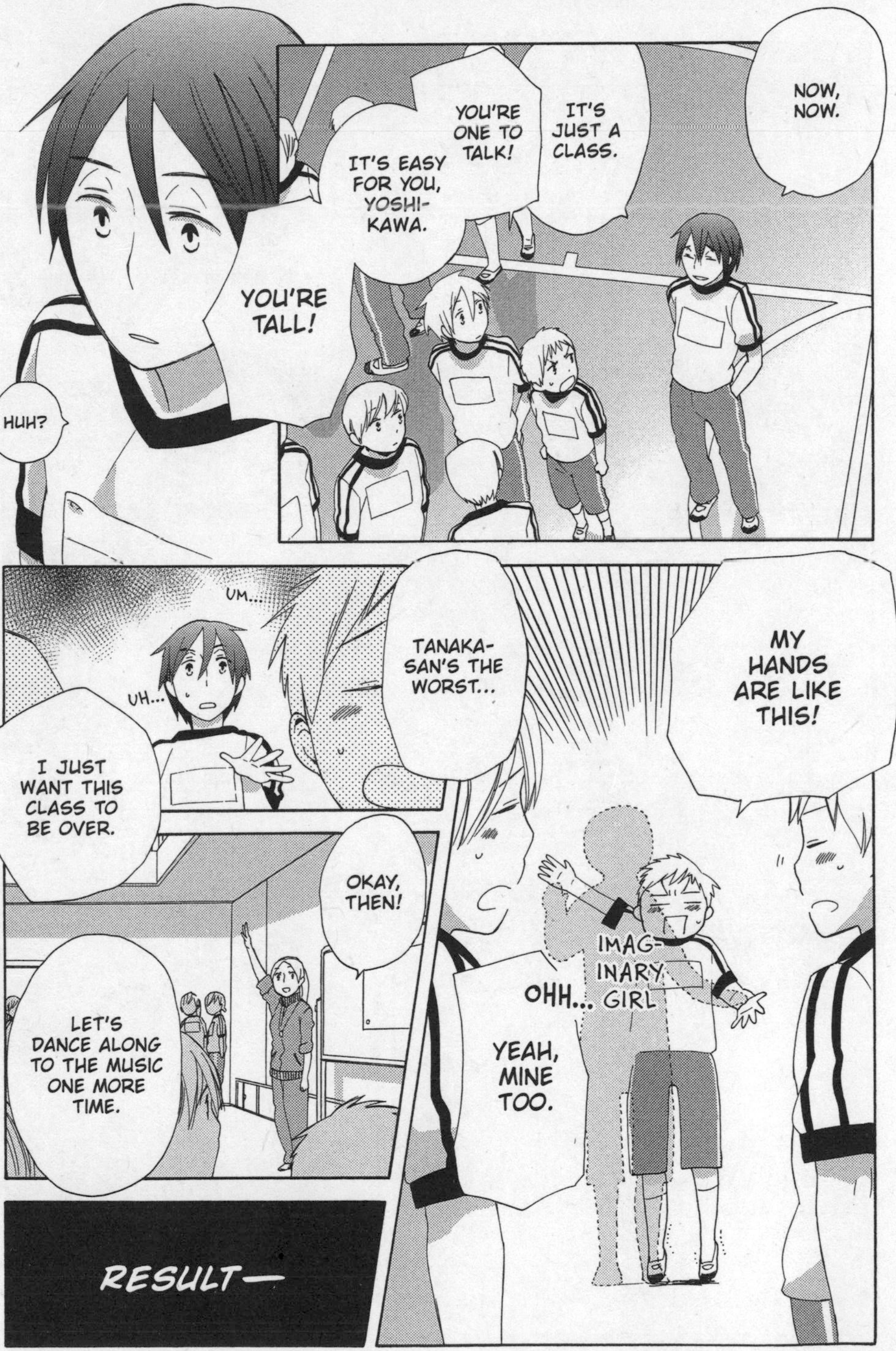
NOW, NOW.
IT'S JUST A CLASS.
YOU'RE ONE TO TALK!
IT'S EASY FOR YOU, YOSHIKAWA.
YOU'RE TALL!
HUH?
MY HANDS ARE LIKE THIS!
TANAKA-SAN'S THE WORST...
IMAGINARY GIRL
OHH...
YEAH, MINE TOO.
UM...
UH...
I JUST WANT THIS CLASS TO BE OVER.
OKAY, THEN!
LET'S DANCE ALONG TO THE MUSIC ONE MORE TIME.
RESULT—

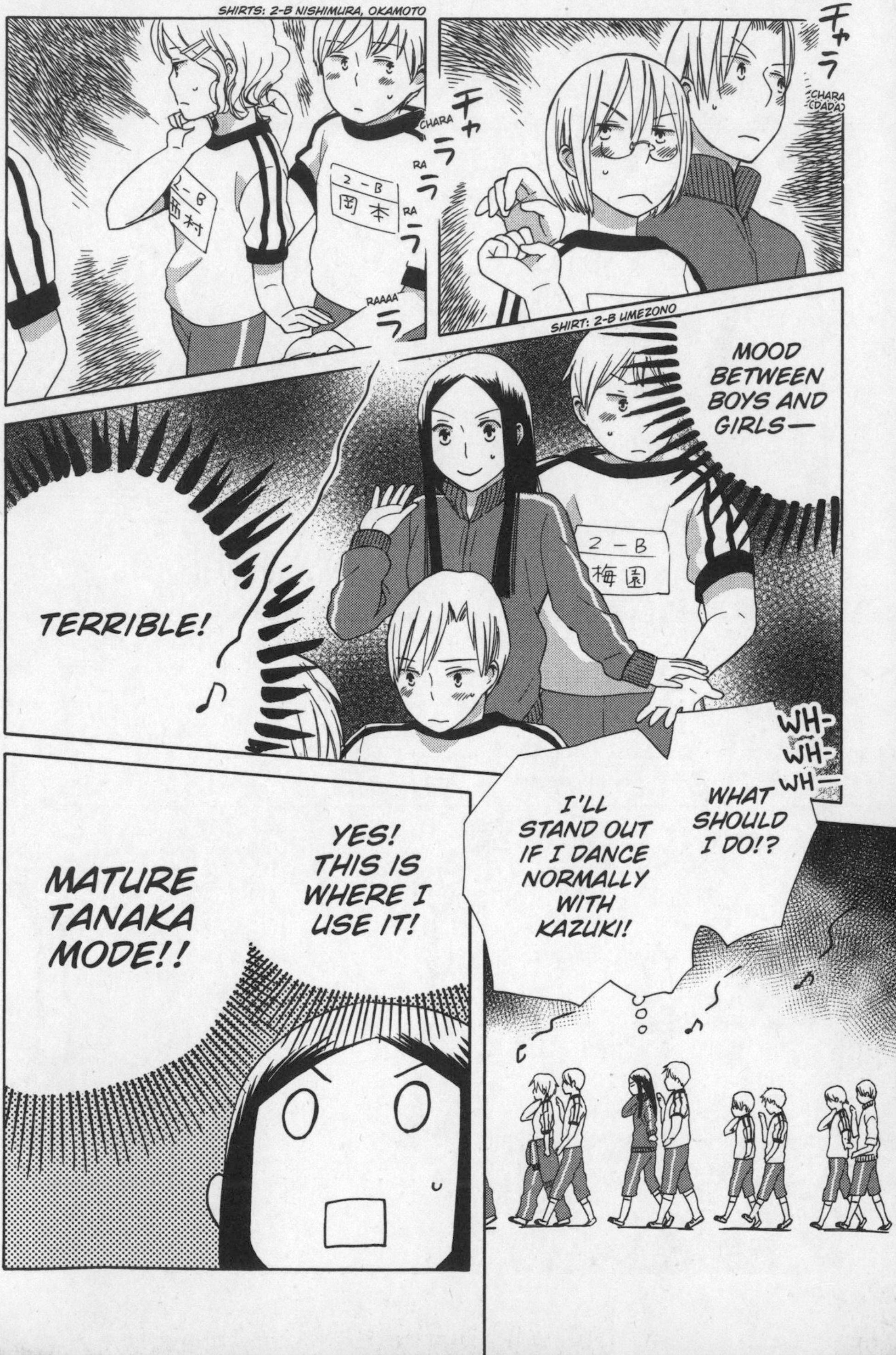
チャラ
CHARA (DADA)
SHIRTS: 2-B NISHIMURA, OKAMOTO
2-B 西村
2-B 岡本
チャララララ
CHARA RA RA RAAAA
SHIRT: 2-B UMEZONO
MOOD BETWEEN BOYS AND GIRLS—
2-B 梅園
TERRIBLE!
WH- WH- WH—
WHAT SHOULD I DO!?
I'LL STAND OUT IF I DANCE NORMALLY WITH KAZUKI!
YES! THIS IS WHERE I USE IT!
MATURE TANAKA MODE!!

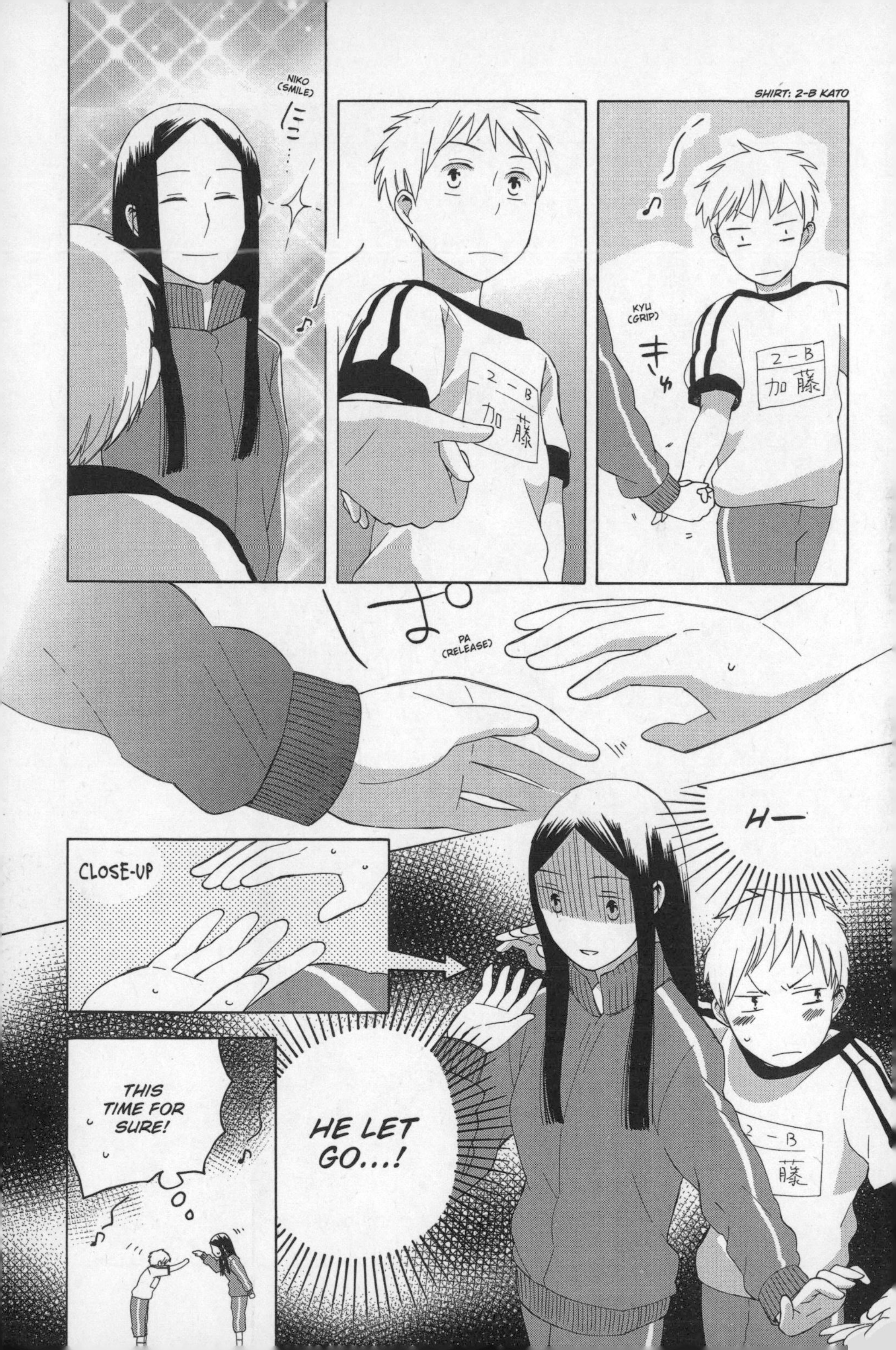
SHIRT: 2-B KATO
KYU (GRIP)
きゅ
2-B
加藤
2-B
加藤
NIKO (SMILE)
に…
ぱ
PA (RELEASE)
H—
2-B
藤
HE LET GO...!
CLOSE-UP
THIS TIME FOR SURE!

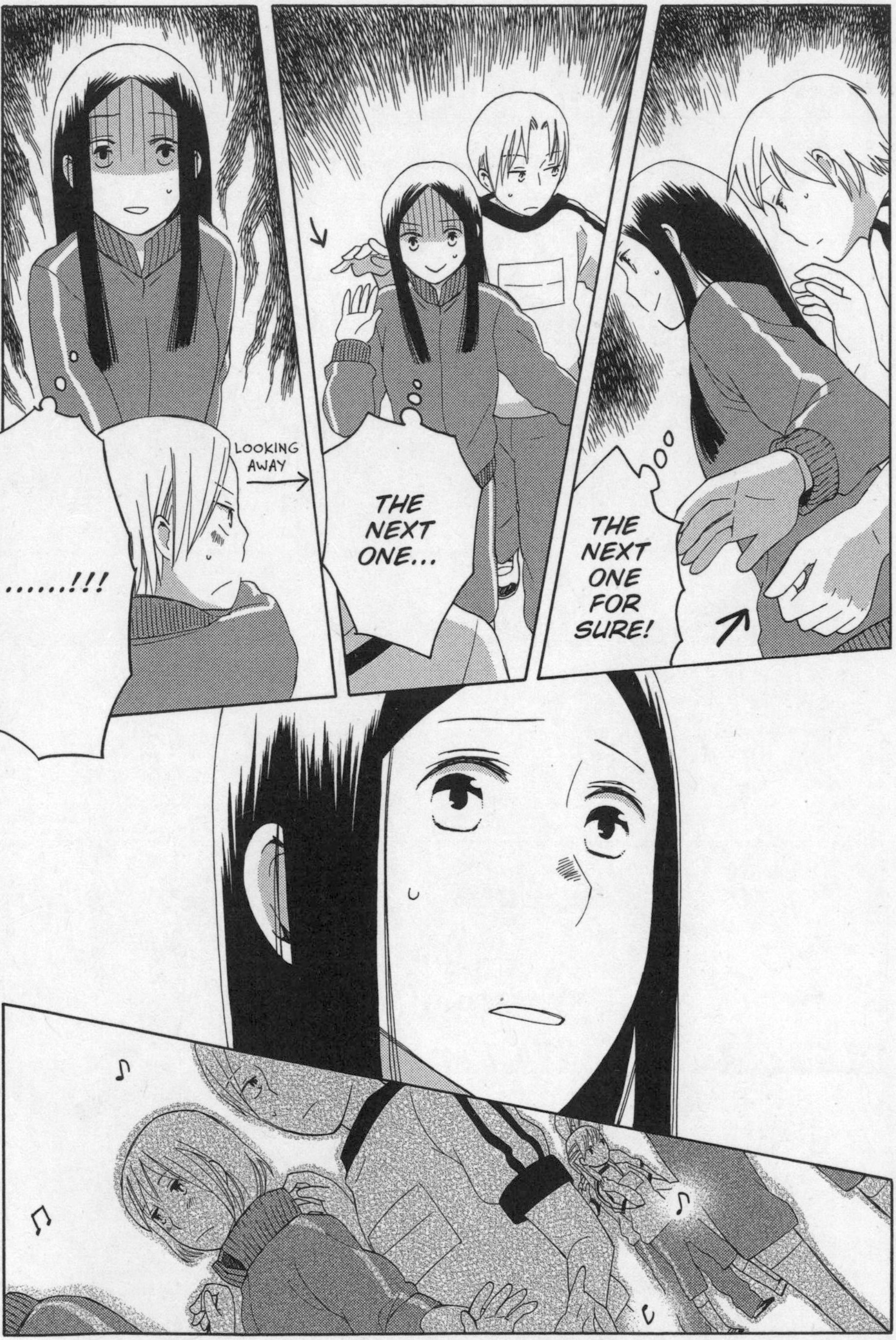
THE NEXT ONE FOR SURE!
THE NEXT ONE...
LOOKING AWAY
......!!!

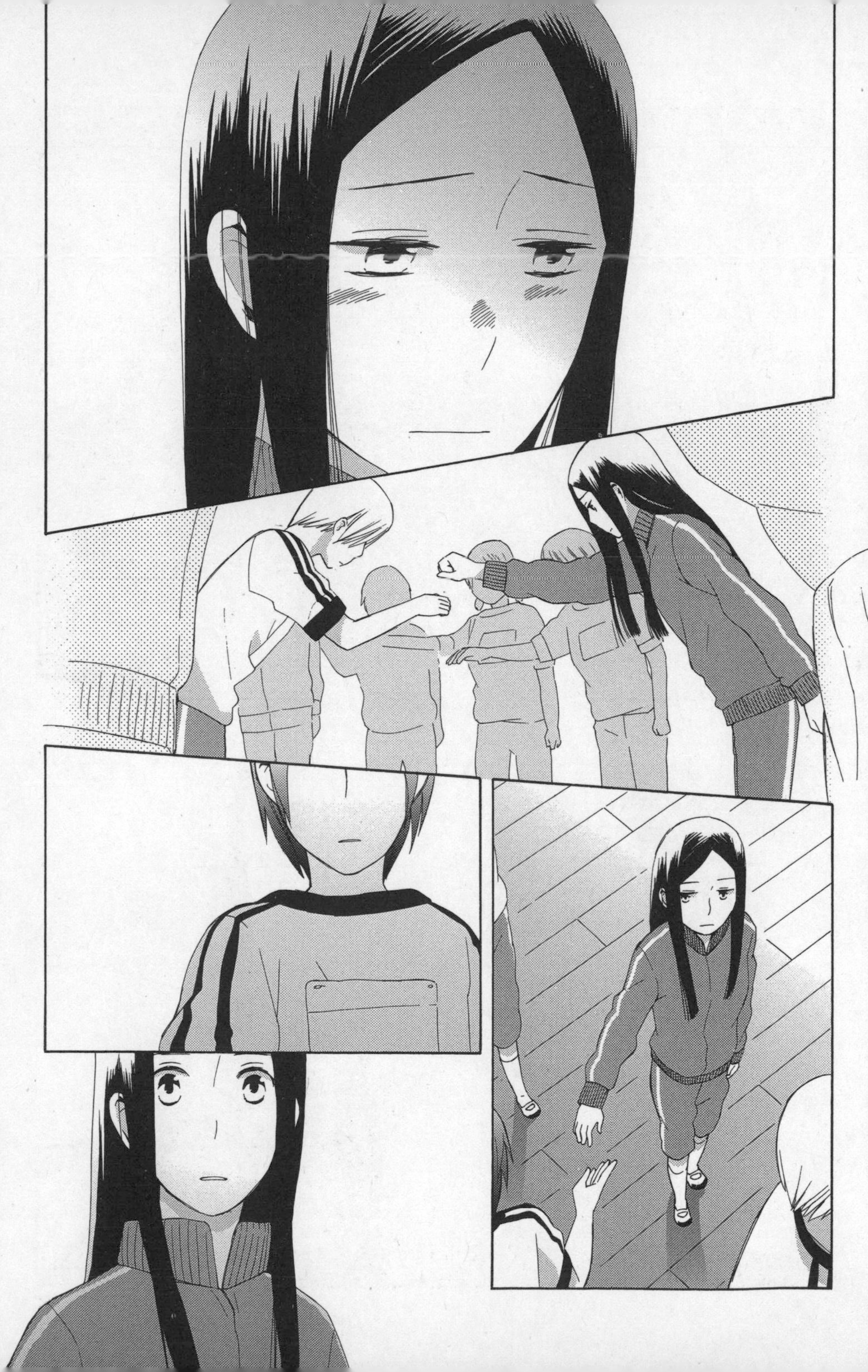

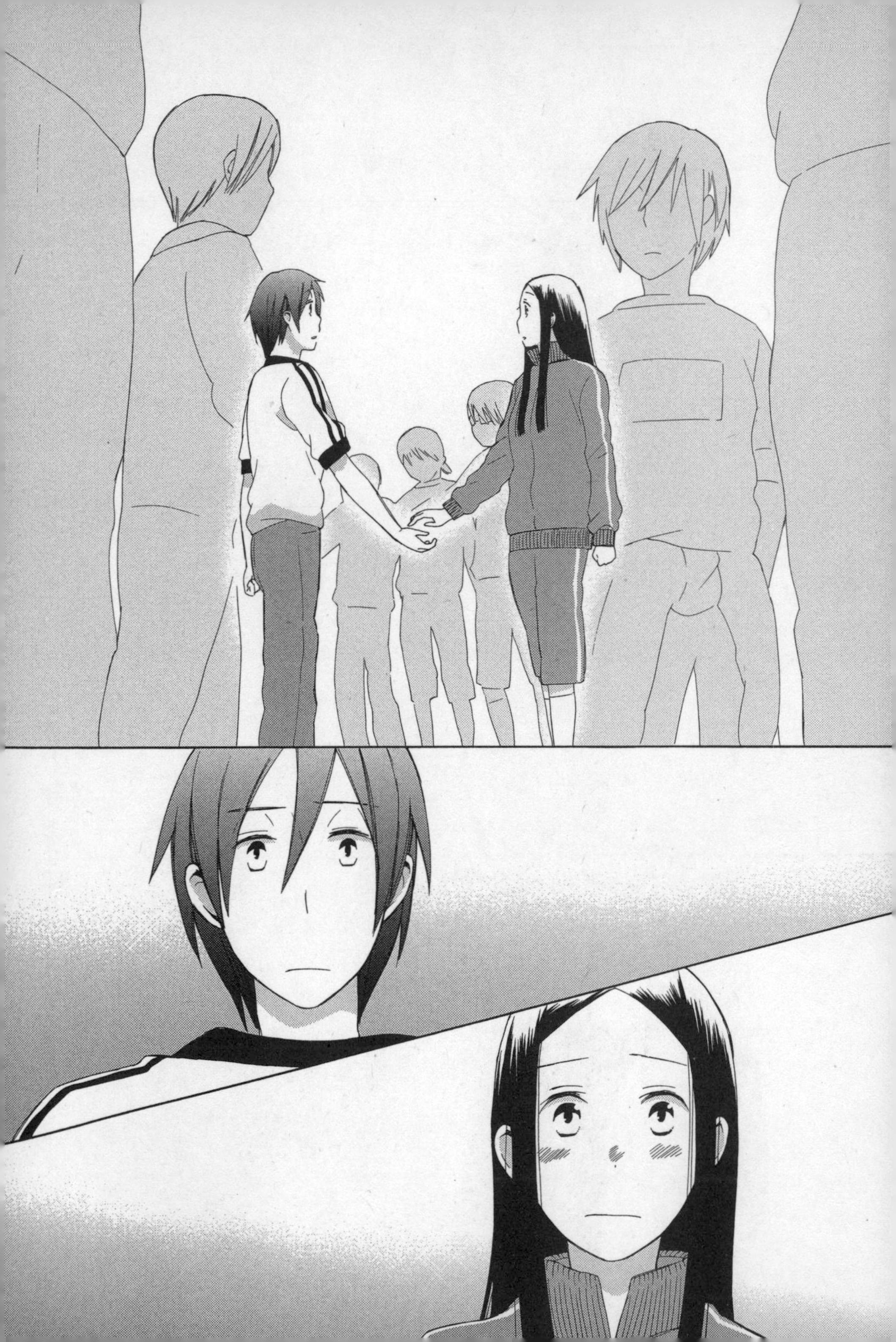

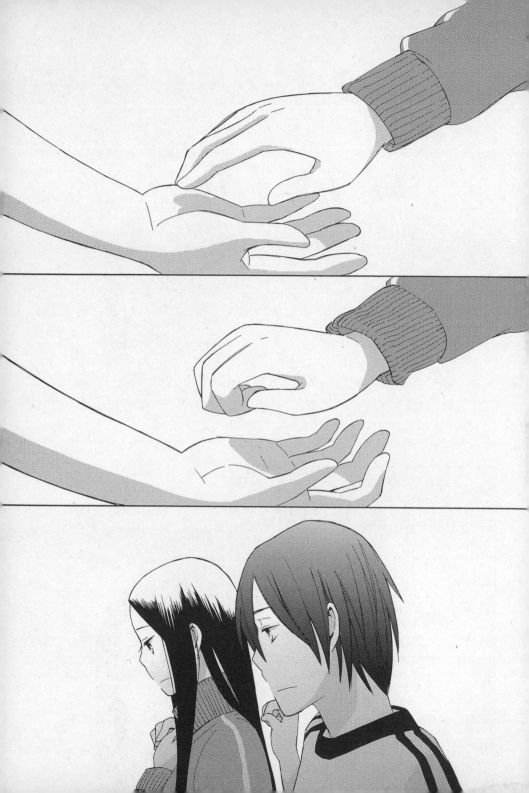

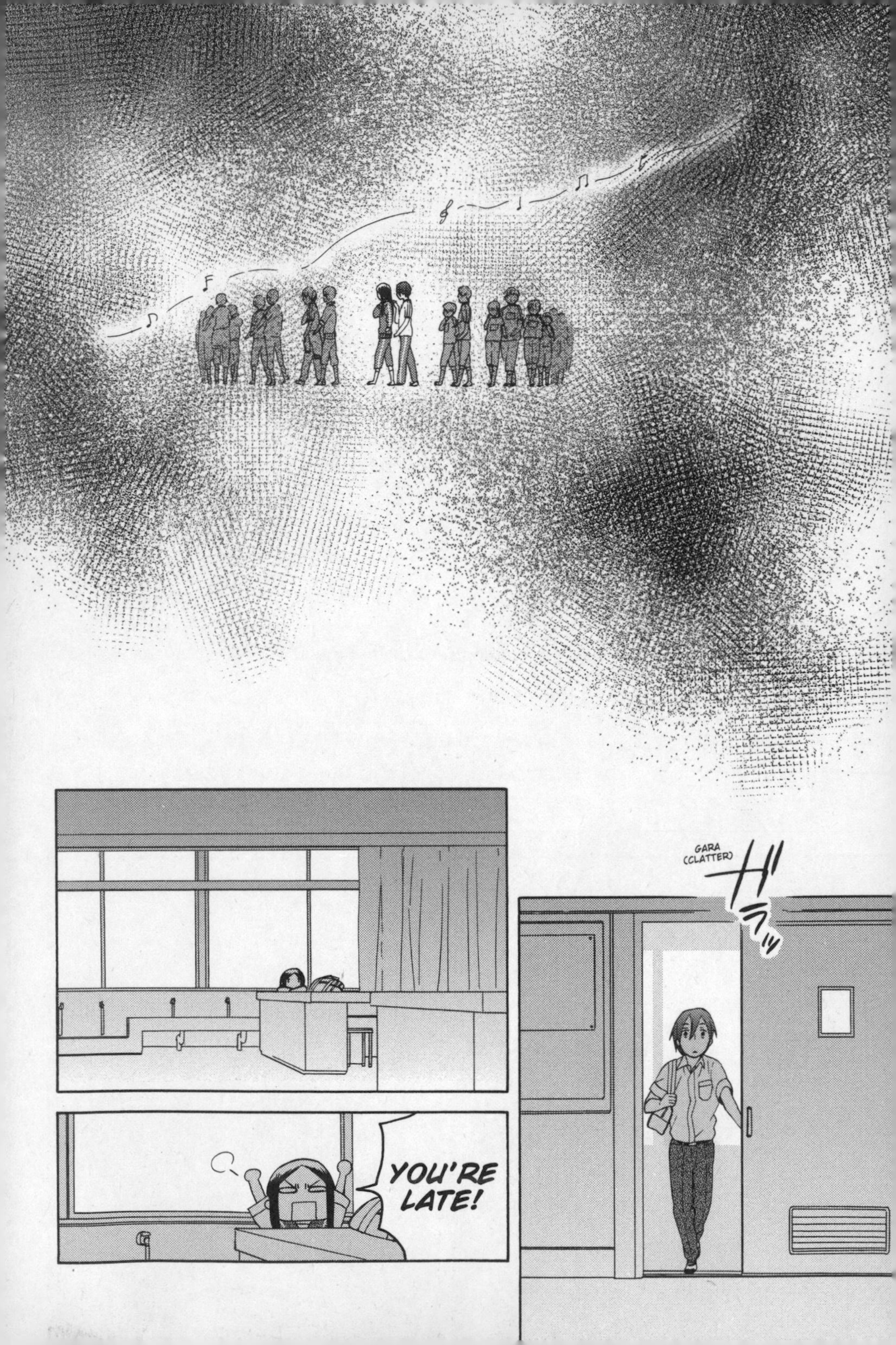
GARA (CLATTER)
YOU'RE LATE!

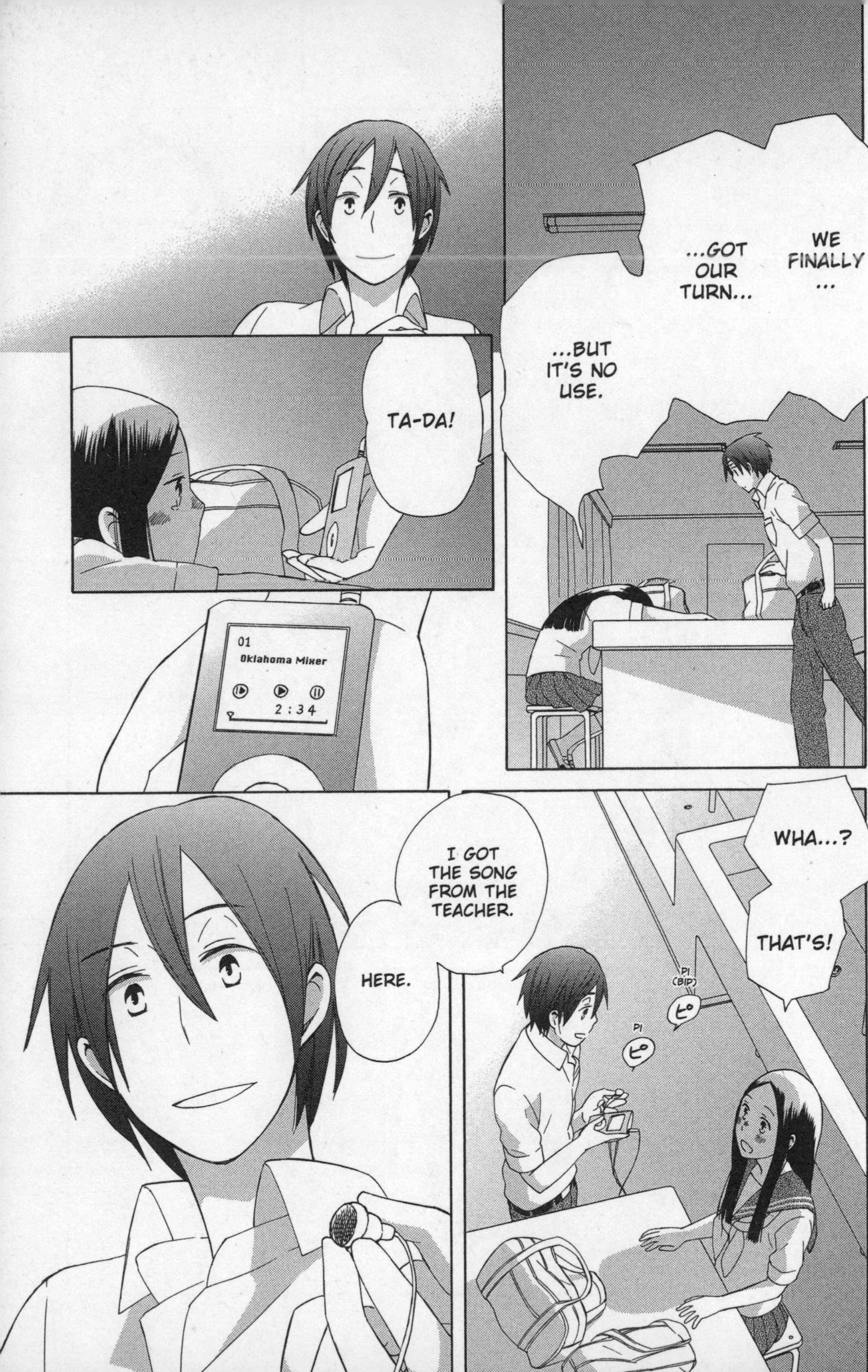
WE FINALLY ...
...GOT OUR TURN...
...BUT IT'S NO USE.
TA-DA!
01
Oklahoma Mixer
2:34
WHA...?
THAT'S!
PI (BIP) ピ
PI ピ
I GOT THE SONG FROM THE TEACHER.
HERE.

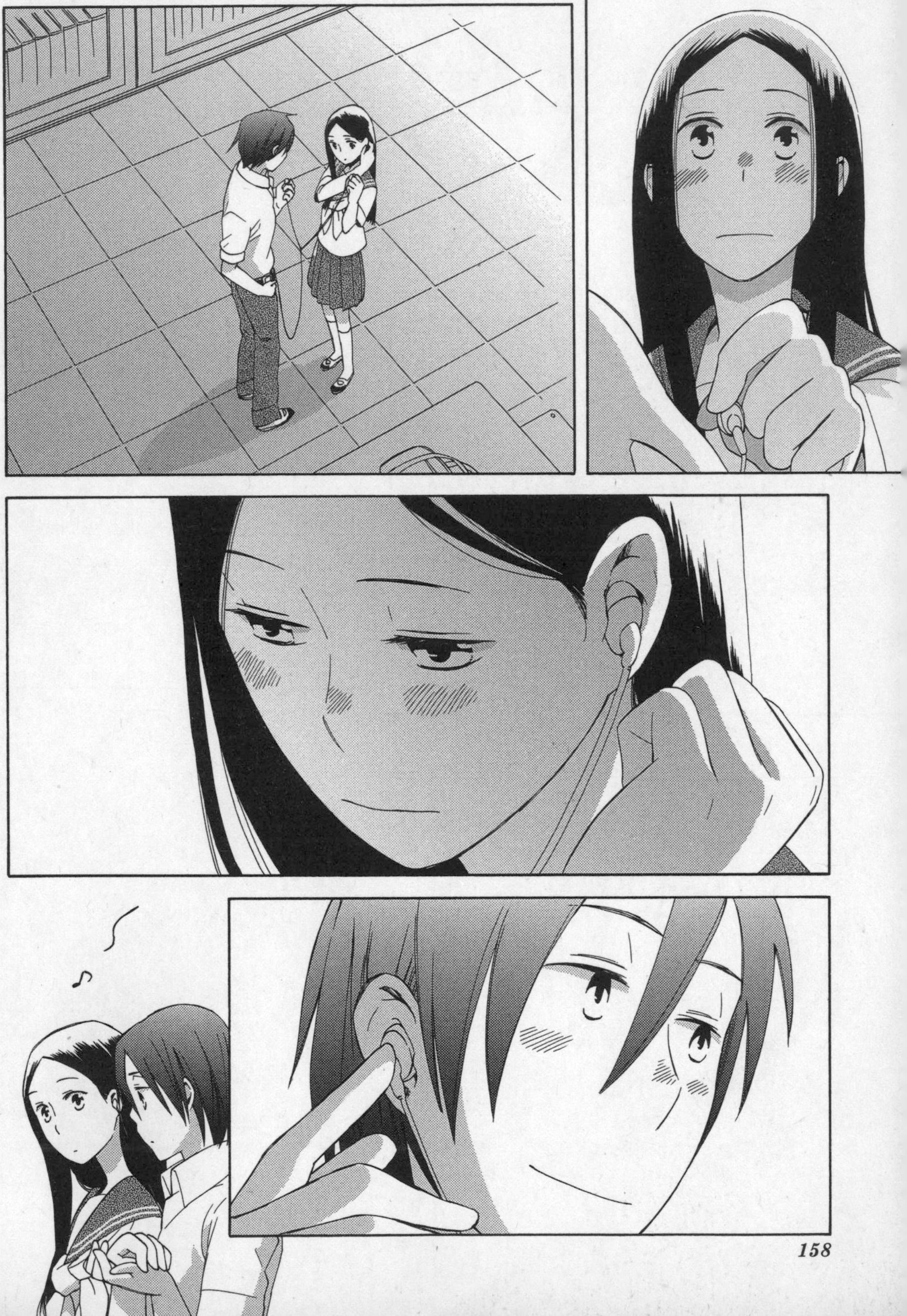

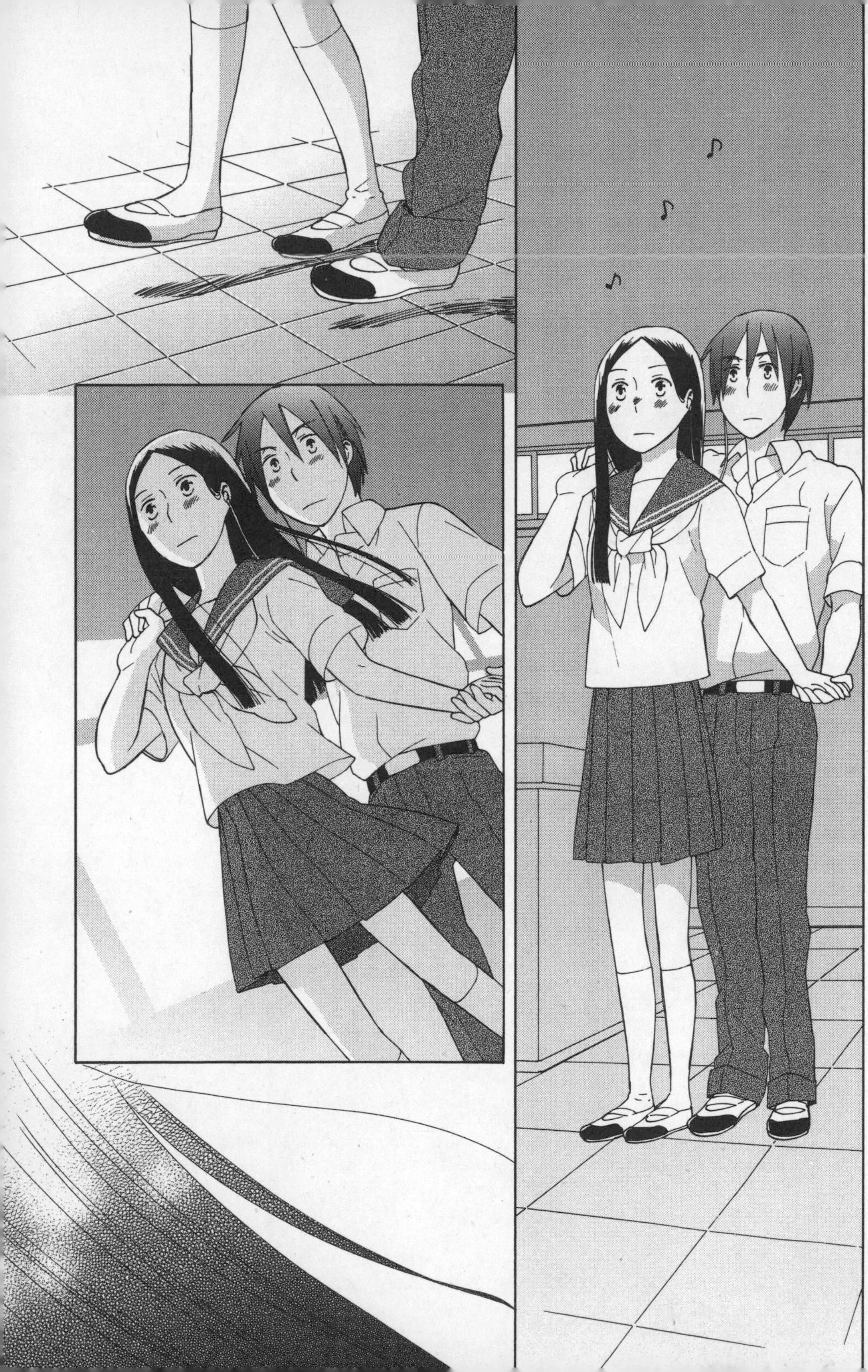

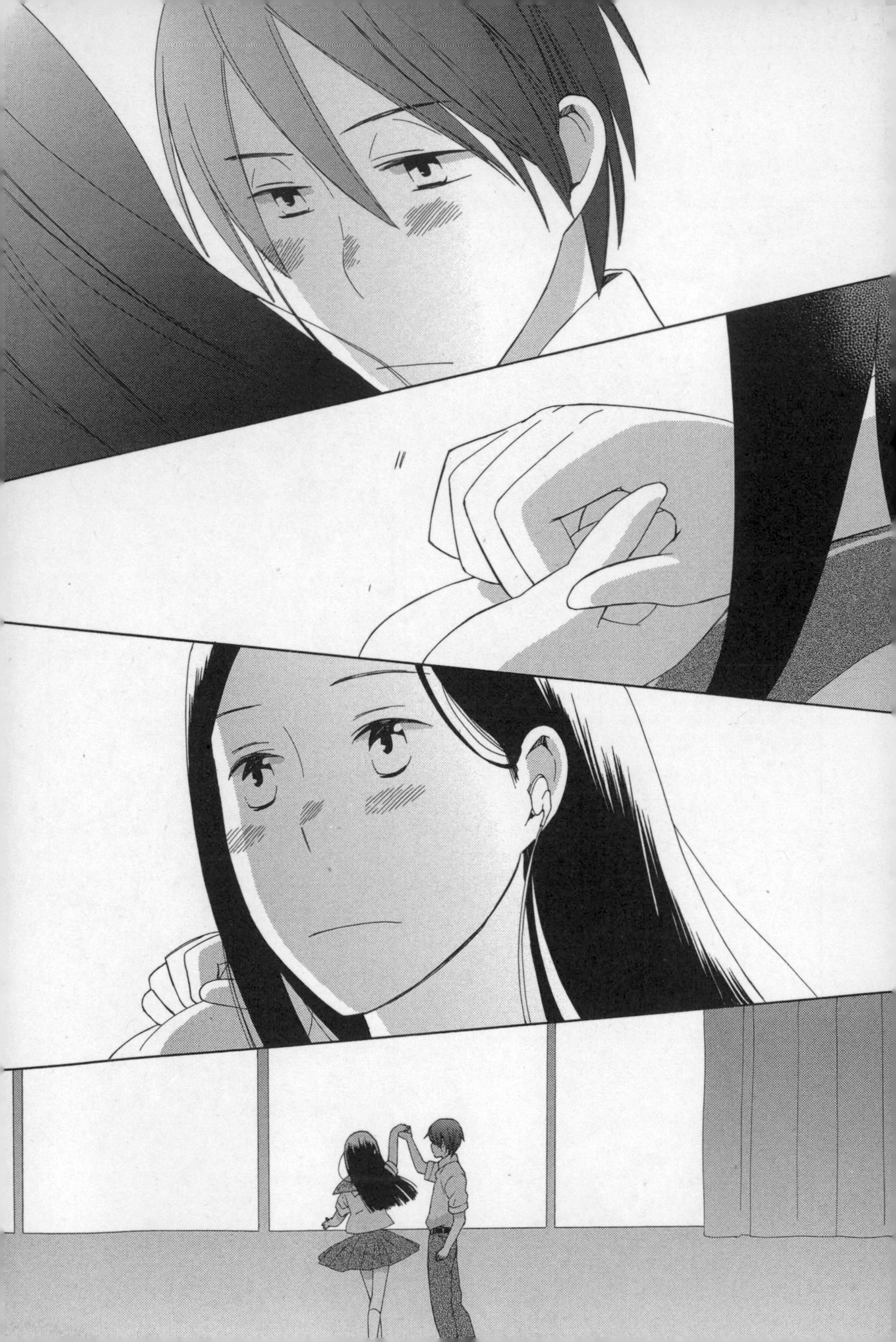

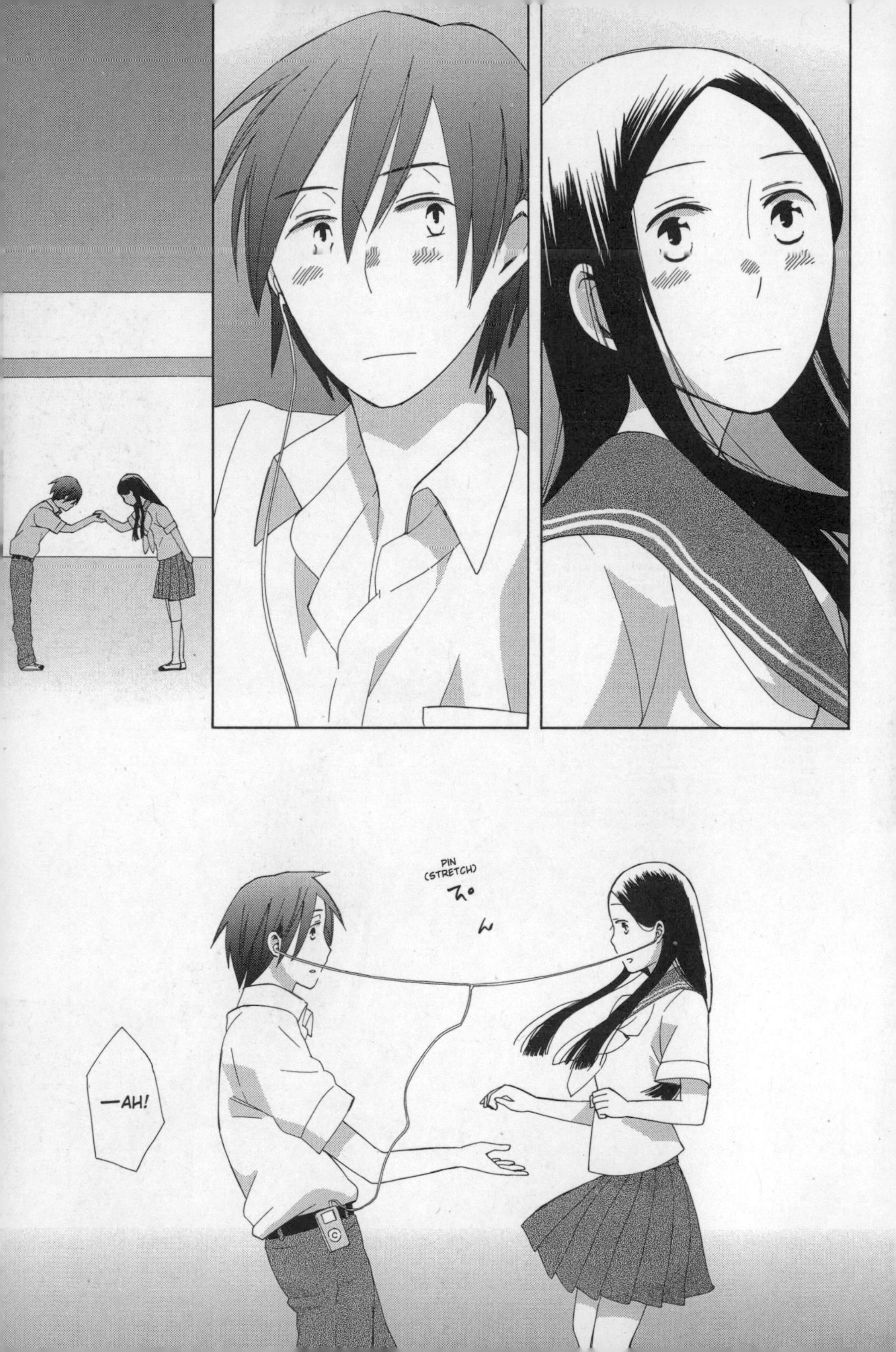
PIN (STRETCH)
—AH!

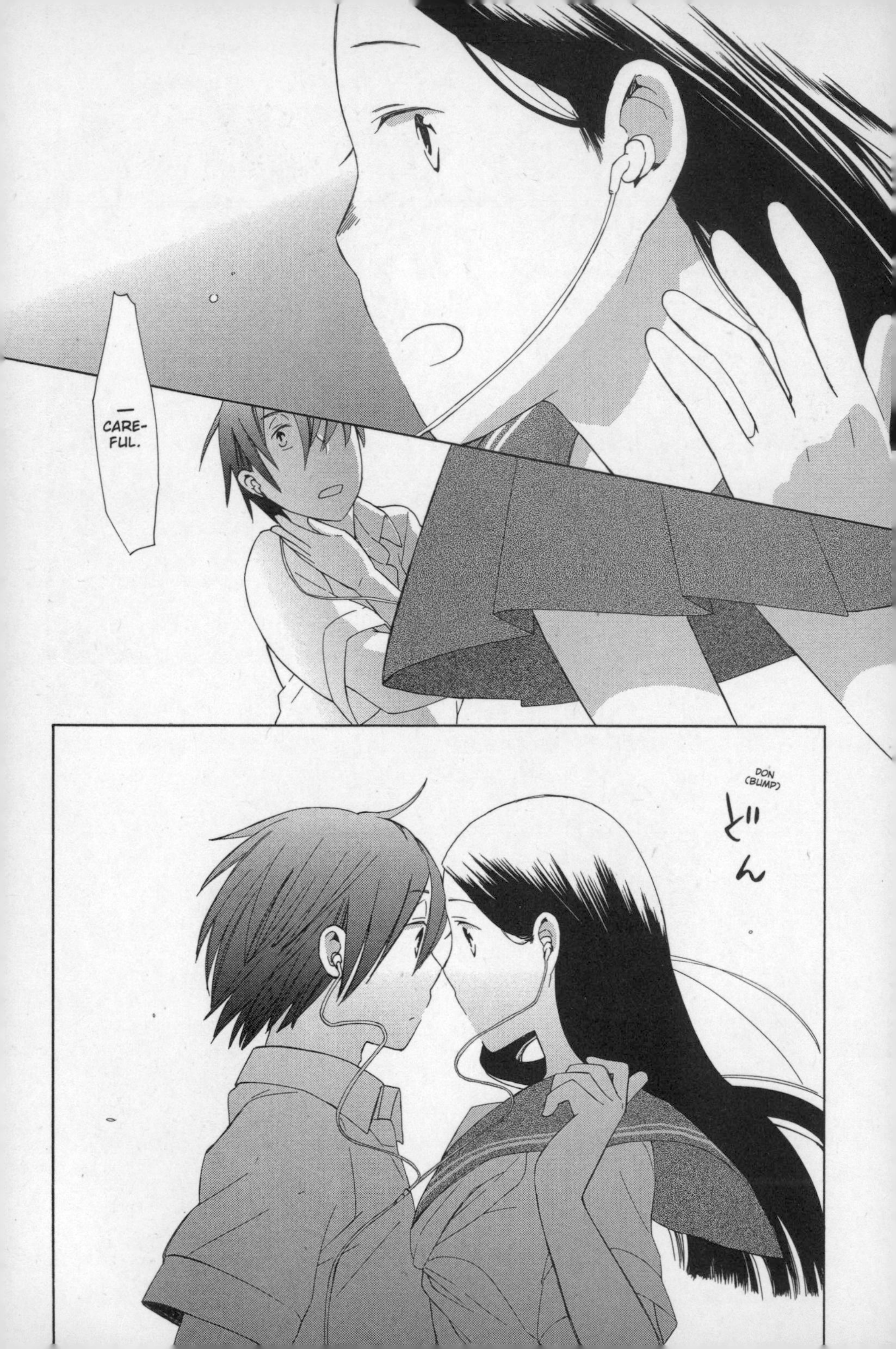
—CAREFUL.
DON (BUMP)
どん

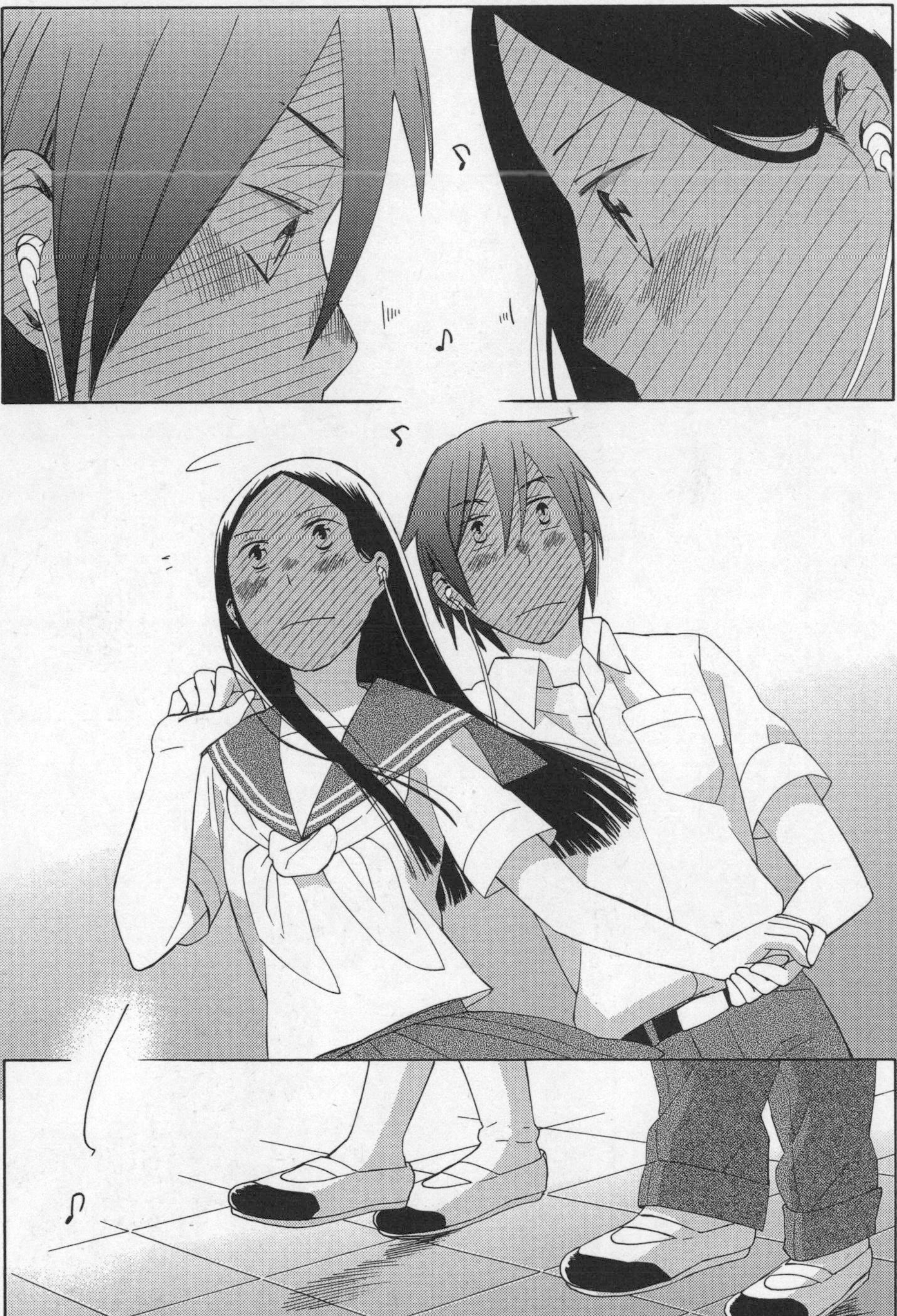

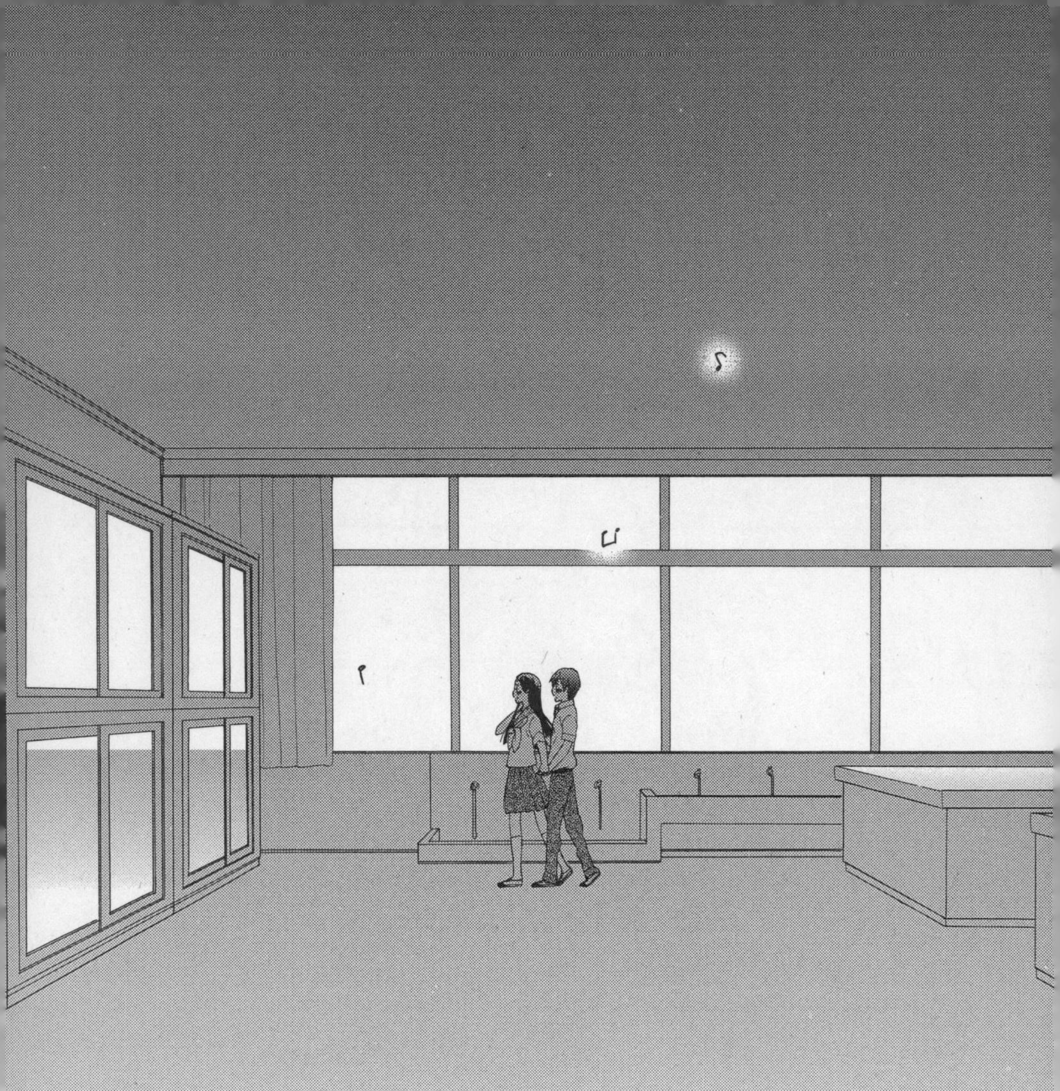

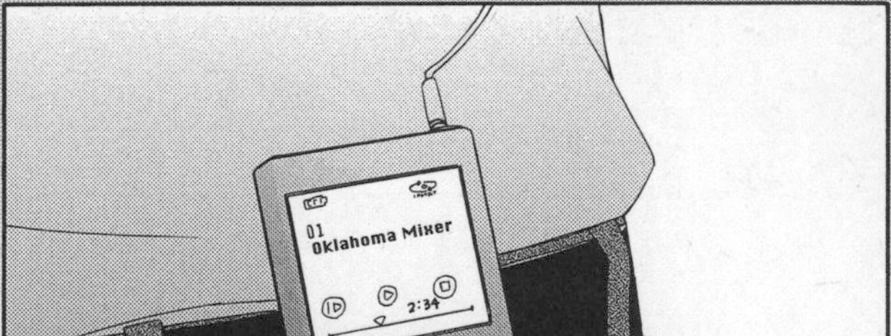
01
Oklahoma Mixer
2:34

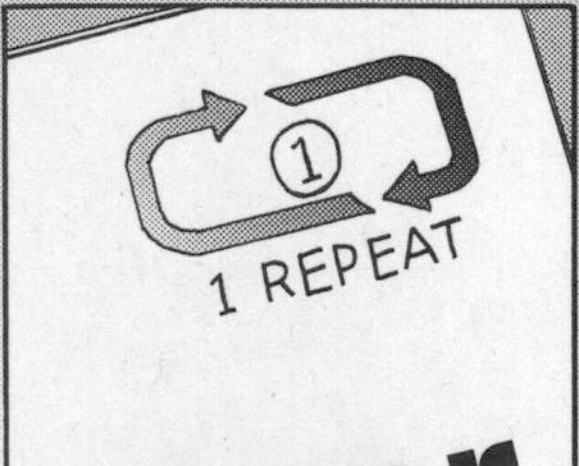
1
1 REPEAT
Mixer

Fin

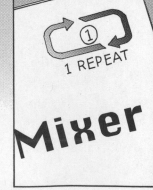

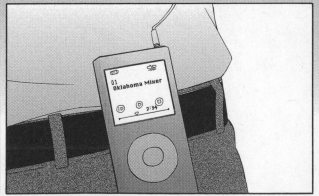

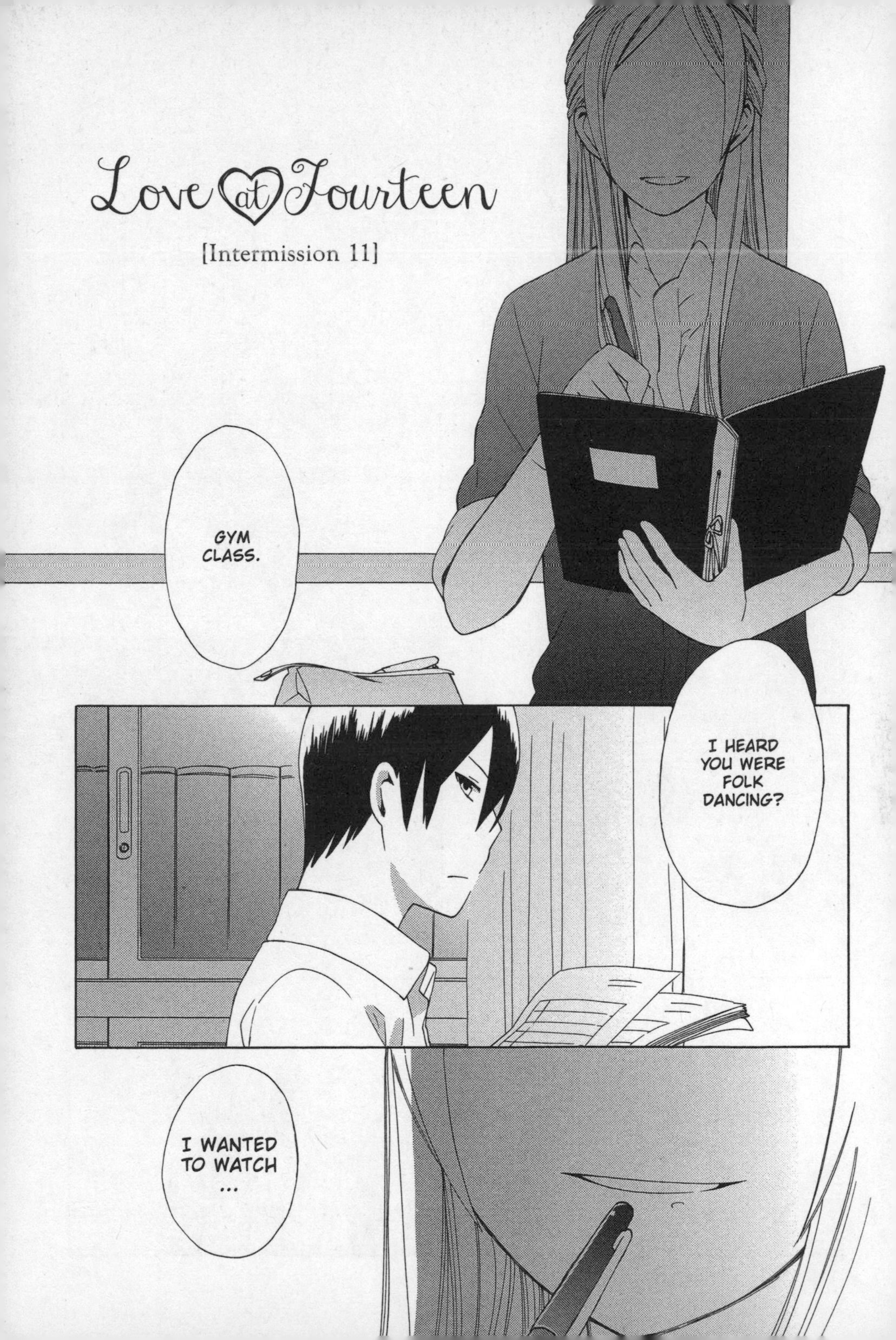
Love at Fourteen
[Intermission 11]
GYM CLASS.
I HEARD YOU WERE FOLK DANCING?
I WANTED TO WATCH ...

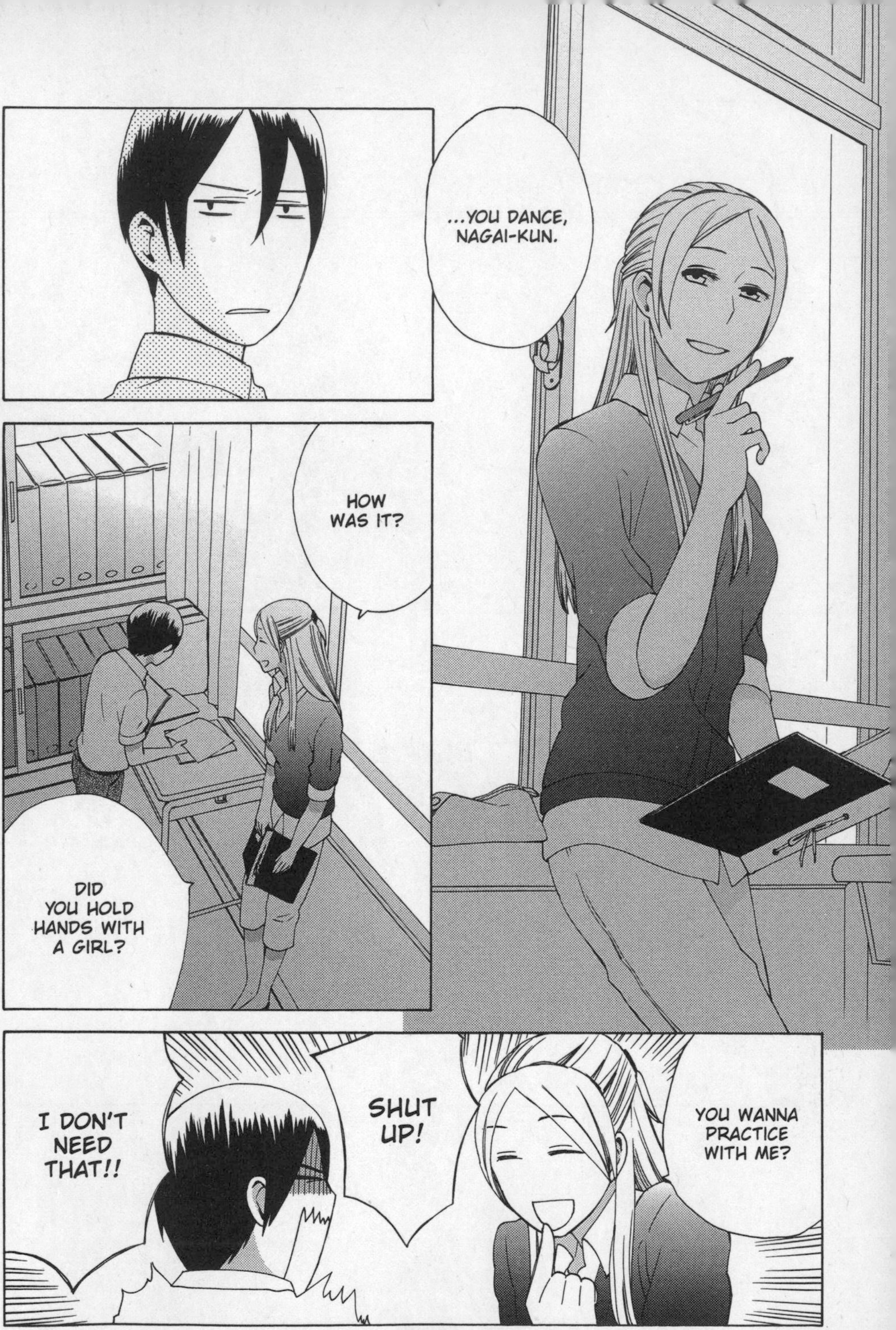
...YOU DANCE, NAGAI-KUN.
HOW WAS IT?
DID YOU HOLD HANDS WITH A GIRL?
YOU WANNA PRACTICE WITH ME?
SHUT UP!
I DON'T NEED THAT!!

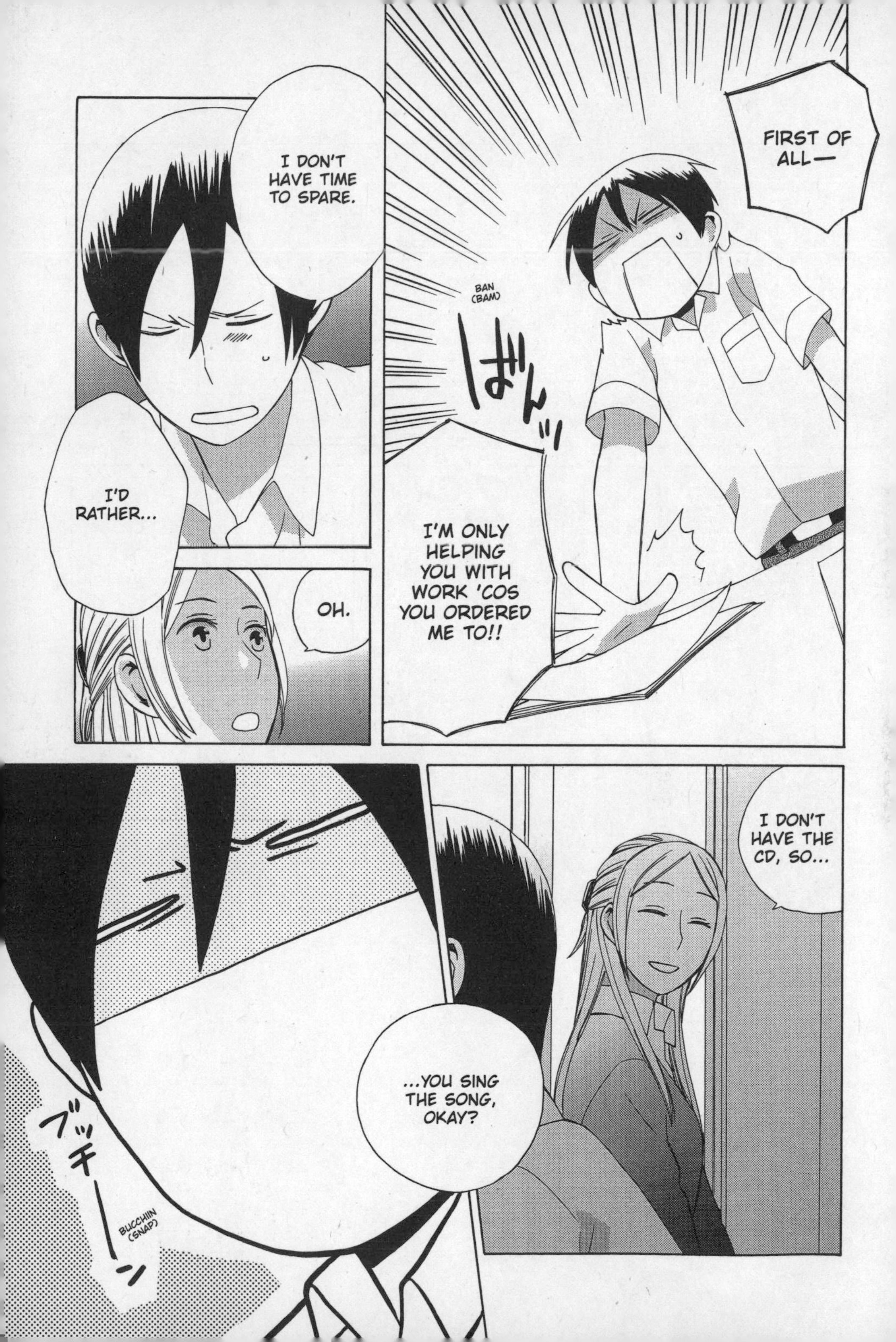
FIRST OF ALL—
BAN (BAM)
ばんっ
I'M ONLY HELPING YOU WITH WORK 'COS YOU ORDERED ME TO!!
I DON'T HAVE TIME TO SPARE.
I'D RATHER...
OH.
I DON'T HAVE THE CD, SO...
...YOU SING THE SONG, OKAY?
ブッチーン
BUCCHIIN (SNAP)

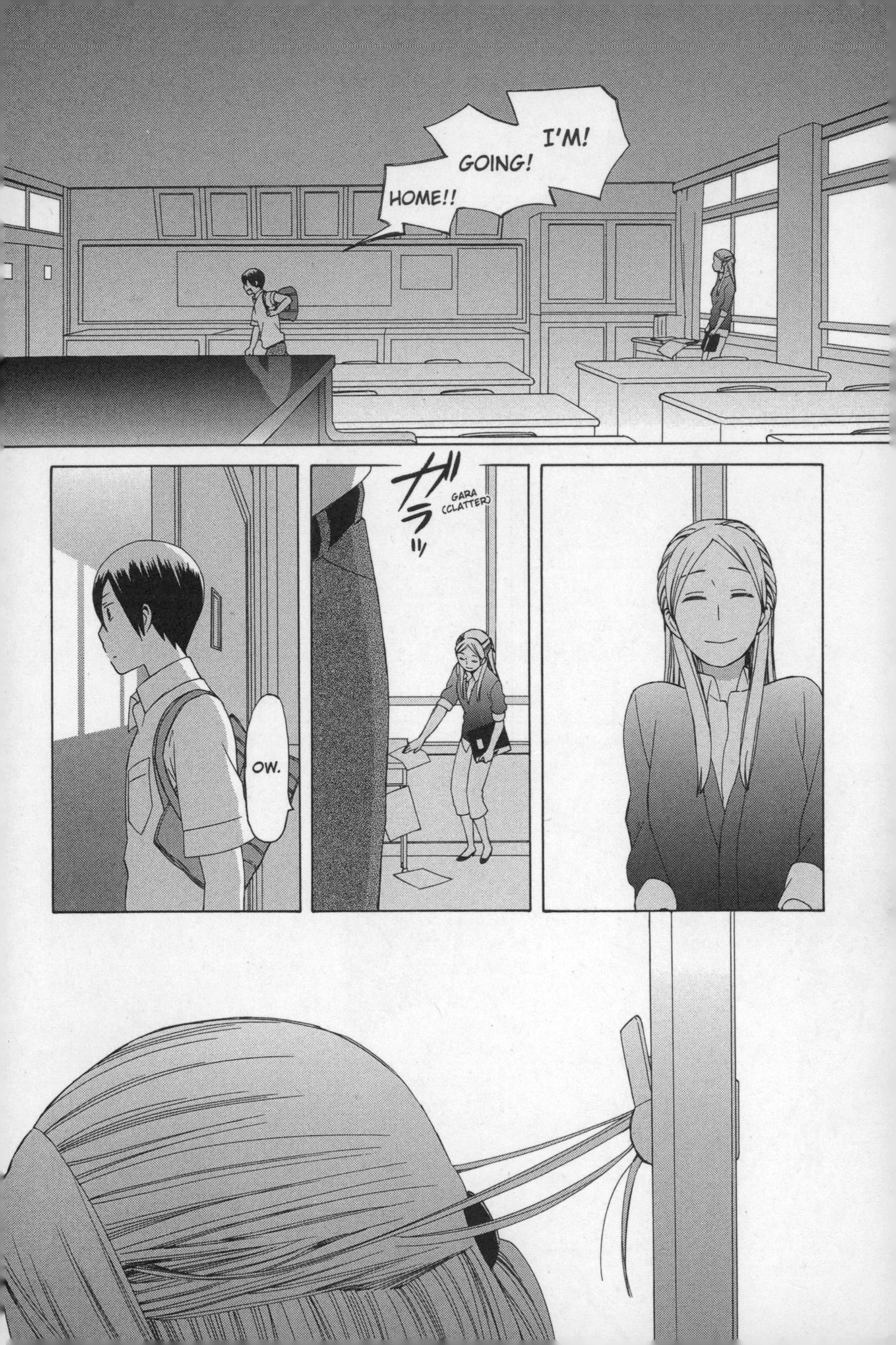
I'M! GOING! HOME!!
ガラッ
GARA (CLATTER)
OW.

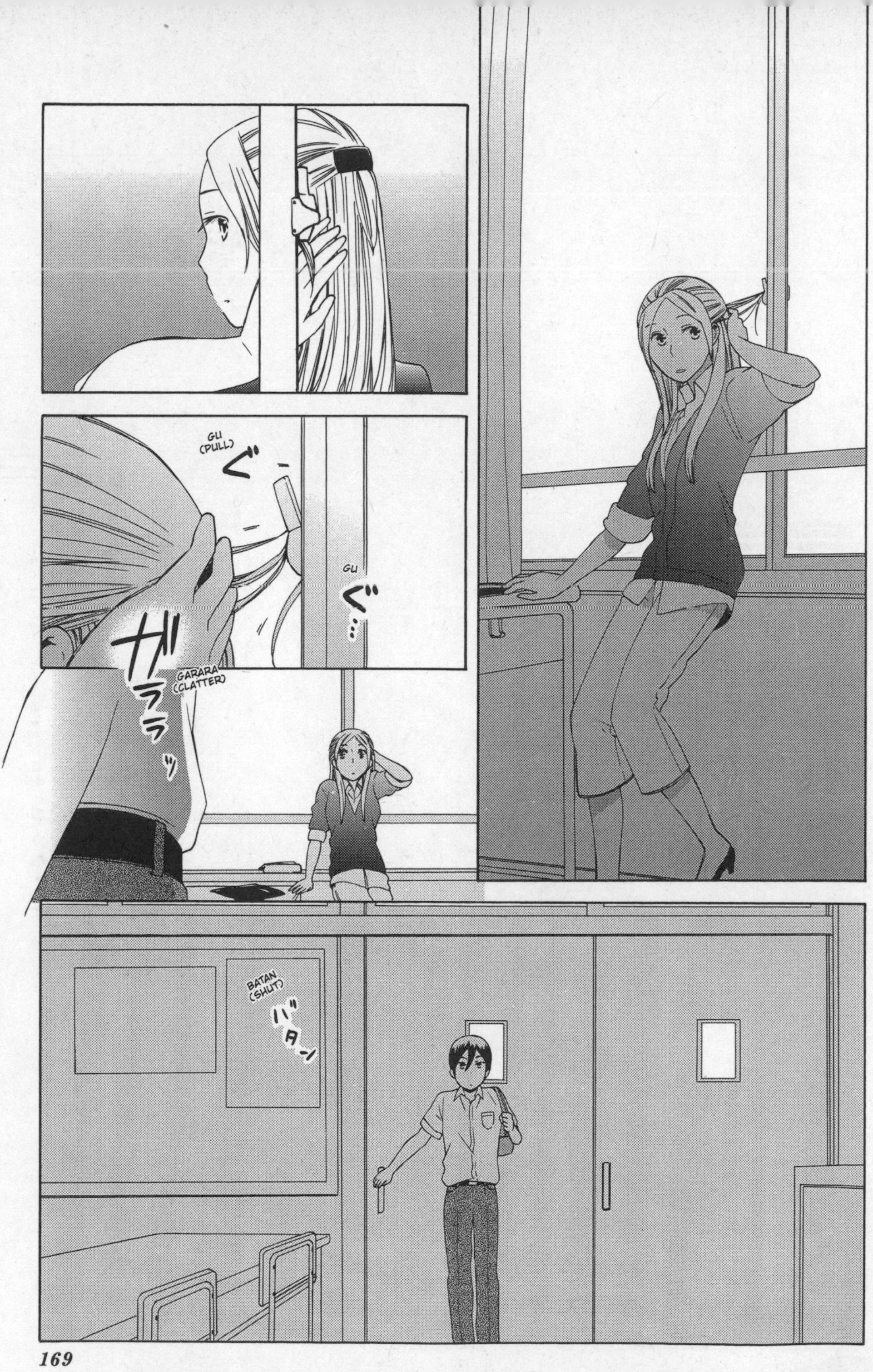
GU (PULL)
ぐ
GU
ぐ…
GARARA (CLATTER)
ガラララッ
BATAN (SHUT)
バターン

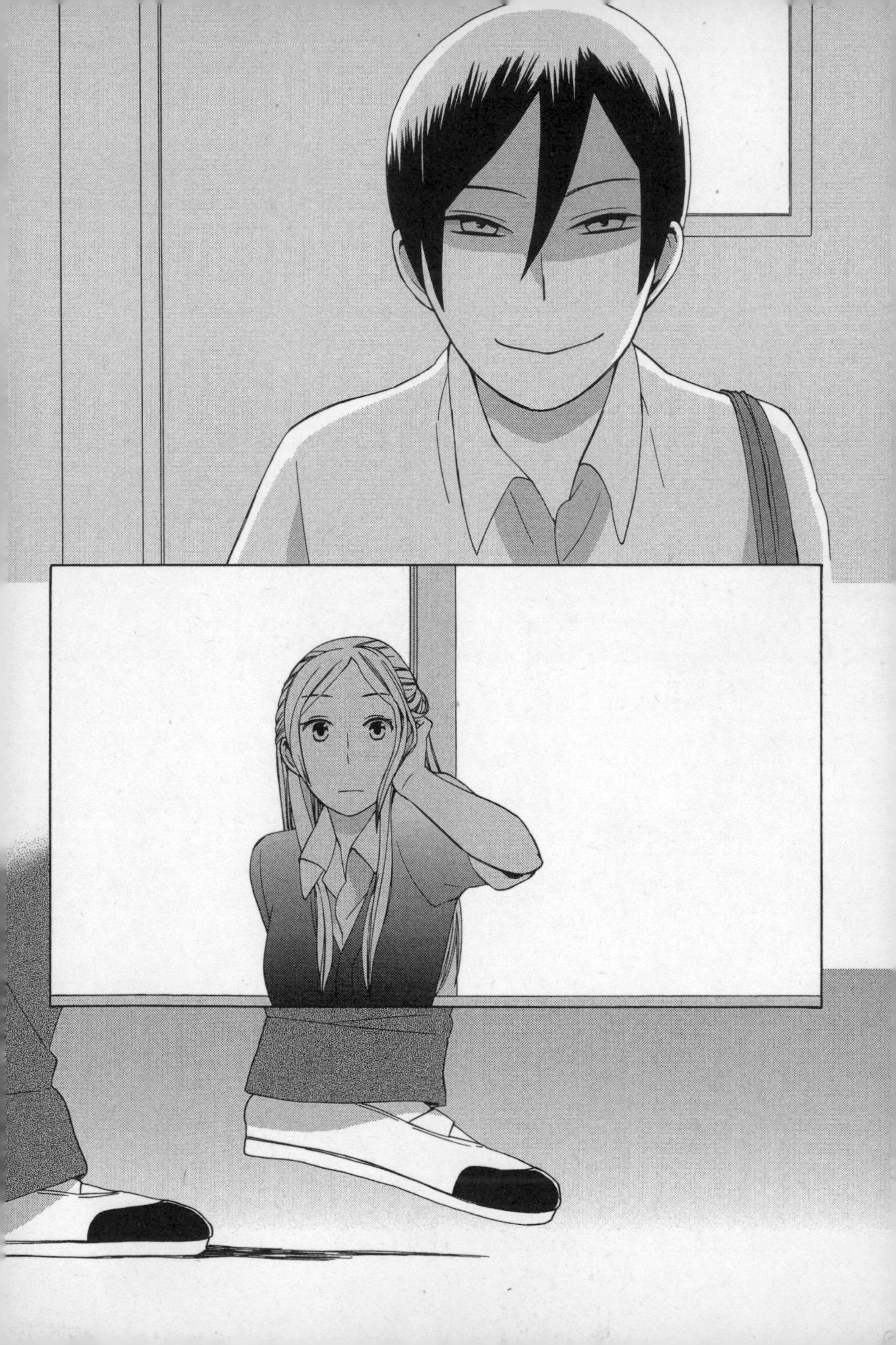

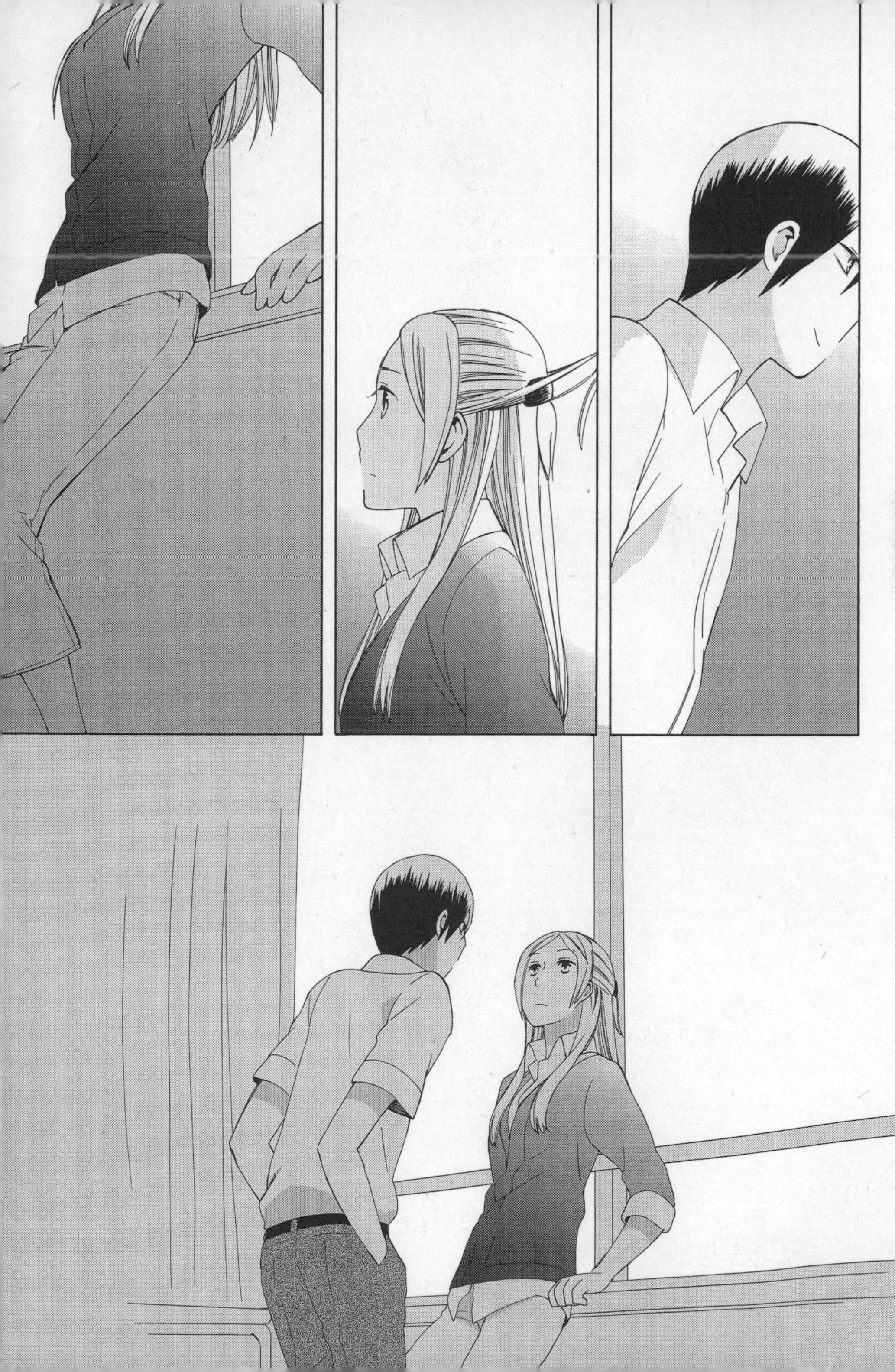

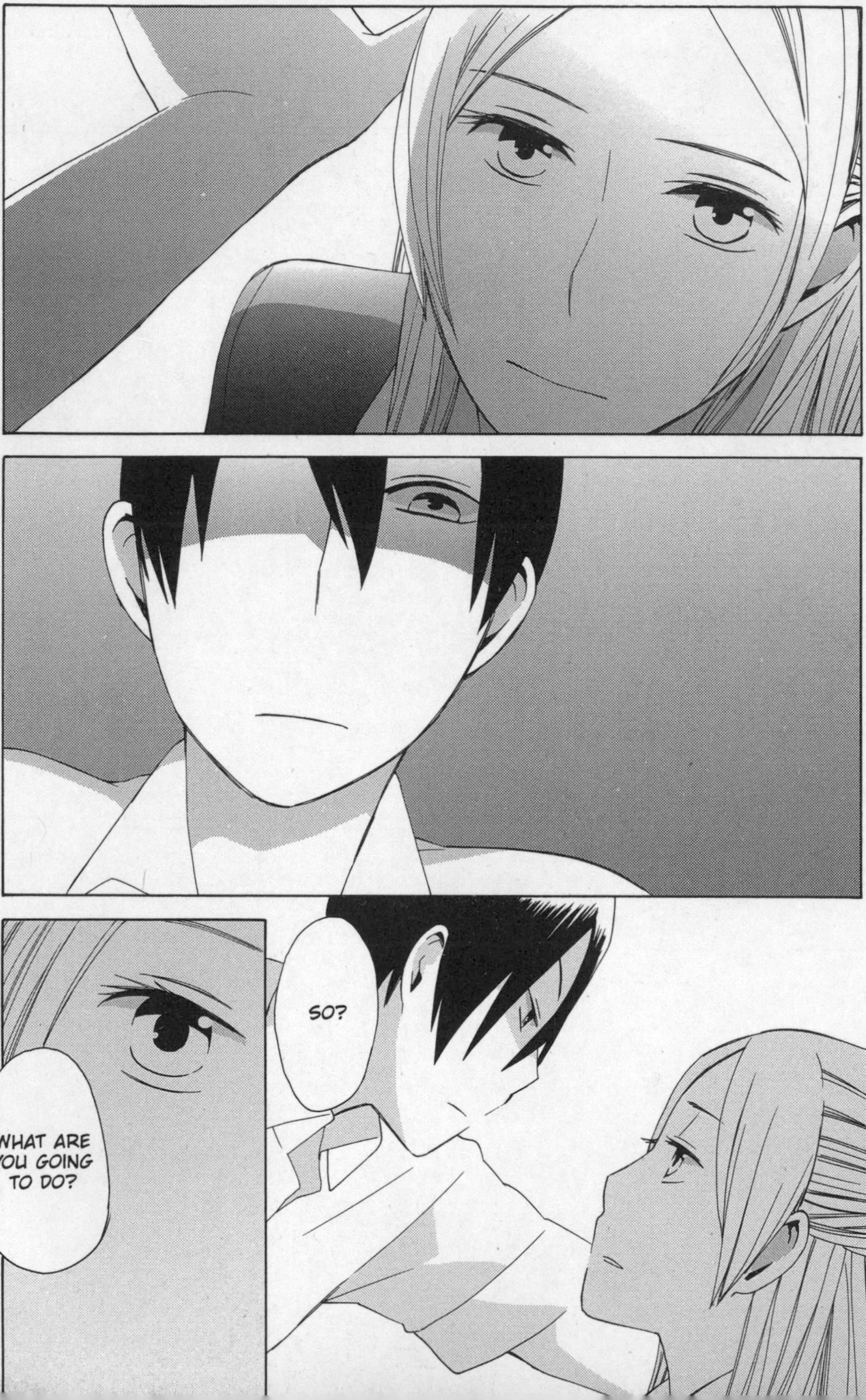
SO?
WHAT ARE YOU GOING TO DO?

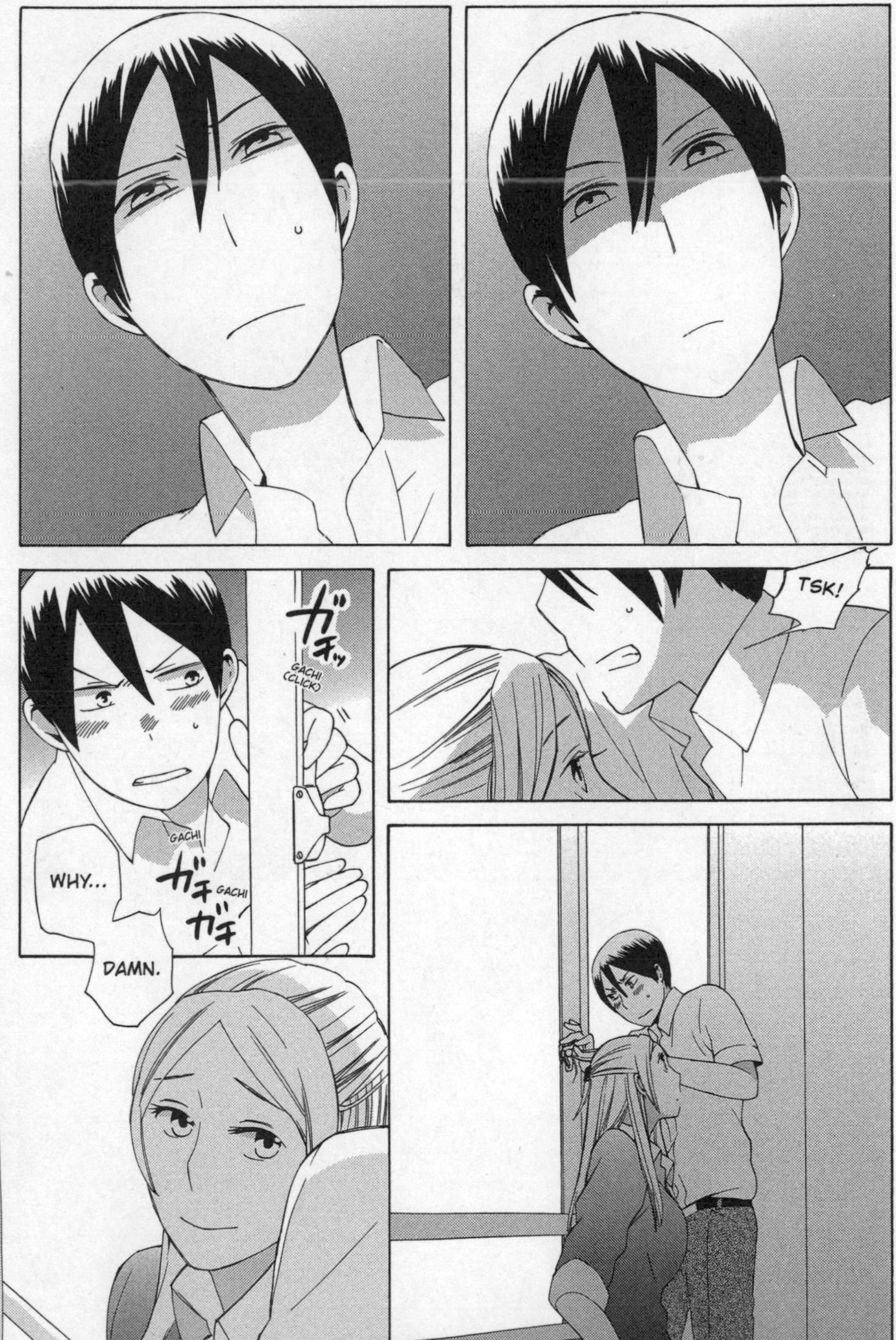
TSK!
ガチッ
GACHI (CLICK)
GACHI
ガチ
GACHI
ガチ
WHY...
DAMN.

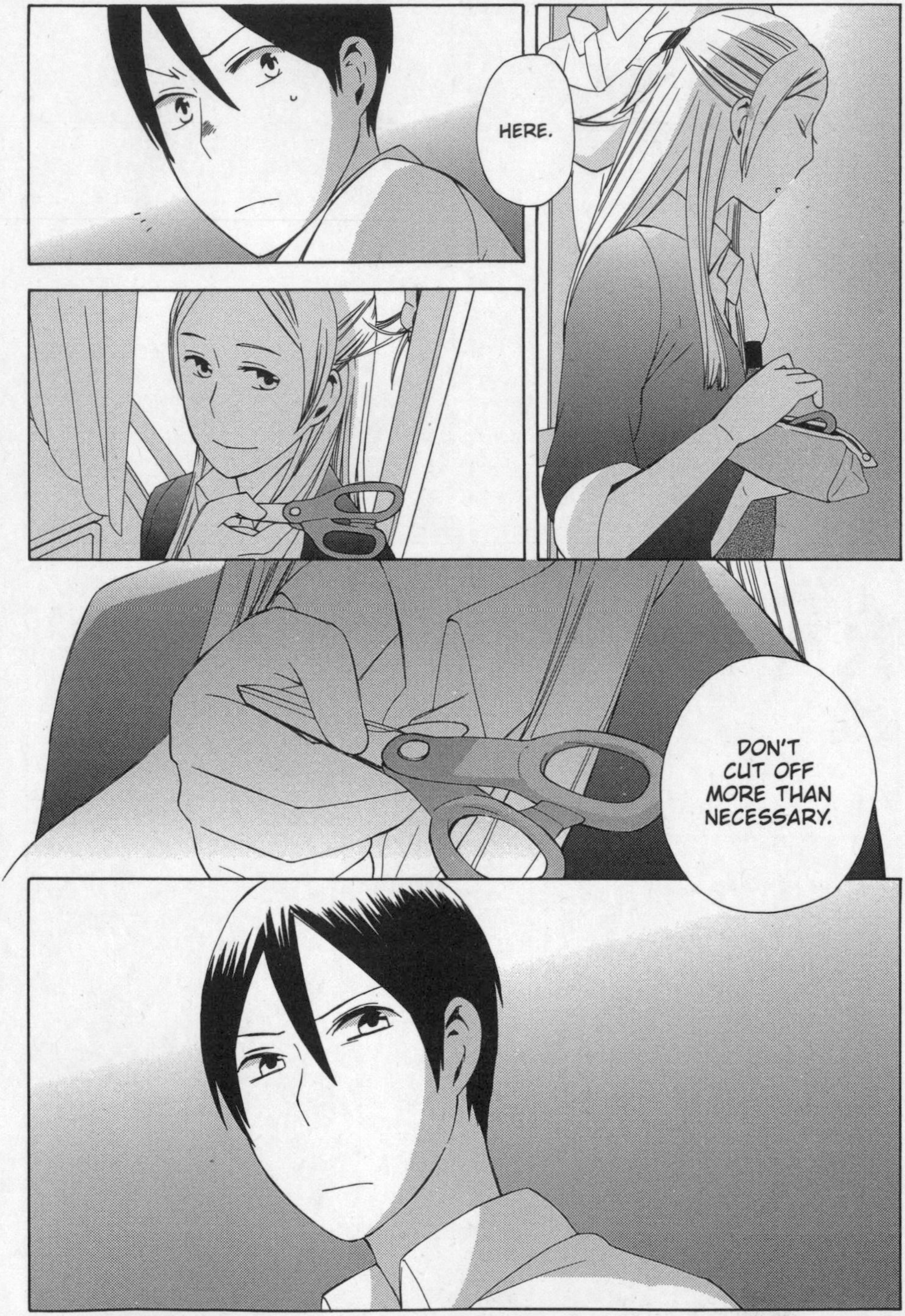
HERE.
DON'T CUT OFF MORE THAN NECESSARY.

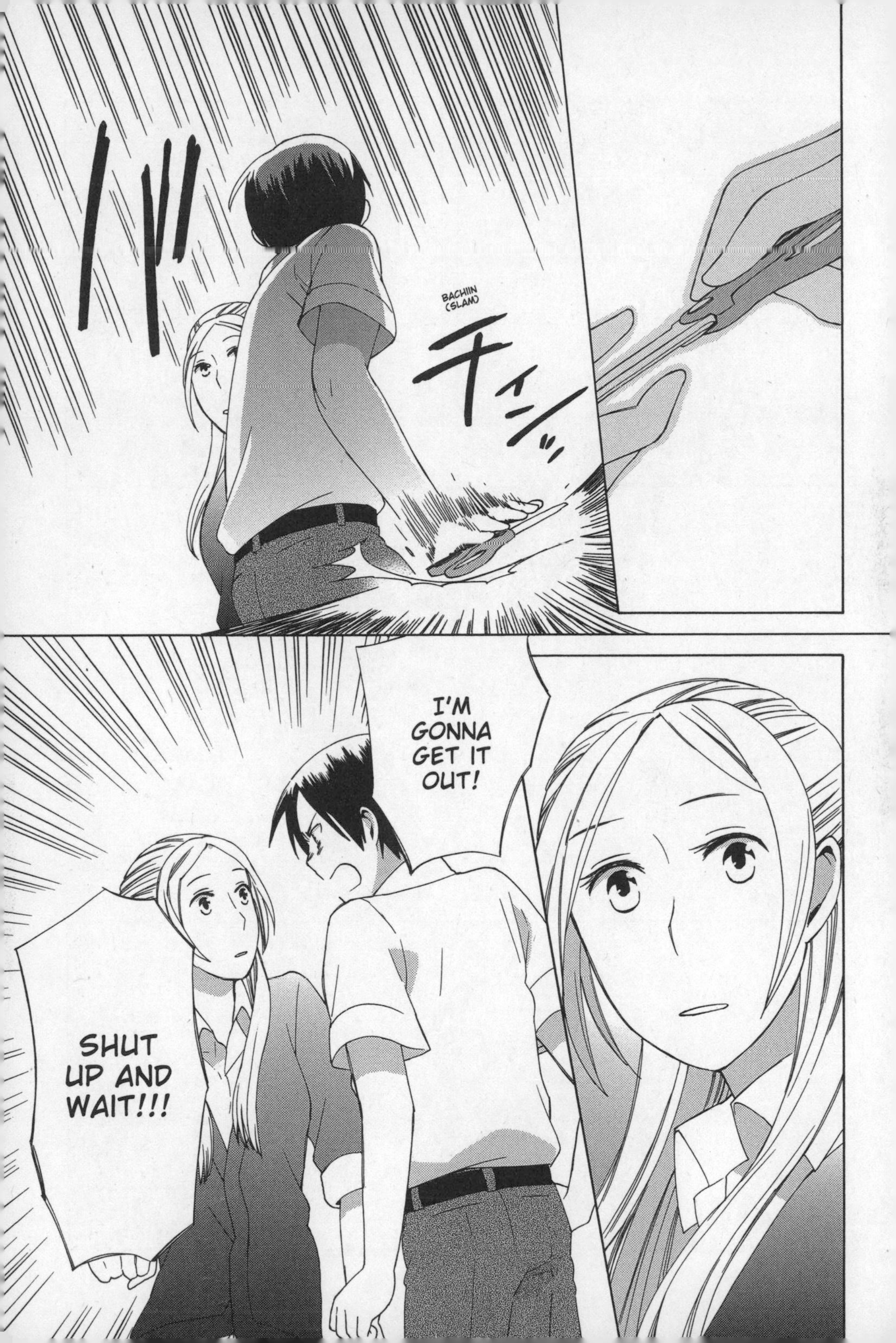
BACHIIN (SLAM)
チィンッ
I'M GONNA GET IT OUT!
SHUT UP AND WAIT!!!

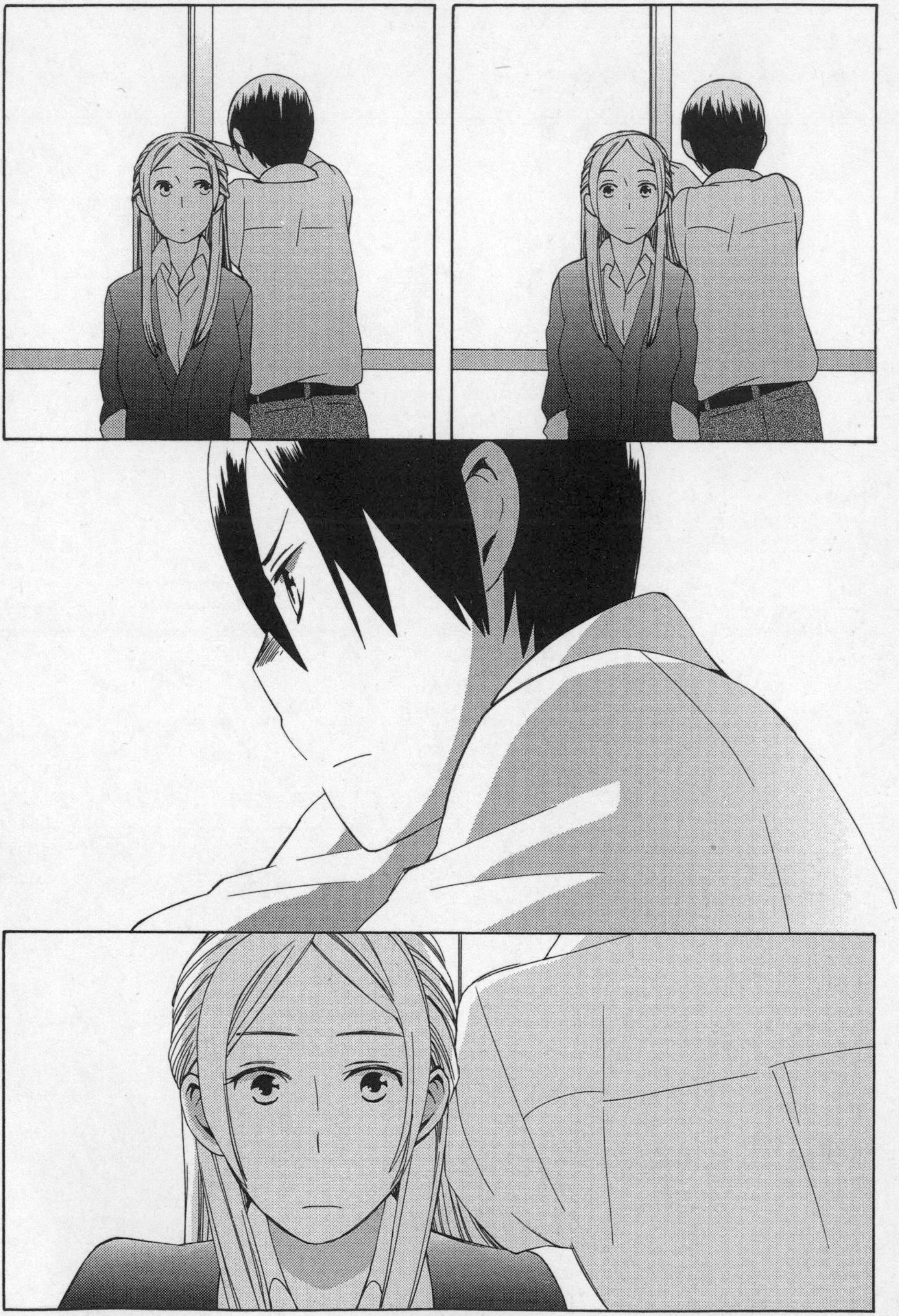

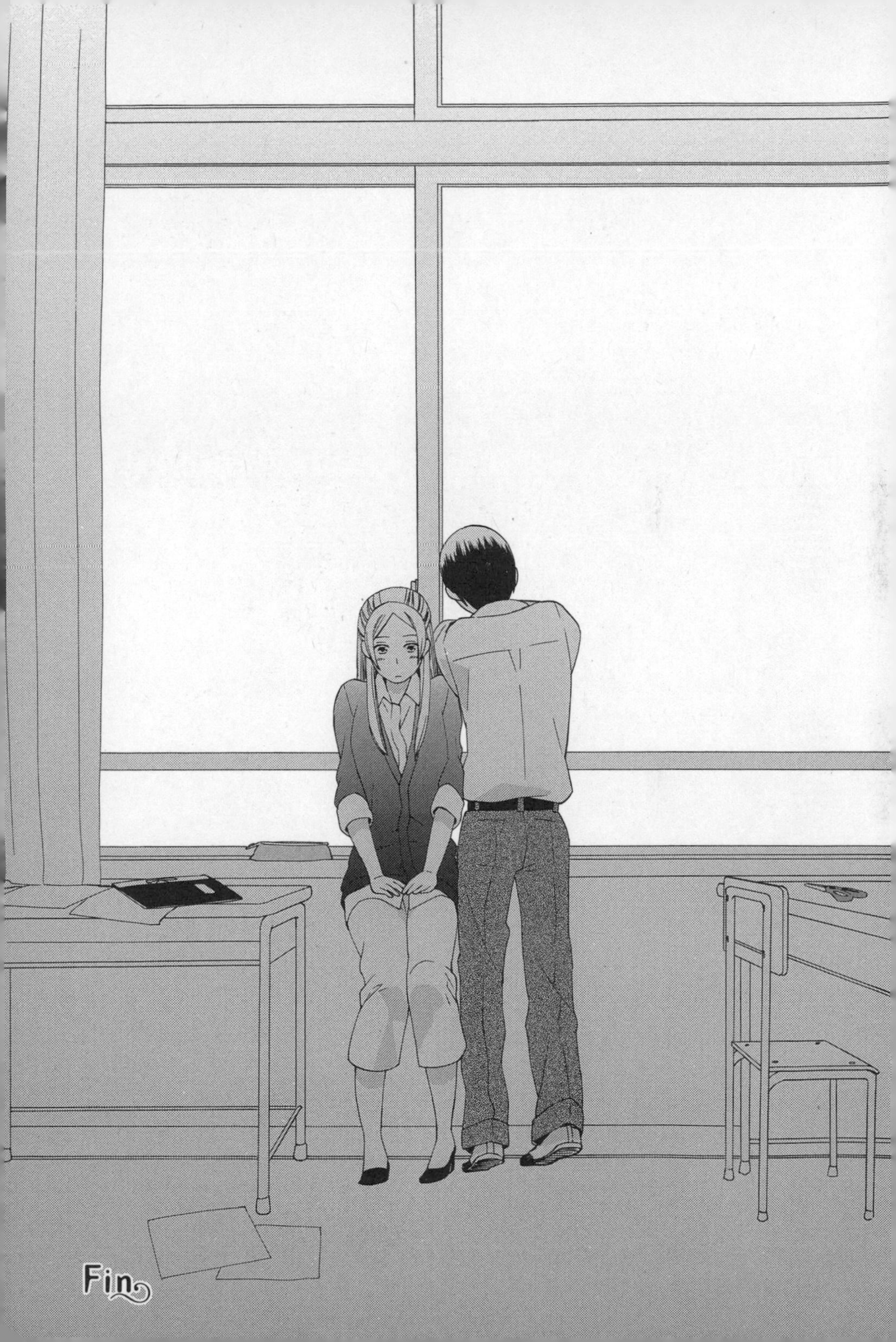
Fin

Love at Fourteen

Fuka Mizutani

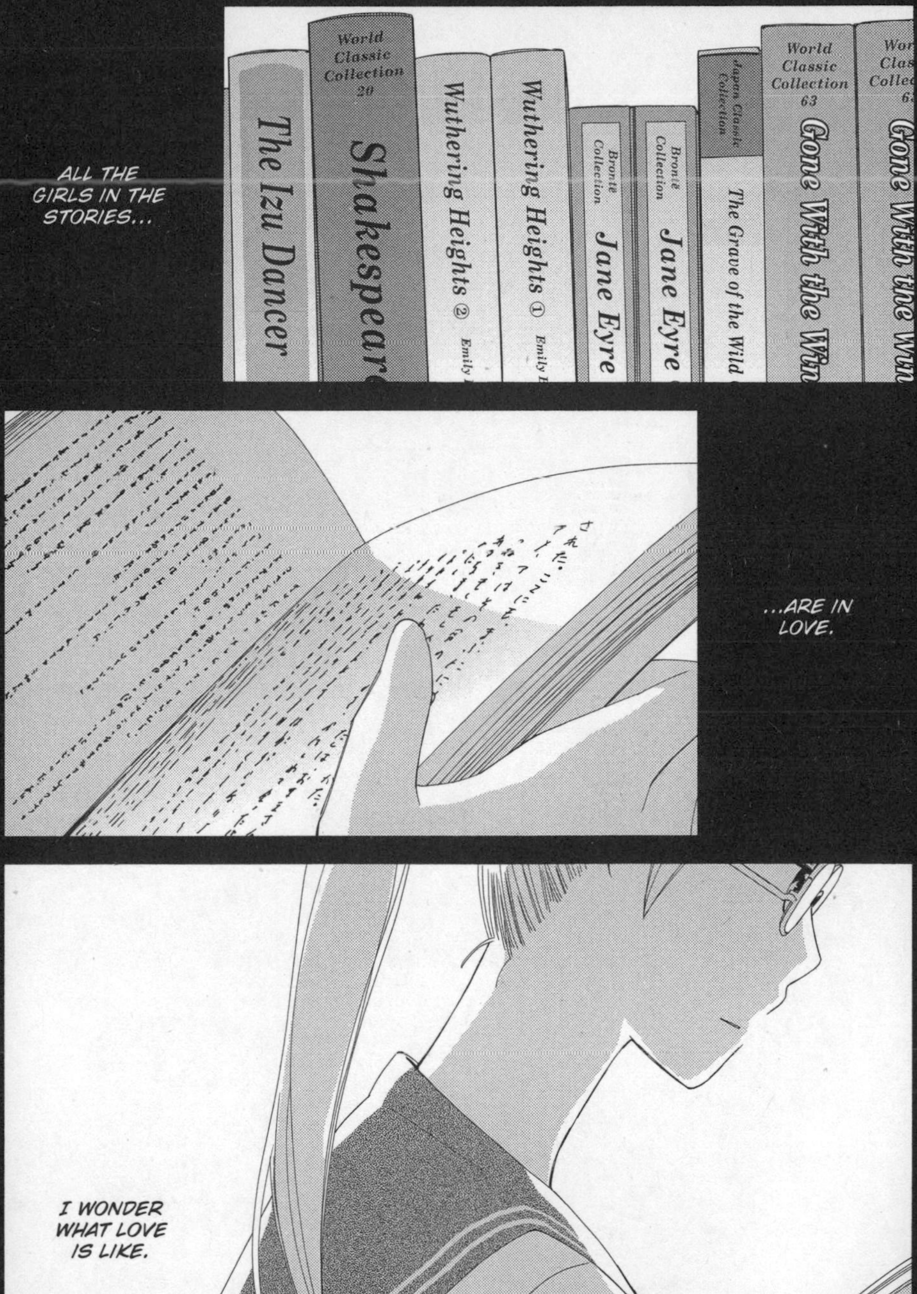

ALL THE GIRLS IN THE STORIES...

The Izu Dancer

World Classic Collection 20

Shakespeare

Wuthering Heights ②

Wuthering Heights ①

Emily

Emily

Brontë Collection

Jane Eyre

Brontë Collection

Jane Eyre

Japan Classic Collection

The Grave of the Wild

World Classic Collection 63

Gone With the Win

World Clas Colle 6

Gone With the Win

...ARE IN LOVE.

I WONDER WHAT LOVE IS LIKE.

An Early Summer of Fourteen

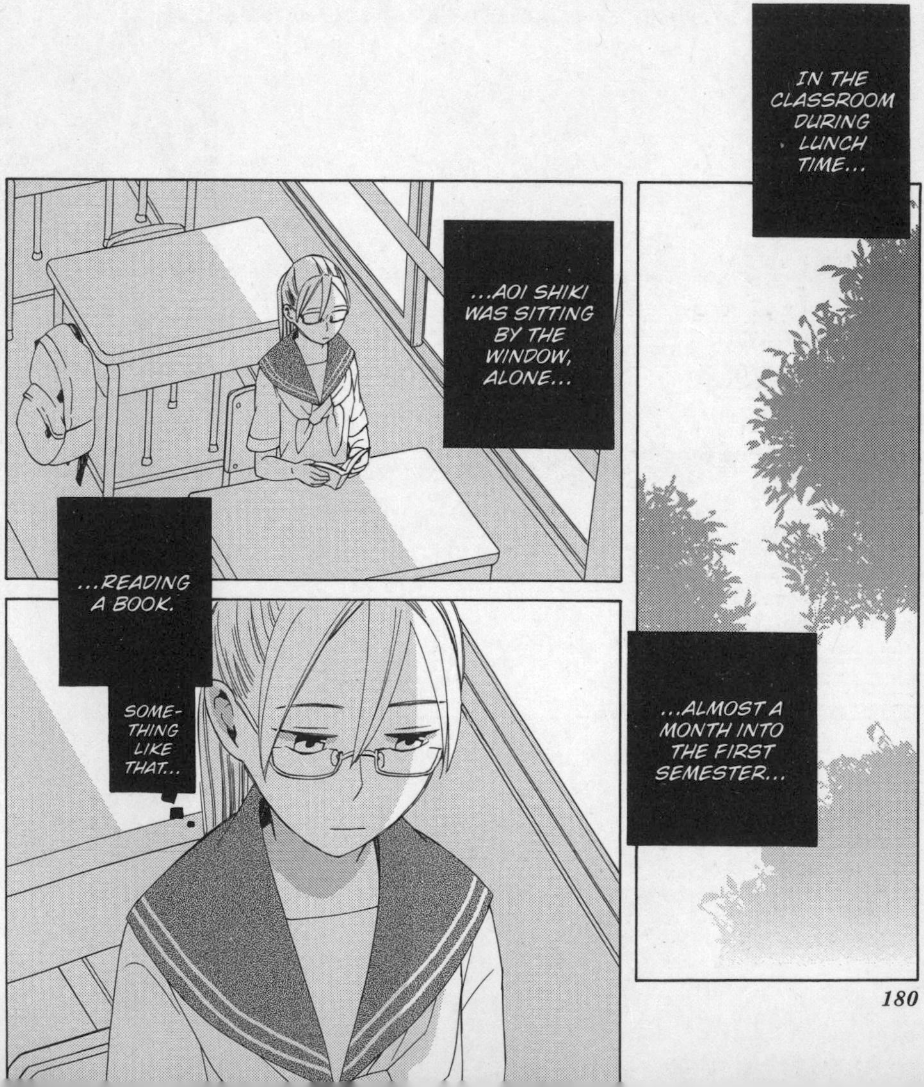
IN THE CLASSROOM DURING LUNCH TIME...
...ALMOST A MONTH INTO THE FIRST SEMESTER...
...AOI SHIKI WAS SITTING BY THE WINDOW, ALONE...
...READING A BOOK.
SOME-THING LIKE THAT...

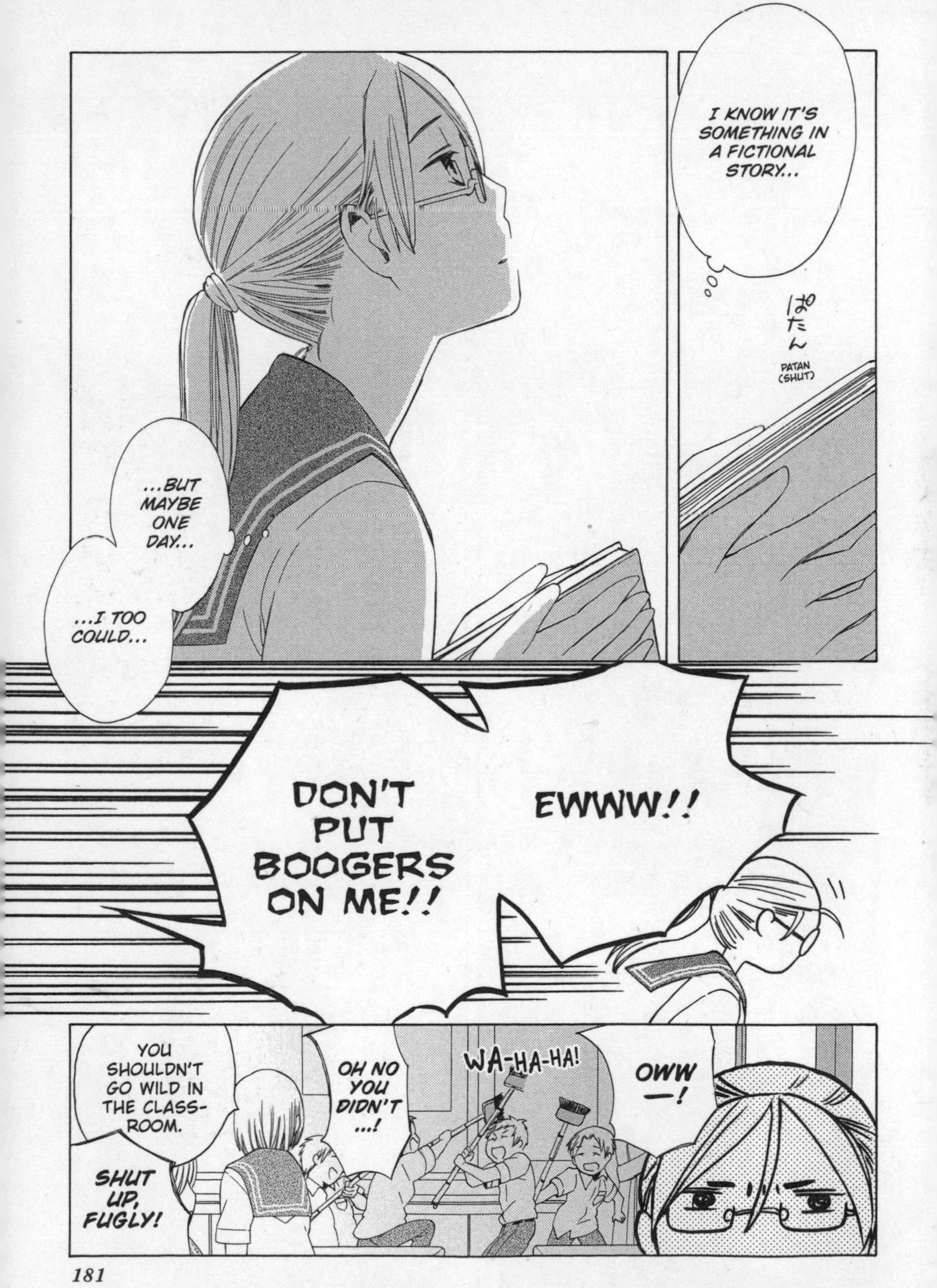
I KNOW IT'S SOMETHING IN A FICTIONAL STORY...
ぱたん
PATAN (SHUT)
...BUT MAYBE ONE DAY...
...I TOO COULD...
EWWW!!
DON'T PUT BOOGERS ON ME!!
OWW—!
WA-HA-HA!
OH NO YOU DIDN'T ...!
YOU SHOULDN'T GO WILD IN THE CLASS-ROOM.
SHUT UP, FUGLY!

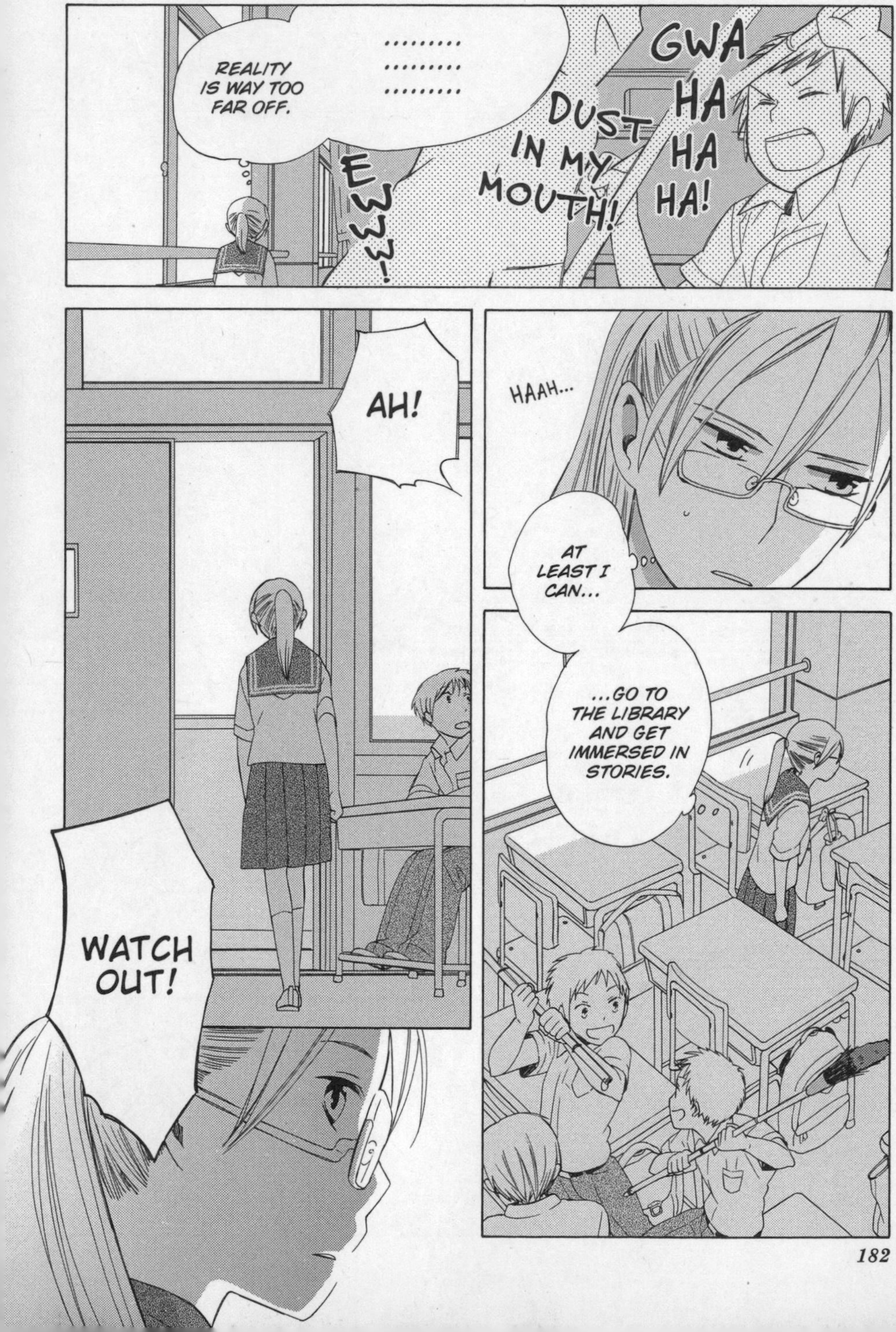
GWA HA HA HA!
DUST IN MY MOUTH!
EWWW!
....
....
....
REALITY IS WAY TOO FAR OFF.
HAAAH...
AT LEAST I CAN...
...GO TO THE LIBRARY AND GET IMMERSED IN STORIES.
AH!
WATCH OUT!

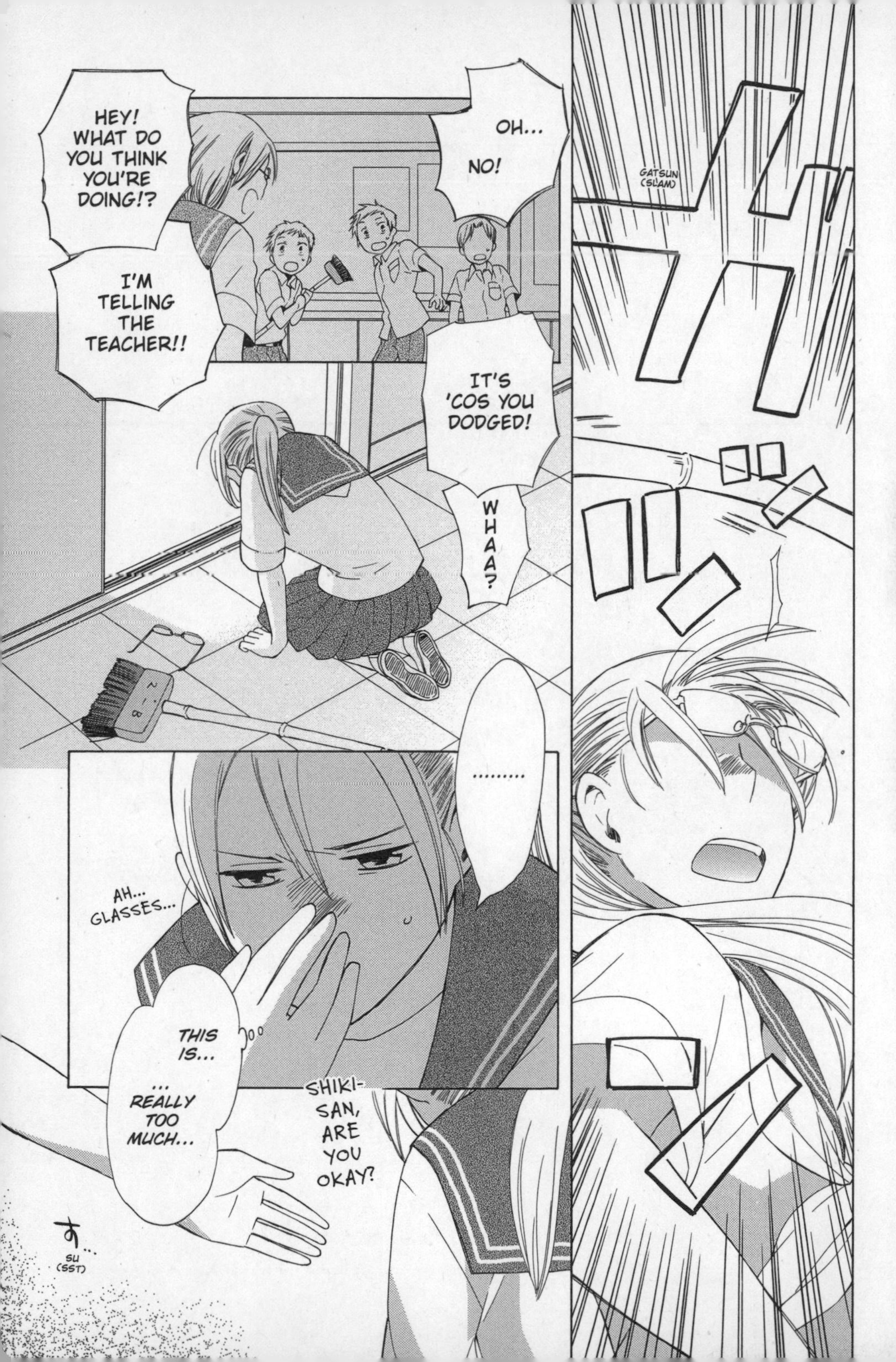
GATSUN (SLAM)
OH... NO!
HEY! WHAT DO YOU THINK YOU'RE DOING!?
I'M TELLING THE TEACHER!!
IT'S 'COS YOU DODGED!
WHAA?
....
AH... GLASSES...
THIS IS...
... REALLY TOO MUCH...
SHIKI-SAN, ARE YOU OKAY?
す...
SU (SST)

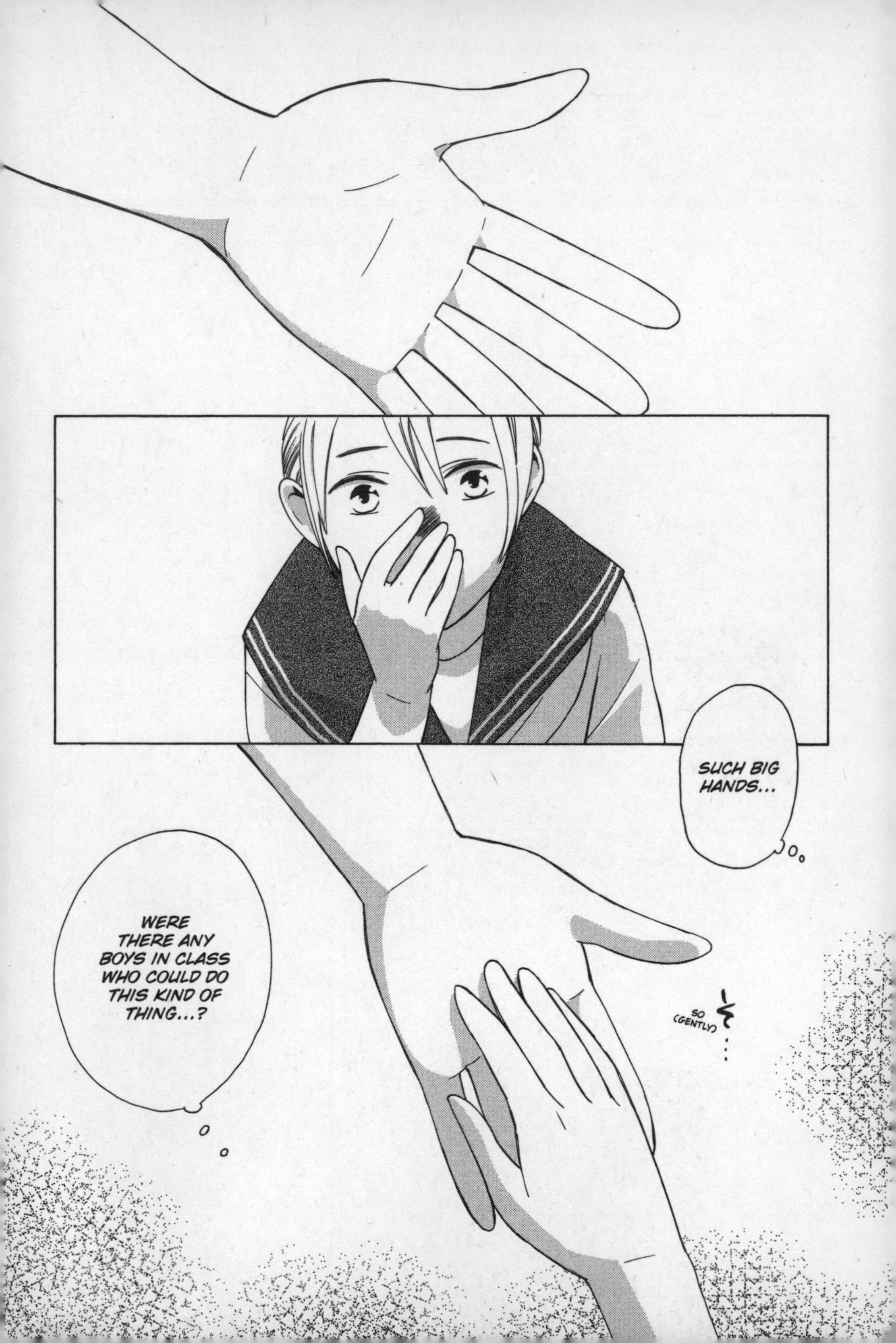
SUCH BIG HANDS...
SO
(GENTLY)
WERE THERE ANY BOYS IN CLASS WHO COULD DO THIS KIND OF THING...?

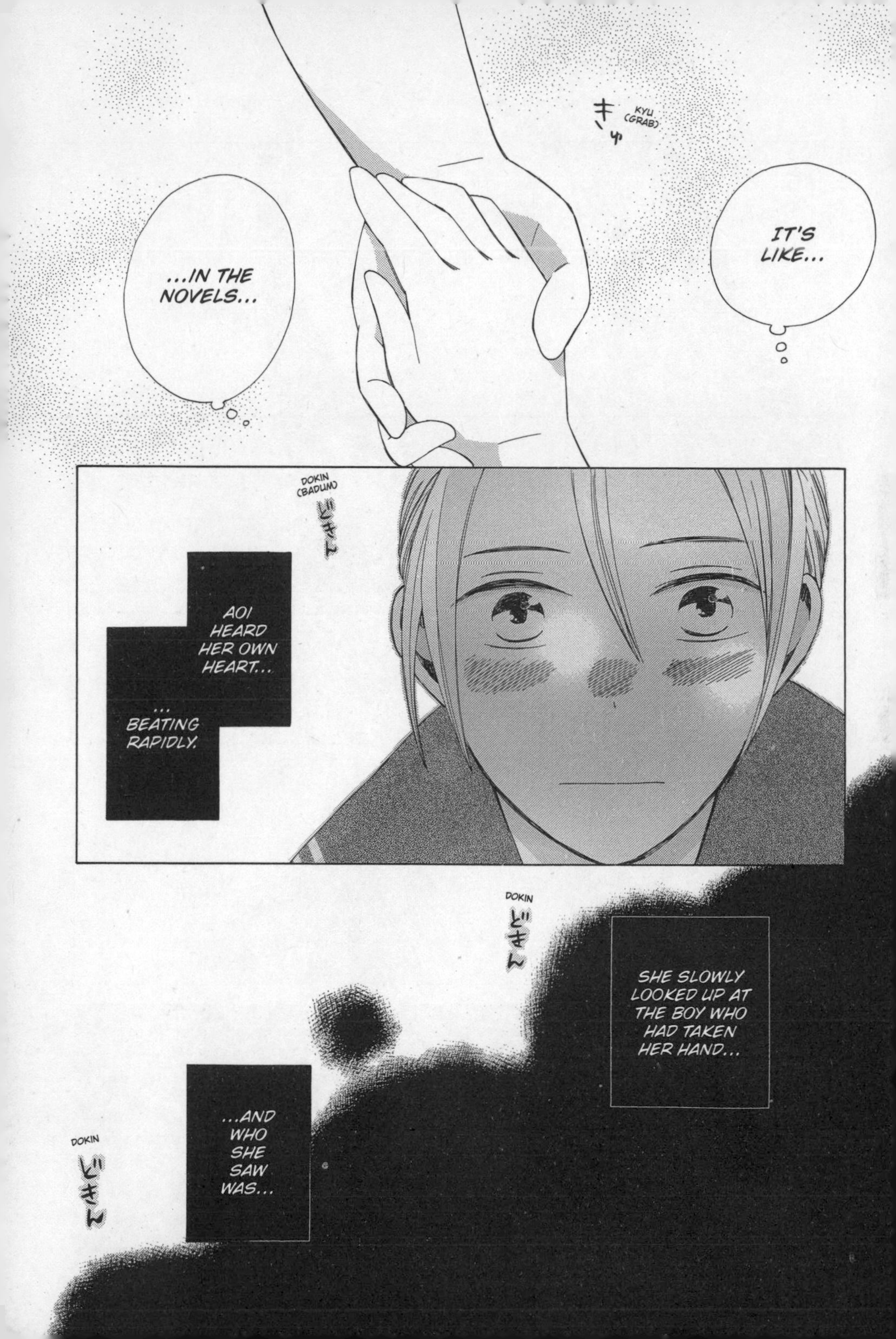
きゅ
KYU (GRAB)
IT'S LIKE...
...IN THE NOVELS...
DOKIN (BADUM)
どきん
AOI HEARD HER OWN HEART...
... BEATING RAPIDLY.
DOKIN
どきん
SHE SLOWLY LOOKED UP AT THE BOY WHO HAD TAKEN HER HAND...
...AND WHO SHE SAW WAS...
DOKIN
どきん

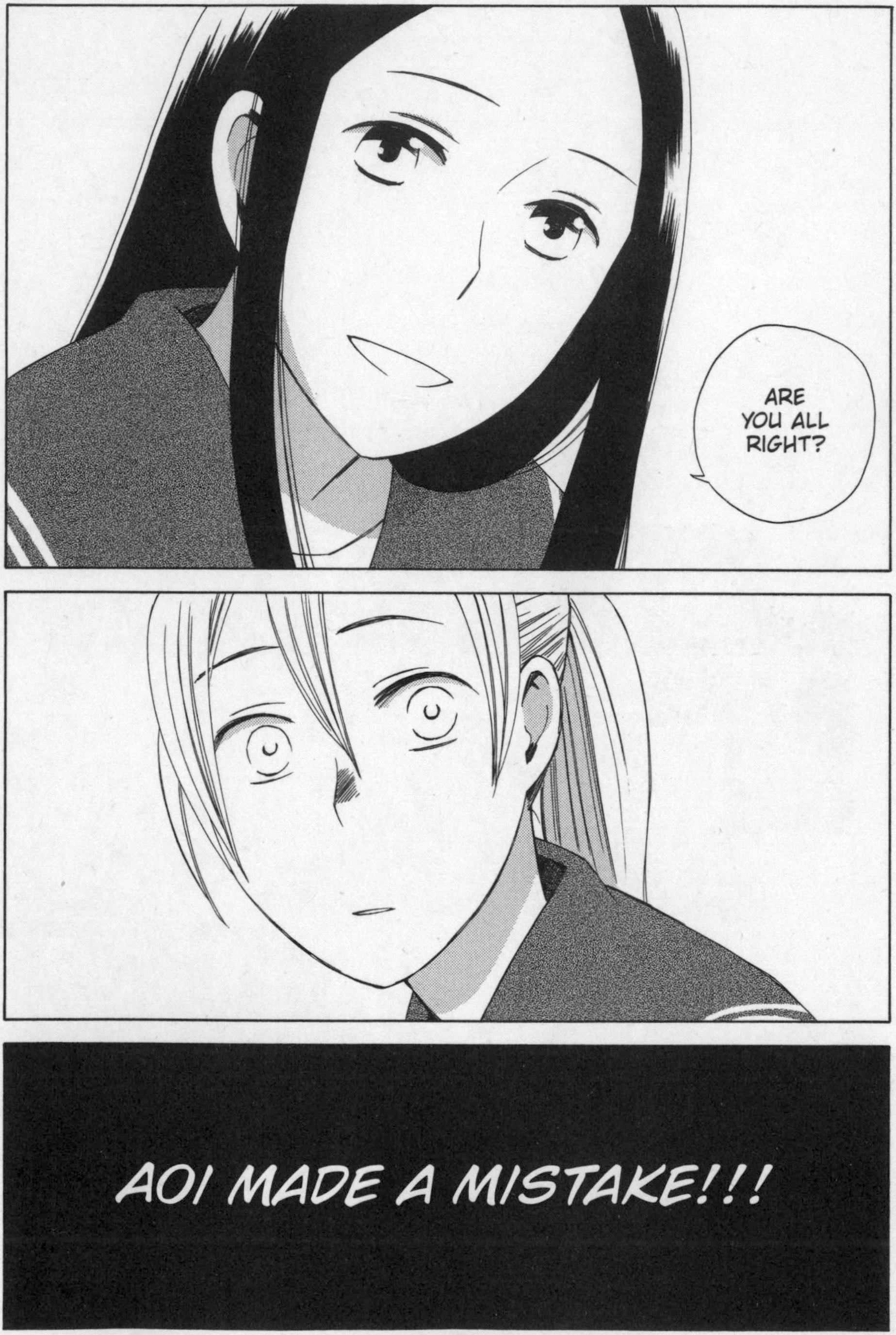
ARE YOU ALL RIGHT?
AOI MADE A MISTAKE!!!

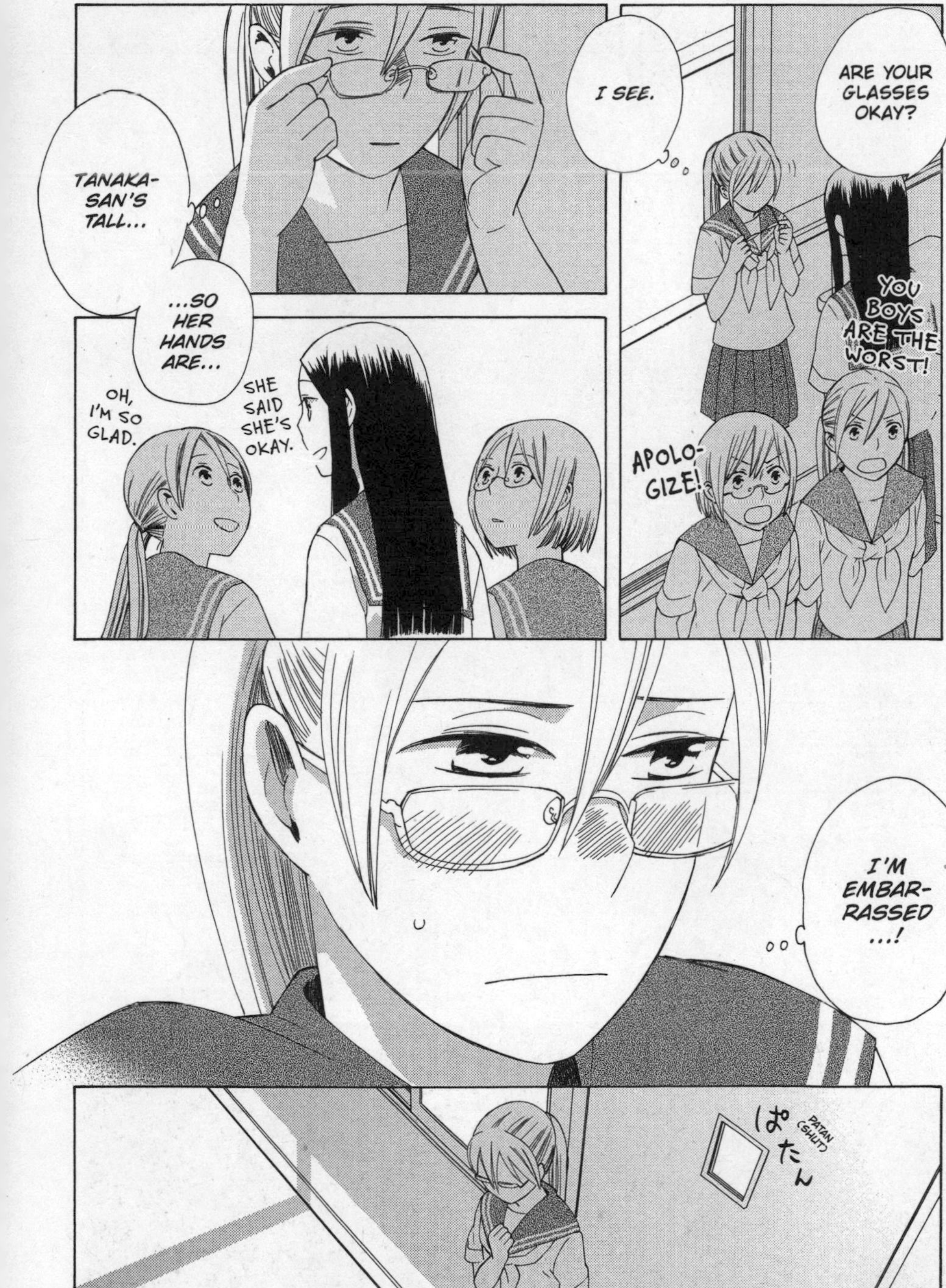
ARE YOUR GLASSES OKAY?
I SEE.
YOU BOYS ARE THE WORST!
APOLO-GIZE!
TANAKA-SAN'S TALL...
...SO HER HANDS ARE...
SHE SAID SHE'S OKAY.
OH, I'M SO GLAD.
I'M EMBAR-RASSED ...!
ぱたん
PATAN (SHUT)

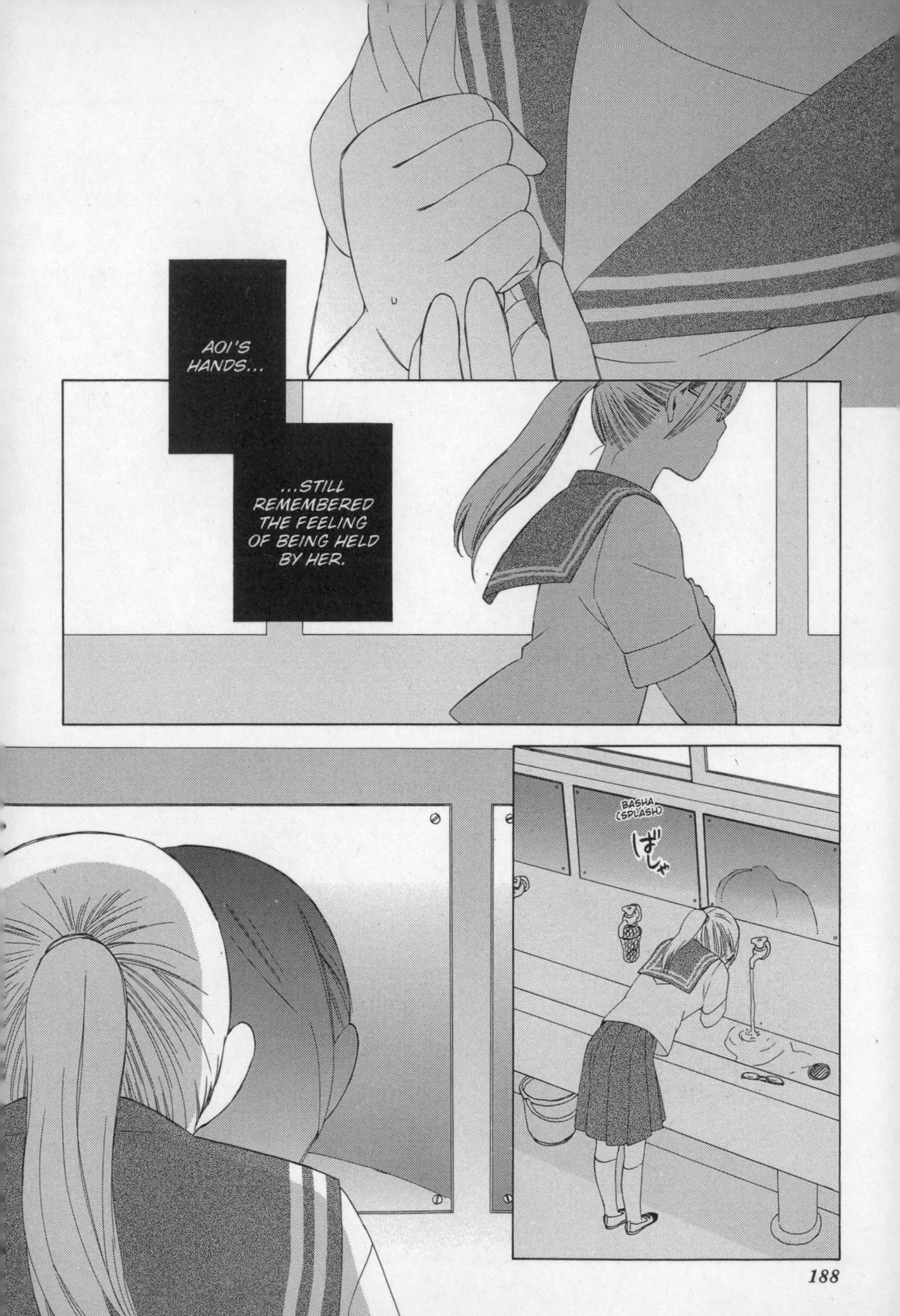
AOI'S HANDS...
...STILL REMEMBERED THE FEELING OF BEING HELD BY HER.
BASHA (SPLASH)
ばしゃ

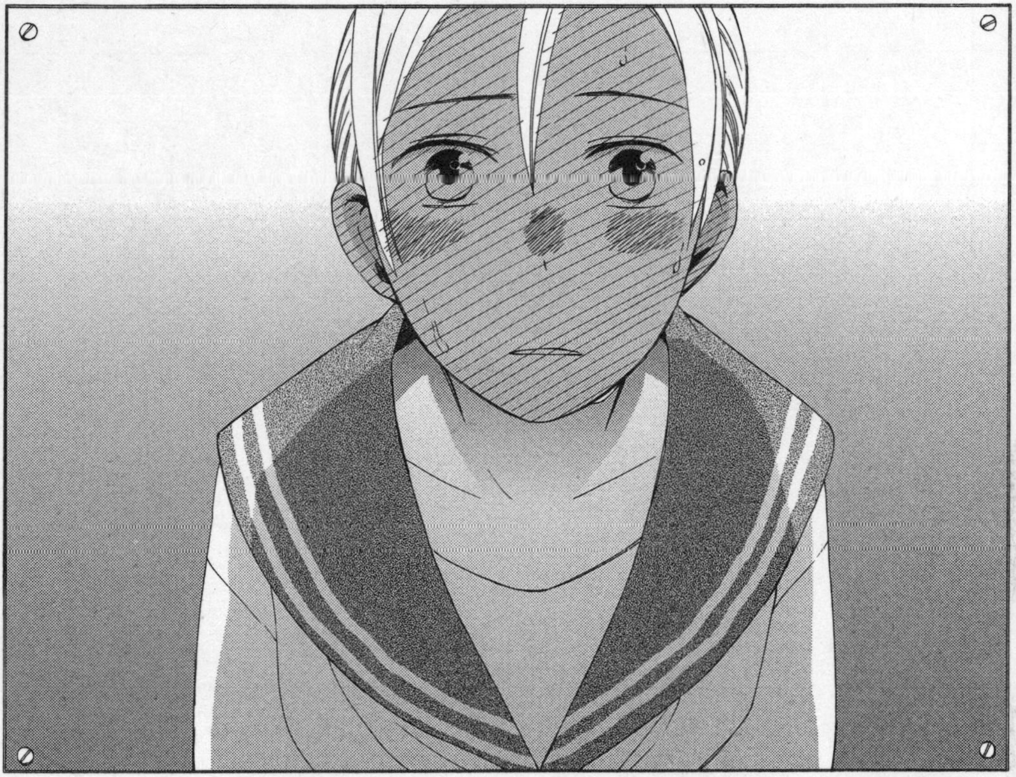

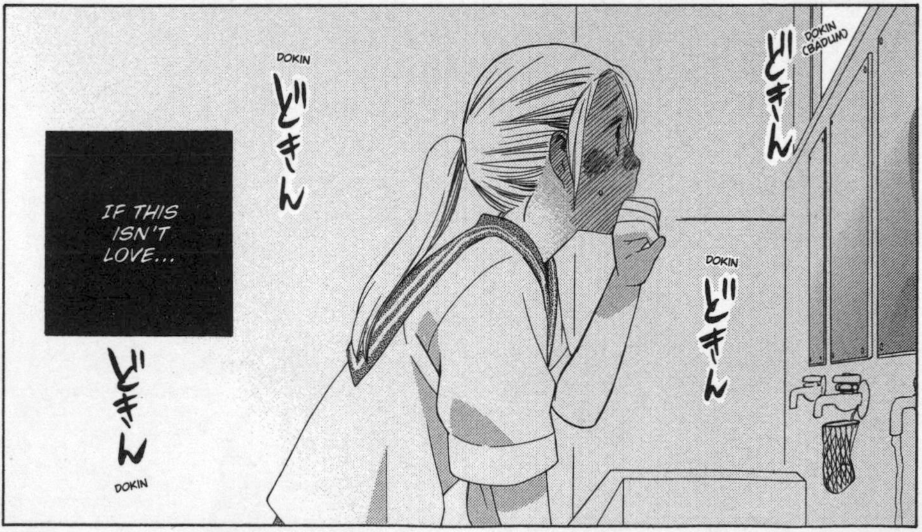

どきん
DOKIN (BADUM)
どきん
DOKIN
どきん
DOKIN
IF THIS ISN'T LOVE...
どきん
DOKIN

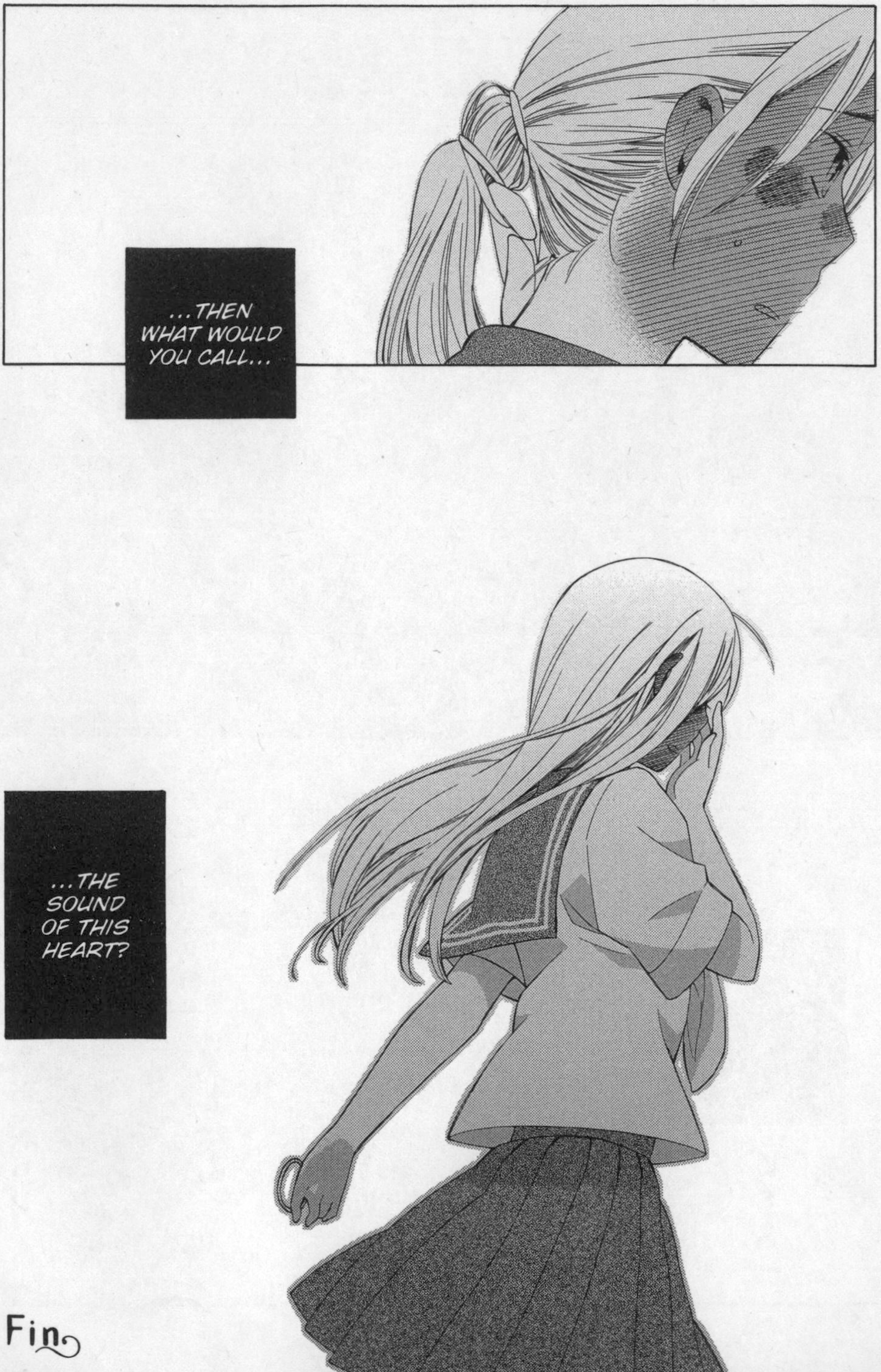
...THEN WHAT WOULD YOU CALL...
...THE SOUND OF THIS HEART?
Fin

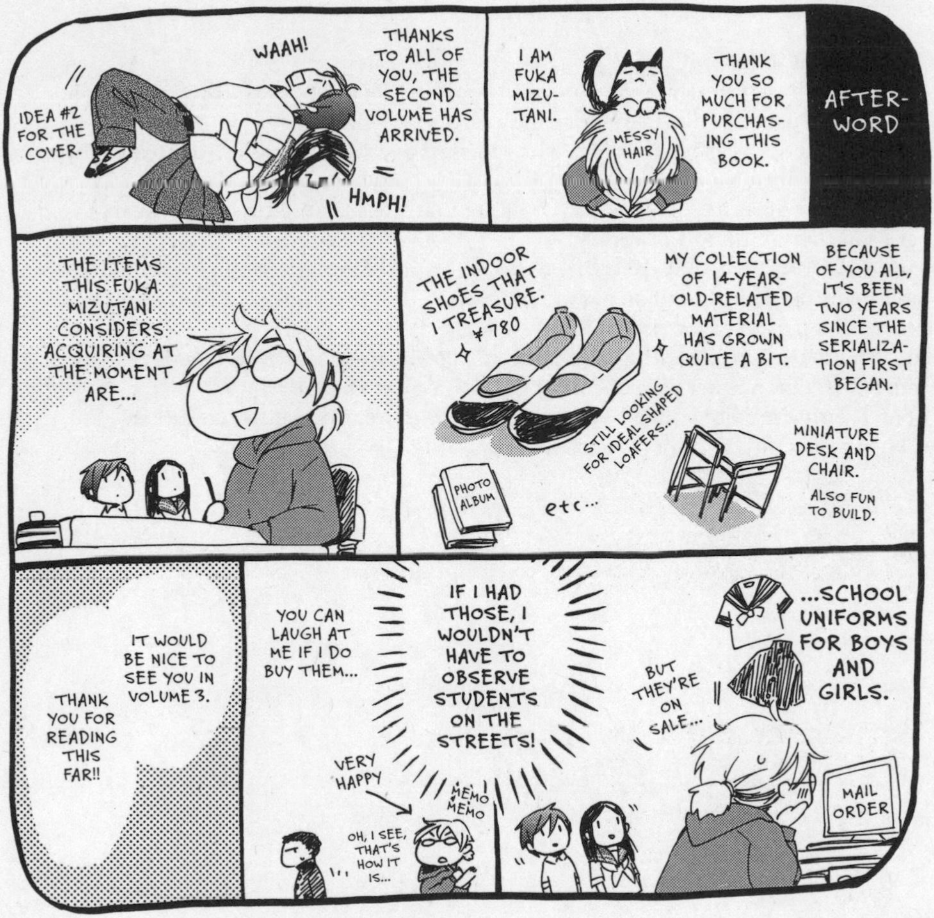
AFTER-WORD
THANK YOU SO MUCH FOR PURCHASING THIS BOOK.
I AM FUKA MIZUTANI.
MESSY HAIR
THANKS TO ALL OF YOU, THE SECOND VOLUME HAS ARRIVED.
WAAH!
IDEA #2 FOR THE COVER.
HMPH!
BECAUSE OF YOU ALL, IT'S BEEN TWO YEARS SINCE THE SERIALIZATION FIRST BEGAN.
MY COLLECTION OF 14-YEAR-OLD-RELATED MATERIAL HAS GROWN QUITE A BIT.
THE INDOOR SHOES THAT I TREASURE. ¥780
MINIATURE DESK AND CHAIR.
ALSO FUN TO BUILD.
STILL LOOKING FOR IDEAL SHAPED LOAFERS...
PHOTO ALBUM
etc...
THE ITEMS THIS FUKA MIZUTANI CONSIDERS ACQUIRING AT THE MOMENT ARE...
...SCHOOL UNIFORMS FOR BOYS AND GIRLS.
BUT THEY'RE ON SALE...
MAIL ORDER
IF I HAD THOSE, I WOULDN'T HAVE TO OBSERVE STUDENTS ON THE STREETS!
YOU CAN LAUGH AT ME IF I DO BUY THEM...
MEMO MEMO
VERY HAPPY
OH, I SEE, THAT'S HOW IT IS...
IT WOULD BE NICE TO SEE YOU IN VOLUME 3.
THANK YOU FOR READING THIS FAR!!

Special Thanks

Iida-sama of Hakusensha

Kohei Nawata Design

My family My great friends

Sayo Murata-chan

And all of you who are reading this now.

Summer 2012

水谷フーカ
Fuka Mizutani

TRANSLATION NOTES

COMMON HONORIFICS:

no honorific: Indicates familiarity or closeness; if used without permission or reason, addressing someone in this manner would constitute an insult.

-san: The Japanese equivalent of Mr./Mrs./Miss. If a situation calls for politeness, this is the fail-safe honorific.

-sama: Conveys great respect; may also indicate that the social status of the speaker is lower than that of the addressee.

-kun: Used most often when referring to boys, this indicates affection or familiarity. Occasionally used by older men among their peers, but it may also be used by anyone referring to a person of lower standing.

-chan: An affectionate honorific indicating familiarity used mostly in reference to girls; also used in reference to cute persons or animals of either gender.

-senpai: A suffix used to address upperclassmen or more experienced coworkers.

-sensei: A respectful term for teachers, artists, or high-level professionals.

Love at Fourteen

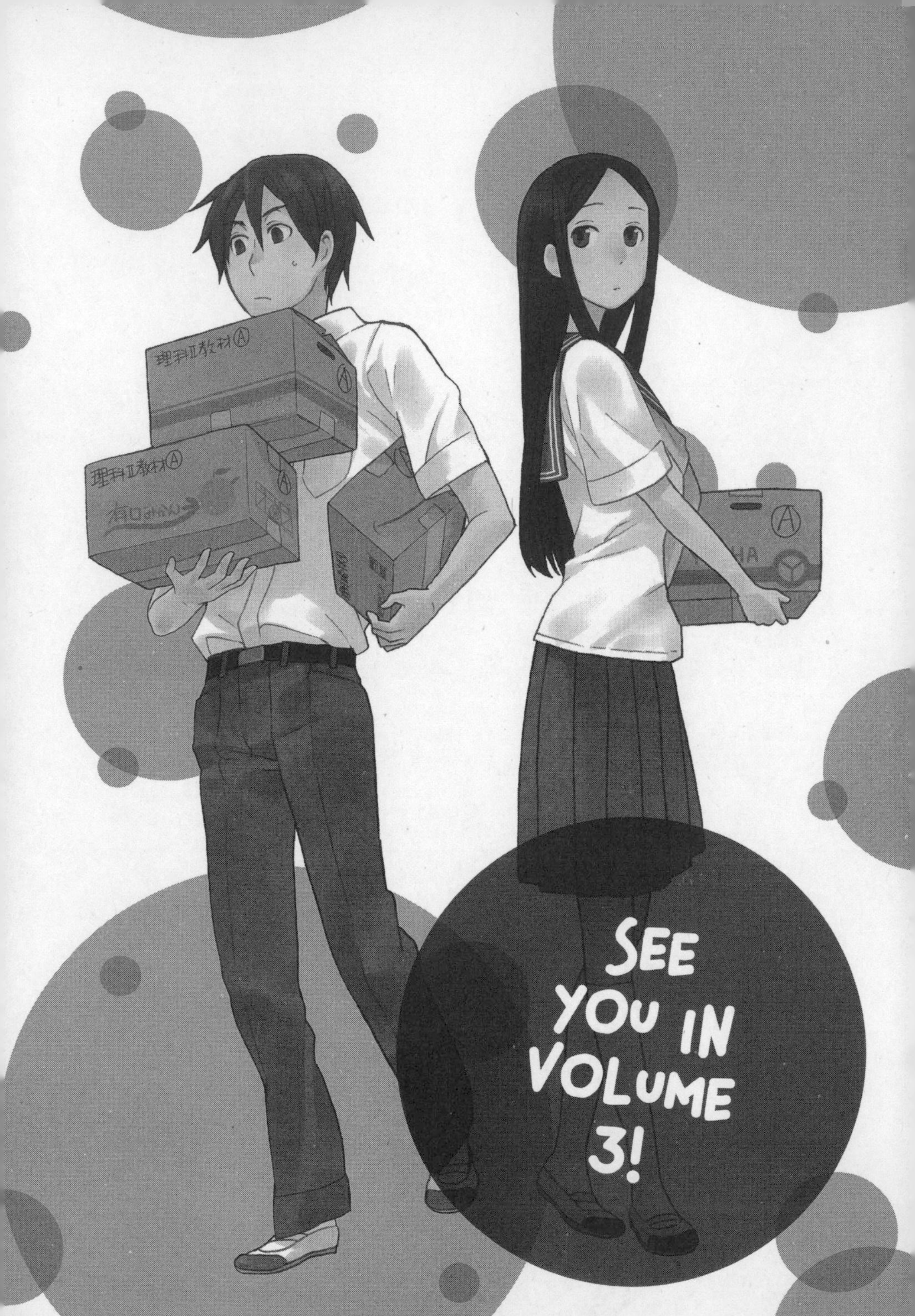
SEE YOU IN VOLUME 3!

BOXES: MATERIALS

Love ♡ at ♡ Fourteen

mrya

LOVE AT FOURTEEN ②
FUKA MIZUTANI

Translation: Yoshito Hinton

Lettering: Lys Blakeslee

JUYON-SAI NO KOI by Fuka Mizutani
© Fuka Mizutani 2012
All rights reserved.
First published in Japan in 2012 by HAKUSENSHA, INC., Tokyo.
English language translation rights in U.S.A., Canada and U.K. arranged with
HAKUSENSHA, INC., Tokyo through Tuttle-Mori Agency, Inc., Tokyo.

English Translation © 2015 by Hachette Book Group, Inc.

Yen Press
Hachette Book Group
1290 Avenue of the Americas
New York, NY 10104

www.HachetteBookGroup.com
www.YenPress.com

Yen Press is an imprint of Hachette Book Group, Inc.
The Yen Press name and logo are trademarks of Hachette Book Group, Inc.

The publisher is not responsible for websites (or their content) that are not owned by the publisher.

First Yen Press Edition: March 2015

ISBN: 978-0-316-29875-9

10 9 8 7 6 5 4 3 2

BVG

Printed in the United States of America

JAN - 1 - 2018